Duquesne Studies
LANGUAGE AND LITERATURE SERIES

VOLUME FOURTEEN

General Editor:
Albert C. Labriola (Department of English, Duquesne University)

Advisory Editor:
Foster Provost (Department of English, Duquesne University)

Editorial Board:
Judith H. Anderson
Donald Cheney
Ann Baynes Coiro
Mary T. Crane
Patrick Cullen
A. C. Hamilton
Margaret P. Hannay
A. Kent Hieatt
William B. Hunter
Michael Lieb
Thomas P. Roche, Jr.
Mary Beth Rose
John M. Steadman
Humphrey Tonkin
Susanne Woods

Major French Milton Critics

Major French Milton Critics of the Nineteenth Century

by

Harry Redman, Jr.

DUQUESNE UNIVERSITY PRESS
Pittsburgh, Pennsylvania

Copyright © 1994 by Duquesne University Press
All Rights Reserved

No part of this book may be used or
reproduced, in any manner whatsoever,
without written permission, except in the case
of short quotations for use in critical articles and reviews.

Published in the United States of America by
DUQUESNE UNIVERSITY PRESS
600 Forbes Avenue
Pittsburgh, Pennsylvania 15282-0101

Library of Congress Cataloging-in-Publication Data

Redman, Harry.
    Major French Milton critics of the nineteenth century / Harry Redman, Jr.
        p. cm. — (Duquesne studies. Language and literature series ; v. 14)
    Includes bibliographical references (p.) and index.
    ISBN 0-8207-0249-8
    1. Milton, John, 1608–1674—Appreciation—France.
2. Milton, John, 1608–1674—Criticism and interpretation—History—19th century. 3. Criticism—France—History—19th century. 4. English poetry—Appreciation—France.
I. Title. II. Series.
PR3587.4.F8R43   1993
821'.4—dc20   93-39661
                                                                                  CIP

Contents

	Foreword	xi
	Introduction	1
1	Abel François Villemain	27
2	François René de Chateaubriand	48
3	Philarète Chasles	78
4	Louis Raymond de Véricour	97
5	Matthieu Auguste Geffroy	123
6	Alphonse de Lamartine	149
7	J. B. Sanson de Pongerville	170
8	Jules Barbey d'Aurevilly	189
9	Alexandre Rodolphe Vinet	200
10	Alfred Mézières	218
11	Hippolyte Taine	232
12	Edmond Gabriel Héguin de Guerle	257
13	Edmond Scherer	289
14	Gaspard Ernest Stroehlin	305

15	Augustin Filon	319
16	A Backward Glance	333
	Notes	346
	Select Bibliography	377
	Index	383
	About the Author	391

For

John R. Redman

Milton Dictating Paradise Lost *to His Daughters* by Eugène Delacroix. This painting was shown at the Salon in 1827. Bought by the Duke of Fitzjames, it was taken to England and dropped out of sight for many years before reappearing in the United States. It now hangs in the Kunsthaus in Zurich.

Foreword

This volume, the fruit of much thought and a corresponding amount of toil, had its beginnings in a seminar paper written many years ago for Merritt Y. Hughes at the University of Wisconsin. Over the years, doing something much more serious on the subject was put aside in favor of projects that, at the moment, seemed more inviting or more feasible. It is a pleasure to return to the topic now with the present study.

Long ago it became clear that John M. Telleen's *Milton dans la littérature française* (1904) left a great deal to be desired. In recent years Jean Gillet's *Le Paradis perdu dans la littérature française de Voltaire à Chateaubriand* (1971) has taken care, and splendidly, of *Paradise Lost* criticism during the French Enlightenment. Gillet's concerns did not, of course, include an extensive consideration of how, in the eighteenth century, the French viewed the rest of Milton's work. For all practical purposes, the French discovered *Paradise Lost* only in the early years of the eighteenth century, and it was quite a while before an appreciable number of them turned their attention to whatever else the poet might have written. It should be noted, however, that not only *Paradise Lost* but also some of the other poems had at least been made available to them at a somewhat early date.

Paradise Regained and several shorter poems were translated in 1730. Bernard Routh's *Lettres critiques sur le Paradis perdu et reconquis* dates from 1731.

The present study, concerned with nineteenth century criticism, does not discuss critics who, though interested, did not examine Milton with enough insight or detail to warrant including them here. Some might be mentioned, however. Etienne Aignan, for example, translated *Comus, Areopagitica*, and *Of Education* in 1823, preceding his work with "notices." Jacques Parmentier's *Histoire de l'éducation en Angleterre* (1896) suggested Rabelaisien influence on Milton's *Of Education* but did not develop the idea. The chapters that follow examine the dozen or so important French critics whose interest in Milton led them to devote a stimulating essay or, in three cases, a whole book to this English poet and prose writer they esteemed. As was true of their predecessors, their chief interest was in *Paradise Lost*, but most of them had something to say about the poet's career and other work as well, and this too is discussed in the pages that follow. Critics are treated, more or less, in chronological order, except for Barbey d'Aurevilly. Although his Milton article was prompted by Edmond de Guerle's book, Barbey belonged, spiritually, to an earlier generation. He has therefore been put in his proper place, among the other romantics.

Many debts have been incurred in writing this study. In addition to many helpful librarians at various institutions, I would like to thank the University of Alabama Research Committee and the American Philosophical Society for generous grants making it possible to work abroad for considerable lengths of time. I would also like to thank *Etudes Anglaises* for permission to reprint the chapter on Lamartine, which, in a slightly different form, appeared in its pages.

In referring to Milton's prose or quoting from it, the edition used in almost all cases is the *Complete Prose Works of John Milton*, published by the Yale University Press from 1953 to 1982. To simplify matters, parenthetically or in notes, references are to *YPW*, followed by volume and page numbers. Similarly, William Riley Parker's *Milton: a Biography*, referred to fairly often, is generally indicated in parentheses, with volume and page numbers.

I have assumed that readers will have some knowledge of French is quoting from the various critics in this study. For longer and more complex passages, however, I have provided English translations.

Introduction

Joseph de Maistre, who admired John Milton, observed that the English considered him "une propriété nationale, une portion de l'établissement, un quarantième article." While they would rather surrender Jamaica than their ownership of such a treasure, one nevertheless wonders how many of the English ever sit down to read what he wrote, according to de Maistre.[1] Educated French citizens *have* read those works, but, aside from the prose polemics, it took them a while to get around to it. Before the nineteenth century, French readers had heard about Milton, but what they knew about him was limited and somewhat biased. To his French contemporaries he was scarcely known as a poet at all, though several of his prose works were disseminated in France.

Anxious to have its cause heard abroad, the English Council of State had Milton's *Eikonoklastes* translated into French. Copies of the translation, published in November 1652, soon made their way to the Continent. The Latin *Pro Populo Anglicano Defensio* had preceded it there. In southern France, the Parlement de Toulouse banned *Pro Populo Anglicano Defensio* and, on 17 June 1651, ordered it burned as subversive. The Parlement de Paris followed suit on 6 July. Booksellers and individuals were instructed to turn their

1

2 Major French Milton Critics

copies over to the authorities, all of which seems to indicate that multiple copies of the book were believed to be circulating. A number of surviving copies prove that not all were turned in. Emeric Bigot might visit and correspond with him, but to most informed French citizens Milton was a scoundrel and a regicide, Claude de Saumaise's vitriolic, implacable opponent.

After the Restoration, the French ambassador, Gaston de Comminges, reported to his royal master on the state of literature in Great Britain. Milton he considered important enough to mention but added that he "s'est rendu plus infâme par ses dangereux écrits que les bourreaux et les assassins de leur roi."[2] Another French contemporary, an author, was Pierre Costar. For Mazarin or Colbert, he drew up a *Mémoire sur les gens de lettres des pays étrangers* in which Milton is listed but with few details. Costar's remarks would be included in Pierre Desmaret's *Mémoires de littérature* in 1726:

> J'ai oublié de mettre au nombre des savants... Milton, Anglois célèbre pour un livre qu'il a écrit contre M. de Saumaise sur le procès du roi d'Angleterre. Il a fait un autre livre contre Morus, qui avoit écrit un livre contre le parlement d'Angleterre intitulé *Clamor Sanguinis ad Cœlum*. Il a, de plus, fait une réponse en anglois au livre de Charles, roi d'Angleterre, et un traité pour montrer qu'un homme peut répudier sa femme quand il en est ennuyé. Il est aveugle depuis quelques années.[3]
>
> [Among the scholars I neglected to list... Milton, an Englishman famous for a book he wrote against M. de Saumaise about the King of England's trial. He authored another book against More, who had written a book against the Parliament of England called *Clamor Sanguinis ad Coelum*. In English, moreover, he turned out a reply to the book of Charles, King of England, and a treatise showing that a man can repudiate his wife when he is annoyed with her. He has been blind for several years].

To the extent that they thought about it at all, the ambassador and his cultivated compatriots, such as Guy Patin and Jean Chapelain, no doubt agreed that the foreign author was an unwholesome, even sanguinary character.

Only toward the end of the seventeenth century did French readers learn that John Milton was not only a prose writer but a poet. Milton the poet began to be mentioned in the 1680s, but not much was said. In 1697 Pierre Bayle's *Dictionnaire historique et critique* discussed *Paradise Lost* along with the polemical works, but the emphasis was on the latter. Though there had been earlier allusions, discussions and reviews in such works as Bayle's *Nouvelles de la république des lettres,* Moréri's *Encyclopédie,* and the *Journal des Savants,* to Gallic readers Milton's real revelation as a poet came when Voltaire, then exiled in England, took a look at *Paradise Lost* in his *Essay on Epic Poetry* (1727), soon translated into French. While he had reservations, Voltaire tended to admire the poem. With successive editions, however, his enthusiasm cooled markedly, and by 1759 it had almost disappeared. That year, in *Candide,* the writer had Senator Pococurante tell two visitors who had noticed *Paradise Lost* on his shelves that Milton was nothing but a "barbare qui fait un long commentaire du premier chapitre de la *Genèse* en dix livres de vers durs," explaining his negative position in some detail.[4] Still, an entry had been made. The French reading public had learned that, during the previous century, England had produced an important epic.

After Voltaire's initial discussion, there were other commentaries. As the decades slipped by, various prose and verse translations and even imitations and parodies appeared. "Lycidas," *Comus, Paradise Regained* and *Samson Agonistes* began to attract some attention also, as did some of the other poems, such as "On the Morning of Christ's Nativity," "L'Allegro" and "Il Penseroso." As Abbé Yart rendered them, *Comus* and *Samson Agonistes,* it is true, bore little resemblance to the originals. The *History of Britain* was examined in the *Journal des Savants* in 1708.

Events were brewing, meanwhile, that would make people remember the prose writer, and soon readers would have reason to take a new look at the political works in particular. With revolution in the air, the pamphlets were timely, and translations and adaptations started popping up.

Until now, books had had to be "licensed" in France. *Areopagitica*, somewhat condensed, was translated as civil disorder broke out. In 1789 J. B. Salaville tendered the public a condensed version of *Pro Populo Anglicano Defensio*, preceded by an essay on the author. The work, sometimes attributed to Mirabeau, had a number of editions and in 1792 was used to help persuade people that the deposed monarch should be given the death penalty. Even the divorce tracts interested Albert Hennet, an author who, invoking their authority, hoped for legislation to enable couples to dissolve problematical marriages.

When the French Revolution came to an end, Milton's works, both in verse and in prose, were thus known to certain audiences. Still, there had not been as much critical comment as one might expect. As late as May 1826, Ernest Desclozeaux complained in *Le Globe* that the sonnets and other minor poems were "peu connus."[5] Less than a decade later, Amédée Pichot added that the prose works had not been studied either.[6] In the early years of the nineteenth century, however, there was to be a new impetus. As Jean Gillet has pointed out, Charles Delalot (1771–1842) discussed *Paradise Lost* in several articles that came out in the *Mercure de France* in 1804. Reacting against the French Revolution, Delalot, a proponent of peace and order, was very conservative. While he considered *Paradise Lost* "la plus grave et la plus sublime des épopées," he had reservations about it. He saw Adam and Eve as being at once sinners and victims. With their sin, they upset the divine order and thus bring on inevitable misfortune. Nevertheless, they are contrite and accept their punishment. Having done so, they become victims and interest the reader more after their sin than before it. This viewpoint would be echoed by a later critic. Delalot applauded their love scenes and the landscape the poet had provided as their décor. Chaos, Pandemonium and the Paradise of Fools he deplored as childish bad taste.[7] He did not discuss his author's other works.

At about the same time, Chateaubriand's *Génie du christianisme* burst upon the scene. Preaching an aesthetic, religious approach to art and literature, it was destined to alter the course of French letters. The book contained a splendid discussion of *Paradise Lost*. Nothing was said here about the other works, but the writer would take care of that later. Meanwhile, the *Génie du christianisme* was the rage. The new book, with its sensitive appreciation of *Paradise Lost*, was devoured, and serious French Milton criticism got a new start. In the pages that follow, we shall see who the major critics were and what they had to say.

As a rule, French literary critics in the nineteenth century wrote for an intellectual élite, cultivated but not necessarily academic. Almost as often as not, the critics themselves were not academics or even the products of universities. Nevertheless, they had a remarkable knowledge of the western world's literary classics and had been given a thorough grounding in French literature as well. They took for granted similar backgrounds on the part of their audience. Constant comparisons with other literatures, ancient and modern, are the norm with these writers. Often *Paradise Lost* evoked such comparisons, but now and then the other poems and prose works did also.

In approaching *Paradise Lost*, French readers were conditioned to accept the idea of a biblical epic. There had been any number of these, many by Milton's French contemporaries. There had been Marc Antoine de St-Amant's *Moïse sauvé* (1653); Antoine Godeau's *St-Paul* (1654); Bernard Lesfargues's *David* (1660); Jacques de Coras's *Jonas* (1663), *Josué* (1665), *Samson* (1665) and *David* (1665); Pierre de St-Louis's *La Magdeleine* (1668); Jean Desmarets de St-Sorlin's *Esther* (1673); Julien Gastien Morillon's *Joseph* (1679); and even others. Most of them were not very good.[8] If the public had not read these epics, they at least knew of their existence. Boileau's *Art poétique* (1674) had showered them with ample scorn.

Aside from his allusions to certain epic poets, Boileau had had negative things to say about the genre itself. He disliked the biblical epic believing Christian doctrine an unsuitable topic for such an endeavor. Pagan divinities were one thing, God was something else. Having more leeway, Greek and Latin epic poets coped with their divinities well enough, but

6 *Major French Milton Critics*

Christian poets have a more sobering problem when they

> Pensent faire agir Dieu, ses saints et ses prophètes,
> Comme ces dieux éclos du cerveau des poètes:
> Mettent à chaque pas le lecteur en Enfer:
> N'offrent rien qu'Astaroth, Belzebuth, Lucifer.
> (*Art poétique* 3.195–98)

Hell and its denizens have no place in an epic. Satan, demeaning the hero while ranting and struggling against God, deserves a place there least of all.

> .... Quel objet enfin à présenter aux yeux,
> Que le diable toujours hurlant contre les Cieux,
> Qui de votre héros veut rabaisser la gloire
> Et souvent avec Dieu balance la victoire?
> (3.205–08)

Best to avoid such things. Christianity is too awesome to lend itself to this. The God of truth should not be made to look like a god of lies, which could happen. Simply stated,

> De la foi d'un chrétien les mystères terribles
> D'ornements égayés ne sont point susceptibles.
> L'Evangile à l'esprit n'offre de tous côtés
> Que pénitence à faire et tourments mérités:
> Et de vos fictions le mélange coupable,
> Même à ses vérités donne l'air de la fable.
> (3.199–204)

The precept was severe, but critics remembered it. More than one had it in mind as he scrutinized *Paradise Lost*. True, he might react against it, but he seldom lost sight of it. Lamartine, even though he enjoyed *Paradise Lost* and wrote some provocative things about it, was one of those who seemed to concur with these strictures. However, once they were able to put their own literature tradition behind them, later French critics began to read *Paradise Lost* in a more independent frame of mind and examine the epic for what it is.

In the nineteenth century, most French Milton critics

were enthusiastic about their author, whatever reservations they may have had about his political commitments and activities. Most knew Joseph Addison's examination of *Paradise Lost*, and some of them also appear to have known Thomas B. Macaulay's famous essay. With François Guizot's *Histoire de la Révolution d'Angleterre*, the background against which John Milton wrote became familiar to those interested in the writer and his period. Generally, the romantics made him conform to their concept of what a hero should be, towering above the masses but compassionate toward them and striving to make their world better. For this he could expect neither thanks nor reward, however. The masses could not understand him and shun or even persecute him, hardly aware of his dedicated altruism. This is how Philarète Chasles, for example, presented Milton. To the realist or naturalist critics, Milton, both in his poetry and his prose, was a creature of the era that produced him, although he was intellectually superior to it. But even the romantics believed that at least the poet of *Paradise Lost* and *Samson Agonistes* would not have been what he was had he not lived through the civil wars and served the Commonwealth.

However, there was one who disagreed. This belated romantic held that what Milton saw and did had nothing whatever to do with his poetic output. This was Jules Barbey d'Aurevilly, who lived to see a school of critics explaining literature in terms of authors' heredity and environment. Barbey was indignant. Using Milton as a weapon, he railed noisily at the literary determinists, claiming that the poet's home life, convictions and activities should have killed whatever talent he had been born with. Instead, the turmoil Milton witnessed left no traces at all on *Paradise Lost*. If Barbey had known more about Milton's private and public life, he might not have been so sure. But Barbey, though well read, was not inclined to painstaking research.

As a rule, the French romantics came very close to viewing Satan as the hero of *Paradise Lost*, though they were not quite willing to say as much. Their admiration is no less clear, however. They were also lackadaisical about strict accuracy in quoting, at least when quoting in translation. Citing passages from Milton's works, they might be translating literally, but, on the other hand, they might be condensing as they went along. Chateaubriand was good at this, and so was Lamartine. Moreover, the tidy modern distinction between quoting and paraphrasing had not been established or was not consistently observed, and occasional surprises could be in store for readers not aware of this. Even though quotation marks are used, it sometimes happens that, again in translation, Milton is made to say something that actually he expressed somewhat differently.

Several nineteenth century creative writers took an interest in Milton. Among these a word should be said about Amédée Pichot (1796–1877), who authored a piece of fiction that several French critics, such as Chateaubriand, Barbey d'Aurevilly and Filon, knew about and liked and to which several of them made allusions. During the romantic period and even later, Pichot was a rather important figure in the world of letters. Journalist and novelist, he was also editor for nearly 40 years of the highly influential *Revue Britannique*.[9] He traveled in England and Scotland several times, notably from 1822 to 1824, and knew the English classics thoroughly. At Cambridge University, anxious to view whatever Milton relics he could, he contrived to obtain a dead branch of the famous mulberry tree. In the *Revue de Paris* in 1830 he published "Milton," a novelette. Later he reworked it and included it in *Le Perroquet de Walter Scott* (1834) and *Les Poètes amoureux* (1858). Several contemporaries, as pointed out above, were to mention it. Pichot considered writing a critical work, in which he would discuss both the poetry and the prose.[10] He was well prepared to do it but never carried out his plan. Nevertheless, in his prose tale and in his *Voyage historique et littéraire en Angleterre et en Ecosse* (1825), he had a great deal to say about the poet and his work.

Relying heavily upon *Defensio Secunda*, Pichot retraces the poet's early years in his novelette, then embroiders a fanciful tale that appealed to his contemporaries' exotic imaginations. Pichot tells his readers that, while a student, Milton lies down to rest one day beneath a tree. Soon he falls asleep, perhaps working out in a dream his *De Idea Platonica*. Suddenly the touch of a hand awakens him. As he opens his eyes, he sees a woman rushing away. Although he cannot see her features, her figure and movements are like those of a goddess and remind him of Virgil's "incessu patuit dea." She is gone, but into his hand she has slipped four lines of poetry in Italian.

> Occhi, stelle mortali,
> Ministri de' miei mali,
> ....
> ....
> Se chiusi m'occidete,
> Aperti che farete?

Pichot does not identify the lines, but they are from Battista Guarini's "Madrigale XI."[11] Presumably, the mysterious sylph was Italian. Young Milton, blushing at the compliment the lines contained, returns to his rooms. There a classmate asks him if he has happened to see an Italian lady who, on a visit to the university, had charmed all of the other students. Thereafter Milton neglects his classical studies somewhat and becomes more and more interested in Petrarch and Tasso. Eventually he decides to visit Italy.

There needed to be a pretext, and, taking a hint from his readings, Pichot finds one. Milton's father, an able musician, is anxious to build a collection of Italian music. Milton will go abroad and assemble it. In passing, Pichot cites a few lines from "Ad Patrem" (ll. 58–60). The Italian journey, with its various halts, is traced in some detail. Finally, Milton arrives in Rome, where he meets the leading intellectuals. Soon he is on excellent terms with Cardinal Antonio Barberini. A writer of Latin verse, the cardinal consults his new friend about poetry and in return helps him choose the music he is collecting. Barberini also invites him to the concerts given at his palace. At one of them, Milton hears Leonora Baroni, and, to his surprise, discovers that she is the mysterious woman of several years before. Pichot weaves a charming little love story about it all. His Leonora Baroni is not only a brilliant artist but also a beautiful, cultivated woman. To her, Milton writes poems in Latin. It is her inspiration, Pichot thinks, that produced some of the Italian poems as well. And it is she who gave him his true appreciation of Italian poetry. The two travel together for a time, though there is no reason to believe that the hero is any less chaste than he claims to have been. For a time, the heroine could hope, she thinks, that her lover might renounce his religion and homeland to remain at her side. One day, however, a letter from his father arrives that puts an end to such dreams. Taking leave of a place and a woman he loves, Milton returns home "pour aller se ranger parmi les ennemis de l'épiscopat et du roi Charles."[12]

Nevertheless, before leaving Rome, Milton goes with Leonora to the Vatican to look at Michelangelo's *Creation*. He also gazes at Baccio Bandinelli's colossal statues of Adam and Eve, which likewise impress him deeply. To prove to him that Shakespeare was greater than the native dramatists, the diva takes him one evening to see Andreini perform his *Adamo*. Pichot summarizes it in some detail, quoting passages here and there. He considers the first scene of act 3, showing the first couple's domestic happiness, a masterpiece of tenderness. Having seen the play, Milton becomes less interested in King Arthur, the Round Table and Merlin. That Milton may have conceived *Paradise Lost* as a drama seems to have whetted few critics' curiosity. Perhaps they agreed with Baron Adolphe d'Avril, diplomat and medieval scholar, who held that epics have a natural dramatic configuration to begin with.[13] At about the time Pichot was writing, Victor Hugo commented that *Paradise Lost* is probably more drama than epic anyway. In the preface to *Cromwell* (1827), he declared that it was "sous la première de ces formes qu'il s'était présenté d'abord à l'imagination du poète et qu'il reste toujours imprimé dans la mémoire du lecteur, tant l'ancienne charpente dramatique est encore saillante sous l'édifice épique."

The Puritan Revolution and the Protectorate came and

went. It was a period of remarkable crimes but also remarkable virtues. "Rien n'est moins rare dans l'histoire que de voir les nations renverser les idoles qu'elles ont adorées, exalter de nouveau les noms qu'elles ont couverts d'opprobre" ("Milton," 29). And so the Restoration took place. On the Continent, or in works sold there, Saumaise, More, Du Moulin and others had written scathing things about "l'adversaire de la prélature, l'apologiste de la république régicide." Perhaps they had been sincere in doing it. One thing was sure. Those who had known Milton as a handsome young poet in Italy would have been dubious that the dour controversialist of later years could be the same individual they had liked and admired a few decades earlier. While he was now on a proscriptions list, the announcement that he had died diminished the likelihood that he would be punished. He never rallied to the new regime. Had he written in its behalf, it might have survived.[14]

Leonora Baroni is curious about the events that have just taken place in Great Britain. Apparently she is aware of the extent to which Milton has taken part in those events. After the Restoration, "encore belle, mais déjà parvenue à l'été de la vie," she arrives in London to see things for herself. One day she happens to meet Thomas Ellwood, whom she agrees to replace as a reader for a certain blind man whose name Ellwood at first withholds. As they approach the man's isolated house, they hear organ music. "Mon maître se prépare par la musique à la poésie," Ellwood tells his new friend. Soon, indeed, a voice is heard declaiming *Samson Agonistes*' address to light. Pichot gives it in French in a splendid translation ("Milton," 35-36). Quickly, Leonora and Milton become friends once more, though not lovers, and are soon discussing literature and events. In most of the rest of the novelette and also in the *Voyage historique et littéraire*, there are frequent quotations from Milton's poems and prose works, generally in French. Much of the personal material in *Defensio Secunda* is quoted.[15]

Pichot knew Milton's prose rather well. In the *Voyage historique et littéraire* he had already talked about it. Generalizing, he had held in the earlier work that "Milton, se dépouillant enfin de tout respect pour les pères et les conciles, en vint à mépriser toute forme de gouvernement ecclésiastique, pour s'en référer à la lumière intérieure de son esprit" (*Voyage* 2:63), an allusion to the poet's evolution in the various religious broadsides. In "Milton," many of the pamphlets—including *Areopagitica, The Tenure of Kings and Magistrates, Eikonoklastes, Pro Populo Anglicano Defensio, Defensio Secunda* and *The Ready and Easy Way*—are alluded to or cited. When Leonora Baroni declares that the republic was scuttled by some of its very leaders, Milton replies that their imprudence should be pitied but that their principles were irreproachable. He explains his part in King Charles's execution, pointing out that his task had been to enumerate the monarch's misdeeds and show the recourse it left his people. However, he thinks that the death sentence, on the whole, may have hurt the republic ("Milton," 43–44).

In the *Voyage historique et littéraire* and the novelette, there are allusions to various poems, including "L'Allegro," "Il Penseroso," "Lycidas" and *Comus*. Sometimes there are quotations. In the *Voyage historique et littéraire* Pichot said of the poet that "il préféra ne pas être compris de son siècle et, après avoir composé les vers chastes de *Comus*, de *Lycidas*, du 'Penseroso' et de 'L'Allegro,' il médita pour l'immortalité la sublime création de son grand poème" (*Voyage* 2:268). In the novelette he has the poet talk to his visitor, during their last conversation, about the epic he hopes to write. In the person of Adam, its main actor will be all of humankind. "Je veux chanter Dieu dans son œuvre la plus merveilleuse, la création de l'homme." Moreover, "Je veux relever l'homme, en montrant le ciel et l'enfer également émus de cette création nouvelle, dont le fils de Dieu daignera revêtir un jour la forme, pour s'associer à son infirmité avant de l'associer elle-même à sa gloire." The plan is ambitious. The poet believes he can achieve what he wishes "en évitant de donner aux figures de mes songes une forme trop matérielle, en décrivant plutôt le symbole que la substance, en ne soulevant qu'à demi le voile du mysère pour laisser à l'imagination de chacun une part dans mes tableaux" ("Milton," 60). Leonora Baroni takes leave of him, reminding him, as he describes Eden, to remember her country, with its "couleurs brillantes" and its "brises embaumées." Pichot thinks that the poet did do. "Il y a dans le *Paradis perdu* des expressions et surtout des concetti" that have caused some critics to declare that at times Milton is more Italian than Tasso ("Milton," 21, 61). Pichot has little more to say about *Paradise Lost* except to praise the description of the Garden of Eden and to extoll Adam and Eve's tender but "chaste" love and its presentation (*Voyage* 1.50; "Milton," 21). Pichot also admired the poem's language. English, he admitted, has been considered an imperfect tool, according to some critics. Still, he pointed out, great writers have always been able to make it do what they wanted it to do. "Le *palais de briques* de Milton n'en est pas moins un magnifique palais" (*Voyage* 2.258).

Shortly after Leonora Baroni's departure, Pichot imagines the poet marrying Elizabeth Minshull. Pichot seems unaware that, less than a year after Milton returned to England in 1639, Leonora had also married someone else.[16] Pichot noted that Edward Bulwer Lytton also wrote a romantic little piece involving Leonora Baroni and Milton. The reference may be to "Milton" in *Weeds and Wildflowers* (1826). However, the Italian girl is given no name in this poem. As William Riley Parker observed, "Much of the romantic speculation about Milton's interest in Leonora is not deserving of serious analysis despite its persistence" (Parker, 2:821). Although the story was totally imaginary, Milton's portrait in Pichot's "touchante nouvelle historique" was a splendid one, according to Chateaubriand.[17]

Although it may be even older, the story about a youthful John Milton, while asleep, having some lines of poetry slipped into his hand by "a fair Italian maid," with no name assigned her, goes back at least to a pair of poems by Anna Seward in her *Original Sonnets on Various Subjects*, published in 1799.[18] The *Defensio Secunda* records that Milton sent home music books while he was abroad. The idea that his travels were for this purpose could have come from William Hayley's life of the poet. Probably Pichot's source was Henry John Todd, where both Hayley and Anna Seward are quoted.[19] One of Seward's poems even quotes the lines from Guarini, but in English and without the author's name. In order to give them more or less correctly in Italian, Pichot presumably would have had to recognize them or hunt them down. It is a little surprising that he did not mention their author.

The numerous outstanding authors who alluded to Milton in their works or correspondence include Balzac, Mérimée, Stendhal, Lamennais and George Sand. Most admired him. Flaubert, curiously, did not. As he told Sand, Milton was "closed" to him; he was unable to understand him. Two French romantic authors were particularly aware of Milton and made him a character in creative works. Both Alfred de Vigny and Victor Hugo had a genuine interest in Milton's work but neither, unfortunately, left a commentary devoted to it.

Alfred de Vigny, the morose but brilliant poet, novelist and dramatist, had much in common with the author of *Paradise Lost* and *Samson Agonistes*, sharing his alleged view of the nature and place of women and the lot of humankind. "La Maison du berger" (1844) and "La Colère de Samson" (1838) extoll and upbraid women, warning that they ought to be kept in subordinate places. "Eloa" (1824), with its Paradise and Chaos, its angels and demons, echoes *Paradise Lost* more than once. In it Satan triumphs, however. At one point, apostrophizing modesty, the poet seems paradoxically to recall the first couple's learning about shame.

> Vous pouvez seule encor remplacer l'innocence,
> Mais l'arbre défendu vous a donné naissance;
> Au charme des vertus votre charme est égal,
> Mais vous êtes aussi le premier pas du mal.
> D'un chaste vêtement votre sein se décore?
> Eve avant le serpent n'en avait pas encore;
> Et si le voile pur orne votre maintien,
> C'est un voile toujours, et le crime a le sien.[20]

And so on.

Stello and the *Journal d'un poète* are peppered with allusions to Milton and his work. Vigny also made the poet an episodic character in his novel *Cinq-Mars* (1826). Here the novelist imagines Milton stopping in Paris on his return trip to England in 1639. While there he attends a social gathering at the home of Marion de Lorme, the brilliant courtesan. Most of the people there, including some authors and courtiers, are rather vapid. Among the intellectuals are Molière, Corneille and Descartes. The hostess announces that John Milton will read some of his poetry. Aware that many of her guests know English, she distributes translations to those that do not. The poet's handsome face is wan, sickly and spiritual but impassioned. Sitting near a table and looking heavenward, the young stranger soon becomes lost in a sublime world of his own creation. Invoking his heavenly muse, he announces "dans ses vers la première désobéissance de l'homme." Next come the rebel angels' defeat and their expulsion into darkness visible. Part of Satan's speech to his cohorts follows. Already it is clear that most of the restive audience neither likes nor understands what it is hearing. Corneille, taking stock of the reaction, urges the young poet to recite some other passage. Milton does so. In a gentle voice, he begins to narrate scenes to which later French readers have been particularly sensitive.

> Il parlait du bonheur chaste des deux plus belles créatures; il peignit leur majestueuse nudité, la candeur et l'autorité de leur regard, puis leur marche au milieu des tigres et des lions qui se jouaient encore à leurs pieds; il dit aussi la pureté de leur prière matinale, leurs sourires enchanteurs, les folâtres abandons de leur jeunesse et l'amour de leurs propos si douloureux au prince des démons.
>
> [He described the chaste happiness of the universe's two most beautiful creatures; he depicted their majestic nakedness, the candor and assurance in their look, then their strolling among the tigers and lions that still played at their feet; he also told about the purity of their morning prayer, their captivating smiles, their youthful, unabashed romps, and their words of love that caused the Prince of Demons so much pain.]

Courtesan that she is, the hostess is touched and even weeps. "L'idée de l'amour dans la vertu lui apparut pour la première fois avec toute sa beauté." Most of the others present do not respond sympathetically, and among her guests the irritation mounts. Milton then recites Raphael's visit to Adam and Eve, with the angel's account of the War in Heaven. It is too much. Mlle de Lorme's visitors cut him off, citing the poet's bad taste and their own religious scruples. Only the hostess, Descartes, Corneille, Molière and François de Thou, a lawyer and courtier, have appreciated the performance.

Romantic hero that he is in this sketch, Milton has been absorbed in his ideas, hardly aware of his audience's reaction. Above it all, "son génie n'avait plus rien de commun avec la terre dans ce moment." He tells one of his hearers, one of those who actually listened, that, disinterested, he is not writing for his contemporaries' plaudits. "Je ne songe pas au succès: je chante parce que je me sens poète." Even knowing that his poem would not be read for a hundred years after his death, he would still write it. Eventually, with Molière, Corneille, Descartes and de Thou, he retires to another room, and the new friends have a memorable conversation. Obviously, Vigny gave his young hero ample reason to dislike the French, at least most of them. Vigny took other liberties as well, needless to say. Proud of his strict morals, John Milton would not have been a likely guest in the home of a courtesan, however fashionable, nor is there any reason to think he ever encountered the great authors with whom he is thrown while there. Of course, that much of *Paradise Lost* had already been written at this time anticipates the poem's probable date of composition considerably. Whatever the case, it is clear that Vigny held the epic in the highest esteem. Regrettably, as indicated earlier, he never wrote an essay about it.[21]

A year after Vigny's novel, Victor Hugo presented a somewhat older John Milton in his play *Cromwell* (1827). Robert Couffignal has pointed out *Paradise Lost*'s influences on Hugo's *La Fin de Satan* (1854) and *Le Sacre de la femme* (1858).[22] In *Cromwell, Paradise Lost* is assumed to be on the drawingboard or even completed, since Cromwell knows about it. Cromwell has become Lord Protector and treats his Latin Secretary with little more than tolerant, slightly amused condescension. Milton, depicted as kind but somewhat petulant, chafes and on one occasion invites his master to be more civil. His influence on the dictator is not remarkable. Begging at one point that Sir William Davenant's life be spared, he is not given a reassuring answer. Cromwell, regarding him as a good poet and a great theologian, likes *Eikonoklastes* but does not care for Satan. Vigny's Milton writes because writing is his vocation and he cannot resist it. Hugo's Milton, knowing that his mind is its own place, bides his time, convinced that posterity will appreciate his great epic one day. Muttering to himself, he declares that

> L'avenir est mon juge. Il comprendra mon Eve,
> Dans la nuit de l'enfer tombant comme un doux rêve,
> Adam coupable et bon, et l'archange incompté
> Fier de régner aussi sur une éternité,
> Grand dans son désespoir, profond dans sa démence,
> Sortant du lac de feu que bat son aile immense!
> Car un génie ardent travaille dans mon sein.
> Je médite en silence un étrange dessein.
> J'habite en ma pensé, et Milton s'y console.
> Oui, je veux à mon tour créer par ma parole,
> Du créateur suprême émule audacieux,
> Un monde, entre l'enfer, et la terre, et les cieux.
> (*Cromwell* 3.2)

Hugo's Milton, like that of Vigny, is a misunderstood intellectual but is a little less modest than his predecessor. Obviously, Hugo had read *Paradise Lost* and admired it. Writing the poem had been an "étrange dessein," he thought. Adam he considered both a righteous man and a sinner. Satan, the despairing but recalcitrant archangel, was a proud, admirable figure as he emerged from the burning lake, beating his huge wings. That Hugo never wrote a commentary on the poem is our loss. His closest approach to doing so is a passage in *Littérature et philosophie mêlée*, which appeared in 1834. Here the author declared with respect to *Paradise Lost*,

> Si jamais composition littéraire a profondément porté

l'empreinte ineffaçable de la méditation et de l'inspiration, c'est le *Paradis perdu.* Une idée morale, qui touche à la fois aux deux natures de l'homme; une leçon terrible donnée en vers sublimes; une des plus hautes vérités de la religion et de la philosophie, développée dans une des plus belles fictions de la poésie; l'échelle entière de la création parcourue depuis le degré le plus élevé jusqu'au degré le plus bas; une action qui commence par Jésus et se termine par Satan; Eve entraînée par la curiosité, la compassion et l'imprudence, jusqu'à la perdition; la première femme en contact avec le premier démon; voilà ce que présente l'œuvre de Milton, drame simple et immense, dont tous les ressorts sont des sentiments; tableau magique qui fait graduellement succéder à toutes les teintes de lumière toutes les nuances de ténèbres; poème singulier, qui charme et qui effraie![23]

[If ever a literary composition bore the deep, ineradicable stamp of meditation and inspiration, it is *Paradise Lost.* An ethical idea that, at one and the same time, touches both of mankind's two natures; a terrible lesson expressed in sublime verse; one of the greatest truths in religion and philosophy developed in one of poetry's most beautiful plots; the whole gamut of creation from the highest to the lowest echelon; an action that begins with Jesus and ends with Satan; Eve lured to her undoing by curiosity, compassion and imprudence; that is what one finds in Milton's work, a simple, immense drama totally dependent upon feelings to achieve its effects; a magic panorama in which little by little all shades of light merge with all nuances of darkness; a different kind of poem, which delights and frightens the reader!]

Another creative writer, this one dating from the latter part of the nineteenth century, admired the poem but never wrote an essay about it. Auguste de Villiers de l'Isle-Adam alluded to Milton several times in his work. "La Machine à gloire," in which the poet is not a character, nonetheless cites him as the most eminent example of an authentic literary genius, to be contrasted with the tasteless scribbler whose work, though highly successful in terms of money, is not destined to survive. In "Les Filles de Milton," not published during the author's lifetime, Villiers took up where Vigny and Hugo left off.[24]

In this short story the poet is presented, once again, as a romantic hero but an elderly one. Though a hero, he is not a pleasant person, and his daughters' dislike is understandable. The time is the Stuart Restoration, and *Paradise Lost* is being written. However, Villiers had not documented himself very well. Mrs. Milton, the reader is allowed to assume, is the mother of the poet's daughters. There are only two of these, Deborah and one named Emma. They are credible; one is even a bit sympathetic. Poverty stalks the household, and food is not always on the table. Understandably, Deborah and Emma are unhappy with their lot, which includes having to write as their father dictates. Deborah is irritated, convinced that the old man thinks of nothing but his epic. Posterity, he believes, will award *Paradise Lost* a magnificent place in literature. As for his contemporaries, he has no illusions. They will not understand, and among them he will be like "un vivant parmi les morts." Such vanity, when the whole brood will soon be in tatters, revolts Deborah. As she sees it, her father, unconcerned about his own and the others' material needs, is driven by only two things, his religious beliefs and his false pride. Like other poets, he is selfish. "Les poètes sont des êtres qui prennent une distraction pour but, au mépris des leurs et des peines qu'ils font supporter à ce qui l'entoure." Deborah mulls over several alternatives to her and her sister's predicament. Solutions are not easy. Deborah would at least like to get out of her father's house. But how?

Finding a husband? Deborah Milton is twenty. Charles II is king, and marriage is out of the question. Who would marry the daughter of a notorious regicide? No one, not even a minister. Her mother reminds her that her father, whatever he did, behaved in accordance with his conscience. Deborah continues to muse. Since she and her sister are attractive, maybe they could take lovers or become prostitutes. Mrs. Milton tells her that she must think about her honor, an idea she dismisses. If Milton would only die, the women could go away somewhere and come alive. Deborah wonders if praying for the poet's death would be a sin.

As for *Paradise Lost*, Deborah's reactions are equivocal. "Peindre le ciel et l'enfer! Et le paradis terrestre! Et l'histoire de l'infortuné couple d'êtres dont nous descendons tous!" To her this is nonsense, "un tintement insupportable de mots vides." On the other hand, there are moments when she relents and thinks that what her father is writing has merit. At the end of the tale, caught up in a surge of intense inspiration, the poet begins to recite lines.

Hail, holy Light, offspring of Heav'n first-born,

he begins. This is followed by a lyric outpouring, "une éruption d'images où des pensées se symbolisaient en grands éclairs.... Un ange passa dans l'inspiration, car il semblait que l'on distinguât des frémissements d'ailes dans les mots sacrés qu'il proférait" (Villiers, 706). As the poet recites, one sees that "les cimes des arbres de l'Eden s'illuminaient d'aurores perdues," one heard "le chant matinal d'Eve, priant auprès des premières fontaines, devant Adam candide et grave, qui adorait en silence." There are also "les reflets bleus du dragon s'enroulant autour de l'arbre défendu." Reciting, the poet is transfiguré. Deborah is stunned and delighted with what she has heard and calls out to him to slow down while she looks for writing materials. The only pen she can find has something the matter with it, and, worse still, there is no paper. This brings Milton back to reality. There is a long silence, the poet shudders and sighs, then tells his amanuensis not to bother, it is too late. He has forgotten the lines he had been reciting. Deborah has already told her mother that this sometimes happened.

Villiers's imaginative dénouement implies that, as the poet conceived them, certain episodes in *Paradise Lost* were not what readers eventually saw in print. Milton had had to reconstruct. Something valuable may have been lost in the process, however. Were the original versions better? One will never know. By showing him as a misunderstood genius obliged to live in a real world that is often harsh, a man given to moments of sacred inspiration yet a victim of capricious fate, Villiers made his John Milton a true romantic. Villiers produced some literary criticism but left no essay on Milton. A fervent monarchist, what he might have said about some of the prose works one can only speculate about.

It is regrettable that several French critics of the nineteenth century who were interested in Milton, knew something about him, and admired his work, never got around to writing an essay about him. Germaine de Staël was such a critic. In *De la littérature* (1800) she praised *Paradise Lost* as a superb intellectual achievement. Along with the awesome tableaux, she liked the treatment of nature. She also liked the poet's characterizations. Adam and Eve are devout and innocent, yet, though not overwhelmed by "le bonheur des jouissances vives," they experience "sensations enivrantes" in their garden paradise. In *De la littérature* and *De l'Allemagne*, de Staël praised another character she admired. Milton had witnessed the civil wars, she wrote, and he made his Prince of Rebels "un factieux gigantesque, armé contre la monarchie du ciel." She then went on to other ideas. Gustave Planche, active during the first half of the century, was another excellent critic. He saw Milton as a brilliant intellectual who dominated the other thinkers of his time. He was an "homme privilégié," a "génie prédestiné," one of those writers who need no advice, no encouragement. Such writers "dominent de trop haut leur temps et leur pays pour avoir besoin d'applaudissements ou de sanction. Ils marchent fièrement et sûrement dans la voie qu'ils ont ouverte, et la postérité se charge de les venger si leurs contemporains ont été pour eux aveugles ou injustes."[25] Planche did not pursue the idea. Another important author who admired Milton but never devoted an article to him was Ernest Renan, who looked upon him as "le blessé des luttes politiques," a poet whose art had been colored by reading the Psalms. Unfortunately, Renan did not expand his remark.[26]

Several authors who did write an article or book on Milton do not qualify, even so, as particularly notable Milton critics. One or two should nevertheless be mentioned. Toward the end of the period, not much needs to be said about Edgar Monod's bachelor's thesis called *Milton théologien* (1882). Aside from some innacurate dates and naïve remarks, this thin little volume added little, if indeed anything, to what was already known about Milton's religious thinking. Along with quotations from *Paradise Lost*, a disproportionate amount of the documentation comes from *Considerations Touching the Likeliest Means to Remove Hirelings out of the Church*, although *De Doctrina Christiana* was used on occasion. The author examined the business of Milton's Unitarianism, rejecting the notion completely. Monod comments, as most of his contemporaries did not, that Cromwell and Milton did not see eye to eye on the matter of church government. Milton called for the church's absolute independence from the state and sought to convince Cromwell. When his plea did no good, the poet desisted and kept quiet until the Lord Protector's death.[27]

M. H. Bailly, though he did not become an outstanding critic, nevertheless published a very good article on Satan in 1881. In the article, entitled "Origines et caractère du Satan de Milton," Bailly all but declared Satan the hero of *Paradise Lost*. According to the critic, Satan does much more than merely stand out in the poem in which he is a character. Other heroes do that. Satan *is* the plot, at least in the first part of *Paradise Lost*. "Il est toujours en scène. Ce sont ses sentiments, ses passions, et les projets qui en sont la suite" that account for all of the action. The reason for this is the fact that the poet originally conceived the work as a drama. Of the three principal characters that he would have had to put on the stage—God, Adam and Satan—only the latter had dramatic potential. God, serene and immutable, seated on a throne that nothing can shake, is not dramatic. Nor is Adam, who is essentially calm and passive in his innocence, as devoid of passion as his maker. However, Satan, whose pride and ambition have already driven him from Heaven, is another matter. Prometheus is literature's only other comparable hero. While Satan's story does not meet the complicated, exacting criteria that a drama calls for, it nonetheless enabled Milton to write "une œuvre poétique aussi émouvante et en même temps aussi simple, aussi régulière, aussi sévèrement ordonnée que la plus noble des tragédies antiques." Cast out and humiliated, Satan rebounds and, more energetically than ever, rededicates himself to his unequal struggle. One admires him whether one wants to or not.[28]

Charles Augustin Sainte-Beuve was France's greatest nineteenth century literary critic. His classical education had been sound, and he wrote several articles on Greek and Latin literature. For the most part he wrote on French letters and themes, but there are articles on such authors as Dante, Cervantes, Gœthe and Heine. Although he claimed to have problems with English,[29] he nonetheless wrote several essays on American and British writers. There are articles, for instance, on Benjamin Franklin, Thomas Jefferson, James Fenimore Cooper, Sir Walter Scott and Byron, but none on Milton. There are, however, numerous allusions, both in letters and in articles on other writers.

Sainte-Beuve liked "O Nightingale." He also liked "les deux célèbres pièces," "L'Allegro" and "Il Penseroso," noting that "dans ces compositions de suprême et un peu froide beauté, le poète n'a pas la passion en lui; il attend le mouvement du dehors, il reçoit successivement ses impressions de la nature; il se contente d'y porter une disposition grave, noble, sensible, mais calme, comme un miroir légèrement ému. Le 'Penseroso' est le chef-d'œuvre du poème méditatif et contemplatif; il ressemble à un magnifique oratorio, où la prière par degrés monte lentement vers l'Eternel." *Comus*'s Lady he compared to Una in the *Faerie Queene*. As for *Paradise Lost*, it was "adorable et riche de toutes choses" (*Œuvres*, 326, 445). Milton had been able to write it "en dépit des obstacles, des oppressions, et des orages." As a senator during the Second Empire, Sainte-Beuve quoted in translation an appropriate passage in a speech having to do with education. He called upon his colleagues on that occasion not to behave like the devils, lost in impractical speculation during their leader's absence. The speech was much admired. Elsewhere Sainte-Beuve admiringly called attention to Adam and Eve's love. Knowing what is about to happen to them, the reader is enchanted, his emotion "se redouble du contraste de ce qui précède ou de ce qui va suivre." Though situated amid the ideal and the divine, the picture is realistic. With his inventive artistic skill, Milton knew how to depict religious truths. "Tout ce qui est beau de Milton est hors de pair; on y sent l'habitude tranquille des hautes régions et la continuité dans la puissance."³⁰

Earlier in the century, a young writer destined to become one of the masters of the short story tried his hand at literary criticism and, in the process, had something to say about *Paradise Lost*. This was Charles Nodier (1783–1844). In 1808 and 1809, he gave a series of lectures on literature. Some of his ideas would be treated by later critics. He considered the epic to be the most serious work the intellect could produce. The *Iliad* he regarded as literature's most perfect one, with the *Aeneid* as second best. Like Raymond de Véricour in 1838, he had little esteem for Lucan's *Pharsalia* and Voltaire's *Henriade*. Turning to Milton, he talked about two dramas, Andreini's *Adamo* (1613) and Masenio's *Sarcotis* (1661), deciding that Milton did not use them. In the War in Heaven, he objected to the use of cannon. Satan's metamorphoses also bothered him. Along with most of his French predecessors and contemporaries, he shuddered at Sin and Death. There were other aspects of the poem that troubled him too. "Milton n'est certainement pas irrépréhensible; peu de poètes offrent des parties aussi faibles, des inconvenances aussi ridicules, des bizarreries aussi grossières." In some respects, however, he felt the poem had no equal.

> Mais il faut reconnaître que peu de parties réunissent à un point aussi élevé des qualités qui semblent s'exclure: la grâce et l'énergie. Les regrets, les fureurs, les imprécations de Satan sont exprimés avec une vigueur de coloris à laquelle rien ne peut se comparer ni chez les anciens ni chez les modernes. La chaste tendresse d'Adam et d'Eve est peinte avec une douceur enchanteresse qui vous pénètre le cœur.³¹

> [However, it must be admitted that, to such an extent, few parts unite qualities that would appear to rule one another out: charm and vitality. Satan's remorse, outbursts and imprecations are expressed in such bold color that nothing can be compared with it, whether among the ancients or the moderns. Adam and Eve's chaste tenderness is painted with a captivating sweetness that goes straight to the heart .]

Nodier was as conservative as Charles Delalot, and he noted that, like Dante, Milton had participated in civil war and revolution. When he wrote *Paradise Lost*, Milton had been involved in a nation's delirious rebellion against a good king. "L'orage cessé, Milton, pauvre et aveugle comme Homère, entreprit de s'immortaliser comme lui." What he had witnessed colored his work. "Il n'y a pas loin de cela à l'idée de la révolte des démons contre le Créateur, et les couleurs dont Milton avait à peindre les rebelles n'étaient pas difficiles à trouver." Fame was slow in coming. The poet died without knowing that he would be immortal (*Cours de belles-lettres,* 112–16).

A few years later, reviewing an edition of *The Divine Comedy,* Nodier would comment once more on *Paradise Lost.* Again, the critic talked about its relationship to other epics.[32] In his opinion, *Gerusalemme liberata* and the *Henriade,* though marvelous here and there, revealed serious weaknesses. With their epics, the authors erected a temple but were unable to provide it with divinities. Moreover, the historical epic is a wornout genre. Flexible and innovative, Milton was one of the rare poets able to produce a new kind of epic. Nodier believed that epics come about in modern times as a result of tremendous social upheaval, upheaval that leaves its mark on language. Milton and Klopstock, as he interpreted them, seemed to bolster his theories. "Je suis très disposé à reconnaître que Milton et Klopstock sont de grands poètes épiques," he wrote. He added that

> le premier est né dans un âge de révolution où le langage et la littérature tendaient à se renouveler; le second a écrit dans une langue déjà ancienne mais à laquelle des circonstances particulières ... avaient conservé son indépendance et son originalité; tous deux, pénétrés de l'idée vraie que le domaine de l'épopée historique était désormais stérile, se sont élancés dans l'espace immense de l'épopée mystique, qui était dans leur langue une création toute nouvelle. La révélation de cette ressource merveilleuse était en eux l'instinct d'un profond génie. (*Mélanges,* 335)

> [the first was born in an age of revolution, when language and literature were attempting to revitalize themselves; the second wrote in a language that was already old but which special circumstances caused to retain its freedom and originality; both,

> convinced that the epic domain had become sterile, leaped into the immense void of the mystical epic, which in their language was something entirely new. The revelation of this supernatural resource was, in them, the instinct of a deep mind.]

Thus instinct led them in the right direction, which meant altering the epic tradition. Up to a point, Dante had done this too. Like Milton, he lived in tumultuous times "parmi ces grands orages politiques qui éprouvent les forces de l'âme, qui les grandissent, qui développent le génie avec les passions qui l'alimentent." Genius, Nodier added, is sometimes passion itself.

Referring to Edmond Scherer, Matthew Arnold, in the *Quarterly Review*, made the curious remark that a foreigner could be more objective and thus was in a better position to assess a literary work than a native. Specifically, "A completely disinterested judgment about a man like Milton is easier for a foreign critic than to an Englishman," Arnold declared. Such a critic is under no obligation to admire "our great epic poet."[33] Presumably, the reviewer allowed for the fact that basic linguistic difficulties had to be overcome. It was a novel position to take. Years before, Abel Villemain had nevertheless pointed out that there are necessarily limitations to what a foreign critic can do with respect to prosody, where the foreigner's ear is almost certainly not going to be as sure as that of the native. However accurate or inaccurate the *Quarterly Review*'s pronouncement, we shall examine in the pages that follow the insights that several French commentators brought to bear upon Milton and his work in a country and in a century that produced some outstanding literary criticism. Those commentators represented its various schools, from neoclassicism to naturalism, that flourished in the century born as the French Revolution subsided and a new era burst into being. Personal, romantic responses to writer and work will be encountered, as will assessments based on a sober consideration of the political and religious milieu in which the poems and prose were written. For the most part, the critics considered all of the work, including the pamphlets, and took a deep interest in the mind that produced them.

1

Abel François Villemain

Of Villemain as a Milton critic, Gustave Planche declared that "dans ces pages si habiles et colorées de nuances si éclatantes, M. Villemain réalise pleinement l'idéal du critique: il pense comme un philosophe et parle comme un poète." Planche knew no English critical studies of Milton that stirred up as many ideas as Villemain's article.[1] Abel François Villemain was born in Paris in 1790 and died there in 1870. To a precocious and brilliant teaching career, he added membership in the Académie Française (1821). Soon he branched out into liberal politics. The July Monarchy named him a Peer of France in 1832. He served the régime as Minister of Public Instruction in 1839 and again from 1840 to 1844. In this position and as Secrétaire Perpétuel of the Académie Française from 1834 onward, Villemain exercised a considerable amount of influence on French intellectual life in his day, especially in the domains of historiography and literary criticism. Most of his criticism deals with Greek, Latin and French literature, but his interests also included a number of more or less modern foreign writers.

In 1819 Villemain published an *Histoire de Cromwell*.

His "Essai historique sur Milton" first appeared in Michaud's *Biographie universelle* in 1821. Two years later, Villemain included it in his *Discours et mélanges littéraires*. It was reprinted many times and soon became one of the standard reference works on Milton. Finally Villemain incorporated it into his *Etudes de littérature ancienne et moderne* in 1846.

Unlike numerous predecessors, Villemain turned his attention not just to *Paradise Lost* but to Milton's other works as well, both prose and poetry. In the main, however, he considered Milton to be the poet of *Paradise Lost*, and this sometimes caused him to dismiss some of the poet's other work with too cursory a nod. His remarks on the novice of "L'Allegro," "Il Penseroso" and *Comus* are an example. "On a beaucoup vanté, parmi ses premiers essais, l '"Allegro' et le 'Penseroso' deux pièces où ne se trouve pas le contraste que promet l'opposition de leurs titres. Le génie de Milton semblait dès lors ami des idées tristes et élevées; et le *Comus*, espèce de comédie-féerie qu'il fit à cette époque, à l'imitation des Italiens, présente plus de bizarrerie que de gaieté."[2] That Milton's purpose in *Comus* could have been something other than mere entertainment does not seem to have occurred to the critic. *Arcades* is not mentioned.

A brilliant Latinist himself, Villemain held Milton's Latin poems in high esteem, although this was sometimes at the expense of the early English ones. To this commentator, the poet's real apprenticeship was done not in these compositions written in his native language but rather in those he wrote in Latin. Villemain declares at the outset, "L'imagination de l'auteur du *Paradis perdu* s'annonçait par des poésies latines où l'on ne peut méconnaître une élégance et une douceur bien rares parmi les latinistes du Nord" (Villemain, 311). Of the Horton period he writes,

> La poésie latine, qu'il aima et cultiva toujours, et la poésie anglaise, qu'il devait embellir d'une gloire nouvelle, servaient seules de diversion à ses travaux. C'est à cette époque, sans doute, qu'il faut reporter la composition de quelques pièces que Milton publia plus tard et qui sont pour peu de chose dans sa renommée. Elles indiquent seulement les fortes études

et le goût profond de l'antiquité qui se mêlaient à son génie original et qui semblent quelquefois le ralentir sous le poids de l'érudition et des souvenirs. Ses vers latins ont beaucoup de correction et d'harmonie: ses vers anglais, qu'il n'osait pas encore affranchir du joug de la rime, sentent l'effort et la contrainte. (Villemain, 312)

[Latin poetry, which he always loved and cultivated, and English poetry, to which he was to give new luster, were the only things that distracted him from his labors. It is to this period, of course, that must be attributed the composition of a few pieces that Milton later published and that contribute little to his fame. They show only the deep study and the predilection for the ancient world that were part of his original turn of mind and that occasionally appear to slow him down beneath the weight of erudition and recollections. His Latin poetry is very correct and harmonious: his English poetry, which he did not yet dare liberate from the yoke of rhyme, shows signs of effort and constraint.]

Villemain commends the Italian verse, which he declares to be "dans le pur toscan," but nevertheless prefers the Latin poetry. Milton's compliment to Manso he calls "des vers latins dignes du siècle d'Auguste."[3] In connection with Leonora Baroni, he is wrong, of course, in saying that Milton celebrated her beauty and her voice "dans quelques vers anglais et dans un sonnet italien."

While it did not go the extremes that later approaches would, Villemain's critical method accorded some importance to a writer's environment, education and occupations. Thus the young Milton's Italian journey was, to Villemain, a major factor in understanding the later man and artist. Contact with Manso and, even more, seeing Andreini's *Adamo* were valuable moments in Milton's preparation for his great work, *Paradise Lost*. Villemain recounts Voltaire's anecdote about Milton's seeing *Adamo* in Milan, pointing out that Samuel Johnson had energetically contradicted Voltaire. To Villemain the anecdote seemed probable, and he adds, as Voltaire had not done, that the second scene of act 1 is a discourse by Satan beholding the sun. There is no denying that this is a weak first draft of Satan's sublime apostrophe to the sun in *Paradise Lost*, Villemain observes. That Milton should have used Andreini by no means

detracts from his magnificent achievement. "Qu'importe ces premières traces d'imitation effacées par l'enthousiasme du poète et perdues dans sa richesse! Au reste, un motif naturel de croire que Milton rapporta d'Italie quelques pressentiments, quelques ébauches de sa grande pensée, c'est que l'on retrouve cette pensée dans les écrits qu'il fit paraître à son retour sur des sujets peu faits pour y préparer son esprit" (Villemain, 315). Here Villemain alludes to "Mansus," where the poet hinted that, in time to come, he might write on King Arthur and his knights. In 1830 Villemain noted in his *Cours de littérature française du moyen âge* that, in his youth, Milton considered devoting an epic to King Arthur and the Round Table. Posterity, the critic held, can be glad the poet renounced this whim, "cette velléité du génie." "Il a bien fait d'abandonner ce sujet pour le plus grand de tous et de sacrifier l'enchanteur Merlin au *Paradis perdu*."[4]

Upon Milton's return to England, he settled in London and devoted himself to the education of several boys, including his two nephews, and to his prose polemics. Villemain refers to *Of Reformation*, *Of Prelatical Episcopacy* and *The Reason of Church Government*. But in the midst of it all, Milton revealed that he was nourishing another enthusiasm. Villemain quotes the "digression toute poétique" in *The Reason of Church Government*, in which Milton announced his plan to write a work "not to be raised from the heat of youth or the vapors of wine... but by devout prayer." Although he used the word "égarements" to describe Milton's partisan involvements at this time, Villemain liked to think that the poet entered the arena reluctantly. "Enfin," the critic writes, still basing his remarks on *The Reason of Church Government*, "jetant un triste regard sur les querelles où il s'engage, il regrette de quitter sa douce et agréable solitude nourrie d'heureuses pensées, pour s'embarquer sur une mer turbulente, emporté loin de la brillante image de la vérité qu'il aimait à contempler dans l'atmosphère paisible et pure de ses études chéries" (Villemain, 317).

A Milton devoted to the private pleasures of erudition and longing for an ivory tower cuts a romantic figure, but Villemain realized that there was another side to his author.

Milton was emerging as a pamphleteer. His activities, essentially of his own choosing, were inspired by partisan zeal. These activities, pure in motive, demonstrate that he had no practical understanding of human nature, no comprehension of life as it is, according to Villemain. Fervent in his dedication to freedom, Milton lived in the "illusion continuelle d'un esprit qui ne voit que ses propres pensées." These, plus his candor and irascible disposition, to all of which he owed his original turn of mind, likewise made it inevitable that he would become the tool of the ambitious men and the fanatics who were about to set England ablaze. Villemain also points to a narrow personal element at work in the "violent" divorce tracts and in their author's no less violent reaction against the Presbyterians, whom the tracts scandalized. He considers Milton's harboring the Powells a generous act, however, and he is glad that Milton was not present at King Charles's trial and execution, assuming this to be the case. But it is not clear what he means when he declares that "Milton s'était abstenu de mettre au jour, avant la fatale sentence, un ... écrit sur la responsabilité des magistrats et des rois...." (Villemain, 318). Villemain appears to have surmised that *The Tenure of Kings and Magistrates* was written prior to Charles's death, but he proposes no reason for why Milton should have "abstained" from making it public at the time he wrote it. Villemain believed that Milton was also busy at this time with *The History of Britain*, which is correct. Regrettably, little is said about *Areopagitica*. Believing in a free press at a time when censorship existed in France, Villemain may have had opinions that would have been unwise or impossible to express. He characterizes the work as "un écrit plein de force."

Another of Milton's "illusions" Villemain admired without reservation, demonstrating that he was in the mainstream of French political thought at the time the Milton article was written. Like most of his contemporaries, French and otherwise, Villemain championed Greek independence in a loud and persistent voice. In particular, he discussed the matter in *Essai sur l'etat des Grecs* and in *Lascaris ou les Grecs au quinzième siècle.* He was pleased to see that the Latin Secretary had held views similar to his own and had even hoped to see his dream translated into reality.⁵

In connection with Milton's service as Latin Secretary, Villemain comments that, as he worked in their interests, Milton made common cause with the Independents and came to share their fanaticism to the point that he whitewashed their blackest deeds. A case in point is *Eikonoklastes.* Little is said about the circumstances that gave rise to the book, nor does the critic go into the matter of Pamela's Prayer, which Milton discovered in *Eikon Basilike* and discussed in *Eikonoklastes.* Quoting his own *Histoire de Cromwell,* Villemain states that Milton's book was beneath him. "Ces attaques contre un roi qui n'était plus, ces poursuites au-delà du jugement, ces insultes au-delà de l'échafaud avaient quelque chose d'abject et de féroce que l'éblouissement du faux zèle cachait à l'âme enthousiaste de Milton."⁶

As Villemain saw it, Saumaise's *Defensio Regia pro Carolo I* was much less admirable than the noble cause it sought to defend. As for Milton's reply, it bristles with savage erudition. At work in it is "le génie pédantesque du seizième siècle, enflammé d'un implacable fanatisme de liberté," its resources marshaled to justify a crime. This was *Pro Populo Anglicano Defensio,* "œuvre odieuse qu'il croyait patriotique." It earned its author an international reputation. Villemain appears never to have heard of Pierre Du Moulin or Alexandre More. He does not look upon the *Defensio Secunda* as an official undertaking, presenting it rather as the author's reaction to his adversaries' attacks. Milton wrote it, Villemain states, because he was "aigri par les haines qu'il avait méritées." Clearly, Villemain was not on the republicans' side. As for the "English people" in the title, this simply meant the despot who governed them. Finally Milton published his own defense. If in the other two he had lost his temper, he is calm and dignified in *Pro Se Defensio.* Villemain seems not to realize that the work is often humorous and vituperative and that it on occasion is almost obscene in excoriating More and Pontia (Villemain, 321).

Villemain commends what he takes to have been the author's disinterestedness, his sincere commitment to the republican banner. As he phrases it, "Les bassesses de l'intérêt ne se mêlèrent jamais aux passions politiques de Milton. Fanatique de bonne foi, il avait sacrifié sa médiocre fortune en dons patriotiques, pour la cause du Parlement." With "fanatique de bonne foi," Villemain coined an excellent phrase to describe Milton at this point in his career. Perhaps more than persuading his adversaries and those of the Republic and Protectorate, Milton convinced himself with rationales that to most readers, then as now, seem so specious and so untenable but into which he threw his whole fund of zeal and principle.

While he readily admitted his author's good faith, Villemain never abandoned his position that Milton was misguided in his stouthearted adherence to the bookish "theological republicanism" in which he lived. Milton saw both events and people as he wished to see them, or rather he convinced himself that what he wanted to see was really there. Thus "la scolastique violente des puritains, la dictature du Long Parlement, lui semblaient une imitation de l'éloquence et de la liberté romaines" (Villemain, 321). When group dictatorship gave way to an individual's despotism, Milton went along with the change. Zealous republican that he was, Milton nevertheless not only served Oliver Cromwell but even showered him with enthusiastic praise. Villemain's explanation is eloquent and plausible, perhaps correct:

> L'homme extraordinaire, qui faisait de grandes choses et de grands crimes, toujours au nom de Dieu, qui appuyait sur ses victoires le mensonge de sa mission, qui jeûnait, priait, pleurait devant le peuple, qui avait toujours à la bouche l'Evangile et la gloire de l'Angleterre, qui, despote dans son pays, humiliait les rois étrangers avec une fierté toute républicaine; ce fourbe, d'une conduite si haute et si ferme, cet imposteur qui paraissait si convaincu, ce Mahomet du nord et de la scolastique, ce génie puissant et inégal, mêlant tous les contrastes de grandeur et de trivialité, de raison hardie et de singularité fantasque, Cromwell, enfin, par tous les accidents de sa fortune et de son caractère, était un héros

assorti, pour ainsi dire, à l'imagination sublime et bizarre de Milton. Il devait à la fois l'inspirer et le dominer. (Villemain, 324)

[The extraordinary man who performed great deeds and committed great crimes, always in God's name, who used his victories to buttress his lie about having a mission, who fasted, prayed, wept in front of the people, who always had the Gospel and the glory of England on his lips, who, a tyrant in his own country, humiliated kings abroad with highhanded republican pride; this scoundrel who behaved with such determined hauteur, this imposter who seemed so convinced, this Mohammed of the north and of scholasticism, this powerful, unequal mind in which all the contrasts of greatness and triviality, bold reason and improbable whimsy mingled, Cromwell in short, by all the happenstances of his character and career, was a hero well suited to Milton's sublime, bizarre imagination. At one and the same time he was to dominate and inspire the poet.]

If Milton remained in Cromwell's service, it is because the Lord Protector overawed him. Thus Villemain does not take into account the poet's possible material need. Nor does he allow for Milton's disillusionment with the pompous, inept Parliament. Perhaps having to choose between Cromwell's resolute dictatorship and Parliament's blunders might not have been too difficult, especially when the dictator went to such pains to look like a servant of the Lord. However, Villemain senses that Milton's accepting the Lord Protector was not without hesitations. Although the sonnet to him is not mentioned, part of the poet's tempered advice to Cromwell at the end of *Defensio Secunda* is brought in.[7] More than once Milton took it upon himself to counsel the dictator, the critic points out. All in all, he was "bold" in doing this, and his efforts do him credit (*Histoire de Cromwell* 2:235).

Of Milton's political treatises in general, Villemain remarks, "Malgré le pédantisme du style et l'absurdité fréquente des raisonnements, ils sont... remarquables par un tour mâle et vigoureux. On conçoit à toute force que le génie violent et passionné qui les écrivait soit devenu le sublime auteur du *Paradis perdu*" (Villemain, 346). Villemain had expanded the idea somewhat in the *Histoire de Cromwell*, noting that the poet's violent controversies paved the way for *Paradise Lost* once the pamphleteer had had to return to private life.

> Nourrie dans les factions, exercée par tous les fanatismes de la religion, de la liberté, de la poésie, cette âme orageuse et sublime, en perdant le spectacle du monde, devait un jour retrouver dans ses souvenirs le modèle des passions de l'enfer et produire du fond de sa rêverie, que la réalité n'interrompait plus, deux créations également idéales, également inattendues dans ce siècle farouche, la félicité du ciel et l'innocence de la terre. (*Histoire de Cromwell* 2:234)
>
> [Coming of age amid factions, accustomed to all the militant zeal that religion, freedom and poetry can entail, this tormented, sublime soul one day, when he could no longer see the world, was to summon up his recollections and in them find his pattern for the tempestuous drives of Hell, and out of the depths of his musing, into which reality no longer intruded, bring into being two creations equally ideal, equally unexpected in that ferocious age, heavenly happiness and early innocence.]

The remainder of Milton's years in public service and then in retirement are passed in rather rapid review. Villemain's principal theme here is that neither Cromwell nor his associates nor the public as a whole had any idea of the real worth of the man they knew as a controversialist and translator of diplomatic correspondence, nor would they have cared. Though not a true romantic, this critic, like the romantics, saw Milton as an isolated genius, disdained and even hated, whom his contemporaries neither would nor could understand.

Of Milton's literary output at this time, the sonnet to his deceased wife is called "quelques vers d'une admirable douceur." Villemain assumes that the wife was Katherine Woodcock. Work on the *History of Britain* and the Latin dictionary is mentioned. Villemain believes that *Paradise Lost* was probably begun toward the end of the Protectorate. As the republican regime was collapsing, new pamphlets made it clear that the author's old illusions were as vivid as ever, but public sentiment was such that no one paid any attention. Charles II ascended his father's throne, and Milton was briefly imprisoned, then released. Whether authentic or not, the story about Davenant's intervening deserves to be true. Free and forgotten, his principles scorned, the old idealist could resume work on his sublime epic. When it appeared, it too was ignored, and Milton turned to other labors. One of these was the *History of Britain*, remarkable for its simplicity.

For *Samson Agonistes* Villemain has little praise. He notes the similarities, which he believes unintentional, between poet and protagonist. In his opinion, *Samson* proves that Milton did well not to write the other biblical dramas he had planned. This one, he feels, does not adhere to the classical rules nor does it possess dramatic movement. "C'est une longue déclamation où brillent quelques éclairs de génie." Those sparks of genius are totally lacking in *Paradise Regained*, the composition of which Villemain seems to place, in point of time, after that of *Samson Agonistes*. The critic dismisses it with the terse comment that it is a "poème en quatre chants que Milton composa comme une suite à son grand ouvrage et qui tomba d'abord dans l'oubli profond où il est resté" (Villemain, 332).

With these poems behind him, Milton resumed his scholarly work. Villemain mentions but does not discuss the treatise he devoted to logic, *Artis Logicæ Plenior Institutio*.[8] Once more Milton also aired his religious and political convictions, this time in *Of True Religion, Heresy, Schism, and Toleration*. "Ainsi cette passion de controverse qui avait possédé sa jeunesse le suivit jusqu'à sa dernière heure; et ce qu'il y a de plus sublime dans l'enthousiasme et de plus gracieux dans l'amour, la peinture du ciel et de l'Eden, semble luire comme un rayon passager sur cette vie toute plongée dans les noirs débats de la scolastique et de la guerre civile" (Villemain, 335). *Paradise Lost* had been a luminous moment in an otherwise murky existence. This is one of Villemain's favorite ideas in his Milton essay, and the critic goes so far as to say of the political treatises that "la postérité, laissant ces diatribes dans l'oubli qu'elles méritent, ne cherche Milton que dans son poème, qui fait un éternel honneur à l'esprit humain" (Villemain, 346). Years later, Barbey d'Aurevilly would say almost the same thing.

Villemain tells his readers that, in the last year of his life, Milton collected and published some of his youthful poems. Villemain seems not to have realized that, with the addition of poems written in the author's middle years, this was a new version of an earlier volume. It was at this time also, Villemain notes, that Milton published "quelques lettres écrites en latin" (Villemain, 332). At the end of his essay, Villemain remembers another of Milton's works, to which, here again, he attaches scant importance. Of the *State Papers*, which are not without their interest to the historian, he says that "cette correspondance ne renferme guère, suivant l'usage, que des mensonges officiels exprimés en beau latin" (Villemain, 346). When he wrote this comment, the critic was not yet a cabinet minister.

Villemain gives the usual details as to the composition and publication of *Paradise Lost*, the public's apathetic reaction, and the new edition in 1674. Several other seventeenth century editions are also mentioned. As time passed, he relates, people began to take notice:

> Addison prouva méthodiquement, dans le *Spectateur*, ce que beaucoup de gens commençaient à soupçonner, c'est-à-dire que Milton était un génie auquel il n'avait manqué que le climat et la langue d'Homère. Il montra même que les grandes idées de la religion lui avaient donné une nouvelle espèce de sublime, qui souvent le place au-dessus de tout parallèle; et il osa dire que si l'on refusait à cet ouvrage le nom de poème épique, il faudrait l'appeler un poème divin. L'Angleterre, si orgueilleuse de tout ce qu'elle produit, se vanta de son Milton comme de son Shakespeare. Cet enthousiasme, justifié par de véritables beautés, ne fit que s'accroître. (Villemain, 333)

> [Addison proved methodically in the *Spectator* what many people were beginning to suspect, that Milton was a mind that had only lacked Homer's climate and language. He even demonstrated that great religious ideas had given him a new variety of the sublime that often places him above any comparison; and he dared to declare that if one refused to call this work an epic poem, it would have to be called a divine poem. England, so inordinately proud of all it produces, boasted of its Milton as it did its Shakespeare. Such enthusiasm, justified by truly beautiful features, only increased with time.]

William Lauder and the Jacopo Masenio business are broached in Villemain's essay. The author believes that Milton imitated a few of *Sarcotis*'s lines but thinks Lauder acted in bad faith. He notes that public opinion rejected Lauder's accusations and admired Milton's original mind more than ever (Villemain, 333–34). To Andreini and Masenio could be added other sources, including the Bible, Homer, Plato, Euripides, the ancient and modern Latin poets, Hugo Grotius and Friedrich Taubmann. Despite the fact that he sometimes borrowed immoderate, tasteless chunks from other authors, Milton nonetheless remains a creative genius. *Paradise Lost*'s subject matter "n'en est pas moins devenu la conquête exclusive du grand poète qui l'a saisi et pénétré tout entier; et autant il était avant lui vulgaire et rebattu, autant il est devenu, sous sa main, sublime et nouveau" (Villemain, 334–35). Villemain best expresses his attitude toward Milton's literary debts with his succinct remark, "Il semble plutôt inspiré qu'enrichi par ce qu'il emprunte" (Villemain, 343). Elsewhere he states that however much Milton read and however much it shows in *Paradise Lost*, the poet absorbed, assimilated, added his own personal touches, essentially struck out on his own (Villemain, 336). Although the poet borrowed from other writers, further, *Paradise Lost* as a whole resembles no known model.

In *Paradise Lost* are summed up all of Milton's intellectual curiosities, all of his worldy experience, all of his ideals, according to this critic. Nothing he ever did or believed is absent from this compendium.

> Les fureurs du fanatisme, l'enthousiasme de la révolte, les tristes joies des partis vainqueurs, les haines profondes de la guerre civile avaient de toutes parts assailli et exercé son génie. Les chaires des églises d'Angleterre, les salles de Westminster, toutes pleines de séditions et de bruyantes menaces, lui avaient fait entendre ce cri de guerre contre la puissance qu'il aimait à répéter dans ses chants et dont il armait l'enfer contre la monarchie du ciel. La religion indépendante des puritains, leurs extases mystiques, leur ardente piété sans foi positive, leurs interprétations arbitraires de l'écriture avaient achevé d'ôter tout frein à son imagination

et lui donnaient quelque chose d'impétueux et d'illimité, comme les rêves du fanatisme. (Villemain, 328–29)

[The rage of fanaticism, the thrill of rebellion, the dismal rejoicing of the winning sides, the deep hatreds of civil war had assailed and exercised his mind at every turn. The pulpits of England, the chambers of Westminster, all ringing with seditious plots and noisy threats, had drummed into his ears that war cry against authority that he loved to repeat in his verse and with which he armed Hell against the monarchy of Heaven. The Puritans' independent religion, their mystic ecstasies, their burning piety bereft of positive faith, their arbitrary interpretations of the Scriptures had finally lifted the last restraint on his imagination, giving it something impetuous and boundless, like fanaticism's dreams.]

In May 1840, reviewing the third and fourth volumes of de Tocqueville's *De la démocratie en Amérique*, Villemain noted that Milton was a democrat with a democrat's passions but added that his violent notions did not keep him from being an excellent painter of the ideal and the supernatural (*Journal des Débats*, 262). Once more, the critic suggests that Milton may have begun *Paradise Lost* during the Republic or the Protectorate.

While the poet's readings and experience left their mark on *Paradise Lost*, basically the poem derives from Milton's mind alone, as Villemain saw it. Mind both creates and sustains the intricate worlds in which the action takes place. *Paradise Lost* is as spectacular an accomplishment as Satan's incredible journey across the void. To be sure, occasional slipping and falling are inevitable in so bold an enterprise. *Paradise Lost*'s blemishes are numerous, and a French reader, more than any other, should be sensitive to them. Shakespeare's unlettered muse, however brilliant, sometimes shocks the reader. So does Milton's, but here it is because the muse is too learned. Milton abuses his audience with tiresome, misplaced erudition. "Des suppositions bizarres et superflues; de fastidieux détails de géographie, de mythologie; des subtilités de controverse; ça et là d'insipides plaisanteries; quelquefois une foule d'expressions techniques et un défaut absolu de poésie: voilà ce qui obscurcit le génie de Milton et diminue le ravissement qu'inspire d'abord son magnifique ouvrage" (Villemain, 339). In addition to these general ones, Villemain has specific complaints, which for the most part are those that French critics have always voiced in discussing *Paradise Lost*. "Quoi qu'en dise l'ingénieux Addison," he writes,

> l'idée de rapetisser les démons pour les faire siéger à l'aise dans une espèce de parlement infernal[9] est une ridicule fiction; et l'épouvantable fiction du Péché et de la Mort renferme plus d'horreur que de génie. La Mort, qui lève la tête *pour respirer l'odeur des cadavres futurs*, est une atrocité anglaise, surchargée de mauvais goût italien. Les anges révoltés tirant du canon dans le ciel, Dieu prenant un compas pour circonscrire l'univers, les diables changés en serpents pour siffler leur chef sont des inventions plus capricieuses que grandes. On ne peut nier non plus que Milton ne soit médiocrement inspiré dans le langage qu'il prête à Dieu et qu'il ne le fasse souvent dogmatiser en théologien. Enfin, et ce défaut paraîtra plus grave, son poème, qui n'offre que deux personnages réels et qu'un seul événement humain, ce poème, soutenu longtemps à force de génie, tombe au dixième chant, aussitôt après la désobéissance du premier homme. Et les deux derniers livres ne sont plus qu'une déclamation fatigante, mêlée de traits admirables. (Villemain, 339)

> [the idea of shrinking the demons in order to make them sit at ease in a kind of infernal parliament[9] is a ridiculous plot element; and the terrifying invention of Sin and Death reveals more horror than genius. Death, which *rears its head in order to smell the odors of future corpses*, is an English atrocity overloaded with Italian bad taste. As plot features, the rebel angels firing cannon in Heaven, God taking a compass to circumscribe the universe, and the devils turning into snakes to hiss at their leader are more capricious than grand. Nor can it be denied that Milton was less than well inspired in creating dialogue he put into the mouth of God, whom he often makes dogmatize like some theologian. Finally, and this flaw is more serious, his poem, which presents only two real characters and only one human event, this poem, long sustained by its author's sheer genius, falls flat in the tenth canto, immediately after the first man's disobedience. The last two books are no more than a tiresome declamation, strewn with admirable flashes.]

Perhaps, too, Milton's Hebrew instrument, dulled by the monotonous northern climate, was less suited to the epic than the more melodious Greek and Italian ones were. Yet, "quels jets de lumière, quelle poésie de l'Orient brillent à travers ces nuages et les colorent d'un éclat céleste!" A true French romantic in this respect, Villemain extols Milton's abundant use of contrast, which authenticates his poetic vocation. Milton could paint pictures that are calm and pleasant or stern and terrible. His varied rhetorical devices, on the one hand soothing, on the other terrible, reveal "le caractère même de l'inspiration poétique: c'est la source de l'intérêt et de la variété. Depuis Homère jusqu'à Dante, depuis le Tasse jusqu'à Racine, l'âme du vrai poète a toujours mêlé ses tons divers. Mais comme jamais les contrastes ne furent plus marqués, jamais l'art du poète n'étonna davantage" (Villemain, 335–38).

However exquisite, it is not in the description of Eden, in which he detects too many bookish reminiscences,[10] that Villemain discovers the Milton that he admires most. Rather, it is the depiction of Adam and Eve that elicits his most unrestricted praise. Here, to the critic, Milton is at his creative best, unrivaled and unsurpassed. Both content and tone are modern. Passion having been rehabilitated in French literature by Rousseau, Chateaubriand and later French romantics, Villemain hails the presentation of Adam and Eve's love as being at once chaste and impassioned.

> Adam et Eve, leur nature fragile et presque divine, leur amour qui fait une partie de leur innocence, l'inexprimable nouveauté de leurs sentiments et de leur langage, cette création est toute au poète anglais. La muse épique n'avait rien inventé de semblable. Malgré le génie de Virgile et les pleurs dont saint Augustin s'accuse, Didon mourante n'égale pas ce tableau chaste et passionné. L'amour conjugal, retracé par Homère, n'atteint pas à cette pureté sublime. Ici la passion est la vertu même, et la volupté semble un des biens célestes que l'homme a perdus. (Villemain, 338–39)

> [Adam and Eve, their fragile and almost divine nature, their love which is part of their innocence, the inexpressible newness of their sensations and language, this creation belongs wholly to the English poet. The epic muse had invented nothing like it. Despite Virgil's genius and the tears St. Augustine confesses he shed, Dido's death

does not measure up to this chaste, passionate tableau. Married love, depicted by Homer, falls short of this sublime purity. Here passion is virtue itself, and voluptuousness seems to be one of the heavenly attributes that mankind has lost.]

Aware of their inherent charm, the poet was able to "varier et prolonger les scènes d'un drame si admirablement simple." But there is more. "Il ne lui suffit pas d'avoir montré dans l'éclat de leur beauté, dans l'innocence de leur tendresse, ces deux créatures nouvelles; il ne suffit pas d'avoir achevé ce tableau de pureté, de gloire, et de bonheur par le contraste d'un témoin invisible échappé de l'enfer et tout ensemble jaloux et presque attendri de la félicité qu'il vient détruire" (Villemain, 338). Satan is the invisible witness, of course.

After Satan, there are the marvelous episodes dealing with the War in Heaven and the Creation, and then the poet returns to Adam and Eve.

> Après avoir fait succéder à ces couleurs naïves et gracieuses les gigantesques images du combat céleste et le spectacle sublime de la création, le poète ... ramène la peinture d'Adam et d'Eve sortant des mains du créateur: il arrête lentement l'imagination charmée sur ce premier amour naissant avec la vie; et il semble recueillir avec un soin religieux toutes les traces du suprême bonheur qui va disparaître. Ce fatal dénouement du poème lui inspire encore des images, non plus animées d'une grâce majestueuse comme l'innocence, mais embellies d'une grâce touchante, comme la faiblesse unie à la beauté. Rien ne surpasse en pathétique la douleur d'Eve coupable et le pardon mutuel des deux époux. (Villemain, 338–40)

> [Having placed one after the other these simple, charming colors, the gigantic images of the War in Heaven and the sublime spectacle of the Creation, the poet returns to the picture of Adam and Eve emerging from the hands of the Creator: he causes the reader's delighted imagination to linger over this first love that springs into being with life itself; and he seems to gather up with religious care all traces of the supreme happiness that is about to disappear. This fatal conclusion of the poem inspires him with even more images, no longer enlivened by a charm that is majestic like innocence but rather embellished by a touching one, like weakness joined to beauty. In pathos nothing surpasses the sorrow of Eve after her sin and the two spouses' mutual forgiveness.]

Villemain sees here, as he does elsewhere, traces of the

poet's own marital experiences and disappointments. Other personal allusions to which the critic calls special attention are the invocation to light; the call to Urania; and "le morceau, si poétique, où il se représente *tombé dans de mauvais jours, parmi des langues mauvaises, entouré de périls et de ténèbres, seul et redoutant le destin d'Orphée*" (Villemain, 340).

Villemain thinks that these private digressions, aside from being one of its most splendid features, draw this poem, which tends to be too involved with the ideal, a little closer to human experience. He hastens to add, however, that this should not be taken to mean that the supernatural characters are not well conceived and well delineated. Satan is a case in point. As has usually been true of French Milton critics, Villemain came close to being a Satanist. We may not agree with Villemain's interpretation, but this character's portrait filled him with awed admiration. "Satan," he declares, "est un des chefs-d'œuvre de l'invention poétique. Ce réveil de l'orgueil foudroyé; ce désespoir incapable de remords; cet amour du mal accepté pour consolation et pour vengeance; enfin, l'hypocrisie, dernier trait d'une âme infernale, forment un tableau sublime d'horreur et de génie" (Villemain, 340–41). While less central than their leader, some of the other diabolical characters are brilliant incarnations of special passions and vices. As to the speeches that are delivered in Hell, "l'expression poétique est portée à un degré de force et d'énergie qu'aucune langue n'a peut-être égalé" (Villemain, 341). This is high praise indeed, all the more so when one remembers the breadth of the critic's readings in ancient as well as modern literatures. Of the rebel angels' harmonious relations among themselves, the writer contends that "rien n'est plus terrible que cette concorde du crime: elle accroît l'horreur des lieux qu'il habite." Milton had seen the Levelers at work, "ces âmes obstinées, féroces avec fanatisme, profondément unies par la haine." Milton had witnessed this "et l'empreinte en restait sur son génie; elle se communiquait involontairement à ses tableaux et mêlait à toutes les images de terreur et d'effroi la fureur unanime et l'invariable complicité d'une faction" (Villemain, 341–42).

Villemain's admiration for Satan and his henchmen—or

at least for the manner in which the poet had presented them—extends to the devils' new abode, which he looks upon as one of the most astonishing feats of the human imagination. He calls particular attention to several aspects. "Voyez," he writes, "au premier chant, les voûtes de l'abîme s'ouvrir et, à travers les *ténèbres visibles*, Satan apparaître sur l'étang de feu, avec la splendeur éclipsée d'un archange." Villemain was all the more excited in that it was on so dramatic a note that Milton had begun his epic, for, he asserts:

> Jamais poète n'a osé, dès l'abord, saisir l'imagination par de si grandes fictions. Cet enthousiasme anime tout le premier chant; il se soutient dans le second par l'éloquence et la variété des discours. Il devient plus merveilleux dans le récit du voyage de Satan à travers le chaos, l'une des inventions où l'emploi de la langue humaine paraît le plus étonnant. L'inspiration s'élève et monte à son plus haut degré en approchant d'Eden, où le beau feu du poète s'épure sans s'affaiblir et jette une si douce lumière. (Villemain, 342)

> [Never has a poet dared, at the very outset, to seize the imagination using such grand fictions. This enthusiasm invigorates the whole first canto; it is maintained in the second by eloquence and the diversity of the speech. It waxes more supernatural in the recital of Satan's flight across Chaos, an invention in which human language seems to have been put to its most astonishing use. Inspiration rises and mounts to its peak as he approaches Eden, where the poet's fire, never flickering, gets purified and casts such a soft light.]

We have seen earlier that, to Villemain's way of thinking, the last two books of *Paradise Lost* diminish in interest. Villemain goes even further, toward the end of his essay, when he says in effect that the entire last half of the epic fails to live up to the promise contained in the first. Despite this reservation, his praise is almost unstinted. "Si les autres parties du poème égalaient les cinq premiers chants, si ces ailes de feu soutenaient toujours le poète, l'imagination n'aurait rien produit de plus grand que le *Paradis perdu*," he writes. "Et même, quelles que soient les langueurs et les disparités qui se fassent sentir dans le reste de l'ouvrage, il y règne un genre de beauté qui rachète toutes les fautes:

c'est le sublime, qui consiste, soit dans la magnificence et la splendeur des images, soit dans le plus haut degré de grandeur et de simplicité réunies" (Villemain). The critic adds that "son génie tendait naturellement au grand et au sublime" and thinks that *Paradise Lost* would provide examples for a treatise similar to the one that used to be attributed to Longinus.

In considering Milton's style in *Paradise Lost,* Villemain declares that with Milton, as with all writers, the manner is inseparable from the person. The diverse elements in the poet's mind and character show up in his poetic expression. The style is

> hardi, nouveau, majestueux, excessivement poétique, quelquefois d'une extrême simplicité et quelquefois bizarre, pénible, et prosaïque. La recherche des termes vieillis, l'imitation des tours hébreux et helléniques lui donnent quelque chose d'antique et de solennel qui convient à l'inspiration du barde sacré. Les règles vulgaires du langage y sont parfois violées. *Notre langue,* dit Addison, *fléchissait sous son génie;* et Johnson va jusqu'à dire que du mélange de tous les idiotismes étrangers qu'il emprunte, Milton s'est formé une espèce de *dialecte babylonien.* Mais ce dialecte est celui d'un homme de génie; il abonde en expressions d'une inimitable énergie; et quoique modifié sur le modèle des langues étrangères, il tient aux racines de la langue anglaise, qui nulle part ne paraît plus pompeuse et plus forte. (Villemain, 343–44)

> [bold, new, regal, excessively poetic, sometimes extremely simple and sometimes bizarre and painful, resembling prose. The quest for archaic terms, the imitation of Hebraic and Greek locutions give it something solemn and ancient, in keeping with the sacred bard's inspiration. The ordinary rules of language are sometimes violated here. *Our language,* said Addison, *sunk under the weight of his genius;* and Johnson goes so far as to declare that by mixing all the foreign idioms he borrows, Milton created for himself a kind of *Babylonian dialect.* But this dialect is that of a man of genius; it abounds in expressions of inimitable energy; and though altered on the model of foreign languages, it sticks to the roots of English, which nowhere else is stronger, more majestic.]

By "pompeuse" the critic means "majestic."

Present in *Paradise Lost* are other traces of Milton's

knowledge of foreign languages. In the versification, for instance, foreign influences make themselves felt

> non seulement par la suppression de la rime, liberté que la mesure et l'accent du vers anglais favorisent, mais surtout par les coupes suspendues, les mots rejetés,[11] les longues périodes, et une marche généralement conforme au vers grec ou latin. Ces caractères étaient assortis à son sujet; et l'absence même de la rime, que Pope lui reprochait, semble donner à son poème un tour plus fier et plus libre. Les Anglais ont loué son harmonie, et l'on peut remarquer souvent dans ses vers un soin curieux de tempérer l'âpreté des sons anglais par des noms propres d'origine italienne. Un critique habile[12] lui reproche cependant d'avoir manqué souvent à cette harmonie première et véritable, qui reproduit dans les sons le caractère des idées et qui est, pour ainsi dire, l'accent de la pensée. (Villemain, 344)

> [not only by eliminating rhyme, a liberty that the measure and stresses of English verse lend themselves to, but above all the suspension of accents, words running over from one line to the following one,[11] the long periods, and a progression that conforms on the whole to Greek or Latin versification. These traits were suited to his topic; and the very absence of rhyme, which Pope held against him, appears to give his poem a cast that is prouder and more liberated. The English have praised its harmony, and one can often detect that in his poetry he had worked to temper the harshness of English sounds by using proper nouns of Italian origin. An able critic nevertheless reproves him for having often missed that basic, real harmony that reproduces with sounds the nature of the ideas and which, so to speak, is the accent of the thought.]

If Villemain does not refute the charge, he at least advances an explanation.

> On aperçoit, dans le *Paradis perdu*, des traces fréquentes de fatigue et de négligence qui peuvent expliquer ce défaut particulier, dont un étranger n'est pas juge. Ce n'est pas en vain, sans doute, que le poète, aveugle et malheureux, se plaignait d'être engourdi par le froid du climat et des ans. Il avait commencé tard son grand ouvrage: il se hâtait de finir; et quand l'inspiration lui manquait, il laissait tomber ses vers, que son siècle n'examinait pas. (Villemain, 344–45)

[One notices, in *Paradise Lost*, frequent traces of weariness and carelessness that may explain this particular flaw, which a foreigner cannot judge. Needless to say, it was not mere talk when, blind and fallen upon evil days, the poet complained of being numbed by the cold that comes with climate and age. He had begun his great work late, and he was in a hurry to finish. When inspiration was not there, he would toss out his lines as they came to him, and his era did not examine them.]

Villemain's essay on Milton is an attempt by a French critic with both romantic and classical tendencies to place the English poet in his historical milieu and treat him as its product. In this respect, the essay is only partially successful. It does, however, reflect a sincere desire to understand Milton's prose and certain parts of *Paradise Lost* in terms of the era and the temperament that produced them. Writing a few years later, Philarète Chasles thought Villemain too severe in assessing Milton's political ideas and activities. On the whole, Villemain did take a harsh stand on the polemical works, but he admitted that the author's Latin style had both charm and elegance. In "L'Allegro" and "Il Penseroso" and the other minor poems he saw little merit, yet for one or two of the sonnets he had a connoisseur's appreciative eye. He considered *Comus* odd and did not bother to mention *Arcades*. As Chasles saw it, Villemain missed the poet's "mérite lyrique."[13] Only rare brilliant sparks relieve *Samson Agonistes*'s monotony, Villemain thought. There are none at all to enliven *Paradise Regained*. Even in *Paradise Lost* there are weaknesses and desiderata, especially in the later books. A contemporary, Alfred Michiels, accused Villemain of expecting too much. According to Villemain's ideas, he wrote, one would scarcely find a Christian epic "dans la *Divina commedia* ni dans le *Paradis perdu* mais dans le *Speculum universale* de Vincent de Beauvais."[14] Yet, with all the reservations, *Paradise Lost* to Villemain was a true epic, in some respects the best one that world literature had produced. On the basis of it, the critic bestowed praise upon "le caractère antique et simple" of its author and forgave him for his pamphlets.

2

François René de Chateaubriand

Toward the end of the nineteenth century, Rémy de Gourmont wrote that "Milton, vu par Chateaubriand, est si grand qu'il touche le ciel et qu'il lutte avec Dieu." Gourmont added that Chateaubriand's Milton may be greater than Milton's Satan.[1] François René de Chateaubriand was a soldier, statesman, diplomat, historian and writer who ushered in French romanticism. For six months in 1791 he roamed about in North America, then returned to fight in the Armée des Princes against the French Revolution. Reverses eventually led his tattered group to disband, whereupon he made his way to England. There, in and near London, he lived on the verge of poverty for seven years, teaching and writing.

In 1800 he returned to France. Stability had settled in, and reaction against the previous decade's excesses was in full swing. One of its manifestations was a new wave of religious enthusiasm. Chateaubriand put himself at the head of the movement with a book started while he was in exile. This was the *Génie du christianisme*, published in 1802.

Its thesis was that Christianity, much more than the heathen religions, inspired and fostered the arts. As far as epic literature was concerned, Dante, Tasso, Camoës, Milton and Klopstock gave him plenty of material. Devoted as he was to the classics, however, he had problems with his thesis, and Homer and Virgil evoked more positive comment than he probably intended to give them. He published a *Paradise Lost* translation, one of the best, in 1836. His comments on the poet and his work are, on the whole, lucid, but there are rare occasions when he saw what he wanted to see in Milton's work.

Chateaubriand was a convinced, though very tolerant, Roman Catholic. He was also a liberal monarchist, dedicated to France's Bourbons. He subscribed to the doctrine that an annointed king's person was inviolate. Of Charles I, he mentions "une tête qu'aucune créature à visage d'homme n'avait le droit de toucher."[2] On the face of it, one might think he would have found Milton, the Puritan regicide, antipathetic. Not at all, or at least not ipso facto. Chateaubriand had much in common with Milton. For one thing, his dedication to legitimate kingship, far from dogmatic, was largely a question of honor and personal commitment, and he was convinced that monarchy would vanish soon enough, replaced by democracies. In any case, Milton was a man of principles, and Chateaubriand could understand that. Both Chateaubriand and Milton knew more than their share of material hardship in their later years. Both were also inveterate pamphleteers. Much involved in public affairs, both had to watch as their political ideals crumbled before their eyes, though both, appealing to their compatriots, made vigorous efforts to stop what was happening. Powerless to check it, both lived on into a hostile era, producing nonetheless some of their best work in an alien milieu they disliked and to which they did not belong. Concluding his *Essai sur la littérature anglaise*, Chateaubriand remarks that "Milton servit Cromwell, j'ai combattu Napoléon; il attaqua les rois, je les ai défendus; il n'espéra point en leur pardon, je n'ai pas compté sur leur reconnaissance."[3]

Chateaubriand claimed that no one is a proper judge of

anything not written in one's own language.[4] Ancient and modern, his own astute pronouncements on literatures other than French belie his statement. Probably his first encounter with Milton came at an early age. Aside from the *Génie du christianisme,* aside from the *Essai sur la littérature anglaise,* his work is peppered with allusions to Milton and quotations from his work. Early in the French Revolution, there were leaders who reminded him of *Paradise Lost.* Marat made him think of Sin. At the tribune, Mirabeau, "sombre, laid, et immobile," looked like Chaos.[5] Napoleon he compared to Moloch in *De Bonaparte et des Bourbons* (1814). Milton is also mentioned or discussed in the *Essai sur les révolutions* (1797), the *Discours de réception* (1811) at the Académie Française,[6] the *Réflexions politiques* (1814). During his tour of the Near and Middle East in 1806 and 1807, viewing the Pool of Siloam on one occasion, Chateaubriand recalled lines from *Paradise Lost.*[7] His prose epic *Les Martyrs* (1809), written shortly after his return, contains situations and lines reminiscent of the earlier epic. Excommunicated, its hero complains at one point that, "Ainsi qu'Adam banni du paradis terrestre, je me trouve seul dans un monde couvert de ronces et d'épines et maudit à cause de ma chute."[8] Along with other things he did while struggling to survive as an émigré, Chateaubriand had made some translations into French. Lines from Milton were among the things he translated.[9] Likewise, it was at this time that he wrote "Milton et Davenant" (1797), a short verse treatment of the anecdote about the two poets' saving each other's lives. Clearly, Milton was one of Chateaubriand's favorite authors.

The *Essai sur la littérature anglaise* (1836) was written as a companion piece to Chateaubriand's translation of *Paradise Lost.* In it, a disproportionate but indicative amount of space is allocated to Milton. Except for a detail or so, Chateaubriand better documented the poet's life than other French Milton critics at the time. True, he believed that the scrivener was noble and that he might have been born in France, but he did not insist. Noting what he called the poet's claim that he used to take on new life in the spring, Chateaubriand disagreed, observing that "la saison la plus favorable aux inspirations de Milton était l'automne, plus en rapport avec la tristesse et le sérieux de ses pensées."[10]

Chateaubriand had a sound knowledge of Milton's work, including the prose and the minor poems. He invokes "Ad Patrem," brings up the prolusions, and affirms that, while still in school, the student poet revealed his talent by composing "des pièces latines et des paraphrases des psaumes en vers anglais." The critic mentions "Elegia Prima" as providing material that the poet's enemies would later use against him. Chateaubriand points to the "Ode on the Morning of Christ's Nativity" as an excellent piece of artisanry, "admirable de rythme et d'un effet inattendu." Parts of the "Letter to a Friend" are quoted, as are the first four lines of "How Soon Hath Time."[11] Without comment, Chateaubriand alludes to *Arcades* and *Comus*. "Lycidas" seems to predict the death of Archbishop Laud, he believes. Concerning "L'Allegro" and "Il Penseroso," Chateaubriand doubts that the two characters have been made sufficiently distinct. There is no mirth in the poet's melancholy, to be sure, but there is a touch of sadness in his joy. The critic notes that the happy man's old age is not accounted for. "Pour le vieil âge de la *gaieté*, Milton ne fait point de provisions; mais il conduit la *mélancolie* avec une grande dignité jusqu'à la fin de la vie" (*Essai* 632–35). Early in life, Chateaubriand himself had refused to become a priest (*MOT* 1:135). He tells his readers that, on leaving Cambridge University, Milton declined to enter the ministry. Anticipating somewhat, he cites the poet's remark in *The Reason of Church Government* about a minister's having to "subscribe slave and take an oath withall."[12]

Like Milton, Chateaubriand had also traveled and lived in Italy. He evokes the young foreigner's friendship with Giovanni Battista Manso, reproducing a few lines from the two men's exchange of Latin verse.[13] He also mentions the visit to Galileo, the "courrier céleste" recalled in *Paradise Lost* (*Essai*, 635). At the time of his own first arrival in Rome, Chateaubriand had been delighted not only with the city but with the surrounding area and had written an enthusiastic *Lettre à M. de Fontanes sur la campagne romaine*

(1804).¹⁴ He was surprised that the English visitor appears to have been insensitive to the remarkable landscape.¹⁵ He notes that at the Vatican Milton got to know Lukas Holste, the librarian. Milton heard Leonora Baroni sing at Cardinal Francesco Barberini's palace, and she thrilled him. Chateaubriand points out that she is mentioned, a little later, in some contemporary French memoirs. "A-t-on jamais remarqué que Léonora se retrouve dans les *Mémoires* de Mme de Motteville, aux concerts de Mazarin?"¹⁶ Because of gathering political storms at home, Milton cut his tour short and did not visit Sicily and Greece (*Essai*, 635-37).

Nevertheless, having returned to England, Milton at first took no active part in the civil disorders then brewing. Soon, however, he would reveal his skill as a polemicist. "Milton est un aussi grand écrivain en prose qu'en vers," Chateaubriand states categorically. When the time came, it was religion that precipitated things. One after the other, Milton wrote *Of Reformation* and several other pamphlets. Against the Church of England, he was calling for freedom of worship. In the process, unfortunately, he treated with disdain a learned and venerable scholar, Archbishop James Ussher. Chateaubriand does not add that, somewhat later, Milton used Ussher's *Britannicarum Ecclesiarum Antiquitates* in writing his own *History of Britain*. Milton's pamphlets, linked to sectarian controversies of the moment, would have no interest for modern readers were it not for the author's stating in *The Reason of Church Government* that he intended to write something in English that his compatriots would not willingly let die. Translating, Chateaubriand quotes several prophetic sentences, running them together as if they were a single paragraph.¹⁷ As for *Of Education*, Chateaubriand thinks *Paradise Lost* could already have been on the poet's mind when he wrote it. From the treatise he plucks the sentence, "The end . . . of learning is to repair the ruins of our first parents by regaining to know God aright. . . ."¹⁸

Assuming that "Elegia Septima" was written when Milton was 19, Chateaubriand summarizes it and states that if the poet stuck to the views it expressed, he must never have loved any of his three wives. He wonders who the girl in the elegy might have been but dismisses the notion that it could have been Leonora Baroni. Whoever she was, she was a "mystérieuse sylphide." As an adolescent, Chateaubriand had been haunted by one of his own, totally imaginary, described and much talked about in the author's memoirs.[19] Having prepared the way, he discusses Milton's first matrimonial experiment. Mary Powell's desertion he attributes to possible political differences, but he allows that there could have been other reasons. Whatever the case, when it became clear that his wife did not intend to return, Milton decided to repudiate her. He made his personal problem a general one. "Pour faire jouir les autres maris de l'indépendance qu'il se propose, son esprit le porte à changer en une question de liberté une question de susceptibilité personnelle" (*Essai*, 639). He wrote *The Doctrine and Discipline of Divorce*.

To Chateaubriand, though he had written on the subject himself, divorce was not a vital issue.[20] He does not tell his readers that there were other divorce tracts. Limiting himself to *The Doctrine and Discipline of Divorce*, he translates the first two sentences of the address to the Long Parliament and the Westminster Assembly, plus a paragraph composed of selections chosen elsewhere. Milton did not really establish all his basic propositions, the critic held, nor did he resolve any specific questions. Instead, he generalized, preaching individual freedom of every kind. Even though he failed to prove his points, this man, who was to hail wedded love, made it clear that he was an ardent champion of divorce. The reconciliation with Mary Powell gave rise to the admirable forgiveness episode between Adam and Eve in book 10 of *Paradise Lost*. "La postérité a profité d'une tracasserie de ménage," Chateaubriand comments—a familiar explanation and probably correct. Chateaubriand had evoked this scene in the *Génie du christianisme* (*Génie*, 634–35). The Presbyterians raised a loud cry when *The Doctrine and Discipline of Divorce* appeared. "L'auteur, irascible, se détacha de leur secte et devint leur ennemi" (*Essai*, 639–41). Among French critics of the nineteenth century, Chateaubriand is one of the few to look into the poet's break with these erstwhile allies and give a plausible reason for it.

In tackling Milton's next cause, Chateaubriand did not know that the poet seems to have tried to get *The Doctrine and Discipline of Divorce* licensed and failed. In any event, Milton next spoke out in the interests of a free press. Probably Chateaubriand could assume that most of his readers were well aware that this had long been one of his own recurrent themes, that writing what he wished despite bungling government efforts at censorship had even landed him in prison three years earlier.[21] This further link with his author added warmth, naturally, to his remarks about *Areopagitica*. When Milton was writing, Chateaubriand notes, the expression "freedom of the press" was still unknown, and so the author subtitled his pamphlet *A Speech for the Liberty of Unlicensed Printing*. Praising its vigorous language, Chateaubriand points out that the author was the first to demand an unshackled press. "C'est lui qui le premier l'a nettement et formellement réclamée." That the author of *Paradise Lost* should also have written this great pamphlet is noble indeed; it is the best thing he ever wrote in English prose. In his habitual manner, Chateaubriand translates the highlights (*Essai*, 642–43).

Chateaubriand does not mention Sonnet 8, written at a time when King Charles's forces were expected to attack London (November 1642). He does believe that in April 1647 General Fairfax and Cromwell were occupying the city. To work in peace, Milton gave up his big house in Barbican and moved to a smaller one in High Holborn.[22] Shortly after arriving in London, Chateaubriand himself had lived in High Holborn for a time (*MOT* 1:435). It was hard to believe, he thought, that one could live and work in a civil war atmosphere, where people representing a thousand viewpoints were at one another's throats and were wading in blood in the midst of ruin and desolation. And yet, "Nous voyons Milton se marier, s'occuper de l'étude des langues, élever des enfants, publier des opuscules en prose et en vers comme si l'Angleterre jouissait de la plus profonde paix." Perhaps he watched Charles I's execution, then came home to prepare a lesson, work on his Latin grammar, or write a few lines of poetry. Often people's behavior in catastrophic times is incomprehensible. Chateaubriand cites examples during the Terror. Engulfed in revolution, the French nevertheless went to the theater and watched sentimental pastoral plays. "Les bergers occupaient la scène quand la tragédie courait les rues" (*Essai*, 643–44).

With King Charles beheaded, the Presbyterians screamed that he had been murdered. Chateaubriand likens them to France's Girondin Party when Louis XVI was tried and executed but tells readers that the Presbyterians, unlike the Girondins, were more sincere and had not actually voted for their sovereign's death. Here, of course, Chateaubriand is wrong. After all, Thomas Pride had purged the House of Commons (6 December 1648). Members disposed to save their king thus had had no opportunity to vote one way or the other. To silence or at least neutralize the clamor that arose after the king's death, Milton published *The Tenure of Kings and Magistrates*, which he wrote during the two weeks that preceded the execution. In it he tried to demonstrate that those who were making the most noise were the ones who had, in effect, sent their monarch to the block. Chateaubriand summarizes the work and translates a few sentences.

Milton's role in defending the king's execution had bothered Chateaubriand for a long time. Years before, in his *Réflexions politiques*, he had described *The Tenure of Kings and Magistrates* as a commentary on Juan Mariana's *De Rege et regis institutione* and had noted that it attracted a great deal of attention. Elsewhere, in the *Analyse raisonnée de l'histoire de France* (1831), he had written that "Jean Petit, sous Charles VI, soutint publiquement...la doctrine du régicide.... Mariana ressuscita la doctrine de Jean Petit avant que Milton l'établît dans la cause de Charles Ier." Chateaubriand disapproved but added that, well prior to the advent of democracy, monarchs had been deposed and put to death. In the *Essai* he added that *The Tenure of Kings and Magistrates* at least invoked Scripture. But then, as opposed to the French one, the Puritan Revolution had an essentially religious character. Both revolutions established the principle of freedom but did so from different perspectives. Treating the idea and developing it somewhat in *Les Quatre Stuarts*, Chateaubriand speaks of the "sentiment religieux qui animait les novateurs de la Grande-Bretagne" as opposed to the "principes d'irreligion qu'affichaient les artisans de nos discordes" (*Essai*, 645; *Réflexions politiques*, 59–61; *Œuvres complètes* 10: 210, 409–10). In another comparison of the two revolutions, Chateaubriand holds that, generally speaking, the French Revolution's pamphleteers were superior to those of the English Civil Wars and Commonwealth. Milton was an exception. On the whole, the English rebels had conviction and a lofty ethic on their side, but they were awkward and obstreperous (*Essai*, 629, 631).

Almost alone among his writer contemporaries, Chateaubriand knew that Oliver Cromwell did not come to power at the outbreak of the Civil Wars or even immediately after King Charles's death. Thus, he points out, it was the Council of State that hired John Milton as its Latin Secretary. Under the Protectorate, Milton stayed on in the same position. Chateaubriand explains that, until this time, English diplomacy had been conducted in French, an obvious choice because the language is so clear. Milton, whose business it was to put official communications in their final state, tried to make Latin the universal diplomatic language. He failed. Even so, rather than adopt French, the British later decided to use English in their official correspondence. The language, Chateaubriand says, does not lend itself to the task.[23]

Hardly had Milton assumed his duties than he was ordered to answer *Eikon Basilike*, an "odieuse commission" that he nonetheless accepted. Milton is cruel in *Eikonoklastes*, but, less dominated by his imagination than in his other political treatises, he is clear and methodical. As for Pamela's Prayer, Chateaubriand repudiates the idea that the pamphleteer could have had a hand in placing it in *Eikon Basilike*. "Rien dans le caractère de Milton n'autorise à croire qu'il eût pu se rendre coupable d'une pareille lâcheté" (*Essai*, 647). Milton and those whose ideas he shared were violent, but they were not scoundrels. These people had intercepted the king and queen's correspondence and published it, not changing a word.[24] "Les interpolations, les falsifications, les suppressions sont des moyens bas que la révolution anglaise a laissés à notre révolution." Intuitively, however, Chateaubriand believes John Gauden worked with notes Charles I left. Selecting various remarks, he expresses his conviction that, facing death, only the king could have written them. "Des sentiments intimes ne trompent pas; on ne peut se mettre si bien à la place d'un homme que l'on reproduise les mouvements d'esprit de cet homme dans telle ou telle circonstance de sa vie" (*Essai*, 648). Basically, *Eikon Basilike* was what it purported to be. Despite his stout republicanism, even Milton was at a loss as to how he should cope with the final chapter, Charles's meditations on death. He solved the problem by *not* dealing with them. By writing *Eikonoklastes*, he shared the regicides' deed and got splattered with the victim's blood (*Essai*, 645–49; *Œuvres complètes* 10:401).

As an accomplished Hellenist and Latinist, Chateaubriand was linguistically prepared to comment on what happened next. With the *Defensio Regia*, Claude de Saumaise "descendit dans l'arène, armé de toute l'érudition de son siècle." Milton was ordered to reply. Chateaubriand thinks Saumaise proved his points (*Réflexions politiques*, 59–61). Milton, he believes, did not. Nevertheless, *Pro Populo Anglicano Defensio* is the book for which Milton was best known during his lifetime. Milton began his rejoinder by insulting Saumaise's Latin. This kind of thing is the rule in learned controversies, the critic notes. "Tout homme habile en grec et en latin prétend que son voisin n'en sait pas un mot." In modern times, most works written in Latin, however good, would have made Roman schoolboys laugh. Milton's broadside is in polished, classical prose, vigorous and tight, but it lacks naturalness. Clearly thinking in English, the author loses his "originalité nationale." Milton went at his opponent "comme un fanatique combat un pédant." For one thing, accusing Saumaise of having been hired to write his book, Milton neglected to add that the thousand pounds he was receiving himself were more than his adversary got paid. Chateaubriand then summarizes the main points at issue and gives some of Milton's retorts. On the whole, he felt, Milton's reasoning was as bad as the cause he was championing. "L'auteur ne répond solidement à rien." Often the comic remarks are in poor taste, and the erudition is inappropriate. All the same, "Milton a remué d'une main puissante toutes les idées agitées dans notre siècle."

Dormant for a century and a half, these ideas were revived in 1789. Concerned as they are with issues that involve the modern reader, Milton's political tracts could have been written in the critic's own day. As for *Pro Populo Anglicano Defensio* specifically, ambassadors representing monarchs called, paid their respects, and complimented the Latin Secretary on his work justifying regicide. When one has seen ambassadors on all fours at the feet of Napoleon's secretaries, this should not come as a surprise. Saumaise's posthumous rejoinder to *Pro Populo Anglicano Defensio* was vitriolic. "Vraisemblablement la colère du savant venait moins de son horreur du régicide que des mauvaises plaisanteries de Milton contre le latin de la *Defensio Regia*" (*Essai*, 649–51; *Réflexions politiques*, 59–61). The comment could have its speculative value. Some years later, in passing, Chateaubriand would refer to the controversy's learned bitterness in the *Vie de Rancé*.[25]

Milton was even more savage in answering Pierre Du Moulin's *Regii Sanguinis Clamor ad Cœlum*, which he attributed to Alexandre More.[26] *Defensio Secunda* is of greater interest than *Pro Populo Anglicano Defensio* for various reasons, according to Chateaubriand. For one thing, Milton appears to champion the Greeks in this second treatise. That the English Homer should do so is as it should be. He had almost visited Greece in 1639, after all. In June 1652 he had written Leonard Philaras that he would like to see English ships and armies deliver Greece, the home of eloquence, from Turkish domination. Now he was praising it anew; again he was a precursor. Quoting one or two of his own parliamentary speeches, Chateaubriand points out that he too had called for Greek independence, another position he shared with the author he was considering.[27]

Defensio Secunda is important in addition because of the plethora of autobiographical data the author gives in it. Along with this information, it also contains curious historical portraits. Chateaubriand cites the writer's admiring words about John Bradshaw, General Fairfax and the Lord Protector. He then has to cope with Milton's praise of the dictator. Preparing his Académie Française speech in 1811, he had remembered what he called the "ostentatious encomium," and it had given him a point of departure. Relating the incident in his memoirs, he translated chunks of the address (*MOT* 2:266). In the *Essai* he points out that in stressing that individual and public freedom, so envied by citizens of other countries, had to be safeguarded, Milton at least tried to do something positive in addressing Cromwell. In a later era, who would have dared tell Napoleon that he owed this to his people?[28] Still, the poet would have done well to imitate those who, realizing that the man was a despot, decided to keep out of the Lord Protector's orbit. These men were true democrats, and Milton, though a convinced republican, was no democrat. Chateaubriand notes his fondness for calling attention to his heroes' illustrious birth. "La naissance joue un grand rôle dans les idées républicaines du poète." Chateaubriand could have added Milton's allusion to the "rude, inconsiderate" multitude excoriated in *The Ready and Easy Way*.

Finally, *Defensio Secunda* stands out as a remarkable, even unique piece of revolutionary propaganda. When Milton states that other countries' nationals applaud and long for the liberties the English people have won, he neglects to add, to be sure, that most of those liberties were snatched back rather quickly. Nevertheless, it was an arresting idea, and Milton put it across eloquently. "Milton seul avait ces idées; on n'en trouve aucune trace dans les révolutionnaires de son temps." Again, Chateaubriand thought, Milton was being prophetic. England has disseminated its political principles and institutions throughout the world (*Essai*, 651–56). In Chateaubriand's discussion, *Pro Se Defensio* is not mentioned among the other prose works.

Chateaubriand talks briefly about Milton's work as Latin Secretary. He loved contrasts and oppositions, and Oliver Cromwell's death and Richard Cromwell's accession inspired a few. Chateaubriand points out that Milton wrote the letters to Louis XIV and Mazarin announcing the Lord Protector's death. In the name of a man "investi d'un pouvoir de quelques heures," Milton was writing to a hereditary, absolute sovereign, one of whose descendants, like Charles Stuart, would die at the hands of the headsman. Louis XIV, a divine right king, went into official mourning for a regicide. Milton, hating not only kings but papists, moreover penned a letter to a monarch who would later revoke the Edict of Nantes. Richard Cromwell, of course, did not last long.[29] On vacating Whitehall Palace, he took with him two trunks filled with the good wishes he had received from the world's illustrious kings and princes at the time of his accession. To Chateaubriand it all proved how little store should be attached to fame and glory. Milton, in all of this, had at least played a role (*Essai*, 659–60; *Œuvres complètes* 10:426).

Among the writers of the period, Milton alone remained faithful to Cromwell's memory. Meditating about it, Chateaubriand was disturbed by Milton's apparent dedication to a man such as the Lord Protector. Insofar as he resolves the problem, he does it by concluding that, in Oliver Cromwell, Milton saw God's agent. In the struggle between God and Satan in *Paradise Lost*, he notes that Milton, despite his deep republican convictions, always makes the King of Heaven triumph. Like the Independents, the poet viewed a theocratic republic as the ideal form of government, on earth at least. But a theocratic republic could mean a narrowly restricted "liberté hiérarchique" under God. By accepting the Lord Protector as God's lieutenant general, Milton could reconcile his religious beliefs with Cromwellian dictatorship, and Chateaubriand implies that he did so. Thus Satan and his cohorts might be those unruly Presbyterians who, refusing to acknowledge Cromwell as God's representative, were repudiating divine truth. What Chateaubriand is doing here, of course, is tantamount to saying that, in a Cromwell representing and therefore answerable only to God, Milton was in effect subscribing to a divine right view of things that he accepted in the Lord Protector but rejected everywhere else. Chateaubriand quotes the Sonnet to Cromwell, as though it bolstered his argument (*Essai*, 695). Elsewhere he quotes a remark attributed to Milton that might give a better explanation for the poet's rallying to the dictator and even retaining a certain amount of retrospective esteem for him in later years. Chateaubriand reports that in old age, when people reproached him for having served a tyrant, Milton used to reply, "He delivered us from kings." Chateaubriand believes that Milton never changed his political opinions. "Demeuré républicain, il s'enferma dans ses principes avec sa muse et sa pauvreté" (*Essai*, 664–65). The question remains, however. Without quibbling over words too much, could one be a republican and still look kindly upon Cromwell's Protectorate?

After becoming Lord Protector, Cromwell was right in keeping Milton in his service as Latin Secretary, Chateaubriand thinks. The Lord Protector sensed the poet's greatness. "Cromwell, par un instinct de gloire, découvrit la gloire cachée de Milton et enchaîna la renommée du héros à celle du poète: c'est quelque chose dans l'histoire du monde que Cromwell ayant pour secrétaire Milton." Basically Chateaubriand looks upon Cromwell as a cunning hypocrite, but in his attitude one nevertheless detects a grudging admiration for the regicide opportunist. Milton's loyalty to the man he had served, however one wishes to interpret it, stands out. "Tandis que de petits auteurs bien vils, bien parjures, bien vendus au pouvoir revenu, insultaient les cendres du grand homme aux pieds duquel ils avaient rampé, Milton lui donnait un asile dans son génie, comme dans un temple inviolable" (*Essai*, 664).

Chateaubriand's sentence, beautiful as it is, suggests that the author of the *Essai* had not read *The Ready and Easy Way* as carefully as he might have. As Chateaubriand himself points out in *Les Quatre Stuarts*, the English Republic lasted only four years, until 1653. With Cromwell's death and Richard's abdication,[30] Milton bestirred himself. The Commonwealth's days were numbered. As Chateaubriand looked into Milton's frantic efforts to prevent a restoration, he no doubt recalled his own fruitless labors to save, then restore, the French Bourbons. "Que faisait Milton pendant cette décompositioon sociale? Voyant la liberté rétrograder, rêvant toujours la république, oubliant qu'il y a des moments où les écrits ne peuvent rien, il publia une brochure." It was Chateaubriand's way of coping with a political crisis, and indeed there were times when his pamphlets did no more good than the one Milton produced at this time, *The Ready and Easy Way to Establish a Free Commonwealth*. Milton thought that now it would be possible to reinstitute the one that Cromwell had abolished or, better still, create a more ideal one. In his pamphlet Milton warns his compatriots not to "build the chief hope of their common happiness or safety in a single person."

Chateaubriand quotes, in his usual manner, Milton's forecast of the evils that a return to kingship would bring about. Was Milton out of tune with his era in declaiming against these evils? Chateaubriand is not so sure and makes a comparison. He notes that Milton had toyed with the idea of writing on Athalia. Racine's *Athalie*, finished in 1691, is considered by many to be the most brilliant tragedy in the French language. It was also written in the shadow of the court of Louis XIV, the quintessential autocrat. Yet, in his play, Milton's devout monarchist contemporary across the English Channel seems to be giving kings, especially absolute kings, as severe a lesson in their responsibilities as Milton could have given them (*Athalie* 4.3). In *Athalie*, Joad, the high priest, tells a young king:

> Loin du trône nourri, de ce fatal honneur,
> Hélas! vous ignorez le charme empoisonneur.
> De l'absolu pouvoir vous ignorez l'ivresse,
> Et de lâches flatteurs la voix enchanteresse.
> Bientôt ils vous diront que les plus saintes lois,
> Maîtresses du vil peuple, obéissent aux rois;
> Qu'un roi n'a d'autre frein que sa volonté même;
> Qu'il doit immoler tout à sa grandeur suprême;
> Qu'aux larmes, au travail le peuple est condamné,

Et d'un sceptre de fer veut être gouverné;
Que s'il n'est opprimé, tôt ou tard il opprime.
(ll. 1387–397)

Milton's apprehensions about divine right kings could not have been better expressed, but neither could his misgivings about the masses *(Essai,* 668–69). As in *Pro Populo Anglicano Defensio,* Milton was prophetic. In the political domain, "Il voyait les longs combats que l'on serait obligé de livrer pour reconquérir ce qu'on allait perdre." Chateaubriand comments on these in *Les Quatre Stuarts* and declares that the process was indeed arduous. As for the prediction that a king would have "a dissolute and haughty court about him," Milton lived to see it become a reality. That king, whose return made the ideal republic Milton dreamed of impossible, was ready to step ashore at Dover.

Chateaubriand regarded Milton's views on the composition of a model parliament deserving of notice. Possibly the restrictions the poet urged upon his readers were needed in his day, but they are less applicable in Chateaubriand's time than they were then. The chasm between landowners and the rest of the people has diminished. Education has played an important role in this. "Les progrès de l'éducation et de la civilisation ont commencé à rendre les électeurs d'une classe moyenne plus aptes à comprendre des intérêts qu'ils ne comprenaient pas autrefois." Modern England has been able to bestow rights upon citizens who, in the seventeenth century, would have made government impossible had they been elected to the House of Commons *(Essai,* 661–62). In a somewhat different context, Chateaubriand observes that a single person at the head of a government is more prone to mercy than legislative bodies are. In the Declaration of Breda, Charles II left it up to the House of Commons to decide what individuals would not be included in a general amnesty. The subsequent "vengeances sanglantes" were the work of Parliament, not the Crown. "Les corps sont plus implacables que les individus, parce qu'ils réunissent en eux plus de passions et qu'ils sont moins responsables" *(Essai,* 663). Chateaubriand was not as idealistic as Milton. Several months before *The Ready and Easy Way*, Milton had published *A Treatise of Civil Power in Ecclesiastical Causes* and *Considerations Touching the Likeliest Means to Remove Hirelings out of the Church*. In them he examined tithes and church revenue and wondered whether, in their functions, ministers should be regulated by law.

In Chateaubriand's day, Milton's prose works were almost never read, and the critic was hardly overstating when he declared them "complètement oubliés." Yet, during his lifetime, Milton owed his reputation to them. Not even *Paradise Lost* can eradicate that reputation. Born of partisan passions, much in the prose was doomed to die when those passions had spent themselves. On the other hand, Milton was far in advance of his times in some respects, as Chateaubriand observes several times when discussing the political pamphlets. This was particularly true, he thought, with regard to representative government. "Toutes les questions générales et particulières agitées aujourd'hui chez les peuples du Continent et dans le Parlement d'Angleterre avaient été traitées et résolues par Milton dans le sens où notre siècle les résout. Il a créé jusqu'à la langue constitutionnelle moderne." Such words as *decrees* and *motions* we owe to this powerful mind, capable of inventing at one and the same time "un monde nouveau et une parole nouvelle de politique et de poésie" (*Essai*, 654, 662–63). As Chateaubriand sees it, the new world and new diction are Milton's poetic and political legacy.

After the Restoration, Milton continued his prose writing. He assembled three volumes of materials eventually used in the Cambridge University *Thesaurus Linguæ Latinæ* published in 1693. In addition, he compiled a Latin grammar. When toil of this kind did not consume all of his energies, he turned to other things. Since history appealed to him, he delved into that. His *Brief History of Muscovia* is "un abrégé amusant par de petits détails de la nature des voyages." Chateaubriand quotes the description of the Kremlin, reminding his readers that this is where Napoleon's reverses began. Relying upon the date of publication, Chateaubriand assigns *The History of Britain* to Milton's later years, unaware that most of it was probably written during the Civil Wars. Stylistically, it is "mâle, simple, entremêlé de réflexions presque toujours relatives au temps où l'historien écrivait." Juxtaposing past and recent events, Milton compares the natives' incompetence when the Romans evacuated their island to the "late civil broils," when the nation's leaders seemed unable to rule. Similarly, at the end of book 6, Milton lists the causes that led to the Saxons' defeat at the hands of the Normans in 1066, wondering whether the moral decay then prevalent could not reappear and make it possible for his compatriots to be subjugated once more. Chateaubriand says nothing about *The Character of the Long Parliament*.[31] The *Artis Logicæ* and *Of True Religion* are mentioned without comment. *De Doctrina Christiana* is not discussed. Several pieces of diplomatic correspondence are quoted, as are letters to Philaras and Peter Heimbach. If Milton was gigantic as a poet, he was also gigantic as a prose writer, Chateaubriand concludes (*Essai*, 655, 658–59, 666, 668, 672, 675).

Though calm and beautiful, *Paradise Regained* is "une œuvre de lassitude," and Chateaubriand lets it go at that. At this point he probably remembered his own Biblical drama, *Moïse*. Staged in 1834, it had not been a success. He had liked it, however, and he liked *Samson Agonistes*, which "respire la force et la simplicité antique." Chateaubriand summarizes it quickly and translates most of the opening monologue. An autobiographical drama, *Samson* reveals that Milton was sensitive to his contemporaries' indifference. Samson perished crushing the Philistines beneath splendid debris, just as "Milton, en mourant, a enseveli ses ennemis sous sa gloire." Fame was long in coming, but when it came, it made him immortal (*Essai*, 631, 675–76).

Whatever his other achievement's, Milton's immortality rests upon *Paradise Lost*. With the Restoration, the old pamphleteer gave up his "égarements politiques," at least as far as externals are concerned. He had no choice, Chateaubriand wrote in 1811.

> Milton, sans être revenu de ses erreurs, se retira d'une société qui se retirait de lui, pour chercher dans la religion l'adou-

cissement de ses maux et la source de sa gloire. Privé de la lumière du ciel, il se créa une nouvelle terre, un nouveau soleil, et sortit, pour ainsi dire, d'un monde où il n'avait vu que des malheurs et des crimes; il plaça dans les berceaux d'Eden cette innocence primitive, cette félicité sainte qui régnèrent sous les tentes de Jacob et de Rachel; et il mit aux enfers les tourments, les passions, et les remords de ces hommes dont il avait partagé les fureurs.[32]

[Milton, without having renounced his errors, withdrew from a society that was withdrawing from him, to seek in religion the alleviation of his ills and the source of his renown. Deprived of Heaven's light, he created for himself a new earth, a new sun, and left, so to speak, a world in which he had seen nothing but misfortune and crime; in the bowers of Eden he placed that primitive innocence, that holy bliss that reigned beneath the tents of Jacob and Rachel; and in Hell he put the turmoil, the passion, and the remorse of those men whose rage he had shared.]

Milton wrote his epic in England. He could not have done it in Paris. In 1812 Chateaubriand told a visitor that Paris, though a center of taste, inhibited literary creativity. "Milton n'aurait jamais fait son poème en France," he declared. The Garden of Eden, Adam, Eve and their love could have been conceived in such an environment but never Pandemonium or Satan's flight across Chaos. "On lui aurait coupé les ailes du génie sur lesquelles il s'est élevé jusqu'aux cieux."[33] Chateaubriand's opinion, though curious, may not be as incredible as it looks. Vigny's *Cinq-Mars*, as we have seen, shows French contemporaries unable to understand when the poet reads and recites episodes from his epic. These Paris intellectuals could not have written the episodes, nor could they appreciate them.

By the time he wrote the *Essai sur la littérature anglaise,* Chateaubriand also knew about the Trinity Manuscript. Thus he was aware that Milton had once planned *Paradise Lost* as a tragedy, and he gives an outline (*Essai*, 669–71). As early as *the Génie du christianisme,* he had observed that all one would need do to convert the poem into a drama would be to divide it into scenes and add the names of the interlocutors. Nevertheless, he insists, as we know it, the epic is more complete and, on the whole, superior to what it would have been had the poet adhered to his earlier plan.[34] Chateaubriand believes Milton started it during the Republic or the Protectorate, probably completing it after the Restoration.[35] Chateaubriand declares in the *Essai sur la littérature anglaise* that, since the *Génie du christianisme*, he has had to change his mind a little about Shakespeare and Dante. His attitude toward Milton, however, has remained the same (*Essai*, 631). In *Paradise Lost* Milton is omnipresent, he feels. For example, the reader sees what kind of republic the poet would have liked to set up. He had already outlined it in *The Ready and Easy Way*. Milton was a nobleman, and he wanted an aristocratic regime, with levels and ranks, so as to avoid "a licentious and unbridled democracy." Curiously, Satan, with his emphasis on the individual's freedom, appears to be his spokesman on the matter in *Paradise Lost*. Addressing his rebel associates, he calls them:

> Natives and Sons of Heav'n possest before
> By none, and if not equal all, yet free,
> Equally free; for Orders and Degrees
> Jar not with liberty, but well consist.
> Who can in reason then or right assume
> Monarchy over such as live by right
> His equals, if in power and splendor less,
> In freedom equal? or can introduce
> Law and Edict on us, who without law
> Err not? much less for this to be our Lord,
> And look for adoration to th' abuse
> Of those Imperial Titles which assert
> Our being ordain'd to govern, not to serve?
> (*PL* 5.790–802)

Satan assembles a real parliament, divided into two houses in which political speeches are made. Now that representative government has become the norm, the speeches, which take up more than half the epic, give the poem added interest. Milton was a tormented man when he wrote *Paradise Lost*. "Encore ému des spectacles et des passions révolutionnaires," he kept the revolution alive within himself but its collapse in the real world left him, so to speak, suspended in space. "Dans l'étonnement de ses illusions détruites, de ses rêves de liberté évanouis, il ne sait plus où se prendre." The confusion extended to his religious convictions. Chateaubriand tries, not too successfully, to disentangle the various threads. In doing so, he raises a number of questions that modern scholarship has not solved to all readers' satisfaction. We must keep in mind that the critic is thinking about *Paradise Lost* and that he seems not to have read *De Doctrina Christiana*.

If Milton was anything, Chateaubriand says, he was an Arian.[36] But he was other things, too. Milton assumed that there had been some kind of preexisting matter, coeternal with the Spirit, but acknowledged no creative act as such. Bringing the universe into being, as he saw it, was merely tidying up some little area of chaos that was always ready, at a moment's notice, to fall back into nebulous disorder. At the very beginning of *Paradise Lost*, the poet declares himself a Socinian with his famous expression about "one greater Man." He does not talk about the Holy Spirit. He never talks about the Trinity, never says that the Son is equal to the Father. The Son has not been begotten since all eternity. Milton even puts the Son's creation after that of the angels. Virtually all of the philosophical systems the poet knew about found their way into the composite of his beliefs. There is Plato, with his doctrine of ideas. There is Pythagoras, with the harmony of the spheres. Epicurus and Lucretius are there too with their materialism, as when the poet lets us glimpse half-formed animals emerging from the ground as they come into being.[37] Milton is also a fatalist, when he has Satan declare that he was born of himself.[38]

Moreover, Chateaubriand continues, Milton is a Spinozist or a pantheist, but his pantheism is of an odd variety. At first he appears to subscribe to the usual kind of pantheism, in which matter and spirit coexist. However, if Adam had remained sinless, man, little by little shaking off his material component, would have taken on the nature of angels. But Adam sins. To redeem his spiritual element, the Son of God, all spirit, is incarnated, redeems humankind, and goes back to Heaven having experienced matter. Thus Christ becomes the vehicle through which matter, juxtaposed with reason, becomes spirit. In the fullness of time, matter, or the material world, dissolves in its opposite principle, spirit. In Milton's view, the human soul will eventually be assumed into the fountainhead of all spirituality. When Milton holds that the Son, with all of the creatures, will be absorbed into the Father's bosom and that God will be one entity, he is likewise preaching spiritual pantheism, which for him has replaced the other, more common variety. Jean Gillet has pointed out that this is not really in *Paradise Lost* and that Chateaubriand was at best stretching things, at worst interpreting rather wildly.[39]

Continuing, however, Chateaubriand asks what one is to make of this vast sea of reason or intellect, one little drop of which, added to matter, is enough to enable one to comprehend the movement of the spheres and inquire into the nature of God. What is the infinite, for that matter? Milton envisions a whole series of worlds within worlds. Diving into these bottomless pits staggers the imagination. Milton could not handle it himself.[40] Nevertheless, underlying the welter of philosophical systems, there is an element that never varies. Consistently, Milton was biblical and Christian. In his own mind at least, he became one of the "saints" and considered himself directly inspired by God. Basically a Puritan, he was at once an Independent, an Anabaptist and a Quietist. His religion was inward and private, and he did not attend church services. In *Paradise Lost* he declares that prayer is the only worship pleasing to God (*Essai*, 694–697). Much later, Paul Chauvet would touch upon some of these ideas in his *Religion de Milton* (1909).

Milton included, Chateaubriand felt that Christian epic poets, given the material they had to work with, had not painted Heaven as skillfully as they might have done. In Milton's case, the problem is largely one of timidity. Reigning over this kingdom is God the Father. Partly because Milton has a blurred image of Him, He is not vividly delineated. But the poet also appears to have been afraid to put mortal words in the divine mouth. God's speeches, which deal with abstract questions of foreknowledge, grace and free will, are only "des discours consacrés par le texte des livres saints et par les commentaires de l'élite des esprits chrétiens dans la suite des âges." Chateaubriand likes Messiah much better. The Son is more carefully drawn than most people realize. Having both a divine and a human essence, He serves the poet well, and, from the reader's viewpoint, the human traits make for credibility. His constant tenderness stands out, even in a situation calling for stern punishment. When the culpable first parents are to be expelled from the Garden of Eden, He it is who pleads their case.[41]

Milton knows his angels and knows them at close hand. In *Paradise Lost* they are well depicted, their characters varied. They look as if Raphael and Michelangelo had painted them, and undoubtedly paintings by these masters inspired them in some measure. Milton "les a transportés de la toile dans sa poésie, en leur donnant avec le secours de la lyre la parole que le pinceau avait laissé muette sur leurs lèvres." In more recent times, J. B. Broadbent, Mindele Treip and Amy Lee Turner have likewise pointed to the similarities between the epic's celestial dramatis personnæ on the one hand and Raphael and Michelangelo on the other. Continuing, the critic notes that the routine bliss of even the saved can get monotonous. To counter this, epic poets should endeavor to "établir dans le ciel une espérance, une attente quelconque de plus de bonheur ou d'une époque inconnue dans la révolution des êtres." Likewise, human emotions and even tears could be attributed to celestial beings. Milton tries this when he depicts the angels as saddened on hearing of humankind's fall (*Génie*, 757–58; *Essai*, 691–92).

Adam and Eve delight Chateaubriand from the start. "Eve a une séduction inexprimable," he writes. "Elle respire à la fois l'innocence et la volupté." If she is a trifle coquettish, she is communicative and charming. However, "elle est légère, présomptueuse, vaine de sa beauté." She is curious and stubborn, too. "Milton n'a pas voulu peindre son Eve parfaite; il l'a représentée irrésistible par les charmes mais un peu indiscrète et amante de paroles" so as to prepare for the disaster that this shortcoming will bring about. After the disaster, her willingness to die or avoid having children is touching in the extreme. Like Shakespeare's heroines, she has about her a childlike aura, and it explains why leading her astray was so easy. As for Adam, the first time we see him he is inexperienced but already a man to be emulated. Just created, he is "noble, majestueux, et tout à la fois plein d'innocence et de génie..., digne d'être respecté par les anges et de se promener dans la solitude avec son créateur." "Simple et sublime, instruit du Ciel et tirant son expérience de Dieu," he has but one weakness, his love for the mate he has been given. Milton could not let this ideal love endure. Absolute happiness bores us, absolute wretchedness repels us. In nature, there has to be more bad than good, however. Milton realizes this. Leaving their garden, Adam and Eve have hope but not bliss (*Génie*, 632, 658–59).

For Chateaubriand, if Milton's art is to be seen anywhere, it is in the couple's love after their sin. The poet paints with the same colors, but the effect is different. Eve is no longer a wife, she has become a mistress. Wandering into the byways of Paphos, the married virgin has become a priestess of Aphrodite. Sensuality has replaced love, enticement has taken the place of chaste caresses. All the poet has to do in order to bring this about is dispense with innocence. Husband and wife awaken, tired from their drunken sleep. On their faces they are ashamed to discover the pale traces of their cavorting. They notice that they are naked and rush to the fig tree. Humankind has fallen, the earth has teetered on its axis, the seasons are thrown out of kilter, and death has taken its first step in the universe. Cain has just been conceived. The only epic poet to do so, Milton ends his poem on a sorrowful note (*Essai*, 688–89; *Génie*, 632).

In Chateaubriand's view, as we have noted, Milton did not make as much of Heaven as he might have done. Similarly, Milton's Hell, like that of Dante and Tasso, is not above reproach. There are nevertheless "quelques morceaux excellents" to prove that, had the whole been touched up with uniform care, Milton's Hell would have been as poetic as those of Homer and Virgil. To Chateaubriand the various demons need no comment. As for Satan, Dante had made him "un monstre odieux." Tasso, by putting horns on him, risked making him ridiculous. Milton's Satan is an incomparable creation. He is handsome, superb, a "bel archange coupable." Not even Homer has anything approximating him. He is loathsome, of course. With the devils' monarch, the poet, who had shared their views and goals, was showing the men of the Civil Wars and Commonwealth, "ces réprouvés, qui firent si longtemps de leur patrie le vrai séjour des démons." Satan epitomizes hatred. His dominant trait is his pride, but he is capable of other emotions as well. For instance, when he looks at Eve, he almost seems to experience love, though it might be lust. He is extraordinarily complex and hence believable.

> Satan, se repentant à la vue de la lumière qu'il hait, parce qu'elle lui *rappelle combien il fut élevé au-dessus d'elle,* souhaitant ensuite d'avoir été créé dans un rang inférieur, puis s'endurcissant dans le crime par orgueil, par honte, par méfiance même de son caractère ambitieux; enfin, pour tout fruit de ses réflexions et comme pour expier un moment de remords, se chargeant de l'empire du mal pendant toute une éternité: voilà, certes . . . , une des conceptions les plus sublimes et les plus pathétiques qui soient jamais sorties du cerveau d'un poète. (*Génie*, 740–41)

> [Satan, repenting on seeing the light that he despises because it *reminds him how high above it he had been raised,* after that wishing he had been created in a meaner rank, then hardening his heart in crime through pride, through shame, even through distrust of his ambitious character; finally, as the sole fruit of his meditations and as though to expiate a moment of remorse, assuming the empire of evil for the whole of eternity: there, certainly . . . , is one of the most sublime, one of the most moving concepts that ever emerged from a poet's brain.]

Chateaubriand lists the sources his contemporaries generally mentioned in connection with *Paradise Lost*. He notes that one could easily add others, such as Du Bartas. St. Avitus's *Eden* has a few scenes that might have been put to good use. With Manso, Milton could also have seen Tasso's *Sette Giornate del mondo creato*. These sources, if indeed that is what they are, do not diminish the achievement of

Paradise Lost. "Ces prétendus originaux ont-ils ouvert leurs ouvrages par le réveil de Satan dans l'Enfer? ont-ils traversé le Chaos avec l'ange rebelle, aperçu la création du seuil de l'Empyrée, apostrophé le soleil, contemplé le bonheur de l'homme dans sa primitive innocence, deviné les majestueuses amours d'Eve et d'Adam" (*Essai*, 679)?

For all his admiration, Chateaubriand admits that *Paradise Lost* has shortcomings in addition to the inadequacies of Heaven and Hell. Already, in 1811, he had mentioned the poem's "beautés incorrectes" and "nombreux défauts" (*MOT* 2:268, 271). As a younger man, he found some of them bothersome. Writing the *Essai sur la littérature anglaise* in 1836, he was less disturbed, especially when viewing the poet in cultural context. There were problems, though. For example, the devils' jokes can be a nuisance. As literary recollections, however, it is easy to explain them away. Quite simply, they are imitated from Homer. Similarly, artillery in Heaven should not come as a shock. The idea is logical enough. The blame for concocting one of humanity's most destructive inventions is placed upon Satan. The invention was, after all, one that preoccupied the poet. Inspired by the Gunpowder Plot, he had written five Latin poems about it. Perhaps a more serious flaw in *Paradise Lost* is the author's habit of smothering his readers with his vast learning, but, if one has to choose, better too much than too little: "Milton a tiré plus de beautés de son savoir que Shakespeare de son ignorance." The devils turning into snakes and hissing their leader has irritated some readers, the critic further observes. This "caprice" should be chalked up to the poet's teeming imagination. However, Chateaubriand continues, there is no denying that the poem has occasional touches of genuine bad taste. For one thing, there is that dinner served a visiting angel that never seems to get cold, no matter how long it is dawdled over. Furthermore, Milton could have done without the lines in which Adam tells Eve that she is nothing but a crooked rib. The insult detracts all the more because it comes in the middle of an exquisite, dramatic scene. In *Paradise Lost*, light sometimes is not as intense as it ought to be; sometimes nuances are not clear. When this occurs, one has to bear in mind that the blind poet is relying upon memory, which nevertheless serves him remarkably well. "La nuit de ses paupières et la nuit approchante de la tombe ont un caractère de mélancolie qu'on ne retrouve nulle part." Finally, one senses now and then that the poet is tired. To this critic, this is not a real problem. "Si le poète montre parfois de la fatigue, si la lyre échappe à sa main lassée, il se repose, et je me repose avec lui" (*Essai*, 680–81).

Unlike several of his fellow critics, Chateaubriand was not particularly interested in comparing *Paradise Lost* to other modern epics, though he did so on occasion. While not insisting upon it, he was more apt to compare Milton to Homer. Now and again, in connection with education, the masses, or the responsibilities that go with kingship, he compared him to some French contemporary. At one point, he calls attention to Milton's concern lest the cold climate in which he had been reared make him a lesser artist than he might have been had he matured in a warmer region, one more conducive to his kind of creativity. Chateaubriand notes that this troubled the poet as he was writing the ninth book of *Paradise Lost* and hints that the concern may have been legitimate. The question arises when Chateaubriand suggests that, on the whole, Homer may have coped with the supernatural better than Milton did. Given the modern poet's natural genius, he could have handled it in a more expert manner had his taste been surer. Undoubtedly, that taste would have been better if he had been reared in France. "On oppose toujours Milton, avec ses défauts, à Homère avec ses beautés," which is unfair. "Supposons que le chantre d'Eden fût né en France, sous le siècle de Louis XIV, et qu'à la grandeur naturelle de son génie il eût joint le goût de Racine et de Boileau." That being the case, the supernatural element in *Paradise Lost* could compete with the best the *Iliad* and the *Odyssey* have to offer (*Essai*, 608; *Génie*, 759). The remark, to be sure, is startling enough at face value. But what Chateaubriand is proposing would not have worked. For the moment the critic has overlooked Boileau's disapproval of Christian doctrine in an epic poem, just as he is forgetting his own remark that certain parts of *Paradise*

Lost could not have been conceived or written in France. Gustave Planche was an important critic in the 1830s and 1840s. Though his birthdate made him a member of the romantic generation, he detested the movement. Chateaubriand, he contended, did not understand Milton.[42] Planche was wrong. While he admitted once that he was drawing upon intuition, Chateaubriand did not allow his romantic outlook to blur his critical vision. Generally his insights were quite good, though one suspects now and then that he may have misread a passage. Both the man and the writer, he knew his Milton very well indeed. The picture he paints is accurate and the judgments, while personal, are sound. He was not preoccupied with the poet's appearance, but he knew what the man looked like. In his youth Milton had been quite handsome and retained his good looks in old age. "Ses cheveux étaient admirables," the critic insists. Standing out against his pale skin, "ses beaux yeux noirs" were so striking that one would not have known that their owner was blind. Perhaps Chateaubriand knew that, like himself, Milton was short. Better than most, Chateaubriand was informed about his author's personal life and even dipped into the familiar letters. As for the poet's domestic life, the critic notes that Milton married three times. Probably Deborah Milton read to her father in various languages. When he had composed several lines, Milton dictated them to his wife or daughters. However, not all was tenderness in the household. Elizabeth Minshull was an excellent companion, but Milton was difficult. And his daughters may not have been the dedicated creatures tradition has made them. "Il paraît qu'il fut peu aimé: ses filles, qui jouent un si beau rôle poétique dans sa vie, le trompaient et vendaient secrètement ses livres" (*Essai*, 664–65, 671–72).

Along with other talents, Chateaubriand was a historian capable of appreciating the political matrix in which the poet lived and wrote. He knew that Oliver Cromwell did not assume absolute power at the outbreak of the Civil Wars. On the contrary, Chateaubriand was aware that "mille partis se déchiraient." Chateaubriand may have been wrong in what he saw as Milton's devotion to Cromwell. What

Chateaubriand interpreted as devotion was probably helplessness. Bringing down a dictator is not something that even the most idealistic pamphleteer is willing to risk his head trying to accomplish.

Chateaubriand had thumbed through virtually all of Milton's works, including the academic exercises and minor poems. With most of the work he was familiar; in his day, this was seldom true of critics. Among the things Chateaubriand is to be commended for is the importance he attached to the prose. In assessing the writer, he insisted upon it. Aside from the light they throw on *Paradise Lost*, Milton's pamphlets made their author, in the political arena at least, a precursor of modern thought. "Il se plaint dans ses vers d'être venu un siècle trop tard; il aurait pu se plaindre dans sa prose d'être venu un siècle trop tôt." Successive revolutions have modernized him for us. "Ses idées politiques en font un homme de notre époque" (*Essai*, 643). Even though he probably did not examine *De Doctrina Christiana*, Chateaubriand was able to isolate, to his own satisfaction at least, the heterogeneous elements making up the codex of religious beliefs that inform *Paradise Lost*. Surely Chateaubriand was exaggerating, however, when he stated that those beliefs had been shaken when the Commonwealth fell apart (*Essai*, 696). Milton's faith was too strong for that.

Chateaubriand found an eloquent sentence or two with which to mark the writer's death:

> Le 10 novembre 1674, la divinité qui parlait la nuit au poète le vint chercher; il se réunit dans l'Eden céleste à ces anges au milieu desquels il avait vécu et qu'il connaissait par leurs noms, leurs emplois, et leur beauté.... Il rendit à Dieu un des souffles les plus puissants qui animèrent jamais l'argile humaine. [This immortal] traîna assez de jours sur la terre pour s'ennuyer, pas assez pour épuiser son génie, qu'il posséda tout entier jusqu'à son dernier soupir. (*Essai*, 676)
>
> [On 10 November 1674 the divinity that used to speak to him at night came to get him: in the heavenly Eden he joined those angels among whom he had lived and whom he knew by their names, their functions, and their beauty.... He returned to God one of the most powerful spirits that ever animated human clay.

[This immortal] sojourned on earth long enough to be weary, not long enough to exhaust his great mind, which he retained undiminished to his last breath.]

Chateaubriand was sometimes struck by curious dates. Milton's demise suggested two. Chateaubriand called attention to the fact that the poet's death occurred at midpoint between two revolutions, 14 years after the Restoration put an end to the Commonwealth and 14 years before the accession of William III drove the Stuarts into their last exile (*Essai*, 677). Another coincidence was that at about the time Milton was being paid his second *Paradise Lost* royalties, Henrietta Maria died in France. The funeral oration, one of the most brilliant sermons in literature, was preached by another of Milton's great French contemporaries, Jacques Bossuet, Bishop of Meaux. As it happens, the oration contains a somber portrait of the Lord Protector, who had helped make Henrietta Maria a widow. There is no reason to think that either Milton or Bossuet ever heard the other mentioned, Chateaubriand believed. "Ces incomparables génies, qui tous les deux, dans des rangs opposés, avaient fait le portrait de Cromwell, s'ignoraient l'un l'autre et n'entendirent peut-être jamais prononcer leurs noms: les aigles, qui sont vus de tous, vivent un à un et solitaires dans la montagne" (*Essai*, 677).

3

Philarète Chasles

While still in his teens, Philarète Chasles (1798–1873) taught himself to read English. Working for a publisher in London from March 1817 to November 1818 gave him a good speaking knowledge of the language. Professor Claude Pichois has called him a "remarquable angliciste." In time, Chasles became an eminent critic, at home in various literatures. In 1835, the year his first Milton article appeared, he gave a course on Foreign and Comparative Literature at the Athénée Royal de Paris. In 1837, when another Milton article appeared, he was named to a librarianship at the Bibliothèque Mazarine. Although he had never finished high school, a waiver allowed him to submit theses and receive a doctorate in 1841. A week later he was appointed Professor of Germanic Languages and Literatures at the Collège de France. Villemain, the Minister of Public Instruction, had created the post for him.[1] Though he once called him "un pédant et un paperassier," Jules Barbey d'Aurevilly had immense admiration for Philarète Chasles as a literary critic. As Barbey phrased it, "Il était né littérateur et critique comme on naît poète. Il avait en littérature le génie de la recherche et de la découverte, qui est le vrai génie de la critique." He was a "rare esprit," a "rude travailleur," a "bénédictin de robe," with "ses vastes connaissances" and "son amour des idées et de tout ce qui ressemblait à une idée."[2]

Chasles was a romantic. This being the case, we must not be surprised when we see him swept away at times by his own verbose enthusiasm. Mostly he wrote for periodicals, assembling articles from time to time and publishing them in book form. Many of the articles, including several on Milton, appeared in the *Revue Britannique*, which he helped to launch, and the *Journal des Débats*. The latter, a liberal monarchist newspaper, aimed, like the *Revue Britannique*, at a broad, cultivated readership. Highly respected, it had a large circulation. The *Revue Britannique* enjoyed great prestige also. Other Chasles Milton articles appeared in the *Dictionnaire de la conversation et de la lecture*, an encyclopedia. One article appeared in the *Dictionnaire* in 1837. Slightly amended and its material moved around somewhat, it reappeared in 1863, when a new edition came out. Chasles's first Milton article, entitled "Milton, ses œuvres, sa vie, et ses opinions," appeared in the *Revue Britannique* in July 1835. Entirely original, it was presented to readers as having been translated from the *Retrospective Review*.[3]

Summarized in several articles, not always correctly, are Milton's essential biographical facts. Chasles was greatly impressed by the early poems. Pointing out in a *Journal des Débats* article that Milton was a Latin poet, an Italian poet and an English poet, he added that he was original in each of the three idioms he used. "Il écrit dans ces trois langues et il les imprègne toutes trois de la même suavité harmonieuse; il mêle et confond les eaux de ces trois fleuves dans le lit nouveau que leur ouvre une poésie nouveau."[4] The Latin poems reveal their author as sensitive, studious and idealistic, equally unsuited to the life of courtier or soldier, "dédaigneux des ambitions vulgaires, soutenu par le sentiment de sa dignité personnelle, incapable de s'abaisser jamais à des occupations sordides ou vénales" (*JD* 4:3). The "Hymn on the Morning of Christ's Nativity," "qui déjà annonçait de grands talents," is mentioned, as is "Lycidas"

(*DC* 1863, 188). Milton's "sentiment de noblesse," his "grandeur" and his "élévation presque céleste" can be detected even in the sonnets. "Le sonnet, ordinairement consacré à quelque galanterie fade, devient sous la plume du grand homme un fragment d'hymne sublime" (*RB*, 63). As an example, Chasles translates "On the Late Massacre in Piedmont."[5]

About "L'Allegro" and "Il Penseroso" Chasles was just as glowing. While Milton set out to paint two opposite states of mind in these twin poems, the reader should not look for noisy mirth in the one or gentle melancholy in the other. What one discovers in "L'Allegro" is calm contemplation, "une douce quiétude, un contentement secret et profond qui reçoit de tous les bruits et de tous les aspects de la nature une sensation agréable." What "Il Penseroso" reveals is "une mélancolie sombre qui sympathise avec tous les aspects tristes, avec tous les sons lugubres" (*RB*, 55). In the first poem, the universe is clothed in "un rayon pourpre et joyeux"; in the second, it is draped in its "voiles mélancoliques." "Toutes les harmonies du bonheur et de l'amour sont dans le premier hymne; tous les accords de la tristesse et de la rêverie sont dans l'autre. Jamais la méditation et l'élan ne se sont plus intimement combinés que dans ces petits chef-d'œuvres de délicatesse et d'unité" (*JD* 6:3).

Comus is, Chasles says, "le premier parfum enlevé par la brise à la fleur qui s'ouvre chaste et solitaire." Lest his poem be considered nothing but a bit of idle court poetry, Milton paid a great deal of attention to his diction, using all the linguistic resources at his disposal, including popular speech. This critic considers the masque to be devoid of plot, movement and passion. On the positive side, it is the work of a young idealist who believes in virtue and the human will. From the Middle Ages and Christian Platonism, Milton borrowed his lofty concept of chastity, developing it "avec amour et grandeur, non comme un symbole de convention mais comme une vérité souveraine et une noble règle de la vie." Like Sainte-Beuve, Chasles compares the Lady to Una in the *Faerie Queene* but thinks Milton made his heroine's situation more credible, giving "bien plus de gravité, de force, et d'éclat à ce thème de philosophie religieuse." The poem is all of a piece, "le plan, le détail, les accessoires, le rhythme lyrique, le fond du tableau, les personnages mis en scène." The result is "un tableau complet, plein de lumière et de vie, où l'air circule, où tout est puissant, où le symbole disparaît sous l'ardeur du coloris, où l'expression crée et l'image saisissante versent à torrents leur réalité passionnée" (*JD* 6:3–4).

Cambridge University, Horton, the Continent. Tracing Milton through all of these, the critic then shows us his hero in London, the Civil Wars about to begin. Before long the poet took a stand on the issues that his contemporaries had to face. Like Chateaubriand in the *Essai sur la littérature anglaise*, Chasles tells readers in his *Olivier Cromwell* that of all the broadsides the Puritan Revolution produced, Milton's are the only ones now remembered.[6] As the poet rushed to arms, he became a schoolmaster, a disillusioned husband and a polemicist.

On Milton at this point in his career, Chasles brought special insights to bear. Chasles's father, who had been a teacher, had also tried his hand at running a boys' school. Somewhat later than is usually the case, he got married. Vitally interested in religious issues, he had been a priest but threw off his cassock at the time of the French Revolution; he entered politics, becoming more and more radical. In the Convention Nationale, he voted for Louis XVI's death and thus became a regicide. Given his background, it comes as no surprise that his son grew up with no religious education. Later, realizing that life would be easier if he were a communicant of some denomination, Chasles chose Roman Catholicism but was never particularly fervent about it.

Chasles believed that Milton's convictions on political, ethical and doctrinal matters informed the whole of his work. It was a remarkably unified system, he believed, with deep roots in Calvinism. Milton wanted "ni temples, ni lieux de réunion, ni heures fixes pour l'assemblée des fidèles, ni prières publiques." He disapproved of "les cérémonies publiques et extérieures qui, selon lui, donnaient un caractère grossier,

82 *Major French Milton Critics*

sensuel, et terrestre à la piété émanée de l'âme." He would even have abolished the Sabbath. Despite such views, Milton crams endless theological dissertations into *Paradise Lost*, with subtle interpretations phrased in an "éloquence bizarre qu'il emprunte aux prédicateurs à la mode" in his world. Unwittingly, he was undermining religion. Religion, as he saw it, made social structures and responsibilities, along with government, obsolete. "Le principe religieux, pénétrant dans toutes les familles, réglant tous les mouvements, traçant à chaque citoyen la route qu'il devait suivre, devait tenir lieu à la société de roi, de magistrats, et d'armée." Milton's ideal republic, founded on individual free will, was impractical, to be sure, but it contained some noble germs. "Milton ne fondait pas sa république sur la salutaire sévérité des lois, mais sur la sévère rectitude et la moralité de chaque individu." Unfortunately, these are fragile bases, and human passions would make short work of them.

Related to all of this is Milton's attitude toward women, whom he looked upon as inferior creatures, the cause of all the woes of humanity. To women "Il ne donne en partage que la faiblesse intellectuelle et physique; il leur attribue toutes les grâces mais aussi tous les inconvénients de la faiblesse." Husbands owe their wives protection but not obedience. Eve's positive feature is her modest charm. When Adam speaks, she listens, quiet and respectful. It is too bad that she also listens to the tempter. After her misdeed, Adam realizes the full thrust of what she has done and what it will cost him. Lashing out at her, "Adam lui fait une vraie querelle de ménage; il entre dans une grande colère, disant à sa femme qu'elle n'est après tout qu'un 'beau défaut de la nature, qu'il est malheureux qu'on ne puisse pas se passer d'elle entièrement, que les choses iraient mieux si les générations humaines se perpétuaient sans la femme'." And so on. Chasles could have drawn additional material from *Samson Agonistes*.

People who had been Cromwell's contemporaries were not surprised at such an attitude toward women, Chasles points out. "Ils approuvaient ce retour aux mœurs de l'Ancien Testament.... Ils protestaient ainsi contre la galanterie des cavaliers, contre l'hommage rendu par eux aux femmes et à l'amour." Mary Powell's behavior had something to do with her husband's views, needless to say. Milton did not stop here, however. For all practical purposes, he went on to do away with marriage by linking it to the individual's personal ethic. "Quant aux rapports des sexes, la conscience individuelle devait les régler; ainsi il abolissait le mariage." In passing, Chasles mentions the divorce tracts and notes that Milton preached polygamy. Taunting Saumaise, Milton trotted out his worst insult, accusing his opponent of being submissive to his wife. The *History of Britain* reveals his unwillingness to accept the idea that a woman could be heroic. "L'acte de courage attribué à Boadicée lui paraît un mensonge historique, un conte absurde" (*RB*, 45–49; *JD* 2:3–4). In connection with these ideas, titles of various prose works are sometimes given, but as a rule the critic prefers to generalize. Milton's thought, he believes, has a remarkable consistency.

Even in the early poems, one discovers the author's "intimes croyances," "la religion de son cœur," and "les luttes de sa pensée" (*JD* 6:3). Did Milton's ideas make him a man of his times, or did they make him a prophet? Chasles was not sure. If one bears in mind what was happening when Milton conceived *Paradise Lost*, one can see that "toutes les passions contemporaines viennent se mêler au tissu de l'ouvrage" (*RB*, 45). Generally, Milton's ethical, political and theological message "se trouve en dissonance complète avec . . . notre époque." The position the poet assigned women linked him to his own era. Likewise *Comus*, with its austere insistence upon rectitude and will, was out of tune with the relaxed mores of Chasles's day. Nevertheless, Chasles asserts, there is the poet's individualism, which we cling to, even though it devours the modern social order. There is also the broad tolerance the writer preached. One or two other notions also show him as a precursor of later times. Chasles considers *Areopagitica* an "excellent ouvrage . . . qui contient tous les principes de la liberté moderne." "Il est impossible de s'élever à une plus haute éloquence" than in this treatise. Today, he says, people aspire to "liberté de la presse, liberté publique garantie par les lois, liberté individuelle fondée sur la morale, enfin l'instruction qui touche aux bases mêmes de la société." Education and freedom, personal and public, are goals later ages have striven to attain, but a prescient thinker and writer called for them several centuries ago. "Assurément le monde moderne compte peu de philosophes qui aient vu de si haut et aussi loin: et ce philosophe a écrit le *Paradis perdu*" (*RB*, 48, 58; *JD* 6:4; *DC* 1837, 173; *DC* 1863, 188).

The Council of State rewarded Milton for *The Tenure of Kings and Magistrates* by naming him its Latin Secretary. After *Pro Populo Anglicano Defensio*, Parliament voted him a thousand pounds (*DC* 1863, 188). That he should have joined the revolutionaries is nonetheless curious. By nature, he did not have much in common with them. It was circumstances that thrust him into their camp. The Cavaliers were dedicated to a cause that was no longer viable, "un passé détruit" doomed to extinction sooner or later. Yet Milton's gentle nature, one would think, should have steered him in their direction. Ushering in an era of "passions féroces et fanatiques," the individuals of the Puritan Revolution were "grands sans être aimables, énergiques et non vertueux." Why did Milton, who *was* virtuous, cast in his lot with such people? Chasles believes it was simply that, "animé d'un ardent amour pour les hommes, philosophe spéculatif, indépendant, sévère, pieux," Milton was closer to them than to the others. Still, not having been cast in the same mold, he was never really one of them. The result was that, while to the Cavaliers he was a scoundrel, to the Puritans, although he served their cause, he was little more than a useful pedant (*DC* 1837, 174; *DC* 1863, 188; *JD* 4:3). Thus, in his life and in his work, Milton is a curious combination. An "aristocrate par la pensée," he became "républicain et calviniste par conviction."[7] "Cette combinaison du raffinement et du luxe de l'esprit, avec la chasteté et la sévérité de la doctrine, produisirent un phénomène sans modèle. Dans ses poésies ainsi que dans sa conduite, la froideur du ton, la sévérité des formes ne sont qu'apparentes: ce calme doux et austère comme celui de la poésie grecque récèle une flamme ardente

et féconde" *(JD* 4:4). Chasles could have added that if the man and poet were unique, so was the pamphleteer. At one point, he labels *Pro Populo Anglicano Defensio* as eloquent as *Areopagitica* (*RB,* 58).

When the Commonwealth was collapsing, Milton tried to save it with *The Ready and Easy Way.* He did not succeed, of course. With Charles II in Whitehall Palace, *Eikonoklastes* and *Pro Populo Anglicano Defensio* were burned. Once Chasles asserts that Davenant saved their author, but elsewhere he claims that no one molested him (*DC* 1837, 174; *DC* 1863, 188). Nevertheless, the Duke of York would have liked to see him punished. In several articles, the critic relates that the duke once visited the poet and chatted with him. The next day he asked his brother why he did not put him to death. Charles II is quoted as having replied that, old, poor and blind, the erstwhile pamphleteer had seen his most cherished illusions wither away and that this was punishment enough. Chasles considers the presumed visit, which he assumes to have indeed taken place, a gratuitous insult. With it, the insensitive heir to the throne was wounding to the quick the "puritain tombé dans la misère," the "ami de la république, dont toutes les espérances étaient trompées." With romantic delight in oppositions, the critic insists upon the contrast between the two men. "Le jeune homme qui attend le trône outrage le vieillard indigent qui attend le cercueil; l'altesse apporte sa tête royale chez un homme qui a fait tomber une tête de roi; le plus ardent des catholiques se pose devant le plus acharné des protestants" (*RB,* 37–38; *DC* 1837, 174–75). Chasles does not report the more usual anecdote showing either Charles or James suggesting to the poet that his blindness is divine retribution.

The Stuarts restored and his dreams gone up in smoke, Milton was alone, "debout sur les ruines de son parti, de ses opinions, et de sa fortune." Almost nothing was left. "La lumière du jour et celle de la gloire, ses plus beaux rêves, ses plus chères espérances, l'estime des contemporains et les rayons de la fortune, tous les soleils dont la vie humaine s'échauffe et s'éclaire, avaient disparu" (*DC* 1837, 174). *Paradise Lost* was written in the midst of a new set of

realities, within earshot of the new court and its noisy revels. Yet the critic points out that there are few allusions to this unfamiliar, boisterous world. In the poem, instead of "imprécations violentes," there are occasional sad "accents étouffés." Even so, "ces plaintes rares et touchantes" seem inadvertent. What stands out in the poem is the author's soul, "qui s'ouvre par intervalles, qui nous apparaît blessée, saignante, fière, résignée." The poet "ne maudit pas, il ne faiblit pas. Il accepte sa blessure, il la regarde en riant." But if *Paradise Lost* was the record of a disillusioned, tormented soul, it was also an enormous intellectual accomplishment that left the critic awestruck. Had he never lived and traveled in Italy, Milton would never have written it, at least not as we know it (*JD* 2:3–4; *JD* 4:3; *DC* 1837, 175).

Chasles was more interested in Milton's language than were other French critics of his day. There are words in Milton, he points out, that are to be found in no dictionary. Several linguistic influences were at work in *Paradise Lost*, Chasles believes. Some words the poet simply took from the vocabulary of contemporary theology. He also drew heavily upon Latin, as he did upon Italian. "Milton a fait passer dans l'idiome anglais et dans la sphère poétique toutes les influences latines et italiennes que cet idiome pouvait recevoir et contenir," the critic observes. Commenting on *Paradise Lost*'s opening words,

> Of man's first disobedience, and the fruit
> Of that forbidden tree..

Chasles notes that, when there was a choice, Milton generally preferred words of Latin origin. In this passage, however, most have Saxon roots: *of, man, first, and, the, forbidden* (Chasles could have added *tree*). As for the others, *fruit* and *disobedience* come from the Latin. One could say of Milton that, to a certain extent, "l'expression de sa pensée puritaine ne fut qu'un emprunt à une civilisation étrangère, fille de la civilisation antique." But if there are romance elements in his diction, one must not forget the Germanic ones. Skillfully, Milton combined the two linguistic resources. "Jamais mélange aussi habile de la suavité italienne et de

l'énergie saxonne ne s'est opéré sous aucune main."
Milton found locutions in other places as well. Here, though, he gleaned not only words but the ideas, patterns of thought, and poetic devices that were transmitted with them. In this domain, Milton's chief providers were Biblical or Hebraic, Greek or Platonic, and Italian, both classic and baroque. Stating his view in its simplest terms, Chasles declares of *Paradise Lost* at one point that "les matériaux de l'édifice sont hébraïques, la disposition en est grecque, les ornements sont italiens."[8] In that the epic is "un sublime développement de la Genèse," the raw materials are Hebraic. The ideological underpinnings, however, are Greek. "Les premiers germes de la pensée miltonienne jaillirent du sol grec, sous l'influence de Platon."[9] As for Milton's mode of expression, much of it derives from Italian poetry, good and bad. "Sa première étude de la forme élégante et de l'exécution artistique eut lieu en Italie, d'après des modèles italiens." The Italian mind is superimposed on the Greek one, in other words. The three major influences making themselves felt in *Paradise Lost* can be observed simultaneously in Adam's tirade when he learns that his spouse has tasted the forbidden fruit. Here Chasles detects a "mélange de sévérité biblique, d'idées platoniciennes, et de mauvais goût italien." Milton's Satan likewise bespeaks triple inspiration. Basically taken from the Bible, he has had a radical overhaul by the time he reaches *Paradise Lost*. In Milton's hands he has become a Greek Titan, given to the "magnifiques colères auxquelles se livre Prométhée sur son roc." He is something else, too. Stripping away the grotesque attributes the Middle Ages had heaped upon him, the Italians made Satan impressive, and Milton remembered it. Michelangelo could have created the Satan we find in *Paradise Lost*. This fallen archangel possesses "une grandeur et une élévation d'âme qui intéresse involontairement le lecteur à cette figure si grandiose." In spite of ourselves, we admire this bold intellectual, "ce représentant de l'intelligence titanique, ce symbole de l'énergie de la pensée dans ce qu'elle a de plus audacieux et de plus impie." Like Milton's alleged view of women, it was a concept that contemporaries could appreciate. It

was suited to a period in which "l'orgueil républicain et l'orgueil du fanatisme se donnaient la main" (*RB*, 43–45, 56–57; *JD* 2:4; *JD* 5:3; *DC* 1837, 180).

Chasles returns to Milton's language in *Paradise Lost*. The poet was creating for his readers a new world, unknown and supernatural. To render it, a new speech was needed, and the poet created this, too. Like Milton himself, it was unique. Milton made it the vehicle for bold poetic expression. Chasles indicates that Milton liked tangible images but sought to bring out their abstract connotations. Even when conceptualizing an act, it was its emotional rather than its physical character that he endeavored to bring out. In a very poetic manner of speaking, he was giving form to idea. Thus, "*Eve ne rencontre pas* son mari: c'est *l'inquiétude d'Eve* qui rencontre Adam. Les *dards ennemis ne sont pas lancés* dans les airs, mais leur *sifflement se heurte* dans l'espace" (*JD* 4:3–4; *DC* 1837, 177).

In his diction, as in so many things, Milton was at once a conservative and an innovator, a purist and a creator of new words. For his poem he devised "le langage le plus composite et le plus étrange dont jamais homme de génie se soit donné le privilège et ait gardé le secret." It is a special idiom. With it "Milton chante un hymne religieux et une révélation divine; il n'a pas besoin de se servir d'accents humains; lyrique et surnaturel à son aise, il monte sa lyre sur un diapason céleste; son langage dépasse les limites du monde connu." That he invented such a tool is one of his titles to immortality (*JD* 2:3; *DC* 1863. 189).

A sustained discussion of the language of *Paradise Lost* occurs in Chasles's *Revue Britannique* article. Since it is one of the critic's best statements on the subject, let us examine it in its entirety:

> J'entends par langage poétique un idiome qui offre à l'épopée ou au genre lyrique des couleurs et des traits que la prose n'admet pas et dont le cachet spécial soit ou la majesté ou la grâce ou l'énergie; c'est l'inversion; c'est la faculté de former les mots composés; c'est l'emploi de certains termes et de certaines locutions plus nobles ou plus élevées, plus élégantes , ou plus gracieuses. Ainsi se compose un idiome

choisi, une langue divine, destinée à reproduire les émotions de l'âme ou à faire briller aux yeux de l'esprit les tableaux de la nature. Cette ligne de démarcation entre le langage du poète et le langage du prosateur existe dans le grec ancien d'une manière un peu plus faible; dans le latin; dans l'italien, par l'emploi des diminutifs et des ellipses; dans l'allemand, par l'extrême facilité d'imiter toutes les syntaxes étrangères; dans l'espagnol, de la manière la plus prononcée; et enfin dans l'anglais. Milton veut-il chanter l'homme et sa chute, sa faute primitive et la vengeance céleste; il ne commence pas son récit à la manière du chroniqueur: "Je vais dire comment la première désobéissance de l'homme a causé son malheur." Il profite des ressources que lui offre l'instrument dont il se sert, il le monte au ton épique et grandiose; la même pensée simple prend un caractère de majesté; il profite de l'inversion pour présenter l'homme et sa chute originelle comme le sujet de ses chants: "De l'homme," dit-il, "la désobéissance première, et le fruit qui cause sa mort...." Et il rejette au sixième vers: *je chante*.

[By poetic language I mean an idiom that offers the lyric or epic genre qualities and colors that prose does not allow and whose distinctive feature is majesty, charm, or energy; it is inversions; it is the ability to create words; it is the use of certain terms or locutions that are more noble or stately, more elegant or more charming. Thus is formed a select idiom, a divine language, destined to reproduce the emotions of the soul or cause the scenes of nature to light up when beheld by the eyes of the mind. This line of demarcation between the language of the poet and the language of the prose writer is somewhat less pronounced in ancient Greek; in Latin; in Italian, through the use of diminutives and ellipses; in German, through the extreme ease with which all foreign syntaxes can be imitated; in Spanish, in the most obvious manner; and finally in English. If Milton wants to celebrate mankind and his fall, his first sin and celestial punishment, he does not start his account of things the way a chronicler would: "I am going to tell how man's first disobedience brought about his misfortune." He takes advantage of the resources the instrument he is using makes available to him, he attunes it to the epic and grandiose; the same simple thought takes on a majestic character; he uses inversion to present man and his initial fall as the topic of his poem: "Of man's first disobedience, he says, "and the fruit that causes his death...." And he postpones until the sixth line: *I sing*.]

Of man's first disobedience, and the fruit
Of that forbidden tree, whose mortal taste

Brought death into the world, and all our woe,
With loss of Eden, till one greater Man
Restore us, and regain the blissful seat,
Sing. . . .

Chasles adds that, with this, it is no longer a historian or a theologian speaking but rather an inspired man, a prophet. Suppressing the articles in this initial sentence heightens still more the "caractère sublime et puissant de l'expression" (*RB*, 51–52).

Like many other Milton critics, Chasles had a few remarks to make about Dante and Milton. Chasles was not interested in Milton's possible sources, though he enumerated those he knew about. However, he did compare Milton and Dante in general terms. Both were lovers, poets, statesmen. For both, things did not turn out well in either love or politics. To Gallic readers, only since the French Revolution had the two poets come into their own. Fittingly enough, because "le feu des guerres civiles avait trempé le génie de ces deux poètes, ils avaient trouvé, dans les passions qui les entouraient, le type de l'enfer, de ses terreurs et de ses fureurs." In Dante's case, when it was all over, the poet went into exile. Milton remained where he was but lost all that he had, including his sight and his friends. Fundamentally, the two men were almost opposites, despite these obvious similarities. One need only look at their portraits to measure the distance separating them. Probably Chasles was thinking of the death mask, in Dante's case. Dante, with his deep lines, tight lips and stern features, was a man "dont l'orgueil allait jusqu'à la rage, dont les sentiments étaient extrêmes, et qui semble n'avoir jamais connu ni exprimé que des pensées terribles et des sensations violentes." For a contrast, look at Milton. Here everything is calm and harmonious. The poet's eyes are closed. There are no painful constrictions. On his wide forehead there are no wrinkles, even in old age. His lips, delicately outlined, suggest quiet, mystical thought. "Il semble jouir intérieurement du monde idéal qui se déroule en lui."

Exile made Dante bitter. "L'âpreté de ses vers, de ses images, de ses réflexions, semble émanée de la lutte d'un

homme inflexible que l'adversité irrite sans le dompter." Reverses did not do this to Milton, however. His material world gone and a licentious new one having replaced it, he created an ideal one and shut himself up in it. "L'harmonie de ses chants ne fut que plus sublime, plus douce, et plus céleste." Dante, whose passions were political, is the poet of despair, pain and violence. Milton, driven by religious enthusiasms, is the poet of a mysterious, infinite universe swathed in a "luxe de beauté, de richesse, et de splendeur," chaste and spiritual. Dante is a sculptor who has hacked his robust characters out of solid, unyielding materials. What Milton has created, however, is like a Claude Lorrain painting in which objects, landscapes and creatures are perceived through a brilliant haze. "La transparence de son coloris est merveilleuse, une vapeur chaude et vague semble régner sur ses paysages et sur ses figures" (RB, 41–45; JD 4:3). Dante is superior to Milton in his vigorous satire. He is superior, too, in that he imagined a triple world, peopled with awesome, terrible characters. Milton's superiority resides in his lyricism, "la fécondité des nuances, la merveilleuse féerie des points de vue lointains, l'audace d'un regard qui plonge dans le monde invisible et nous associe par une magique création à ses mystères inconnus."

For all Dante's harshness and Milton's serene contemplation, Chasles notes, there are times when the two poets switch natures. On occasion, Dante is gentle; at times, Milton is strident. Take their attitude toward women, for instance. Normally so violent, Dante nevertheless saw woman as a tender, ethereal creation. His Beatrice is the delicate, transcendent incarnation of heavenly purity. The critic has already discussed what Milton thought about women. Eve he treats "durement et sans façon, même sans pitié." Dante's presentation of Heaven is another case in point. On the whole, Dante rendered Heaven better than Milton. Only three elements—music, light and movement—are used to describe it and the pleasures of those who dwell there. The picture is simple yet powerful. "Vous nagez au milieu de ces étoiles qui changent de forme, de ces lumières harmonieuses, de ces mélodies lumineuses." There is nothing sensual, nothing

violent. "Pour le poète méridional, la joie céleste est dépouillée de tout vestige mondain." In Milton's Heaven, early reminiscences abound. "Pour le poète septentrional, les voluptés terrestres vivent dans le ciel. Il y a du nectar qui pétille, des beautés ravissantes, et de suaves odeurs. Les plus belles plantes de la terre, l'or et les diamants qu'elle recèle dans ses entrailles, Milton les a prodigués pour embellir son Paradis." But there are other worldly echoes in *Paradise Lost*, unpleasant ones. Milton put subtle preachers and ranting politicians in his poem, men he had seen and known. "La trace de l'époque est ... flagrante dans le ton violent, démagogique, insultant que le ... poète attribue à ses anges du ciel, anges qui parlent comme des tribuns du peuple et qui ne ménagent pas les outrages à leurs ennemis." To Milton's contemporaries, accustomed to such behavior, this would have been expected. Seeing Heaven "représenté sous des couleurs terrestres" did not bother them either. Nor did "toutes les joies voluptueuses prodiguées aux élus." Good citizens, this was their due. For Chasles, however, these things are flaws in *Paradise Lost*. "Voilà des taches qui, malgré le noble génie de l'auteur, nous blessent et nous révoltent aujourd'hui" (*RB*, 46). Chasles does not develop the idea.

Chasles notes, not without surprise, that, despite historical allusions going back only two centuries, it was Milton, not Dante, whose epic had become obscure. Everyone understands *The Divine Comedy*, this critic believes, but *Paradise Lost* requires commentary. From canto to canto, it is easy to follow the topography of Dante's three realms. The imagery is palpable, nothing is vague. The reader's ear picks up sounds that provoke delight or terror. Dante has been translated into every language, usually with success. But even with awkward translations, *The Divine Comedy* is so powerful that it survives. This is not true with *Paradise Lost*, which bad translations have hurt.[10] Nuances, so hard to render, have usually been lost. Yet, to produce the effects Milton had to achieve, they are vital. "La délicatesse, la transparence, la variété des teintes" are indispensable to the poem because they are qualities "qui forcent le lecteur de croire à l'invraisemblable et de voir l'invisible; qui font illusion; qui le transportent dans les sphères lointaines; qui le placent tour à tour devant le trône de Dieu et devant le trône brûlant occupé par l'archange tombé" (RB, 44; JD 6:3).

Chasles devotes little space in his articles to works Milton published late in life or that were published after his death. The *History of Britain* and *A Brief History of Muscovia* are only mentioned. Chasles thinks the Latin dictionary had been finished, perhaps published. Though it appeared a decade before his first article, he does not discuss *De Doctrina Christiana*.[11] *Paradise Regained* is scarcely alluded to. Chasles admires *Samson Agonistes* very much, though, and calls it a "drame lyrique," "quelque chose de sublime"; he quotes almost all of the protagonist's long soliloquy at the beginning of the poem.[12] *Samson* was written when its author was old and blind and when life had handled him roughly. Nevertheless, the critic says, the poem shows us an uncompromising survivor determined not to give in to a callous, relentless fate. "Samson exprime le dernier combat de la vieillesse indomptée contre le destin qui l'écrase." Writing his final article, Chasles likes the poem a little less but praises its emotional impact springing from the highly personal element in it. Reading the poem, one should remember *Comus*, in which a young, idealistic poet had spoken his mind on personal ethics and the human will. In *Samson Agonistes*, old and deserted, the same poet was commenting on more or less the same issues. "Comprendre *Comus* et *Samson*, c'est traverser la journée du poète, depuis son matin jusqu'à son couchant" (JD 6:3; DC 1863, 188).

Chasles regarded Milton as a phenomenon in English literature. There had been nothing like him before, there has been nothing like him since (JD 4:4). Chasles's admiration is obvious, his insights splendid. Still, there are desiderata. One could wish, for example, that, instead of lumping all of these men together as "Calvinists," Chasles had detected political or doctrinal nuances in those who, having overthrown Charles I, rushed into a cold, at times indecorous scramble for arbitrary power themselves. We might disagree with him over Milton's reasons for going with the Puritans in the Civil Wars. In addition, Chasles believed that Milton took stands on people and issues and that these positions remained more or less static. It would have been better had he allowed for more evolution in the writer's religious and political thought. For instance, he did not delve into how or when the poet became a republican. Occasionally, he was just plain wrong, sometimes about a title or a date. Once in a while, though rarely, it is more serious. A case in point is the reason he gives, a reason at least subject to interpretation, for Milton's break with the Presbyterians. "Tant que les Presbytériens furent militants, il combattit sous leur bannière; quand il les vit triompher et prétendre à la tyrannie, il s'éloigna d'eux." This is part of Chasles's concept of Milton as an idealist, but what about divorce, what about regicide? "Ces hommes, jadis ses amis, qui, après avoir revendiqué la liberté de la pensée, essayaient de la monopoliser à leur profit, devinrent ses ennemis" (RB, 59).

Chasles is too generous, and also a little inconsistent, in evaluating his author's independence. "Jamais les préjugés et les opinions qui régnaient autour de lui ne le dominèrent et ne le subjuguèrent" (RB, 59). Though opposed to despotism, there is no record that Milton spoke out when his compatriots were placing their well-being in the hands of Oliver Cromwell. "Au lieu de s'armer contre des erreurs de détail, Milton frappe toujours la racine même des abus" (RB, 59). Probably Saumaise would have had another opinion about Milton and matters of detail. Chasles's most unfortunate remark along these lines is the sentence declaring that "Jamais sa massue ne tombe sur un parti déjà vaincu; il laisse la tourbe des écrivains vulgaires se charger de cette tâche ignoble et frapper un ennemi à terre" (RB, 59). This is to pretend that Milton wrote neither *The Tenure of Kings and Magistrates* nor *Eikonoklastes*. Chasles liked to stress that Milton died unaware that in time he would be considered one of the world's great poets. He also made the puzzling comment in several articles that the poet's fame began in 1680. "La renommée poétique de Milton ne s'éveilla qu'en 1680," he observed (DC 1863, 188). Why 1680? Perhaps

Chasles meant 1688, the year of *Paradise Lost's* fourth edition. Eventually, to be sure, the moderate constitution we now know having been established, an intellectual climate settled in that made it possible better to appreciate some of the poet and pamphleteer's views. That Addison's *Spectator* articles came out in 1712 was probably, even so, a coincidence.

Refreshingly, Chasles makes no effort to explain away Milton's position on regicide. As other French romantics were prone to do, he overemphasizes the picture of the later Milton as a lonely hero, neglected, abandoned, even ridiculed. To make realities conform to the picture, he even discards the wife and problematical daughters.

> Il était privé de la vue et n'avait plus de famille; tous ses amis avaient teint l'échafaud de leur sang, gémissaient dans les cachots ou mendiaient leur subsistance à l'étranger. Il était en butte à la haine d'une cour dépravée et d'un peuple inconstant; on le montrait au doigt, et des poètes dont le talent ne s'élevait pas au-dessus de la médiocrité, dont la moralité était encore inférieure à leur talent accaparaient les faveurs de la cour et de la fortune. (*RB*, 42)

> [He could not see and his family was gone; all his friends had either stained the scaffold with their blood, were moaning in prison cells, or were begging their bread in foreign countries. He was the butt of a depraved court and a faithless people's hatred; he was pointed out, and poets whose talents did not rise above mediocrity, whose morality was even inferior to their talent won the exclusive favors of fortune and the court.]

Over and over the critic modulates on the theme in his articles. Despite the mistreatment, however, the poet had a serene old age, and there are no hints that it was marred by discord in his household.

Chasles was almost obsessed with Milton's physical appearance. A suggestion of this has come up in connection with Dante. In his article on the minor poems, Chasles calls attention to Milton's good looks as a youth, to "ce beau visage aux boucles flottants, cette tête d'Apollon du Nord" (*JD* 6:3). Elsewhere, he declares that "les longues boucles de ses cheveux ondoyants accompagnent une tête qui dans la jeunesse ressemble à celle d'un ange." Milton was handsome in old age as well. Here Chasles recalls the "belle tête, calme et harmonieuse, sans ride sur un large front; ses longs cheveux argentés tombant en boucles sur ses épaules, et ses beaux yeux noirs d'aveugle brillant sur la pâleur de son visage." It was the face of an apostle. This is the Milton of the later works, with his soul "qui s'ouvre par intervalles, qui nous apparaît blessée, saignante, fière, résignée (RB, 43; DC 1837, 174; JD 4:3). Milton's resignation, somewhat developed in several articles, is not quite consistent, needless to say, with the critic's remark about *Samson Agonistes* showing the poet defiant in the face of adversity.

Chasles's articles are irritatingly disjointed, but, amid some torrential rhetoric, they contain remarkable insights. Although he said little about them, Chasles had probably read Milton's Latin poems more carefully than most of his fellow critics had done. Also worth noting is the attention he paid to Milton's language in *Paradise Lost*. While he tended to confuse it with style (RB, 178), Chasles was unusually perceptive about it and what the poet had been able to do with it. The neologisms and the new meanings given to old words are part and parcel of all this, but so are "l'organisation de la phrase" and "toute la tenue du discours" (DC 1837, 180). That language and style, new and inspired, helped account for the author's uniqueness, Chasles believed. We can also be grateful to Chasles for his contrasts, shrewd and illuminating, between the authors of *The Divine Comedy* and *Paradise Lost*.

4

Louis Raymond de Véricour

Louis Raymond de Véricour was a teacher, historian and literary critic about whom, today, rather little is known. He seems to have been a religious man, and he appears to have been a liberal in politics. After teaching in Paris, he moved to the British Isles. At one point he was Professor of Modern Languages and Literature at Queen's University, Ireland. Much of his work is in English. On 11 June 1869 he was elected a Fellow of the Royal Society in London. He died around 1879. In addition to his historical studies, his interests centered on literature, on the epic in particular, and he wrote a book on Dante. In the 1830s he gave a course on Milton at the Athénée Royal de Paris. He published the course in 1838, calling its 12 chapters "lessons." The book is entitled *Milton et la poésie épique*.[1] Reviewing it in July 1838, the *Monthly Review* commended its "judicious criticism."

Since the book treats all of Milton's career and work, the title is something of a misnomer. Occasional errors of detail slipped into the text, but in general the critic was meticulous.

Domestic and otherwise, he was very much abreast of what earlier critics had said about his author. Now and then he borrowed a phrase or an idea from Philarète Chasles and Chateaubriand but did not hesitate to take exception with his predecessors. He disliked Chateaubriand's *Paradise Lost* translation, or so he said, but nevertheless quoted from it. Dealing with Milton's prose, he also quoted selections Chateaubriand had translated and put into the *Essai sur la littérature anglaise*. In the case of passages not in the *Essai*, he produced other renderings, presumably his own. For the audience he sought to reach, he generally quoted Milton in French. Since Véricour's lectures were given at the Athénée Royal de Paris, its appeal was to a cultivated public not necessarily working toward university degrees. People attended because they wanted to.

Véricour told his hearers, soon to become his readers, that Milton was "le premier de tous les poètes lyriques anglais" (Véricour, 110). Véricour was selective in choosing the minor poems he would comment on, however. He reminds readers at one point that the poet, remembered as a dour, puritanical republican, had quite another side to him. "Milton avait vu le monde, et le monde le plus élégant," and he had written for it. He was not a courtier, but much of his work could have been read at court. His English, Latin and Italian poems have a "suavité harmonieuse," "une énergie, une douceur et un abandon inconnus avant lui." The sonnets are a multitude of little masterpieces. Singling out "On the Late Massacre in Piedmont," the critic notes that whereas sonnets generally deal with amorous matter, with this poet a sonnet can become a sublime hymn (Véricour, 102, 123–25). Among the minor poems, "On the Morning of Christ's Nativity," with its remarkable structure, evokes special praise: "Le poète eut ici l'idée d'encadrer un tableau de l'univers idolâtre dans une série de 27 strophes, et dans chacune de ces strophes il dépeint les temples païens s'écroulant et les idoles tombant en poussière à l'aspect de la crèche de Bethléem." Perhaps this ode, "une admirable composition lyrique," is the best thing ever written on Jesus' birth (Véricour, 102). In "Lycidas" the poet "touche d'abord le cœur par la simplicité d'une douleur juste et naturelle et élève ensuite l'esprit par des images magnifiques, ennoblies par l'enthousiasme de l'affection et du dévouement." The poem will be admired as long as "la tendresse, l'imagination et l'harmonie seront considérées comme les vraies sources de ce genre de composition" (Véricour, 102–03).

Véricour believed that "L'Allegro" and "Il Penseroso" were written at Forest Hill, by which he of course meant Horton. The two poems, both calm, are "deux tableaux de la vie rurale et des différentes impressions qu'elle produit sur l'esprit contemplatif." In the one, there is "une douce quiétude, un contentement secret et profond qui reçoit de tous les bruits et de tous les aspects de la nature une sensation agréable." In the other, there is "une mélancolie sombre qui sympathise avec tous les aspects tristes, avec tous les sons lugubres." The critic stresses the somber atmosphere. One should not be misled by the poems' titles, he insists. "Si vous cherchez dans l'un l'expression de la gaîté bruyante, de la joie folle, dans l'autre celle d'une douce mélancolie, vous n'y trouverez rien qui justifie les titres que vous aurez mal interprétés" (Véricour, 103–04).

Arcades is a "bouquet poétique," though not discussed. *Comus* the critic likes very much. He tells his readers that masques were "certaines pièces dont l'intrigue reposait principalement sur l'intervention d'êtres surnaturels." He then mentions the circumstances that gave rise to this one, noting that it was performed at Ludlow Castle and leading readers to think that it was in 1633 rather than 1634. The poetry is excellent. Milton's inventive art has taken a simple action and swathed it in exquisite verse. The critic summarizes the work, giving several passages in translation. Comus's call to pleasure is described as "une des plus poétiques romances de la langue anglaise." Also stressed is the Lady's reliance upon her conscience and virtue as she addresses the night in the lines beginning "Else O Thievish Night" (*Comus*, ll. 195–220), given in translation. This "morceau ravissant" Véricour describes as "tendre au plus haut degré," adding that he knows nothing superior to it "en sentiment noble, profond et mélancolique." The lines are, moreover, a statement of religious faith. "On trouve rarement dans les compositions modernes ce mélange de sentiment et de providence, de poésie et d'esprit religieux." Sabrina's incantation is likewise extolled. When the Attendant Spirit returns the children to their parents' castle, there is a brilliant epilogue, after which the Spirit concludes with the moral, also translated (*Comus*, ll. 1012–023). Once Véricour calls the work an opera but does not insist on the term. As drama, he thinks that it does not measure up to the usual criteria, but neither does he believe the poet intended it to. Classifying it does not matter, needless to say. What does matter is that, "sous la plus riante fiction, le poète a placé une grande idée morale et que dans ce cadre ... l'auteur ... a richement semé les produits de son inépuisable et éblouissante imagination. Cette production de ses premières années n'a été surpassée en poésie par aucun de ses ouvrages subséquents." The critic adds that "*Comus* mérite d'être placé parmi les fruits les plus heureux du génie." Written in the poet's youth, it is superior to *Paradise Regained*, dating from his final years (Véricour, 95–101). With the possible exception of Taine's, this tribute to *Comus* is the most enthusiastic any French critic awarded it in the nineteenth century.

Except for "On the Late Massacre in Piedmont," Véricour does little to situate the minor poems in contemporary events, private or public. The prose works are something else. All of one chapter and part of another are devoted to these. Underlying them, Véricour notes, are Milton's very personal religious tenets. "Milton était très pieux, mais à sa manière." Yet, in his writings, paradoxically, Milton worked against religion. "Sans le vouloir, il détruisait presque toute espèce de lien religieux." He did not like public ceremonies and temples, but predicated individual worship instead. One's inner religious convictions should regulate domestic life and make social institutions obsolete. Such an outlook, Véricour believes, natural enough for the author, was too much for the rest of humankind. So it was with politics. Intertwined with his religious views were his republican principles. In political matters, as in so much else, his guide was Plato, but his republican ideal, founded on virtue and free will, was as impractical as that of his master. His system, grandiose and chimerical, can be seen in the numerous pamphlets, discourses and treatises that he turned out. Idealized, it can also be seen in *Paradise Lost*. Throughout, Milton was sincere and disinterested (Véricour, 55–57).

Véricour turned his attention to the prose works themselves, several times using translations from Chateaubriand's *Essai sur la littérature anglaise*. The best of the prose works, the critic holds, was unquestionably *Areopagitica*. In this excellent discourse, the poet called for "liberté entière pour les livres, pour cette essence vivifiante et précieuse d'un esprit supérieur, recueillie, concentrée avec soin, destinée à une vie au-delà de l'existence." Milton, beginning with the observation that censorship is powerless against bad books, moves on to his point about not killing a book, which is tantamount to killing reason. Using Chateaubriand's much condensed translation, Véricour quotes most of the famous lines (Véricour, 63–65). With *The Tenure of Kings and Magistrates*, Milton talked about monarchs' responsibilities and asserted that a bad king could be called to account. As for *Eikonoklastes*, it must be seen in the context that produced it. Because of the centuries that have intervened, Véricour says, we can look at it dispassionately now. Perhaps the viewpoint was reprehensible, but the intention was sincere and noble. King Charles was stubborn, but in this book to which he is so central, "Il n'y règne aucun esprit de férocité, mais la haute raison d'un républicain . . . loyal et désintéressé. Milton pouvait être victime d'une erreur, mais rien dans son caractère n'autorise à croire qu'il eût pu se rendre coupable d'une lâche cruauté." The book is clear and methodical, austere and noble. Far from being aimed at an individual, it is directed at absolute rulers as a class, urging future ones to restrain themselves (Véricour, v, 46–47, 61–63). But from this point on, Milton's diatribes grew bitter and violent.

Saumaise got what he deserved, on the whole, according to this critic. Instead of insisting that despots were inviolable, he should have established that King Charles was no despot, which would not have been hard to do. Saumaise, unequal to the task, earned his opponent's scorn and came out of it all looking like the "défenseur absurde de la tyrannie" (Véricour, 48, 65). *Pro Populo Anglicano Defensio* and the *Defensio Secunda* are admirable pieces of Latin prose, elegant and classical, even if the author did allow himself some vicious words now and then. He was only doing what his contemporaries did. "C'était un vice du siècle." Besides, the invective was needed. Now, the *Defensio Secunda*, vindicating people rather than principles, is more interesting than the earlier volume, Véricour asserts. He likes the portraits in it as well as the exhortation to Cromwell, which he cites along with the magnificent personal digression. Probably Véricour liked his author's political tracts much more than he was willing to admit. He points out that, while he lived, the poet owed his reputation to these prose works, later forgotten and then resurrected in modern times to charm liberal, progressive minds. "Triste réputation que celle de cette âme ardente, qui ne connut point sa douce et impérissable renommée de poète..., qui n'eut d'autre gloire, d'autre source pour alimenter son génie que ces résultats des tempêtes politiques, résultats qu'il savait devoir expirer avec elles, comme tout ce qui se rattache aux passions momentanées des partis." A poet, Milton died knowing that he would be remembered for his prose polemics but unaware that these works, laid to rest with the events that occasioned them, would one day be revived and used by later generations (Véricour, 65–71).

Aside from those mentioned above, Véricour names several other prose works but says little about them except for the simple, virile *History of Britain*, which contains passages so applicable to the author's own times. With its praise of Alfred the Great, the work demonstrates that, though a republican, Milton was "l'ami sincère des rois qui savent mériter les bénédictions et l'amour des peuples." The book also demonstrates the author's bias against women. Dismissing Queen Boadicea's courage, Milton called the account of her bravery against the Romans an absurd tale. Milton was consistent in his attitude and, when contradicted, could cite authorities to substantiate it. Dueling with Saumaise, his worst, most persistent insult was that his opponent was not much more than his own wife's slave. In *Paradise Lost* Eve, with all her modest charm, is still a subordinate creature. Milton advocated polygamy (Véricour, 49, 72–77, 83).

Véricour was at great pains to show the poet's conduct and prose works in their best light. Sometimes he went rather far afield. Not mentioning the divorce tracts, he tells his readers that Milton broke with the Presbyterians only when, having come to power, they turned despotic. Like Chasles, Véricour claims that Milton never attacked his opponents on matters of detail. Equitable critics would not agree. Echoing Chasles again, Véricour also contends that the poet never belabored a fallen enemy, which would suggest that he had not pondered *The Tenure of Kings and Magistrates* and *Eikonoklastes* as carefully as he might have done. Véricour holds that, neither Puritan nor Cavalier, Milton was a true individualist. In connection with the minor poems, we have already seen the critic insisting upon the poet's aristocratic proclivities. He brings the matter up again. No uncouth zealot, Milton "emprunta aux classes les plus élevées cette élégance noble et ornée, cet amour des arts, ce sentiment du beau," that characterized him. "Il s'élève au-dessus des masses divisées de son époque par son caractère, sa piété, son zèle, son génie et son désintéressement. Les puritains le regardaient comme un pédant, parce qu'il savait le latin; les défenseurs de la monarchie le flétrirent comme un infâme, parce qu'il voulait la liberté publique." Milton excoriated what he considered wrong, wherever he saw it. "Dans la solitude de sa pensée, dans son mépris pour les préjugés contemporains, il attaque sans crainte les idoles puritains et les superstitions royalistes." He was "sévère, chaste, résolu, indomptable, comme les plus honnêtes des puritains." Like them, he hated despotism. In its place he advocated constitutional government. If he served Cromwell, it was in the hope that, while doing so, he could serve important causes. He did not hesitate to remind the Lord Protector of his political duties. In this and other things, he was a precursor.

Comme Bacon et Locke, il sert d'éclaireur à son siècle. Les axiomes qu'il émet et qu'il défend sont, aux yeux de ses contemporains, ou des paradoxes insoutenables ou des erreurs criminelles.... Toutes les thèses dont les écrivains modernes se sont emparés se retrouvent dans les œuvres de Milton: la liberté de la presse avec des lois restrictives et non préventives; la légitimité du divorce; la nécessité d'une éducation moins pédantesque et plus populaire.... Enfin, toute sa carrière est... féconde en résultats dont l'avenir a profité. (Véricour, 83)

[Like Bacon and Locke, he serves his era as a herald. The axioms he utters and defends are, in the eyes of his contemporaries, indefensible paradoxes or criminal errors.... All of the theses that modern writers have seized upon are to be found in Milton's work: the freedom of the press with restrictive and not preventive laws; the legitimacy of divorce; the need for more popular, less pedantic education.... In short, his whole career... generated results from which a later age has profited.]

Véricour admired Milton's prose for a variety of reasons. Several works, of course, contain important material concerning the author's life and aspirations. In addition, the style is remarkable. Anyone wanting to acquire a feeling for the power of the English language should delve into the prose. "On y trouve des passages d'une éloquence sans parallèle" where the author "est aussi élevé que dans les passages les plus sublimes de son épopée," where one is struck by his "élans de ravissements lyriques, d'enthousiasme et de patriotisme." In short, "Il est à regretter que ses ouvrages en prose ne soient pas un objet d'étude plus générale" (Véricour, 86–87, 91–92). As a final example of that prose, Véricour gives a condensed translation of Milton's letter, then newly discovered, to John Bradshaw recommending that Andrew Marvell be named assistant secretary to the Council of State. Véricour sees this letter as additional evidence of the poet's "largeur d'âme."

Véricour's enthusiasm for *Paradise Lost*, "la poésie la plus haute qu'il soit donné à l'esprit humain d'atteindre," was almost limitless. The critic alludes to William Lauder and passes in review the various sources the poet is said to have used. To sources as such he attaches little importance. After all, Virgil extracted all of his gold from Ennius's *Annals*, a "dunghill." And we do not even know what preceded the *Iliad*. Probably Milton knew Andreini's *Adamo* and St. Avitus's *De Initio Mundi*, which contains, "au milieu de ses descriptions diffuses et noyées dans une masse de vers latins, quelques éclairs assez vifs qui auraient pu servir de germe au *Paradis perdu*." Whatever the case, it does not matter much. *Paradise Lost* towers above the works that may have furnished its author a detail or two (Véricour, 159–63). Véricour devotes most of a chapter summarizing the poem, noting some of his impressions as he goes. Satan has "colossal" proportions. When, stunned but reviving after his sudden defeat, he assembles his legions around him, the critic sees a compellingly realistic military scene. "Tous les chefs de tant de bataillons, tous ces fiers capitaines semblables à des dieux, ce tableau d'une armée ralliée par un homme de génie après une déroute, sont empreints d'un caractère profond de vérité. Le poète développe ici toutes les richesses de son imagination, toute l'énergie de son pinceau." Two decades later, in his *Life and Times of Dante*, Véricour is a little less exubérant, noting that, as fallen angels, they were "of an equivocal nature," "not representing much more than abstract vices."[2] In 1838, however, he considers them marvelous. Their council meeting was gigantic, a "tableau immense, formé des esquisses des autres poètes." In inventiveness, Milton had surpassed his predecessors.

Sin and Death derive from Hesiod, Virgil, the Bible and the poet's brilliant imagination. An "image grandiose," they are destined to "porter la ruine et la désolation dans le monde que Dieu avait créé si beau et si parfait." Satan, on reaching the Garden of Eden, is thrilled at what he sees, and so is the critic, who draws on his readings to make another comparison. "Ici le poète prodigue les couleurs les plus ravissantes pour la peinture de ce délicieux jardin. Cette description rappelle celles d'Homère, Spenser, le Tasse, l'Arioste et Marino mais les surpasse de beaucoup en richesses variées et délicates." Similarly, in depicting Adam and Eve's physical love, he outdoes Homer and, even more so, Virgil. Milton reveals what the Latin poet took such care to hide.

The result is that "la vérité nue, mais pleine de grâce, est plus chaste que le voile dont la délicatesse de Virgile a voulu la couvrir." Book 5 is filled with splendid scenes. Sticking to the Bible, the poet managed to preserve "le caractère primitif du livre sacré jusque dans les ornements qui l'embellissent." The book contains "à la fois la poésie la plus magnifique, les plus riches descriptions, et un ensemble qui respire je ne sais quoi de simple, un mélange de grâce et de modestie inconnu des Grecs et des Romains."

The next book details the horrors of war. No poet has ever equaled Milton "dans des descriptions d'une nature aussi terrible et grandiose," Véricour writes. In book 7 Adam and Eve listen, enchanted, as Raphael tells them about the Creation. Again, Milton has excelled. As narrative, the episode is superior to Virgil's Dido pressing Aeneas to recount the disasters that ruined Troy. It is also better than Fénelon's Calypso, eager to learn about Telemachus's adventures. At Raphael's conclusion, Eve remains silent, while Adam warmly expresses his pleasure. In the *Aeneid*, not only does Dido remain silent, readers do not even find out how the scene ends. Leaving his characters onstage, so to speak, "le poète latin oublie de nous apprendre comment et dans quelles dispositions ils en sont sortis." Eve's seduction and how it is presented elicit the critic's additional praise. Milton's psychology and rhetoric here are superb.

> La malice, les desseins couverts, la marche oblique, les savants détours, l'art de saisir l'entrée favorable du cœur, les précautions oratoires, la modération du langage, la douceur de l'accent, l'éloquence insinuante, et par-dessus tout la flatterie ... mêlée aux apparences de la bonne foi, qui la rend si puissante, se trouvent réunis dans cette création de Milton. Jamais allégorie aussi juste, aussi vive, ne nous montra plus à découvert la marche habile des passions qui viennent nous surprendre. (Véricour, 151–52)

> [Malice, guile, devious shortcuts, skillful detours, the art of knowing when to try to make a point, rhetorical precautions, linguistic moderation, soft speech, insinuating eloquence, and above all flattery ... mingled with the appearance of good faith, which makes it so powerful, are combined in this Milton creation. Never did so exact, so living an allegory expose so nakedly the clever

progression of the passions that can catch us off guard.]

Especially in the last two books, Milton is imitating Virgil but, as usual, surpasses his model. "Ce n'est pas un seul peuple, ce n'est pas le seul empire romain que le poète anglais présente à nos yeux, ce sont tous les peuples et le monde entier." As far as Michael's revelations to Adam are concerned, Addison may have been right in saying that Milton should not have presented the first of them in a vision, then the remaining ones in a narrative. On the other hand, notes the critic, this change of pace keeps the reader's attention and perhaps leads into the dénouement better. Ablaze with marvelous poetic effects, the conclusion is worthy of everything that precedes it in this divine poem. It is also appropriate.

> Milton ne pouvait couronner plus dignement son poème que par la rédemption du genre humain. La sublime espérance de ce bienfait arrache Adam et Eve au désespoir et les encourage à mériter sur la terre les récompenses du ciel, où, purifiés de toutes les souillures du péché, ils doivent jouir à jamais de la présence du Dieu qui venait les visiter dans le Paradis au temps de leur première innocence. (Véricour, 159)
>
> [There was no better way Milton could crown his poem than by redeeming the human species. The sublime hope that this will come about snatches Adam and Eve from despair and encourages them on earth to earn the reward of Heaven, where, purified from all sin, they may enjoy forever the presence of the God who used to visit them in Paradise at the time of their first innocence.]

Paradise Lost's framework, with its wealth of ravishing detail, is at all times grandiose. But there is the plot also, which, considered in the abstract, is even more sublime than that of the *Iliad*. Based on the most ancient traditions, it deals with the universal human being. Always curious about our origins, we humans have sought them in religion. Contradictions within this domain have led us to poetize our uncertainties. *Paradise Lost* is a superb response to these needs. The poem is immortal. If some revolution were to sweep all else away and only this epic remained, it would be "comme un monument isolé, devenu l'élément et la base à la fois d'une civilisation nouvelle." As for Milton's place in literature, it is as imperishable as humanity, as vast as the universe (Véricour, 7, 29). This is hearty praise indeed.

It is not to say that the poem is flawless, however. This "longue suite variée de chants divins" has its defects, which Véricour also delineates. Overall, the reader staggers beneath the author's ponderous erudition and has to put up with an immoderate penchant for disputation, a complaint that, a couple of decades later, Taine would also make. More serious is the poet's having assigned functions to his supernatural characters that sometimes clash with the characters' spiritual essence. Then there are bothersome individual episodes. A case in point is the demons' shrinking in order to squeeze into their council chamber, which is in bad taste. So are the puns used in describing the rebels' defeat in the War in Heaven. In book 9, Adam and Eve's domestic squabble, "beaucoup trop verbeuse," could have been dispensed with (Véricour, 163–64, 321–22).

In his first chapter, Véricour had defined the epic, adding a detail or so later, as a long poetic narrative divided into cantos. It should be serious, lofty and religious. Through "le merveilleux idéal," it should perpetuate in a people's memory "les actions des dieux, les hauts faits des héros, les fondations des états, les subversions des cités, les belliqueuses entreprises, les grandes découvertes sur les continents ou sur les mers." It should also depict a people's private and public mores (Véricour, 3, 168 n. 1, 221–22). To write such a work demands imagination, intellect, learning, eloquence and poetic fire. True epics are rare. There are Homer's *Iliad*, Virgil's *Aeneid*, Tasso's *Gerusalemme liberata*, Camoës's *Lusiadas*, Milton's *Paradise Lost* and Klopstock's *Messias*. At times the *Odyssey* seems to be on Véricour's list, and a case could also be made, he believed, for the Bible, *The Divine Comedy*, and Ossian. With his *Pharsalia*, Lucan falls short of what he could have achieved, given his topic. Ariosto's *Orlando furioso* has much to recommend it, but in it there is too much narration, too much inappropriate plot material, too much clownishness to put it in the same class as *Paradise Lost*. While it has interesting descriptions, noble speeches and wondrous deeds, Ercilla's *Araucana* suffers from its arid subject matter and remains tedious throughout. Voltaire's *Henriade* does not measure up, either. Despite its well-knit action, Fénélon's *Télémaque* is excluded as well, chiefly because it was written in prose rather than verse. These works could be called "épopées du second ordre." France has no real epic, even though its history, more than that of any other nation, abounds in epic events (Véricour, 4–26, 336). The *Chanson de Roland*, only recently discovered, was not published until February 1837. Presumably Véricour did not know about it yet.[3]

Véricour knew the other epics quite well. From various technical viewpoints and with numerous quotations, his book is largely devoted to comparing *Paradise Lost* with the major ones. The author looks at exordia, for instance. These should be simple and concise, as in the *Odyssey* and the *Aeneid*. The *Henriade*'s exordium is weak; the *Pharsalia*'s is bombastic. In the *Lusiadas* Camoës was too enthusiastic and pompous. With his exordium, Klopstock introduced something novel. Like him, Milton declared that he was doing something new but did not get carried away by it. The beginning of *Paradise Lost* "ne possède ni la vivacité ni le commandement impérieux de celui de l'*Iliade*; il n'a rien de la douceur de celui de Virgile et du Tasse, de l'ardeur extrême de celui de Camoës, ou du mysticisme très élevé de Klopstock." Instead, it is serious, solemn, appropriate, and so noble, so imposing that it creates in the reader the peace and respect one should experience on entering a holy place (Véricour, 167–74). Véricour also examines invocations and expositions. Homer mixed his in the *Iliad* and the *Odyssey*. Perhaps Milton alone has imitated him in this, Virgil and most of the other epic poets having kept them distinct. Véricour mentions Tasso's invocation to a sacred muse. Klopstock abuses invocations in *Messias*, where, almost at random, they are introduced in all of the cantos. Milton inserts them with sober restraint and when he needs to do so. An example is the invocation to Urania in book 7. A new invocation is warranted at this point, since the poet cannot descend to earth without his muse's help. Here, as elsewhere, Véricour quotes from the Chateaubriand translation, which he claimed to find wanting.

Véricour distinguishes between episodes on the one hand and, on the other, narratives recited by various characters. Though useful, narratives should not be overworked, as with Camoës. Episodes are really digressions. Incidental to the main story, they nevertheless derive from it and should enhance it. The basic plot determines how many there can or should be. The *Odyssey* and the *Aeneid* meander, lending themselves to a series of adventures that, while more or less related to each other, are not tightly linked. The same is true of *Gerusalemme liberata*. The *Iliad* is different. Tightly constructed, it hurries along to its conclusion, leaving no room for deviations from the main plot. Véricour feels that much the same is true of *Paradise Lost*. This epic "forme une masse tellement puissante, tellement régulière dans ses progrès" that it too cannot accommodate numerous lengthy episodes. Episodes there are, however, "variés et admirablement adaptés au genre du poème." Early on, Sin and Death provide one of the most important, "un vrai prodige d'imagination" that Addison liked and Voltaire did not. The two monsters' reappearance in book 10 is a worthy sequel. Other splendid digressions are the Paradise of Fools and the description of Eden. In addition, Adam's narrative in book 8 is filled with "petites digressions qui, sans être des épisodes proprement dits, répandent sur le récit un charme qui est en quelque sorte du domaine de l'épisode" (Véricour, 214–21).

Véricour raises the curious question of how long the principal action of an epic should last. There need be no exact limit, he thinks. What happens in the *Iliad* takes 40 days. Less than six months are used up in the *Lusiadas*. The *Odyssey* requires two months. A year goes by in the *Aeneid* and in *Gerusalemme liberata*. Strictly speaking, *Paradise Lost* takes a week, if one decides that the action consists of humankind's temptation, sin and punishment. Skillfully, Milton has contrived not to spin things out, thus maintaining the appearance of a short time lapse. He has achieved this in part by using narratives, needless to say.

Something else he has done is show events in *medias res*.

> Quand la fable, trop surchargée d'événements qui se sont succédés, lui paraît trop longue, il entre en matière au milieu ou près de la fin du sujet et rappelle ensuite les choses antérieures par le récit qu'il met dans la bouche de quelque acteur de la fable. Le passé, se reployant ainsi sur le présent par un ingénieux artifice, raccourcit l'action en la complétant et varie ses formes en resserrant leur étendue.
>
> [When the story line, too encumbered with a succession of events, strikes him as being too long, he starts toward the middle or the end of an episode and then recalls what led up to it in a narrative that he puts in the mouth of some actor in the story. Thus the past, linking up with the present through this ingenious trick, shortens the action while completing it and varies its forms while narrowing their scope.]

To the critic, this is a remarkable device for coping with the time element (Véricour, 263-65).

Arranging material in some kind of order makes demands upon an epic poet's skill. Above all, there has to be diversity. And so there is in the *Odyssey*, the *Iliad*, the *Aeneid*, and most of the other great epics. Because of their subject matter or their own limitations, Lucan, Dante, Voltaire and Klopstock were not able to achieve it. For Véricour, then, Milton's accomplishment in this domain is awesome. If *Gerusalemme liberata* "déroule une succession de chants gracieusement ordonnée, portant dans toutes ses parties l'empreinte d'une brillante et fertile imagination et d'une connaissance profonde de l'art," so does *Paradise Lost* with its incredible scenes, descriptions, characters, emotions, deeds, events, all kaleidoscopic (Véricour, 187-93).

Unity is an essential feature in an epic. By unity, Véricour means that there should be but one central action, although now and then the critic is concerned with unity in its broader sense. With regard to technical unity, Homer and Milton are the great masters. The *Iliad*'s beginning, middle and end are Achilles' quarrel, his refusal to fight and his taking up arms again. What actually happens in the epic is a mere incident in the final days of the siege of Troy, despite the fact that any number of related events are brought in. "Cette mesure exacte et convenable de l'action est le résultat de l'unité, mais de cette seule unité de fait que nous venons de vous signaler." Along with *Gerusalemme liberata, Messias* is another outstanding example of unity. In this respect, however, *Paradise Lost* still remains unsurpassed. Like the other epic poets, Milton treats a single action. Even so, he manages to penetrate the deepest recesses of the human heart and reveal the origin of our woes. "Rien au monde ne touche plus les hommes que les malheurs des hommes" (Véricour, 233–40).

And then, an epic must have its supernatural element. To the possible the impossible must be added. "L'action de l'épopée, devant être grande et héroïque par elle-même, exige, puisqu'on doit l'agrandir encore, qu'à son élévation, qui atteint au plus haut degré des choses possibles, on ajoute encore le merveilleux, l'extraordinaire, l'incroyable, et le sublime." In this, allegory can be a brilliant component. Nevertheless, allegory is less powerful than the divine supernatural, and no one proves this better than Milton. While there are examples of epic allegory in *Paradise Lost,* better ones are Dante's Hypocrisy, clothed in its garment of lead; Camoës' Adamastor, the giant representing the Cape of Good Hope; and Lucan's Rubicon, where a deified Rome tries to arrest Cæsar on its banks. The French call the epic supernatural "le merveilleux." Véricour defines it as "l'image sensible et personnifiée du surnaturel," adding that it includes

> toutes les substances célestes ou infernales qu'on suppose en relation avec les hommes, toutes les forces motrices de la nature morale et matérielle, tous les êtres fantastiques nés de nos rêveries spéculatives et créés par notre imagination. Il embrasse toutes les religions, tous les phénomènes, toutes les passions, toutes les idées. Le merveilleux est essentiellement caractéristique de l'épopée, et l'on en trouve les fondements dans les profondeurs du cœur humain.
> (Véricour, 240)

> [all the celestial or demonic substances regarded as having a connection with man, all the motive forces of spiritual and material nature, all the fantastic beings born of our speculative meditations and created by our imaginations. It embraces all religions, all phe-

nomena, all passions, all ideas. The *merveilleux* is a basic characteristic of the epic, and its foundations lie in the depths of the human heart.]

Deities and their abodes provide the most spectacular kind of *merveilleux*, needless to say. Homer's Jupiter is a prime example. Milton, Homer's only true rival, provides others. God, the Son, Satan are memorable. So are their deeds. No reader is likely to forget the Creation or Satan's revenge, humankind's ruin. It is true that the devils' using the cannon in their war is unnecessary and even ridiculous, but we need to remember that, in the poem, demons are the ones who invent this instrument of death and destruction. With the lethal machines coming from Hell, not Heaven, the poet made an authoritative moral statement. But Homer hated war, too. "Le but d'Homère en chantant les batailles était d'en faire abhorrer les causes et d'en plaindre les désastres." Like the marvelous creatures that visit or live in them, Milton's Chaos, Pandemonium, Eden, and Heaven are splendid (Véricour, 240–52, 258, 364).

In an epic, as in other genres, characterization is important. Of course, many of the characters will be supernatural and will thus have dimensions one is not accustomed to. Milton's Satan is almost in a class by himself. "Jamais . . . le génie de l'homme n'a plus puissamment caractérisé un héros dramatique," Véricour writes. "Nothing can be more sublime than his lofty, indomitable pride, his haughty challenge to the Almighty, and his sinister delight in the eternal revolt, although writhing in eternal sufferings," he adds 20 years later (*Life and Times of Dante*, 255). But in an epic, mortals, like spirits, have to be made to come alive also, and they must have their motivations. Camoës "n'a fait qu'esquisser ses caractères sans les achever; sa touche est fière mais trop rapide; elle ne détermine pas assez les traits." Voltaire failed to distinguish between portrait painting and characterization. "La *Henriade* est remplie de ces physionomies ressemblant à certains personnages de l'histoire, que l'auteur a très bien dessinées et coloriées; mais on ne voit pas un seul acteur se mouvoir et se caractériser lui-même par ses faits et par ses discours." On the other hand, the *Iliad*'s

Hector is a living human being. A model of civic and military virtue, a patriot, he stands out as a "citoyen vertueux, mari tendre, bon père, parent sensible, courageux soutien de sa famille et de sa ville menacée." Virgil's characters, less well drawn, are not as good as those of Tasso. Milton's are remarkable. In *Paradise Lost* the poet "n'a pour acteurs qu'un homme et qu'une femme; mais il trace en eux, avec une supériorité admirable, la dignité, l'élévation de l'homme, la grâce et la pudique vertu de la femme; il les peint tous deux de couleurs célestes qui embellissent encore cet idéal état d'innocence." Adam and Eve, with their tender, ideal love and their other innocent attributes, impress us as somehow real. After their sin, they become even more real as they take on characteristics that we recognize as being, unfortunately, very human. Having learned vanity, anger, recrimination, lust, shame, and a remorse never needed before, they are now people we encounter every day and whom we know (Véricour, 253–55, 257–58, 263).

An epic, further, must be sublime, or it is not an epic. Without always sticking to it, Véricour provides another definition. Unlike the supernatural, the sublime can be envisaged in human terms. Whereas the *merveilleux* deals with supernatural beings and what they do, "le sublime se fonde sur l'extraordinaire réel et possible, pris dans la plus haute élévation des choses, sans pourtant sortir du cercle des idées accessibles à l'intelligence humaine.... Le sublime ne s'élève qu'aux grandes actions, aux nobles sentiments des hommes et des êtres réels. Toute passion, toute qualité, toute vertu portée... à un degré supérieur est sublime." The supernatural produces wonder; the sublime convinces the reason and awakens admiration (Véricour, 276–79). In Véricour's opinion, all of the *Iliad* is sublime. Pointing out Emmanuel Kant's claim that Virgil and Klopstock are more noble than sublime, the critic does not discuss the idea but adds that each of the poets has his moments. Tasso's sublime is too uniform, too moderate, too shy. More than from anything else, it arises from the pure flow of the style and the very nature of the action involved. Dante's, though more varied, is marred by things that are simply unusual, even horrible. Camoëns had a gift for the *merveilleux* but was rarely sublime. In the *Henriade*, the sublime is totally missing. Lucan, who intoxicates his readers with his verbal skill, shocks their good sense and is a perfect example of the "false sublime" (Véricour, 281–87). *Paradise Lost* abounds in examples of the sublime, with all its variations. Véricour cites the Garden of Eden and its inhabitants, for instance. Adam and Eve delight the imagination. "Leur âme intacte et céleste trouve une source de plaisirs innocents dans la nouvelle création qui s'élève et qui sourit autour d'eux." This is truly sublime, as is the "inexprimable nouveauté de leurs sentiments et de leur langage," all of it simple, touching, admirable. Likewise, with their tender words to each other, Adam and Eve's rising in the morning is sublime. Sublime also is the couple's reluctance to leave the Garden. Eve is distressed at leaving her flowers, and Adam will not be able to show his children where God appeared to him (Véricour, 288, 291–92, 299–301).

In addition to its other features, Véricour holds that an epic has to be didactic. Indeed, he says, the great epics have survived in part because of the moral teachings inherent or predicated in them. *Gerusalemme liberata* and the *Lusiadas* abound in useful truths, maxims, even philosophy. Aeneas's adventures demonstrate that the only way to establish nations is to persevere, letting justice and religion be one's guide. In *Paradise Lost*, the rebel angels are chastised, human beings sin and are driven out of their garden, and ethical values triumph. The poem overflows with "récits naïfs qui remuent le cœur et enfantent les émotions généreuses par l'expression élevée des sentiments les plus nobles, les plus touchants, les plus pieux, les plus vrais et les plus charitables" (Véricour, 229–31).

Véricour had a special interest in Dante and, as we have seen, would later write a book about him. Not surprisingly, in addition to those we have seen above, the critic makes other comparisons. "Milton était, comme Dante, homme d'état, amant et poète; tous deux avaient été malheureux dans la carrière politique et dans leurs amours." Winding up on the losing side, both had witnessed civil wars, and both had seen human passions make earth into a hell. While cultivating their own artistic individualities, both poets respected the epic models. As for Homer, however, Dante followed his lead less than Milton did.[4] Though treating them differently, both poets chose somewhat similar topics and are "prodigieux et sans rivaux dans le sujet qu'ils ont adopté." In *The Divine Comedy* Dante was dealing with three worlds, Véricour tells readers, not two as in *Paradise Lost*. Dante's Hell stands out better than his Heaven, whereas Milton painted the two with equal skill. Dante's best scenes depict physical and spiritual torment or else political violence. Bitter and satirical, Dante is the poet of hatred and vengeance. Milton's creations, human and divine, have their disputes and even their revolts, but, generally speaking, the tone of *Paradise Lost* is pure and serene. This is because, within him, the poet sees an ideal world, religious and grandiose. Compared to his medieval predecessor,

> Milton est plus pittoresque, plus varié dans ses couleurs. Dante a une force plastique, il crée pour ainsi dire des statues. Si le poète anglais s'égare quelquefois dans le vague et l'obscurité, l'italien, par la précision des contours formés d'une manière dure et violente, tombe quelquefois dans l'exagération.
>
> [Milton is more picturesque, with more variety in his colors. Dante's strength is plastic; he carves statues, so to speak. If the English poet sometimes wanders about in vagueness and obscurity, the Italian, with the precision of his contours molded in a harsh, violent manner, is sometimes guilty of exaggeration.]

Moreover, "Dante est souvent plus puissant et plus caractéristique." Milton compensates, however. His characters, whether ideal humans or supernatural entities, are better, and he provides his readers more material for speculation. He opens "à la pensée un espace illimité." But the poets are also alike in several ways. Both are omnipresent in their poems, for example. In both there is "ce même contraste d'une audace de génie et d'une foi respectueuse et vive, une imagination qui règne partout dans leurs magnifiques inventions, réunie à une naïveté extraordinaire." Their "in-

spirations opposées" and their "mélange de sentiments divers" guarantee them an eminent and durable place in literature (Véricour, 305–35). The comparison is a well-informed personal view, but Véricour has erred in remarking that Milton, unlike Dante, dealt with two worlds rather than three in his epic, since *Paradise Lost* takes place in three spheres also: Heaven, Hell and Earth.

After Dante, Véricour has some additional comparisons and contrasts to make, this time between Milton and Klopstock. There can be no doubt that Milton influenced the German poet, he holds. Yet *Messias* is not in the same class as *Paradise Lost*. Its merits, though real, are outnumbered by its defects. Milton's Hell is better conceived and described than that of his emulator. His Satan is better motivated as well. Klopstock's Heaven is well drawn, but it overpowers us. To start with, making God an active character, like Homer's Jupiter, was not a sound idea. In the *Génie du christianisme* Chateaubriand had felt the same way. God's presence, as Véricour sees it, led to episodes that impugn common sense. Having God watch the Crucifixion makes us wonder whether we ought not "accuser de barbarie l'auguste témoin d'une agonie si douloureuse." Jesus is well delineated but, on the cross, should not have been casting venomous looks at enemies, however evil. Nor did Klopstock have any business prating about theology. "Commentateur imprudent, interprète sans mission, il s'expose à faire déraisonner les personnes divines de la manière la plus étrange." It seems not to disturb Véricour that Milton has been accused of much the same thing. Véricour continues, pointing out that Klopstock was too enthusiastic about nature and devoted too much space to it. Moreover, his epic is vérbose, and there are tedious sections in it. In short, Messias "n'a rien de la grandeur chaleureuse, homérique, du *Paradis perdu*. Klopstock n'a pas assez resserré les diverses parties de son poème; il succombe à la tentation continuelle de son mysticisme; il abuse du dialogue, et ses discours sont d'une longueur désespérante; il manque d'imagination dans l'art de faire agir ses personnages...." Klopstock, then, was an

able writer but, when compared to Milton, comes out the loser (Véricour, 341, 348–70). The *Monthly Review* thought Véricour's comparisons of Milton with Dante and Klopstock "the most novel and instructive to the English reader" (*Review*, 346).

As we have seen earlier, Véricour believed that an epic should have only one basic plot. He considered that no epic poet had observed this rule better than Milton. In *Paradise Lost* the plot is human disobedience. God has given Adam and Eve but one commandment, and they violate it. Milton prepares for this with consummate art. A celestial visitor has warned the couple. "Adam, resté près de sa chère Eve, la confirme dans la résolution de ne jamais transgresser l'ordre divin, et pour mieux la préserver de tout écueil, il désire ne plus se séparer d'elle." But Satan has been at work. Eve is now curious, less docile, and insists on going about her work alone. She and her husband exchange tender words, but she is no less determined to have her way. Taking leave of her spouse, she speeds off to tend her flowers. This act, which the author invented, is what sets everything in motion. In the epic, this is "le véritable point de l'intérêt central." The poet has paved the way for the irreparable misfortune which, now, will be unavoidable (Véricour, 272–76).

Paradise Lost is hard to read, Véricour tells his listeners and readers, but the effort is more than worth it. The language may seem difficult, but this obstacle is more apparent than real. There are neologisms, to be sure, but the basic linguistic structure is pure. "Quoique modifé sur le modèle des langues étrangères, le *Paradis perdu* tient aux racines de la langue anglaise, qui nulle part ne paraît plus pompeuse et plus forte" (Véricour, 378–80). With the raw materials at his disposal, Milton created "un édifice immortel," which Véricour urges his audience to read and reread. Milton's intellect, shining through it, will reward those who do. "Son esprit était un vaste foyer de toutes les connaissances anciennes et modernes. Doué d'une lucidité prodigieuse qui lui permettait de tout embrasser sans être superficiel...., il possédait cette universalité qui est le cachet de l'ordre le plus élevé de l'intelligence humaine." Véricour is not sure that the proper critic, the one eminent individual prepared to understand and explain the poet, has come along yet. For one thing, Milton inspires too much blind veneration for one class of critics to touch him. Others have been too concerned with textual matters to lift the veil that partially hides "la grandeur et les beautés peu comprises de toute vraie poésie" (Véricour, 375, 378).

Véricour's book is chiefly concerned with *Paradise Lost*, but the author also awards high marks to *Paradise Regained*, which he says should be read by all people with discriminating taste. Other than that, he says rather little about it, however. Worthy of its author, the poem is "une œuvre calme et belle" but is devoid of action. Quoting William Hayley, Véricour combats the notion that it was its author's favorite work. In the first book, God ordains that the Son will be tempted but will resist and win out. According to the critic, this decree undermines somewhat the poem's dramatic interest. To tempt Christ, Satan presents a panorama of all the passions that assail humankind, which leads to the long speeches encountered throughout the poem. The process served the author's purposes in a most poetic manner. "Ainsi lorsque Satan met en jeu l'appât des grandeurs, il déroule magnifiquement . . . un brillant tableau de la gloire des Romains." For Véricour, it is the fourth book that sparkles the most. "Satan, après avoir épuisé tous les moyens, fait usage de la tentation de la science et des succès attachés aux lettres et à la philosophie. Milton a placé ici une espèce de revue poétique de tous les systèmes grecs et des merveilles des arts et de l'éloquence d'Athènes." Satan renews his attacks, invents other wiles. "Satan revient toujours à la charge, il se présente toujours de nouveau, et il est toujours réfuté: le poète le compare à une vague qui revient sans cesse frapper le rocher, bien qu'elle en rejaillisse en vaine écume" (Véricour, 113–16).

Véricour has even less to say about *Samson Agonistes* than he did about *Paradise Regained*. A "beau drame lyrique," *Samson* reveals "partout l'inspiration d'un génie élevé." The work, "quoique moins poétique que *Comus*, est cependant plus richement semé des produits de l'imagination du poète et beaucoup plus dramatique." Like *Comus*, it is in dramatic form, although the author did not intend it to be staged. Yet staging it would be possible, Véricour notes, although it probably would not succeed. "Le langage en est si grave et le style si majestueux qu'elle produirait sans doute par cette pompe soutenue un effet fatigant à la représentation." To his unworthy era Milton had just offered *Paradise Lost*, which had gone unnoticed. *Samson Agonistes* was his eloquent revenge, or perhaps his acknowledgment that he was beaten. Véricour assumes that, in the blind captive, Milton was depicting himself. "On est frappé, en lisant ce poème lyrique, des passages d'une sensibilité énergique qui présentent à notre imagination le tableau de la tristesse, des souffrances, des sensations du poète mêlées à celles de son héros." The poem "respire un charme pathétique qui ne se retrouve pas dans les compositions de ce genre. On est ému de cette heureuse idée, de cette félicité du génie qui épanche ainsi un cœur accablé de douleur et d'indignation." Singling it out for special praise, Véricour mentions the opening monologue, "la belle ... apostrophe touchante sur la perte de la lumière, malheur affreux sur lequel Milton revenait souvent avec un plaisir douloureux." The critic gives his readers an excerpt (Véricour, 108–13).

From what precedes, it is clear that Véricour's admiration for Milton was very real. The critic worked too hard, it is true, to make Milton the pamphleteer look disinterested. While insisting upon the poet's rigid independence, he neglected to account for Milton's not raising his voice against Cromwell's dictatorship. Yet Véricour did much to make up for these shortcomings. As Geffroy was to do, he called attention to the pamphlets' modern ring. In addition, labeling Milton "le premier de tous les poètes lyriques anglais" (Véricour, 110), he was one of the few French critics of his day to call attention to such minor poems as "On the Morning of Christ's Nativity," "On the Late Massacre in Piedmont" and *Arcades*. He was also one of the few to notice *The History of Britain*. Interested in comparative literature, his main object, of course, was to discuss *Paradise Lost* in terms of the other great western epics, which he appears to have studied carefully. *Paradise Lost* he considered superior to them all, except perhaps the *Iliad*. Unlike Lamartine, he did not try to downplay the conviction, so often attributed to Milton, that women are an inferior breed. Nor was he appalled at Sin and Death, as so many French critics have been. Not all readers are as willing as he was to discount the violence and evil in *Paradise Lost* and insist that, on the contrary, it is the serene and the ideal that dominate in the poem. But if there is an area where the critic is to be admonished, it lies in his having spilled too much ink explaining away the poet's position regarding Charles I's judgment and execution. He tells us that Milton was a creature of his times and that, in any event, he did not really approve of what was done.

> Nous avons essayé de vous expliquer... comment Milton peut être lavé de toute accusation sanglante, sans que le peuple soit exempt des sentiments d'horreur qu'il a inspiré. Le noble défenseur de toutes les libertés anglaises a mis trop d'aigreur, il est vrai, dans sa controverse; il a lancé avec trop de violence, contre l'absolutisme et contre ses ennemis, l'anathème de son éloquente invective. Mais, nous ne craignons pas de le répéter, dans quel temps vivait-il? Quelle terrible contagion de haine et de fureur s'était répandue autour de lui? Ce guerrier jeté dans une mêlée sanglante pouvait-il mesurer tous ses coups? (Véricour, 79)
>
> [We have sought to explain... how Milton can be cleansed of all bloody accusations, without the people's being exempt from the feelings of horror he inspired. The noble defender of all the English liberties put too much bitterness into his controversies, it is true; against absolutism and against his enemies he hurled with too much violence the anathema of his eloquent invective. But, we do not fear repeating, what era did he live in? What terrible contagion of hate and fury had caught on around him? Cast into the bloody melee, could this warrior have measured all his blows?]

Milton and likeminded people abhorred the bloody deeds of those in authority. At least the critic believed this to have been the case, his personal conviction sounding very much like wishful thinking (Véricour, 79).

Regardless, Véricour helps prove that the bases for deterministic literary criticism were in the air a couple of decades before Hippolyte Taine codified them. According to Véricour, if Milton's political views expressed in the prose works can be attributed to the climate of the times, something similar can be said for the poetry. Its particular character springs from the author's having been English. In connection with Villemain's *Histoire de Cromwell*, Véricour notes somewhere that "la poésie lyrique, cet accent musical des passions, est sans cesse en rapport avec la nationalité" (Véricour, 110).

5
Matthieu Auguste Geffroy

Matthieu Auguste Geffroy (1820–1895) handled the English language well and did some of his research at the British Museum. Planning to be a historian, he entered the Ecole Normale in 1840. He received his doctorate in 1848. Soon he was named to a history professorship at the University of Bordeaux, then went on to the Ecole Normale Supérieure and the Sorbonne. Many of his articles appeared in the *Revue des Deux Mondes*. In 1874 he was elected to the Académie des Sciences Morales et Politiques. *Etude sur les pamphlets politiques et religieux de Milton*, written during the February Revolution, was one of his two doctoral theses in 1848.[1] A note tells the reader that the introduction was written in January, while the thesis approval date was 15 March. In the meantime, the July Monarchy had been swept away and replaced by the Second Republic. The thesis could not have been more timely; liberal ideas were in the air, and these ideas are found in Geffroy's thesis. We have seen Véricour's admiration for the prose works. Geffroy was to go into them in great detail.

In his introduction, the author claims that "la renommée glorieuse de Milton poète a étouffé le mérite très réel de

Milton prosateur." While this is as it should be, it was the author's involvement in the controversies of his era that groomed him for his more important role as an epic poet. "Ardent patriotisme, généreux désintéressement, sincère amour des hommes, toutes ces mâles vertus ont de bonne heure ouvert et préparé le cœur de Milton aux plus sérieuses et aux plus profondes inspirations de la poésie." Studying the prose works, in which these characteristics are illustrated, enriches one's understanding of *Paradise Lost*. One must not forget that, in spite of his poetic instincts and his gentle inclinations, Milton was a publicist and pamphleteer before he was a great poet. But why, with these peaceful instincts and inclinations, did he descend into the arena at all, Geffroy asks? He concludes that a sense of duty pushed him there (Geffroy, 2-3). Geffroy was to reiterate this opinion.

However, aside from what it tells us about *Paradise Lost*, Geffroy believes there is another reason for scrutinizing this thinker's prose. In France, the Enlightenment and the Revolution of 1789 did much to accredit liberal ideas, but the process had started much earlier on the other side of the English Channel. There the French "philosophes" had encountered the ideas in books and clubs. Taken back to France, the ideas were nurtured and they blossomed. "L'Angleterre avait fait jaillir la flamme; la France y ajouta une ardente et fécondante chaleur." Milton was one of those who had planted the seed.

> Liberté entière d'interprétation pour quiconque admet que la Bible contient la vraie parole de Dieu, libre et volontaire soumission à tout chef élu en vertu d'un contrat social, respect de la dignité et de tous les droits naturels de l'homme, distinction nette et précise entre l'église et les pouvoirs laïques, liberté d'examen, liberté de parole, liberté de la presse, libre divorce et libre éducation, Milton a tracé dans ses pamphlets tout ce programme d'une société nouvelle. (Geffroy, 6-7)
>
> [Total freedom of interpretation for whoever acknowledges that the Bible contains the true word of God, free and voluntary submission to any leader elected by virtue of a social contract, respect for the dignity and all the natural rights of man, clear and

precise distinction between the church and civil authority, freedom of inquiry, freedom of speech, freedom of the press, free divorce and free education, Milton outlined in his pamphlets this whole program for a new society.]

Standing on the threshold of the modern world, Milton announced his noble ideas, missing but few of the great issues of our time. Geffroy sees his author as an idealistic precursor.

As Milton had done in *Defensio Secunda*, Geffroy divides the tracts into those dealing with religious freedom, those concerned with freedom of thought, those advocating domestic freedom. These are the liberties one needs in order to live in some measure of comfort. The classificiation, in its general outlines, happens to be chronological. Geffroy's introduction follows Milton up to the moment when, hardly back from his travels, the young reformer leaped into the fray with his earliest pamphlets. From pamphlet to pamphlet, the relevant circumstances, public and private, are sketched in, assuring biographical and historical continuity. Each pamphlet or group of pamphlets is thus seen in context. References to other prose works, to the correspondence, even to *Paradise Lost* and *Samson Agonistes*, occasionally indicate worthwhile parallels. Geffroy quotes at length, translating his material or paraphrasing.

On returning to England, John Milton took stock of things. To start with, what he saw in the church displeased him. His ideal church was being humiliated and repressed. Picking up his pen, he came to its defense by attacking the institution of bishops. His first assault was *Of Reformation*. Geffroy considers it together with *Of Prelatical Episcopacy* and *The Reason of Church Government*. Never, he believes, had a pamphleteer hurled himself into a debate with more enthusiasm or conviction. The brochures show what Milton disliked in the Church of England and what changes he demanded; he found fault with its organization and called for it to be revamped along Presbyterian lines. Geffroy cites long passages from *Of Reformation* and points out that all three tracts appeared the same year as the Grand Remonstrance, which Parliament passed on 22 November 1641.

Quoting the Grand Remonstrance, Geffroy calls attention to the similarities: "Il est curieux de voir la libre éloquence du pamphlétaire servir de commentaire, ardent et passionné..., aux griefs exprimés dans cet acte officiel." The critic hastens to add that the Presbyterians had attacked the Church of England as rivals, with an axe to grind. Milton had attacked it as a citizen and as a patriot. Little did he realize that what his allies planned to do was simply grab their enemies' power and despotism for themselves (Geffroy, 31–48).

Milton took on such renowned adversaries as Bishop Hall and Bishop Ussher. The religious tracts that followed *Of Reformation* are sectarian, ironic, bitter and violent. At times the author's eloquence is "un singulier mélange de faux goût et de noble simplicité, de bizarres images et de spirituelles allégories, de mordantes satires et de sublimes aspirations." These works would interest us but little were it not for their style, which, in spite of everything, often manages to be "spirituel, toujours chaleureux et poétique," filled with impressions and ideas dictated by "une vive imagination et un cœur toujours ému." To some extent, the invective is relieved by candid moments such as the poet's autobiographical digression in *The Reason of Church Government*, which, in French and with much condensation, the critic reproduces.[2] The digression promises a poem such as *Paradise Lost*. While it reveals Milton's concern for his intellectual labors, it also bespeaks his commitment to other ideals, equally demanding. "Toujours la voix impérieuse d'un admirable dévouement le rappellera vers sa grande et laborieuse tâche. Cet irréstible élan pour les grandes choses et cet ardent amour de Dieu et de la liberté deviendront les plus habituelles comme les plus fécondes inspirations de sa muse poétique. Ce sera là sa récompense." By writing pamphlets, Milton was not frittering away his poetic gifts; he was, rather, serving the same causes that would produce *Paradise Lost* (Geffroy, 50–53). As William Riley Parker was to do, Geffroy observes that the *Apology for Smectymnuus* ended Milton's first period as a controversialist (Parker, 1:224).

Perceiving at last that the Long Parliament Presbyterians

were as domineering and intolerant as the Established Church, Milton became alarmed at their attitude toward education and censorship. He decided to take them on, just as he had taken on their opponents. He had become, in his own home, a schoolmaster. "C'était continuer l'œuvre à laquelle il voulait consacrer sa vie, éclairer et élever ses semblables." True worship is best experienced when it is the product of "une généreuse et libérale éducation." Geffroy reminds his readers that, to Milton, the purpose of education is to know, love and approach God (*YPW*, 2:366-67). Milton was appalled at how backward university education had remained. So were Bacon and Hobbes, whom Geffroy invokes. Paraphrasing more than he translates, this historian delves into Milton's pedagogical ideas. For one thing, Milton reproaches current educational practice for teaching languages for their own sake, through tedious ritual and with no concern for the ideas they are supposed to help one acquire. Equally bad, the analytical method was being neglected. Victims of inept education, children were growing up and entering professions unprepared and with no vocation. Milton would replace grade schools and universities with a new kind of institution that would keep students busy from the ages of 12 to 21.

Again with much paraphrasing and translating, Geffroy sums up the program, which he likes. Perhaps Milton was asking too much too soon of his theoretical young scholars, but, in doing so, he was demonstrating that he was a man of his times. Already a republican, he was looking to his country's future and demanding that education provide it—and quickly—with learned administrators, excellent generals, and dedicated, devout preachers. Was Milton too demanding? One may retain or discard details in the ambitious program, but if one believes that teachers have a divine mission, that if they put their hearts into their work, and that if they have prepared themselves by patient toil, then "tous les programmes seront également bons et ils se modifieront à l'empreinte" of the teachers' virtue. Geffroy points out that, with his letters, Milton remained in touch with some of his charges after they moved on to the world beyond the classroom (Geffroy, 76-77, 55 n. 1). What Geffroy does not say is that, while the new curriculum may or may not have been more practical than the one its author hoped it would supplant, Milton was at least as doctrinaire about it as the proponents of the old one were about theirs. Geffroy fails to add that much later, in keeping with his ideas, Milton even prepared a textbook, the *Accedence Commenc't Grammar*, which upon its publication was as much ignored as *Of Education*.

Areopagitica, published the same year as *Of Education*, was another plea for freedom of thought. Presbyterians at first had wanted a free press, but, their goals achieved, they set out to dismantle it so as to silence their opponents. The Long Parliament, their agent, reimposed the old restrictions on 14 June 1643.[3] Courageously, Milton raised his voice "non en tribun qui insulte et qui brave, mais en homme d'état qui propose et délibère." Demonstrating his concern for the public weal, his pamphlet appeared in November 1644. Geffroy claims that the manuscript, at least at the time the critic was writing, was in the Bodleian Library.[4] Step by step, he leads his readers through the book. Pointing out how difficult it is to select, he nonetheless tries to call attention to the most striking passages. He adds that Milton was not exaggerating. When *Areopagitica* inveighs against the complicated imprimatur process then being used in Florence, Geffroy notes that it was even worse in Spain and Portugal. Milton was the first person in England, perhaps in the world, to understand and call for the people's right to a free press. God had given human beings the ability to think.

> Puisque la pensée ne se manifeste que par le langage, écrit ou parlé, il est évident que le droit d'exprimer toutes ses idées par l'écriture ou la parole n'a pu être conféré ou refusé à l'homme par aucune loi humaine, que c'est là un de ses droits naturels... auquel il ne peut renoncer qu'en abdiquant sa qualité d'homme.... Un livre, c'est une âme d'homme, un reflet de la divinité. (Geffroy, 83)
>
> [Since language, spoken or written, is the sole means by which thought can be conveyed, it is clear that the right to express all of one's ideas by speaking or writing could not be granted or refused man by any human law, that this is a natural right...

he can give up only by renouncing his status as a man.... A book is a human soul, a reflection of the godhead.]

Geffroy considers *Areopagitica* eloquent, compliments its "spirituelle invective," but complains that the author probably sprinkled his text with too many Greek and Latin phrases. Even so, compared with his contemporaries, he was rather modest in this respect. Geffroy implies, correctly, that Milton's petition went unheeded. He does mention that Mirabeau translated and summarized *Areopagitica* as the French Revolution was getting under way. "Ainsi, aux deux plus solennelles époques des deux plus grands états du monde, s'est venu placer Milton, pour invoquer la liberté et annoncer au peuples son heureux et prochain avènement."[5] Geffroy could have added that freedom of the press, legally at least, fared no better as a result of the French Revolution than it did during and after the Great Rebellion. He does not go into Milton's own reservations about freedom of the press, nor does he mention that eventually Milton became a licenser himself, taking on the responsibility for seeing to it that Marchamont Needham's *Mercurius Politicus* did not get out of line, for instance. Apart from Milton's express reservations, it appears not to have occurred to the critic that the poet might have been less than sincere, that he may have changed his mind eventually, or that he simply learned to compromise with realities he ultimately could do nothing about.

Geffroy rightly declares that the period around 1644 and 1645 was a busy time in Milton's pamphleteering. After tackling education and making a case for unlicensed printing, the erstwhile poet was ready to have a look at divorce. Geffroy's chapter on this aspect of Milton is one of his shortest. Except for the remark that the wedding took place in 1643 instead of 1642, the account of Milton's first experiment with matrimony is accurate enough. So, no doubt, are the reasons given for the bride's decision not to return to her husband's house once she left it soon after the marriage. The atmosphere in which Mary Powell had been reared was diametrically opposed to the one in which wedlock was about to shut her up.

La jeune dame, habituée aux fêtes et aux danses au milieiu desquelles elle avait grandi, dans le monde léger et insouciant des Cavaliers amis de sa famille, se vit avec dépit et chagrin transportée dans l'intérieur grave, silencieux et sévère d'un sectaire et d'un républicain dont la journée se partageait seulement entre le travail solitaire et quelques leçons de latin ou de grec données aux enfants qui l'entouraient. (Geffroy, 91)

[The young lady, accustomed to the parties and dances she had grown up among in the careless, frivolous society of her family's Cavalier friends, was disappointed and annoyed at being set down in the serious, austere, silent home of a zealot and a republican, whose day was devoted to nothing but solitary work and a few Latin or Greek lessons administered to the children who surrounded him.]

Then, too, who was going to win the war that was splitting the country apart? Mary's family "crut au prochain triomphe de Charles Ier et put prévoir avec effroi que la cour, recouvrant son ancienne prospérité, n'aurait plus de faveurs pour une famille dont l'héritière avait épousé un républicain, un ennemi de l'Eglise Etablie. On peut admettre les deux explications. . . ." Was Milton already a convinced republican at this stage of things? Geffroy does not raise the question. In his writing Milton was still alluding to "realms." In any event, resolving to get rid of his wife, Milton typically made his cause that of everyone whose marriage had gone wrong and who might want out of it. He wrote *The Doctrine and Discipline of Divorce.* Since his bibliography lists it, Geffroy must have been aware that there was a 1643 edition. However, he seems to have used only the one that came out in 1644, because he states that the work was dedicated to the English Parliament. Thus he misses the ironic point that Milton originally dedicated the work to the Westminster Assembly. Only when those worthies ignored his proposals, no doubt thoroughly scandalized, did he turn to the secular arm, asking it, along with the religious body, to reinstitute divorce. Again Geffroy translates and paraphrases, selecting the most eloquent and most important passages. He also summarizes. As he had done in previous tracts, Milton tried to win over his readers by convincing them that the "abuses" he wanted them to correct had their roots in the Catholic and then the Anglican Churches. Eliminating the ban on divorce was simply part of putting some finishing touches on the Reformation. Reduced to its simplest terms, Milton "voyait dans l'interdiction du divorce la cause de tous les désordres domestiques." Rebutted, he gave *The Doctrine and Discipline of Divorce* a few sequels. Geffroy tended to think him sincere in all of this but nevertheless realized that "il savait interpréter subtilement en sa faveur."

As we know, *The Doctrine and Discipline of Divorce* provoked a storm. Herbert Palmer and Joseph Hall protested and called down all the wrath they could muster.[6] Worse still, the Westminster Assembly, instead of ignoring the matter, now became incensed. It asked the House of Lords to take action, but, for whatever reason, the House of Commons absolved the scandalous author. Meanwhile, Milton and Mary Powell were reconciled. As pointed out above, Geffroy believes that Milton was honest in what he was preaching. He had proclaimed that marriage is a union of souls, not bodies. He had superior people in mind, however. When a virtuous individual finds himself or herself shackled to an incompatible mate, there should be a way out. To Milton, the woman, generally, is at fault. "La femme est toujours, à ses yeux, la cause première des malheurs du genre humain." No matter who is responsible, there are practicalities that Milton, too much the idealist, did not really address, such as what happens to the property and the children. Still, Milton was convinced that happy unions are possible, and this conviction made it possible for him to hail wedded love in *Paradise Lost* (Geffroy, 99–113).

From the divorce tracts, Geffroy moves on to the prose works demonstrating Milton's belief that, in government, there is a fundamental social contract. The first of these is *The Tenure of Kings and Magistrates*. Here again, according to the critic, the author is disinterested, his motivation springing from pure patriotism. Until the death to Charles I, he never wrote a line against monarchy. On the contrary, he defended it against the Anglican Church. Whether he realized it or not, however, he had embarked on a course that would inevitably put him in opposition to the Crown. Since church and throne were inseparable, damaging the one meant damaging the other. From the first, Milton had taken the side of the Long Parliament, with all that that implied. Add to this his disillusionment with the Presbyterians, whom he had come to view as timid and conservative on the issues that had attracted his attention up to this time. Instead, Milton looked to the Independents, who seemed more willing to bring about radical changes. It just happened that they were also the declared enemies of King Charles. Seizing control after the Presbyterians had discredited themselves, instead of reforming, the Independents set about destroying. One of the things they destroyed was the king. Milton, while he did not share "le désordre de leurs idées," nevertheless found himself in their camp, and there was no turning back. "Par son amour inquiet de la liberté et par sa piété enthousiaste, Milton se trouvait rapproché des hommes de ce parti." There were not many choices. This meant, however, that he was rubbing elbows with men whose relentless quarrel with the king would result in the latter's death.

Geffroy liked to think that Milton "s'affligea en voyant cette révolution tant souhaitée ensanglantée dès le berceau." Amédée Pichot had had him tell someone that the execution had probably damaged the republic. Perhaps Milton hoped the sacrifice would be acceptable and would lead to something good, Geffroy continues. "Une sainte république allait succéder à une monarchie" that, when all is said and done, had been despotic. Maybe this would be the dawn of a new and better era. In the meantime, one way or another, John Milton had become a republican (Geffroy, 115–18). Perhaps he had been one all along. He could tell himself, in any event, that he had had nothing to do with the bloodshed. The Presbyterians were the ones who had dethroned their monarch and sent him to the block, thus making the country a republic.

Whether Milton had desired the king's death or not, he willingly accepted the consequences. The first of these was the disestablishment of the Anglican Church, which could not fail to make him happy. His happiness and optimism stand out in his pamphlet. The very title of *The Tenure of Kings and Magistrates*, with its claim that people have the right to punish a wicked king, leaves no doubt that the work springs from what, by now at least, was an ardent commitment to democratic principles on the author's part. Characteristically, "le désintéressement et l'amour de la patrie lui avaient seuls dicté ses paroles." Even when Milton was getting his ideas down on paper, some were not altogether new. Still, no one had expressed them quite so distinctly. The doctrine of regicide is clearly stated, but there is also lofty talk about government responsibility and where true sovereignty lies. One will find "dans ces pages républicaines un généreux plaidoyer en faveur des grandes idées de la souveraineté du peuple, du contrat social, de la responsabilité des rois, et de la liberté de penser." Once more, Milton was anticipating the French eighteenth century. Good sense, of course, has made people turn away from the idea of regicide, but, on the other hand, in Milton's short treatise are notions that modern France has adopted and developed. Jean Jacques Rousseau would prove to be a more engaging champion of the social contract, but this does not diminish his predecessor's achievement in enunciating the concept a century earlier. That Milton should have been propounding such ideas at the time is amazing, Geffroy asserts, when one bears in mind that, a short distance away, Bossuet and Fénelon were getting ready to sanction divine right with all the authority of their genius.[7] Geffroy does not add that one of the places Bossuet would sanction it was in the majestic sermon he preached at the funeral of Henrietta Maria, Charles I's widow.

The History of Britain is not a pamphlet, needless to say, and Geffroy does not treat it as one. He brings it up, however, notably in connection with Milton's attitude toward kings and kingship and toward the Church of England. As modern scholars tend to do, he believes that most of the work was written much earlier than the book's publication date would lead one to suppose. He thinks Milton went to work on it just after *The Tenure of Kings and Magistrates*, although he slips once and calls the whole book a work "de son âge mur." Whatever the case, it can be seen as evoking some of its author's earliest illusions, "ses premières espérances et ses premiers combats" (Geffroy, 131–32).

Milton had justified the fledgling republic to the rest of the world. The Republic was grateful. Soon he was Latin Secretary to the Council of State. Because it had been used in the important negotiations that had just culminated in the Treaty of Westphalia, French had virtually established itself as the language of diplomacy. England, jealous and a little apprehensive, tried to impose Latin. Milton's dispatches would be in that language. Before long, though, it became clear that he would have to use Latin it for another purpose, likewise international. Controversies arose at once. Did Milton answer John Lilburne's *England's New Chains Discovered*? The Council of State ordered him to do so. If he did, this brochure is still to be identified (Geffroy, 128, 132, 134–35). Early on, he refuted *Eikon Basilike* with *Eikonoklastes*. Geffroy determines that the work was not commissioned; it was the patriotic service Milton calls it in his preface. Only later does one discover the Council of State getting involved and ordering a second edition. Obviously, Geffroy did not read the preface as carefully as he might have done or he would have seen, in the second paragraph, the author's disclosure that his task had been "a work assigned" him.

It did not take Milton long to realize that Charles I probably had not written *Eikon Basilike* himself, but Geffroy rejects the notion that Milton had anything to do with slipping Pamela's Prayer into John Gauden's book. Milton tore *Eikon Basilike* apart chapter by chapter, sentence by sentence, almost word by word "avec un style que nulle part il n'a montré plus soutenu, plus précis et plus mordant." Milton is violent, accusing the late monarch of every crime he can think of. Every word attributed to him "est commentée avec malice et prend une odieuse signification." "Toutes ces souillures viennent s'accumuler sur une tête encore sanglante et la traînent dans la fange." Geffroy admired Milton but found *Eikonoklastes* "une œuvre de colère et de ressentiment," disheartening. One looks in vain for great ideas here. "C'est, il faut l'avouer, un triste spectacle que de voir un noble et religieux esprit, l'auteur du *Paradis perdu*, s'égarer si profondément dans ces ténèbres des guerres civiles." Geffroy continues to see the author as a patriot but, in this instance, feels that he was a misguided one.

The Milton of *Eikonoklastes* reminds Geffroy of a French writer he has just invoked in another context, Fénelon. In the political domain, Fénelon's thought foreshadowed the Enlightenment. During the last decade of the seventeenth century, anonymously, Fénelon wrote a *Lettre à Louis XIV*, destined to become a landmark in French political thought. While it never occurred to Fénelon to doubt his king's divine right, according to the critic, he nevertheless warned the ruler that things were seriously amiss in the realm and that, if not corrected, would leave him answerable to his maker. Geffroy did not want to overstate the case, but he detected similarities. "L'indignation qui leur est commune prête à leur éloquence une même terreur par un même artifice de style. Fénelon, par ses phrases brèves et coupées, renverse pierre par pierre cet édifice d'orgueil et de magnificence extérieure construit par Louis XIV sur tant de misères; de même, chaque paragraphe de Milton, court, précis, irrité, apporte un nouveau coup sur cette image de roi et la fait voler en éclats." Chateaubriand, it will be recalled, had compared Milton's view of absolutism with the one expressed in Racine's *Athalie*. Milton's book excited the reading public at home and even abroad. A French translation appeared. France, by now in the throes of a civil war of its own, did not balk at the ideas it contained (Geffroy, 132–43). Nevertheless, the ideas were not to make much overt headway for a long time.

Charles I's death produced an outcry. Perhaps commissioned, Claude de Saumaise's *Defensio Regia* (1649) appeared almost immediately.[8] On its heels came a French translation. Geffroy thinks Saumaise made it himself. Like *Eikonoklastes*, but in a different milieu, the work was well received in France, where the alarmed court was happy to see a renowned scholar coming to a monarch's rescue. The English Council of State ordered Milton to answer *Defensio*

Regia, and he did. His new book was *Pro Populo Anglicano Defensio*, a sequel to *The Tenure of Kings and Magistrates*. The beginning is calm and majestic. Unfortunately, the tone soon gives way to irony, satire and invective, and between these two scholar adversaries the political quarrel degenerates into raucous, ponderous insults. Who won the duel? Saumaise was to boast that he had made Milton go blind, while Milton liked to think he had caused Saumaise to die of mortification. Still, Milton's book was a great international success. In France, it was read everywhere—and even burned. It cost Milton his sight, Geffroy relates, but in it, for his contemporaries and for posterity, Milton had spelled out the "premiers rudiments du droit moderne" (Geffroy, 143–56).

Indeed, the poet was now totally blind. Very freely, Geffroy translates Sonnet 22, including the lines in which the poet refers specifically to his eyes.

> .... What supports me dost thou ask?
> The conscience, friend, to have lost them overplied
> In liberty's defence, my noble task.
>
> (ll. 9–11)

Also in French, Geffroy gives Milton's letter to Philaras on 28 September 1654. Blindness, he notes, did not put an end to the Latin Secretary's career as a pamphleteer. Geffroy mentions John Rowland's and Pierre Du Moulin's rejoinders to *Pro Populo Anglicano Defensio*, as well as Milton's obstinate conviction that they were the work of John Bramhall and Alexandre More. What followed was a thoroughly "odieuse polémique." Milton dictated the *Defensio Secunda* (1654), filled with "belles réponses, auxquelles seules les pamphlets de ses ennemis doivent l'honneur d'être aujourd'hui cités." Specifically, the book was aimed at More, whom Milton held responsible for the *Regii Sanguinis Clamor ad Cœlum*. To those who claimed that he owed his blindness to divine punishment, he replied that he had always been guided by the loftiest motives, including patriotism and religion, and that his conscience was at ease. What makes *Defensio Secunda* one of his Milton's curious pamphlets is the light it sheds on his character and ideas, according to Geffroy. The ideas show a new concern, as Milton admonishes the people to be virtuous. Is he implying that they need to keep their eyes open as well? The *Defensio Secunda* "exprime des craintes, presque déjà des regrets, au lieu des espérances que contiennent les écrits précédents. La face des affaires avait... changé" (Geffroy, 157-62).

On 16 December 1653, Oliver Cromwell had become Lord Protector. Except for the title, he was king. He was more: he was dictator and much more powerful than a king. Why did Milton, the republican patriot, stay on as Latin Secretary? Was it because the Lord Protector was giving his country international prestige? Perhaps. Nevertheless, Milton was worried. "Malgré toute la grandeur du gouvernement de Cromwell, Milton ne tarda pas à comprendre que la liberté était en danger, et la *Seconde Défense* a été écrite sous ce funeste pressentiment." Hence the address to Cromwell, advising him, reminding him of his responsibilities, urging him to maintain private and public freedom. To Geffroy, none of this seems ignoble or calculating. Basically, Milton was thanking a great soldier and a great statesman. At the same time, in a voice both stern and beseeching, he was calling upon him to respect the trust that had been placed in him. That there was an anxious tone cannot be denied, however. "Milton avait évidemment placé sur la tête de Cromwell toutes ses espérances; il le considérait comme le lieutenant de Dieu sur la terre et comme le sauveur de la république; mais les dernières lignes montrent combien le faisait souffrir la crainte de quelque déception" (Geffroy, 164-70). Not particularly interested in *Pro Se Defensio*, Geffroy observes that More, harassed by Milton, "chercha inutilement à détourner ses coups sur du Moulin et implora son silence." More published his *Fides Publica* and *Supplementum*, and Milton replied with *Pro Se Defensio* and a *Responsio*.[9]

Afterward, Milton continued his work as a government functionary and was asked, in 1655, to draw up *A Declaration of the Lord Protector* against the Spaniards, in which Geffroy detects "toute l'élégance de sa plume exercée." That Milton had a hand in this is anything but certain, actually.[10]

During these years he also worked on "un vaste dictionnaire latin ... dont les matériaux très nombreux mais incomplets et confus servirent depuis aux compilateurs du grand dictionnaire latin imprimé à Cambridge." Probably by the time Cromwell died, most of Milton's illusions were gone. As we have seen, Geffroy pointed out Milton's likely suspicion that, in matters political, the Lord Protector was not a trustworthy guardian of the public weal. Nor, in religious matters, had he paid any attention to the sonnet Milton had addressed him in 1652.[11] When a new Parliament convened in January 1659, the poet took hope that where the soldier had refused to listen, the peoples' representatives might be induced to protect religion along the lines he had in mind. To its members, he addressed two new pamphlets, *A Treatise of Civil Power in Ecclesiastical Causes* and *Considerations Touching the Likeliest Means to Remove Hirelings out of the Church*. Thus, "vieux et infirme," he was returning to an occupation of his younger days. "Il s'engagea dans une lutte nouvelle en faveur de la liberté religieuse, de laquelle, à ses yeux, dépendaient toutes les autres" (Geffroy, 171–72).

A Treatise of Civil Power is based on the concept that the state has no business involving itself in church affairs. Each individual has an innate, sacred right to personal religious convictions. No magistrate is competent to regulate them and should not have the authority to do so. If the object is to prevent "scandal," one should remember that forcing people to subscribe to teachings or participate in ceremonies they do not believe in jeopardizes their souls by making them hypocrites or sinners. Essentially, religion consists of two things, belief and obedience. Because it is divine in nature, it ought to come from God alone (Geffroy, 175–80). *Considerations Touching the Likeliest Means to Remove Hirelings out of the Church*, a logical consequence of the earlier tract, appeared several months after it. At the time, a momentous public issue was whether or not ministers should be paid salaries, especially by the government. Milton thought not. "Un salaire légal institué par l'état et donné régulièrement par lui au clergé lui semblait avilissant pour l'église." As in the earlier pamphlet, Milton was calling for the total separation of church and state. "Il lui répugnait de voir profaner par une puissance de la terre le domaine des consciences." Ministers willing to accept such salaries ought to be dismissed. As paid public servants liable to "la séduction des délices temporelles," they might be tempted to forget their real vocation. "Le salaire par lequel Dieu a voulu que les travaux de son église fussent récompensés doit être . . . une offrande libre. La liberté et la charité chrétiennes doivent seules y contribuer, et dans la mesure qui leur semblera juste." If not entirely voluntary, such contributions should not be accepted. Geffroy reminds readers that Milton was not alone in espousing such views. He then translates the letter Moses Wall wrote to Milton on 26 May 1659.[12]

If religion, given Milton's outlook, was in a bad way, government was faring no better. Milton realized that the disordered state of things was preparing the way for monarchy to make a quick, easy return. To ward this off, according to Geffroy, Milton addressed three short pamphlets to General George Monck. These were the *Letter to a Friend*, *The Ready and Easy Way to Establish a Free Commonwealth* and *The Present Means and Brief Delineation of a Free Commonwealth*. Geffroy is being a bit free and easy here. While the correspondent in the *Letter to a Friend* has never been identified, it was almost certainly not Monck. Geffroy does not realize, either, that *The Ready and Easy Way* underwent serious emendations and that it had two editions. A bit simplistic in his approach, the critic tells his readers that *The Ready and Easy Way* developed and expanded the ideas laid out in the *Letter* and *The Present Means*. In all three, Milton was proposing "un singulier système de gouvernement." There would be no king, of course. There would be a Council of State. There would be no House of Lords. No House of Commons either, for that matter. Instead, there would be a Grand Council, its members to serve for life or else be renewed by periodic elections. Aiming as he was at stability, Milton did not really like the rotation idea, but it was a concession he was willing to make. "Obsédé par les objections et les griefs de tous les partis, cherchant du reste à concilier ses idées démocratiques avec les intérêts de la paix générale, il acceptait une partie des réformes proposées par les autres écrivains républicains." Milton wanted his system to have guarantees, however, and the most important of these would have been to restrict electors and the kind of candidates they would be able to choose. "Milton avait raison de redouter l'élargissement du cadre des électeurs." Recent history had justified Milton's reservations, Geffroy contends, although, generations later, English citizens would finally prove their absolute trustworthiness as voters. Milton concluded with an encomium, "un éloge pompeux du gouvernement démocratique, seul véritable asile, à son avis, de la liberté d'esprit et de conscience, seul refuge honorable de la dignité humaine," and a patriotic diatribe against monarchy. In warning his contemporaries to take care lest, in a restoration, they lose the advantages it had cost them so much to gain, Milton was prophetic. "Moins de trente années après que le poète eut écrit cette prédiction, la Glorieuse Révolution prit soin de la vérifier" (Geffroy, 188–95).

Milton made a last attempt to induce his compatriots to hang onto the republic that was fast eluding their grasp or that they simply no longer wanted. This was in the *Brief Notes upon a Late Sermon*, which Matthew Griffith preached on 25 March 1660 and dedicated to General Monck. The preacher, a former chaplain to Charles I, derided the republicans, embarrassed the general and the government, called for a speedy restoration, and got sent to jail. Milton exulted but must have known that it was all over. Still, he had the courage not to recant and, indeed, the courage to utter some harsh words. Far from accusing him of personal desperation or fear, Geffroy points out that, given the tenor of the times, it took bold convictions to do what Milton did and to declare that, during the Civil Wars, Charles I had been "the chief enemy" and that "in all right" he had "ceased to be the king." Geffroy does not make much of this pamphlet but remarks that "C'en était fait de toutes les illusions de notre poète; pas un seul corps de l'état n'avait assez de force morale pour prendre en main les affaires, et les principes républicains n'avaient pas assez pénétré dans les esprits pour que le peuple lui-même rompît avec tout le passé" (Geffroy, 195). Charles II was at the door, and his subjects were eager to let him in.

Geffroy paints a spirited if somewhat lopsided picture of Restoration England, insisting upon the loose morals and exaggerating the reprisals. French manners and mannerisms, even in literature, took over.[13] "Une littérature vaine, futile, railleuse, remplaça les mâles et vigoureux pamphlets de l'époque républicaine." Gone was the "ardente et consciencntieuse étude des questions les plus graves qui puissent occuper l'esprit des hommes.... Quant aux grands et éternels principes pour le triomphe desquels les hommes de la révolution avaient livré tant et de si durs combats, ils étaient... relégués dans l'oubli; liberté de penser, liberté d'écrire et de parler, réforme électorale, libre instruction, on étouffa tous ces vœux de l'avenir; la presse reçut de nouvelles entraves...," and so on (Geffroy, 201). All these new abuses that disturb the critic had flourished, as we have seen, during both the Republic and the Protectorate. Geffroy repeats the usual stories about Milton's going into hiding, his arrest and imprisonment, Davenant's alleged intervention. He also repeats the "vague tradition" that the poet's friends staged a mock funeral. Geffroy feels one thing is certain. The prompt burning of *Pro Populo Anglicano Defensio* and *Eikonoklastes* demonstrates that the former Latin Secretary had not been forgotten. Whatever saved him, it was not his reputation as a poet. As yet, he had not published his great poetic work, and it was "ses écrits en prose qui faisaient précisément son crime." Somehow he got off. But old adversaries like Pierre du Moulin were still there to taunt him. "Du Moulin, voyant abattu celui qui l'avait fait trembler, renouvela sans courage ses viles attaques, et d'autres ennemis du poète publièrent tout ce que Saumaise, à son lit de mort, avait inventé de calomnieuses accusations" (Geffroy, 204–06).

Once sure he would not be molested, Milton retired to his study. His fighting spirit may have been daunted, but it was not gone. There are passages in *Paradise Lost* where the vigorous old champion steps into the arena once more to battle for his ideals, even if by now he comprehends that they have little chance of being translated into reality on this earth. In this work, Geffroy says, Milton could "déplorer la faiblesse de l'homme mais en même temps se convaincre que ce gouvernement de Jésus-Christ n'était pas fait pour le monde mortel et enseigner à ses concitoyens dans quelles hautes régions ils le rencontreraient et quelles vertus leur en ouvriraient l'entrée" (Geffroy, 210–11). Milton's *Artis Logicæ Plenior Institutio*, based on Pierre de La Ramée (Ramus) and accompanied by a life of the French Renaissance thinker, could be considered another education tract. "C'était probablement une attaque dirigée contre les universités." La Ramée had done his part to free the academic world of scholasticism. He, "l'un des premiers, était venu troubler le repos de l'école et jeter au milieu de l'enseignement de hardies opinions, que Cambridge et Oxford laissaient volontiers tomber dans l'oubli" (Geffroy, 212). Geffroy could have added that Milton, no matter what he was writing, was not one to pass up an opportunity to blast the universities. For example, on 21 September 1656, in a letter to his old pupil Richard Jones, he commented on the lad's studies at Oxford. "You adduce nothing to make me believe that you have got any good there or been made any wiser."[14] Whether Milton's admonition had anything to do with it or not, Jones did not tarry at Oxford. Soon he was off to the Continent, making the Grand Tour. Nine years after Milton's death, the critic notes, the universities got revenge on their old enemy. In July 1683 they presented Charles II a document condemning 27 propositions from the works of Milton, Knox and others (Geffroy, 218, 275–82).

Milton wrote one final pamphlet. This was *Of True Religion*, published in 1673. With no legitimate children, Charles II was thinking about the future. His brother and heir was a Roman Catholic and, openly or not, so were a goodly number of his subjects. On 15 March 1672 he issued a Declaration of Indulgence that guaranteed freedom of conscience to all recusants, as long as they were fairly discreet about it. Milton should have been pleased; he was not. He had always championed freedom of worship—except for

Papists—and here was the monarch about to permit them to go to mass. As it happened, the king's indulgence did not last. Parliament made it impossible, legally at least. Taking alarm, on 12 March 1673 it passed the Test Act, making it obligatory for all officeholders to receive communion according to the rites of the Church of England. Still, there continued to be talk that something was in the works to relieve dissenters. And what about dissenters who did not hold office? Were they to be allowed to worship as they pleased? Tolerating Popery was something John Milton could not brook. The critic relates that Milton, taking up his pen, or rather having it taken up for him, flew into action and dictated. *Of True Religion* appeared in the spring of 1673. This time Milton took the position that the real danger lay in Protestant disunity, and now he seemed ready to join forces with erstwhile opponents. As in *The Ready and Easy Way*, he showed that he could compromise. "Persuadé cette fois que les divisions du protestantisme expliquaient ses revers, il entreprit de faire cesser toutes les querelles intestines.[15] Il n'avait plus désormais de ressentiment ni contre les presbytériens ni même contre les anglicans; il devenait tolérant, mais à force de haine contre le Papisme, qui restait à ses yeux une faction dangereuse et toute dévouée à un maître étranger." This was Milton's last broadside. Its author died 8 November 1674.

De Doctrina Christiana was not a pamphlet, and Milton never published it. Geffroy had little to say about it. Probably he did not do much more than thumb through it. Relegating it to an appendix, he does discuss the manuscript's history, discovery and publication. He describes the book as "une longue série de citations bibliques réunies sous différents chefs et auxquelles Milton mêle à peine quelques phrases pour résumer et conclure," which is hardly true. He believes that the preface, which he translates, condensing a little, reveals the author's intent and demonstrates what his religious views were at the end of his life. Geffroy did not know that the work, in some state or other, came into being much earlier, although it underwent emendations at various times. He assumes that the Mr. Skinner who came into possession of the manuscript at Milton's death was Cyriack Skinner, rather than Daniel Skinner Jr. Haste no doubt accounts for Geffroy's blunders here. A footnote tells us that one of his sources was Henry John Todd's *Some Account of the Life and Writings of Milton*. Geffroy had not read his source carefully. In editions that followed the discovery of *De Doctrina*, Todd had gone into considerable detail about what had become of the manuscript at its author's death. Among other things, he had repeated Edward Phillips's remark about a "tractate" begun in the 1640s and had taken great care to establish that the younger Daniel Skinner was the person to whom, eventually, it had been given.[16] In French, Geffroy gives all but the complimentary close and postscript of Daniel Elzevir's 20 November 1676 letter to Sir Joseph Williamson, Secretary of State, promising that he would have nothing to do with publishing the manuscript. After translating the preface, Geffroy explores *De Doctrina* no further (Geffroy, 283–92).

Summing up his book, Geffroy declares that Milton's pamphlets, because of their style and the importance of their ideas, are a literary monument. They contain too many long parentheses, too many quotations, and too many theological subtleties, but the age that produced them was given to this kind of thing. In Milton, other stylistic features redeem it:

> Une constante élévation d'âme, une continiuelle émotion pour tout ce qui est grand et beau, de naïves aspirations vers Dieu, la Patrie, l'Eternité, de ferventes prières interrompant tout à coup le récit, une grande vigueur d'expression dans les emportements d'une indignation généreuse, infiniment d'esprit dans la peinture ironique des travers et des vices, le style majestueux et poétique de l'enthousiasme religieux, la légère et facile parole d'une libre conversation ou de la plus fine comédie, tous les mérites du pamphlétaire se retrouvent chez Milton. (Geffroy, 219–20)

> [An ever lofty soul; a continual concern for all that is great and beautiful; simple aspirations toward God, Country, Eternity; heartfelt prayers suddenly interrupting a narrative; great vigor in expressing anger inspired by noble indignation; boundless wit in painting foibles and vices; the majestic, poetic style of religious

enthusiasm; the light, easy speech of a free conversation or the most delicate comedy: all the gifts of the pamphleteer are found in Milton.]

After the Restoration, the political pamphlets went unheeded. The universities remained as blind as ever, censorship returned, and the Church of England, proud and unabashed, went on its way unchecked. Not much happened, in short, until the Revolution of 1688 gave impetus to ideas Milton had advanced. Soon, says Geffroy, the French Enlightenment would take them over, but it would do so with a difference. It would use reason, the universal guide, as its point of departure, whereas with Milton it was the individual. Because his brand of Protestantism carried with it some encumbrances that he would not or could not shake off, Milton was not as truly independent as he thought he was. He had his hesitations, even his contradictions. For example, "il balbutie plutôt qu'il ne proclame les nouveaux droits de l'homme, et, il faut le dire, il n'aperçoit pas tous ses devoirs." Similarly, in his individualistic approach to religion, "Milton ne s'aperçoit pas que si, acceptant d'abord la tradition chrétienne, la brisant ensuite par une subite révolte, il lâche ainsi d'une main les brides qu'il resserre de l'autre, l'essor est interrompu, la marche se mêle et devient incertaine." Beyond a doubt, he was sincere, nonetheless.

As for his political beliefs, there is disorder and contradiction, Geffroy concludes. Milton was no practical statesman, and his ideal republic was a pure utopia, even though it evolved somewhat over the years. Basically, he had no one consistent program. His hatred for monarchy did not take shape until Charles I was brought to justice for his misdeeds. If he defended regicide, he did it because, in the political context of the moment, he deemed it conducive to individual freedom. Later, when he saw the Commonwealth threatened by reaction from within, he proposed a republican aristocracy, hardly a democratic form of government. If there is a unifying thread in Milton's pamphlets, it is the notion of freedom, which their author loved passionately. "Il a consacré à la défense de cet éternel et

fécond principe sa vie tout entière, avec une élévation d'esprit, une générosité d'âme qui le distingue de tous ses compatriotes et de tous ses contemporains." He was indeed ahead of his time. "Il a mérité d'être mis au nombre des précurseurs de notre dix-huitième siècle, et ses écrits offrent à l'historien et au philosophe le curieux et imposant spectacle d'une société nouvelle qui commence à naître" (Geffroy, 220–25). Geffroy was writing in a year when revolution swept across western and central Europe. Milton's pamphlets were being resurrected under auspicious circumstances.

In the *Etude sur les pamphlets politiques et religieux de Milton*, Geffroy probably quotes too much, as he accuses the poet of doing. His translations show a good feeling for Milton's prose, but numerous liberties are taken. Factually, Geffroy occasionally makes mistakes that historians should not make. His chronology is not impeccable, and now and then his dates are wrong. He did not know that Milton's reply to Alexandre More was simply an addendum to *Pro Se Defensio*, just as he failed to notice that Milton published two versions of *The Ready and Easy Way*, the second quite different from the first. Once, purporting to be quoting from the *Apology for Smectymnuus*, he is actually quoting *The Reason of Church Government*. And so on. He may not have been absolutely consistent, either. His observation that Milton never wrote a line against kingship before the execution of Charles I would suggest that, as the critic saw it, the poet accepted monarchy up to that time. This does not square with his theorizing about Mary Powell's prolonged visit to her parents' home and the reasons for her return in 1645. Geffroy believed, no doubt correctly, that, depending on how well the royal cause was doing at a particular moment, uppermost in the parents' thinking was concern over the relative liabilities and advantages of having a republican son-in-law. Milton already a republican in 1642, not 1649? Discussing *Of Education*, Geffroy declares that Milton was giving his ideas on the kind of education republican leaders ought to receive. But *Of Education* was before 1649 also. To make Geffroy consistent on this point, one would have to take the position that, although a republican at heart somewhat earlier, Milton did not actually *write* against monarchy until Charles I's execution.

Despite the few reservations he made in his summary, Geffroy saw Milton as probably more forward-looking, more progressive than he really was. In particular, *Areopagitica* is not the all-out plea for an unrestricted press that the critic makes it out to be. One could wish, too, that in talking about Milton's long quotations Geffroy had pointed out how carefully the publicist always chose his authorities, avoiding or rejecting outright those who did not agree with him. Finally, one is a little astonished at the ease with which Geffroy reports, and sometimes appears to accept, some of the Milton anecdotes. To several he gives his own personal touch. One of these has to do with the bad relations said to have existed between the poet and his daughters. No reason is given, but Geffroy tells us that Deborah Milton did not share her sisters' ill feelings. In heaping opprobrium upon the Restoration, Geffroy claims that Lady Claypole, one of Cromwell's daughters, was among those exhumed and hanged along with her father and other prominent dead regicides when the new regime took over. Geffroy does not say where he got this story, which is totally false. Another story is even more ghoulish. According to this one, at the Restoration it was Charles I, not Cromwell, who was disinterred and hanged.[17]

> Une singulière mais incertaine tradition veut que le cadavre de Charles Ier lui-même, substitué par de prévoyants républicains à celui du Protecteur, en 1658, ait..., par un bizarre coup de la fortune, subi des émissaires de son propre fils les outrages destinés à son mortel ennemi. (Geffroy, 203)
>
> [A peculiar but uncertain tradition would have it that in 1658 the body of Charles I himself, switched by farsighted republicans for that of the Protector..., suffered, by an odd twist of fate, the indignities that agents of his son had in store for his mortal enemy.]

These caveats disposed of, Geffroy's study is a highly creditable one. He believed too many anecdotes, it is true, but so did many of his contemporaries. He stresses his conviction that, in the pamphlets, Milton was driven by a sense of duty (Geffroy, 207). Like his English, Geffroy's Latin was good.[18] He was in a position to observe that Milton could be less than perfect in that language, though he had no reason to develop the idea. When jeering at his opponents' linguistic blunders, the pamphleteer was overlooking the fact that his own Latin poems are "fréquemment entachés de mauvais goût et que les fautes de quantité y sont nombreuses." And Geffroy gives examples (Geffroy, 155 n. 4). Knowing Milton's Latin and English poetry and now and then citing it, Geffroy has the advantage of not having to examine the prose as an isolated hunk of the writer's total literary output. Perhaps he would have done well to look into *De Doctrine Christiana*, for in it he would have found illuminating parallels to what his author says in the brochures on divorce and religion. His remark about the Council of State ordering Milton to answer John Lilburne reminds us that Milton may have authored pamphlets not yet attributed to him, at least not convincingly. In addition, seeing Milton as an important precursor of the French Enlightenment and Revolution is a pertinent and worthy tribute to the writer's place in the history of thought. As for Geffroy himself, he went on to become a distinguished history professor. Curiously enough, his research never took him back to the Puritan Revolution or, for that matter, to any aspect of the English seventeenth century. The French seventeenth and eighteenth centuries were something else, and he wrote probing works on Princesse des Ursins, Mme de Maintenon and Marie Antoinette. He also became interested in Scandinavian history.

6

Alphonse de Lamartine

In 1820 Alphonse de Lamartine (1790–1869) married an English girl, Marianne Birch. Through her, could he have had a connection with the Thomas Birch who, in the eighteenth century, had edited Milton's prose works? Like Milton, Lamartine was a poet. Like Milton also, he was a government insider for a time. Again like Milton, especially late in life, he was to come up against some harsh financial realities. However, despite these similarities, we shall see that an attitude toward one very serious matter divided these two poets who were writing a couple of centuries apart.

Lamartine was the first of the great French romantics. His *Méditations poétiques*, published in 1820 and followed by various other collections over the next few years, quickly assured him an enviable and durable place in French letters. He continued turning out poetry, but as diplomat, member of the Chamber of Deputies, and minister in the Provisional Government of 1848, he was likewise involved in government during the Restoration, the July Monarchy and the Second Republic. A candidate in the presidential elections of December 1848, he was trounced by the future Napoleon III. His political career at an end and harassed by creditors, he then turned to writing prose, hoping to find in it a speedy means of paying off his debts. Sir Walter Scott had set him an example. But then, had a time not come when, for a very different reason, Milton himself more or less abandoned poetry, temporarily turning to prose? For the most part, what Lamartine wrote during this period consists of novels, memoirs, histories and literary criticism. Initially his "Cromwell" and "Milton," essays dating from 1853 and 1854, appeared in *Le Civilisateur*, the critic's own periodical. A year or two later they were tucked into the *Vie des grands hommes*. Eventually, in his vast complete works, Lamartine found a place for them in the three volumes he called *Vies de quelques hommes illustres*. Though studded with provocative insights, the two essays are punctuated by considerably more than their share of factual mistakes. As a historian, Lamartine remained a romantic. Generally interested in movement, not matters of detail, he was not one to concern himself with "painstaking research," as someone has observed.[1]

Despite his rush, Lamartine proposed to use a biographical approach in examining Milton. "C'est un caractère du temps actuel de prendre plus d'intérêt à l'homme qu'au livre," he remarks.[2] With this in mind, he traces Milton's career, situating the author's work in it. Lamartine is incorrect, of course, in stating that Shakespeare was dead when Milton was born, and he is stretching a point in claiming that Milton's parents were nobility. He awards Milton more than one brother but fails to mention a sister. Milton's three daughters show up, but nothing is said about a son. Lamartine is wrong, too, when he asserts that Milton spent "de longues années" in Italy (*Vies* 3:21, 28; 2:331). Quoting the sonnet "Qual il colle aspro" in French, Lamartine appears to date it, like the Latin epigrams to Leonora Baroni, from the poet's Italian sojourn. Assuming that a love involvement with the singer had existed, the critic wonders how it ended. Amédée Pichot's little tale seems not to have contaminated him. Returning from his travels, Lamartine's Milton found Parliament and King at war. For three years, Milton meditated in solitude without appearing to take sides. Then all at once he leaped into the fray, "armé de harangues, de controverses, de pamphlets, ces armes quotidiennes du peuple en révolution" (*Vies* 3:7). Lamartine appears not to have known that when Milton's earliest pamphlet burst into print, it was not its author's first published work; several poems had already appeared. In Cromwell, Lamartine thinks, Milton saw a prophet and the people's champion. But Cromwell needed a champion himself. With no time to write and with enemies attacking him on every hand, he "accueillit avec empressement ce talent viril, éloquent et imagé que Milton mettait à son service." Cromwell would be the nation's sword, Milton would be its spokesman. Nominally a secretary, Milton would be "en réalité le ministre du protectorat." Milton's name "devint une puissance, sa fortune s'accrut à la hauteur de ses fonctions." Further, the minister's brothers lost no time in coming to live with him in his "maison opulente" in London.

Lamartine also evokes Mary Powell and Milton's marital problems, although only one "dissertation sur le divorce," with no title given, is mentioned. The reader is told that Milton obtained his divorce and that, relenting, he then agreed to take his wife back, the reconciliation followed by "années de paix et d'amour" (*Vies* 3:8–10). If by now there was peace in the poet's household, there were momentous problems on the national and international scene. While Lamartine was in the process of reverting to his earlier conservatism as he wrote these lines, he still remembered his own recent involvement with republican government. As for Milton, he believes that the poet, with his pamphlets, gave an "accent immortel aux passions passagères de son temps."[3] The critic seldom identifies specific pamphlets, even when quoting from them. In connection with Milton's pamphleteering, as he will do again and again, Lamartine devotes a great deal of space to Milton's position on regicide. He had already examined the question in his essay on Cromwell. Lamartine's own opposition to the death penalty informs his remarks.[4] Lamartine does not distinguish between the Republic and the Protectorate, believing—another of his errors—that Cromwell assumed absolute power long before he actually did so. As Lamartine sees it, Milton considered Charles I a despot, Cromwell a liberator. Having contracted "la noble passion de la liberté républicaine," Milton "crut servir la cause opprimée des peuples en combattant le privilège de l'inviolabilité de la vie des rois" (*Vies* 2: 374.) Although he does not name the work, Lamartine has *The Tenure of Kings and Magistrates* in mind, and his comments presuppose that the pamphlet was written before the king's death, perhaps during his trial, but not immediately after his execution. Thus he sees Milton's apology for the grim sentence about to be handed down and carried out as partly an effort to justify the real culprit.

Lamartine had treated revolution himself. "Les révolutions," to which he eventually assigned a place in the *Harmonies poétiques et religieuses,* had warned that such upheavals bring about harm as well as good. Condemning the French Revolution's excesses, *Jocelyn* calls attention to how the blood of innocent people

>................... massacrés par centaines
> Coule dans les ruisseaux comme l'eau des fontaines
> (2.187–88)

once the masses take control. "Contre la peine de mort," another poem that found its way into the *Harmonies,* declares that when a just man is put to death, the real criminals are those who sent him to the block:

> Il est beau de tomber victime
> Sous le regard vengeur de la postérité
>   Dans l'holocauste magnanime
>   De sa vie à la vérité!
> L'échafaud pour le juste est le lit de sa gloire:
> Il est beau d'y mourir au soleil de l'histoire
>   Au milieu d'un peuple éperdu!
> De léguer un remords à la foule insensée,
> Et de lui dire en face une mâle pensée,
>   Au prix de son sang répandu.
> (ll. 51–60)

To Lamartine this was as applicable to Louis XVI as it was

to anyone else. *Jocelyn* depicts the "peuple ivre de sang" as worse than whatever previous abuses there could have been and expresses "douleur" and "effroi" that

La terre du royaume a bu le sang du roi.
(2.186)

In his *Histoire des Girondins*, Lamartine asks a question for which he has a ready answer. "La nation avait-elle le droit de juger en tribunal légal et régulier Louis XVI? Non: car pour être juge il faut être impartial et désintéressé, et la nation n'était ni l'un ni l'autre." Basically Louis was an innocent victim, his inexcusable "murder" an "immolation." Reviewing his work somewhat later, the historian added that, on the basis of what he had had to say in his book, "La question de la mort du roi ne peut laisser aucun doute sur ma réprobation du régicide."[5] It was with these ideas in mind that Lamartine turned his attention to Charles I, Milton and *The Tenure of Kings and Magistrates*.

Generously, Milton could have urged sparing the vanquished, imprisoned king. He could at least have broken with the regicides and washed his hands of their crime. But, Lamartine reports, he chose not to do this. Instead, "Milton, qui avait suivi le protecteur dans la guerre, le suivit dans le crime. . . . Il ne témoigna ni hésitation, ni pitié, ni horreur" (*Vies* 2:374, 3:10). Available to Milton was the position that "les rois, n'étant que des hommes investis comme tous les autres magistrats, d'un pouvoir conditionnel et nécessairement responsable, n'ont pas pour leurs crimes le privilège de l'impunité" (*Vies* 3:10). Apparently Lamartine thinks Milton did not exploit this argument as thoroughly as he might have. But had Charles really committed a crime? Milton needed to establish three theorems that he failed to demonstrate. First, that Charles, attacked and deposed by his rebellious Parliament, was a criminal for using force to defend his throne, constitution and people against armed rebellion. Secondly, that this crime, if such it was, deserved death. Thirdly, that it was "juste, équitable, humain, et religieux à une armée victorieuse d'immoler son roi vaincu, désarmé et prisonnier." With his false logic, Milton proved none of this. On the contrary, Lamartine argues, what he demonstrated was that even a poet's heart can be hardened by overzealous political commitment or that even a superior mind can be complacently opportunistic. Both suppositions incriminate the poet's memory equally.

> Si la pitié était proscrite du monde, elle devrait se retrouver dans le cœur du poète, le résumé vivant de toutes les vibrations pathétiques des choses humaines. Et quant au génie, le génie n'est pas une excuse, il est une aggravation; car, s'il s'abaisse devant la puissance jusqu'à laver ce sang de l'échafaud sous ses pas, le génie est plus coupable de cette adulation sanglante que le vulgaire, car il se courbe de plus haut et il s'incline plus bas. (*Vies* 3:11)

> [If pity were to be outlawed in the world, it ought to reside in the poet's heart, which is the living epitome of all sympathetic vibrations of things human. And as for genius, genius is no excuse, it makes the deed all the more heinous, for if, in the presence of power, it lowers itself to the point of washing the scaffold blood beneath its feet, genius is more guilty of sanguinary adulation than common people are, because it means stooping from a higher sphere and bending lower.]

In short, Milton was either bloodthirsty or ambitious. One way or the other, "Milton a cherché ... lui-même l'éternelle éclaboussure de ce sang royal à son nom: qu'elle lui reste. Ce sont de ces taches que la gloire ne rend que plus sombres sur une vie illustre, parce qu'elles y sont éclairées de plus de lumière." Lamartine adds that a great person's accomplishments and misdeeds are equal components in the reputations such individuals leave behind (*Vies* 3:10–11). Morally speaking, Milton's apology for regicide was damaging enough, but Milton compounded his guilt when, in the same work, he had "la lâcheté de plaider la cause du meurtrier contre celle de la victime" (*Vies* 2:374). If Lamartine was thinking about Cromwell here rather than the country's new republican rulers, he blundered, of course. Cromwell is not mentioned in *The Tenure of Kings and Magistrates*, although, in passing, he comes in for lavish praise in *Observations upon the Articles of Peace*, published a few months later.

A little later still, he would be complimented in *Pro Populo Anglicano Defensio* and, much more heartily, in *Defensio Secunda*.

Lamartine continues his historical inaccuracies. "En récompense de ce fanatisme cruel ou de cette complaisance servile, Milton fut élevé par Cromwell à la place de secrétaire d'état pour la langue latine. On avait besoin de son éloquence pour réfuter un livre" (*Vies* 3:11). Except that it was the Council of State and not Cromwell distributing the reward, Lamartine is correct in assuming that *The Tenure of Kings and Magistrates* won Milton his appointment as Latin Secretary.

The book Milton was expected to answer was *Eikon Basilike*. While tending to accept his authorship, Lamartine was not much interested in whether the late king had actually written the book or not but pointed out that, like Louis XVI's will on the heels of the later king's execution, the document had a tremendous impact, unleashing a mammoth wave of public sympathy for the beheaded monarch and his cause. The book was "le cri du sang, la voix de la conscience après celle de la passion," arousing "un remords qu'il fallait à tout prix apaiser." Liberally quoting it in French, Lamartine describes the book to his readers as "un plaidoyer céleste qui justifiait après le supplice les intentions et le cœur du supplicié," in which the victim "ne demandait que de la miséricorde à Dieu, de la pitié à son peuple, de la mansuétude à son fils." Too many people were taking this "livre sorti du tombeau," these "pages retrouvées dans un cercueil," to heart. A rebuttal was needed. Milton provided it. With arguments and insults, *Eikonoklastes* endeavored to make "les larmes et le sang du roi immolé" look absurd (*Vies* 3:11–13). All Charles did in the book, Milton claimed, was demonstrate that he had read a great deal and that he had poetic talent. Lamartine did not take up Milton's charge that the king, or whoever was writing in his name, had borrowed Pamela's Prayer from Sir Philip Sidney's *Arcadia*.

Milton's pen was soon needed to answer an attack from abroad. "Bientôt les invectives qui assaillaient de France et de tout le continent le peuple anglais pour lui reprocher son régicide obligèrent Milton à venger son pays. Le patriotisme l'inspira mieux que le régicide. Il publia la *Défense du peuple anglais* contre l'écrivain français Saumaise" (*Vies* 3:13). From *The Tenure of Kings and Magistrates* and *Eikonoklastes*, Lamartine moves on to a discussion of Claude de Saumaise's *Defensio Regia* and Milton's reply, *Pro Populo Anglicano Defensio*. Both authors, the critic reports, were paid for their labors: Louis XIV gave Saumaise a hundred gold pieces, whereas Cromwell, always Cromwell, awarded Milton a thousand. As we know, both stories are suspect.[6] Agreeing with both labels, Lamartine mentions Voltaire's charge that Saumaise was a "pédant" and Milton a "bête féroce." Lamartine adds on his own that "Chaque phrase de Saumaise sentait la lampe; chaque phrase de Milton suait le sang." Perhaps this is an allusion, here again, to Milton's bloodthirstiness.

Lamartine calls attention to Milton's having been one of the first to realize that the Puritan Revolution's shock waves might reverberate on the European continent. Milton wanted this to happen. Consciously, in the form of freedom, he hoped he was introducing the other nations of the earth to a special product from his own country.[7] As it turned out, his anticipations were correct, but the export item ran into difficulties. To serve a lofty purpose, a noble aspiration such as freedom must not be tainted with innocent blood, the critic contends. In the long run, when a people's conscience is blocking the way, achieving genuine freedom is problematical. The scaffolds on which Charles I and Louis XVI died cast shadows making it hard for freedom to find its way. In any event, neither Europe not England was ready for a republic. Taking the one his compatriots had created, Cromwell turned it into a dictatorship buttressed by soldiers. Then, predictably, soldiers betrayed even this.

If Lamartine condemns Milton for defending regicide, he commends his loyalty to the republic he had hoped to see grow out of it. In the short interval between the Lord Protector's death and the Restoration, when it was no longer wise to do so, Milton stuck to his convictions, calling upon his compatriots to persevere rather than lose what they had achieved. He urged them to maintain parliamentary freedom and called for a wiser election process. Without naming it, Lamartine is referring to *The Ready and Easy Way to Establish a Free Commonwealth*.[8] In adhering to the principles he had espoused much earlier and at a time when the public was almost certain to repudiate them, Milton stands out, the critic feels, in his stubborn dedication to those principles. Lamartine does not consider the possibility that, desperate, Milton may have been terrified at what might lie ahead for him personally if the republic were scuttled and if the son of a king he had so maligned were to come to power. Lamartine, not too practical in political matters himself, chooses to take the position, quite the contrary, that Milton was reminding his compatriots of tangible political realities in saying what he did. While certainly knowing that a restoration was in the wind, Milton was nevertheless pleading for the improvement and perpetuation of the republic he loved and believed the nation could still save. "Ses derniers écrits d'homme d'état attestent en lui une expérience mûrie par l'exercice du gouvernement en un sens politique qui répugnait aux chimères, même dans sa cause" (*Vies* 3:15). Milton's pleas fell on ears that were unwilling to listen. Acting on supposition, Lamartine claims that the Latin Secretary resigned his government post and disappeared (*Vies* 3:15). Actually, Milton had prepared no letters of state since May or June 1659, although he was still being paid (Parker, 1. 526, 538). Masson believed that the Council of State let him go in March or April 1660.[9] While there is no known record of his resignation, his work naturally ceased with the Republic's demise. Lamartine, of course, had seen his own political dream vanish, replaced by the Second Empire.

Dispossessed but proud, Milton did not renounce his political credo even when the Republic went under for good. Lamartine applauds him for it. "Il ne fit ni d'ignobles excuses ni de lâches palinodies devant les Stuarts triomphants." Far from seeking refuge abroad when such a course might have seemed advisable, Milton remained where he was, not only unashamed of the role he had played but willing to take the consequences, "avec la responsabilité de ses opinions et de ses actes, prêt à donner son sang à la liberté" if need be. Inevitably, then, the Restoration took place. However courageous he may have been, Milton was persuaded to go into hiding. Some of his friends are even said to have announced his death and to have staged a mock funeral. Lamartine accredits the story, attributing the initiative to the beleaguered author himself.[10] "Pour mieux effacer son nom du ressentiment des royalistes, il fit répandre le bruit de sa mort et célébrer, lui vivant, ses propres funérailles." Somewhat inconsistently, Lamartine adds that Charles II knew where his father's old antagonist was hiding and pretended to think that he was indeed dead. Charles was not vindictive, but, his personal inclinatioins notwithstanding, there were some proscriptions, and the blind poet had a few close calls. Eventually, however, it became clear that he was not going to be seriously molested, and thereafter he was free to come and go as he liked. Lamartine repeats the anecdote about Charles's encountering Milton and suggesting that the poet's blindness might be divine punishment. Chateaubriand, in his *Essai sur la littérature anglaise*, had mentioned the story also. Neither Chateaubriand nor Lamartine gives the anecdote's variant, making it the Duke of York rather than King Charles who accosted the poet in this manner. Lamartine asserts that the new king offered to give Milton his old position as "publiciste du gouvernement, s'il voulait consacrer ses talents à la cause royale."[11]

On leaving power, honest public servants carry away nothing material to sustain them in retirement. Lamartine knew this all too well, and he emphasizes Milton's financial straits during the Restoration. He notes that Milton wrote several works at this time in the hope that they would bring in money needed for his family's upkeep and for his daughters' dowries. Milton's name on the title pages did not help sales. A work Lamartine specifically attributes to this period is *The History of Britain*, most of it written much earlier (*Vies* 3:17). No other titles are singled out. Probably Lamartine had *Of True Religion* in mind. Perhaps, too, he was thinking of such works as the grammar and logic, especially if he was being guided by publication dates. Nothing is said about the posthumous *Brief History of Muscovia*.[12] Lamartine points out that Milton's economic distress survived him, noting that his widow "languit dans l'obscurité et dans l'indigence et mourut d'isolement peu d'années après lui. Les filles épousèrent de pauvres artisans du faubourg qu'elles avaient habité avec leur père" (*Vies* 3:31). The critic specifies that the artisans were weavers but does not venture a guess as to whether dowries were ever provided.

The Republic throttled, his political career at an end, his livelihood precarious despite his prose endeavors, Milton returned to poetry. As a young man, Lamartine notes, it had been a distraction for him. Now, with his involuntary leisure, it proved to be a consolation. Milton was picking up where he had left off. From Italy he had brought back the idea of a grandiose poem. More than ever now, he was tossing it about in his head. What he was doing was also an escape from a real world to which he no longer belonged. "Le monde imaginaire l'enlevait délicieusement au monde réel," writes Lamartine (*Vies* 3:17). Thus Milton began *Paradise Lost*. Several times, in discussing it, Lamartine uses the word "pathétique," by which he means "moving."

Fancifully, Lamartine decides where at least one segment of the poem was dictated. This segment is the invocation to light. Lamartine, whose *Méditations poétiques* contained an "Hymne au soleil," admires the passage. "C'est au pied d'un chêne exposé au midi, sur la colline d'Hampstead, que Milton dicta un jour cette pathétique apostrophe à la lumière, début de son troisième chant" (*Vies* 3: 18–19). To Lamartine, it demonstrates the superiority of pure feeling over imagination itself. Lamartine quotes it at length in French, calling it "une des plus belles pages du poème, parce que là le poète est plus l'homme et parce qu'au lieu d'imaginer, il sent" (*Vies* 3:20). Lamartine may have seen paintings, now lost, showing the poet out in the open, dictating. "Les meilleurs portraits de Milton," he writes:

> le représentent ... assis au pied d'un chêne, au coucher du

soleil, le visage tourné vers ses rayons, dictant ses vers à sa bien-aimée Déborah, attentive à la voix de son père, tandis que sa femme, Elisabeth, le regarde comme Eve regardait son époux après la faute et le châtiment. Ses deux plus jeunes filles lui cueillent des fleurs des prés pour lui faire respirer quelques odeurs de l'Eden qui viennent de parfumer ses songes. . . . Le poète, ainsi reproduit, est plus pathétique que le poème. (*Vies* 3:35)

[show him . . . seated at the foot of an oak tree at the setting of the sun, his face turned toward its rays, dictating his poetry to his beloved Deborah, who is listening attentively to her father's voice, while his wife Elizabeth is looking at him the way Eve used to look at her husband after the sin and punishment. So that he can enjoy a few scents from Eden, his two younger daughters are gathering him flowers from the fields, flowers that have just perfumed his dreams. . . . The poet, thus reproduced, is more moving than the poem.]

Lamartine's comment about Eve's looking at Adam in a certain manner suggests that the critic had a good knowledge of the Fall as a theme in art. On the other hand, his having Milton dictate to Deborah while the "younger" girls pick flowers shows his unawareness that the amanuensis was herself the last of the poet's brood to come into the world and survive. Whatever the case, Richard Westhall's *Milton Composes his Paradise Lost*, exhibited at the Royal Academy in 1802, shows the blind poet pretty much as the critic describes him, dictating his epic in an open air décor.[13] This is only one painting, however. Lamartine's reference to "portraits" or paintings seems to indicate that, at one time, other canvasses showing Milton outdoors, composing, must have existed. Today, they appear to have dropped out of sight. Had Lamartine viewed them on trips to England?

As far as it goes, Lamartine's admiration for *Paradise Lost* is sincere but not without restrictions. The French critic knew about Milton's prediction that one day he would produce a work that would give English literature added glory.[14] Realizing that the times were not propitious, the poet hurled himself instead into the controversies of the Civil Wars, the Commonwealth and the Protectorate. With the Restoration, his partisan labors over, he set to work on

Paradise Lost. That the poem's actual composition might have begun earlier is not considered.

The French poet's enthusiasm for the invocation to light has already been noted. Another passage the critic praises is the reconciliation scene between Adam and Eve. On the whole, Lamartine believes that Milton had taken Elizabeth Minshull as his model for Eve. "Sa femme, l'Eve sans crime..., dont il avait célébré la grâce, l'amour et la fidélité sous le nom de la première épouse de l'homme, fut un modèle de dévouement et de patience dans ses adversités," he writes (*Vies* 3:28). Nonetheless, Mary Powell had to have inspired the reconciliation episode. Evoking the arranged meeting that led to Milton's taking his first wife back, the critic alludes to "les repentirs, les larmes, les embrassements" which "laissèrent à Milton une impression si délicieuse qu'il en fit plus tard, dans sa vieillesse, une des scènes les plus pathétiques de son poème" (*Vies* 3:9). And Lamartine quotes, condensing as he goes, from *Paradise Lost* 10.909–1009.

"L'imagination languit dans les régions intermédiaires, dans les climats trop tempérés; il lui faut des excès de température. La poésie est fille du soleil ou des frimas éternels: Homère ou Ossian, le Tasse ou Milton," Lamartine writes in his *Voyage en Orient*.[15] Lamartine had read *Paradise Lost* during his formative years. For example, Milton was one of the English poets he was reading in 1810.[16] Later, on a visit to the Holy Land, he gazed at the Pool of Siloam, and it reminded him—as it had reminded Chateaubriand—of Milton.[17] Like Milton, Lamartine had his ideas about the Creation and the world's first couple. Eve, in particular, had caught his attention. "L'Humanité," in the *Harmonies poétiques et religieuses* (1830), had described her as "un marbre aux divins contours," "noble et légère."

> Sa chevelure qui s'épanche
> Au gré du vent prend son essor,
> Glisse en ondes jusqu'à sa hanche,
> Et là s'effile en franges d'or;
> Autour du cou blanc qu'elle embrasse,
> Comme un collier elle s'enlace,

Descend, serpente, et vient rouler
Sur un sein où s'enflent à peine
Deux sources d'où la vie humaine
En ruisseaux d'amour doit couler!
(ll. 55-64)

A sensuous creature indeed. But to Satan gazing at her for the first time, Milton's Eve had been just as seductive, with "the flowing gold of her loose tresses" barely concealing her naked "swelling breasts."

She as a veil down to the slender waist
Her unadornèd golden tresses wore
Disheveled, but in wanton ringlets waved
As the vine curls her tendrils..........................
(ll. 4:304-07)

The *Paradise Lost* episodes that Lamartine likes best are the tender ones between the two spouses. As he phrases it, "On ne peut lire sans un éblouissement d'admiration les scènes amoureuses et pathétiques de l'apparition d'Eve à Adam et d'Adam à Eve dans le jardin de l'innocence; on ne peut lire sans un frisson de chaste volupté les dialogues à la fois purs et passionnés entre les deux premiers amants de la race humaine." Lamartine adds that "Les historiens qui accusent Milton de n'avoir jamais aimé les femmes que comme les servantes de l'homme calomnient la nature." Based on his descriptions of Eve, Lamartine concludes, Milton could not possibly have considered woman an inferior creature, deserving a secondary place in the domestic order of things. An apostle of romantic love, Lamartine is seeing what he wants to see, needless to say. Probably, as we shall observe later, he never read *Samson Agonistes*. Nor did he notice, apparently, that in *The History of Britain* the author had been willing to fly in the face of historical tradition in order to make Queen Boadicea, usually presented as a heroine, look like an incompetent shrew. To Lamartine, only "un cœur fécond d'enthousiasme pour la beauté et de respect et de tendresse pour la femme" could have written lines such as those having to do with Adam and Eve's waking up, Eve's troubled dream and Adam's soothing words, followed by the couple's prayer, "une exclamation d'admiration, de reconnaissance et de félicité." These lines are "aussi harmonieux que les teintes fugitives du matin" (*Vies* 3:22, 24; *PL* 5.1–223; *PL* 9.192–398). Similarly, the critic dwells upon the spouses' reactions to one another after their sin. Once again he invokes moving lines from *Paradise Lost*'s tenth book, translating a little differently this time (*Vies* 3:22–26; *PL* 10.909–46).

Clearly, Adam and Eve's domestic happiness is what most appeals to Lamartine in *Paradise Lost*. The critic also likes the descriptions of Eden. But what he finds hard to stomach is the bard's proneness to belabor his readers with religious dogma. Viewed from this angle, *Paradise Lost*, he says, is a disappointment, "une Bible en vers et non un drame humain." Apart from the passages he had singled out, perhaps the only ones the epic contained with which one could in some measure empathize, "le reste est imaginaire, fanatique, et froid....," he believes. Basically, the plot comes from the Bible, but mixed in with this material is a tangle of wearisome rhetoric and equally wearisome deeds. As for the tedious theology, half Biblical and half personal, it gets in the poet's way and tires the reader. God and the Son of Man, with partisans and adversaries among their own creatures, talk like ordinary mortals. And they talk, and talk, and talk. But they are far from alone in this. With their endless speeches, the bewildering factions, all at odds with each other, are astounding. "On discute dans le conseil de Dieu comme dans le parlement. Il y a des orateurs du gouvernement céleste et des tribuns du peuple infernal qui demandent la tête du Très-Haut comme Milton celle de Charles Ier." Between speeches, the orators fly at each other's throats. Angels and demons war in space with mechanized weapons, killing one another but not dying, all because of an insect called a human being who lives on a grain of dust lost in chaos known as the earth (*Vies* 3:20–21).

In judging *Paradise Lost*, Lamartine was speaking from a certain amount of experience with this kind of poetry. Years before, he had attempted an epic, never completed, of his own. Two segments, though, had been published. Both have their great moments but do not, as a whole, rank with Lamartine's most successful work. *La Chute d'un ange* (1838) shows us an angel that, having committed the sin of falling in love with a mortal, is condemned to live among mortals. Contemporaries considered the poem Miltonic (Partridge, 164). *Jocelyn* (1836) concerns a priest who likewise experiences deep human love. In both poems the characters are gentle beings. In both the religious element, though important, is not overpowering. Theologically, the viewpoint is unobtrusive, humane, tolerant. Rather than dogma, it is the love theme, gloriously secular, that stands out. It comes as no surprise, then, that certain aspects of *Paradise Lost* attracted the author whereas others bothered him.

But there was another problem, more serious. Perhaps with his own two epic fragments, Lamartine thought he had learned something. Already, *Jocelyn*'s preface had declared that epics could have social as well as religious meaning. By the time he examined *Paradise Lost*, Lamartine had gone a step beyond this and had reached the conclusion that the Christian epic is a contradiction in terms. Dogma and poetry, by their very nature, do not mix. Boileau had said the same thing a century and a half earlier. There is nothing poetic about sin and penance, Lamartine asserts:

> Le christianisme est la philosophie de la douleur...; elle sèvre rudement l'homme de tous les songes; elle lui présente sans cesse la triste image de sa déchéance, de sa misère, et de sa rédemption par la pénitence. Ses dogmes gémissent et ne chantent pas: sa morale proscrit toute les voluptés, même celles de l'imagination.... Une image même est presque un crime aux yeux d'une religion toute spiritualiste, qui abat les sens pour faire triompher l'esprit. Il n'y a pas de poètes à son berceau, il n'y a que des apôtres, des croyants, et des martyrs. Le génie du christianisme, c'est l'austérité; le génie de la poésie, c'est la fiction: ces deux génies antipathiques ne se marient jamais sans se dénaturer l'un par l'autre. (*Vies* 3:26–27)
>
> [Christianity is the philosophy of sorrow...; it rudely weans mankind away from all his dreams; it never stops confronting him

with the sad picture of his downfall, his wretchedness, and his salvation through repentance. Its teachings groan rather than sing: its ethic forbids all sensuality, even that of the imagination. . . . Even an image is almost a crime in the eyes of a religion that is completely spiritualistic, which batters the senses in order to make the spirit triumph. Beside its cradle are no poets, only apostles, believers, and martyrs. The nature of Christianity is austerity; the nature of poetry fiction: these two antipathetic natures never wed without the one causing the other to become distorted.]

Dante, Camoës, Tasso and Milton have succeeded as epic poets only because they have Homeric Heavens or Virgilian Hells, which, after all, are not consonant with Christian theogony. Strictly speaking, austere religions would do well to outlaw poets. "Quand on chante ses dieux, on est bien près de les profaner." Christianity has no place for gods and goddesses with human reactions and passions; it only has room for "un calvaire et un instrument de supplice, où les gouttes de sang d'un martyr divin lavent les souillures de la terre." With *Paradise Lost* Milton did not escape the dilemma. *Paradise Lost* is not really poetry, it is "de la métaphysique en vers." Perhaps *Paradise Regained* should have made the critic reconsider his position, but he does not explore its possibilities. Of all modern epics, Klopstock's *Messias* alone has succeeded in reconciling poetry and theology, he holds. But then, "la *Messiade* n'est pas un poème, ce n'est qu'un sanglot de l'humanité aux pieds de la croix d'un rédempteur." Lamartine's romantic credentials are good here, but the argument is rather weak (*Vies* 3:3, 26–27).

Romanticism also dominates the splendid image with which, with all his personal reservations, Lamartine sums up the later Milton:

> La vieillesse semblait donner un accent plus pathétique à sa voix. Son âme était comme ces instruments à cordes qui ont peu de son quand ils sortent des mains de l'ouvrier, mais que la vétusté du bois rend plus sonores et dont ce qu'on appelle l'âme gémit plus mélodieusement dans le bois presque vermoulu de l'instrument.
>
> [Advanced age seems to have endowed his voice with a more moving articulation. His soul came to resemble those string instruments that produce little sound when they leave the crafts-

man's hands but which, when the wood gets old, become more sonorous and whose souls, if we may call them that, whimper more melodiously when the instruments' wood is almost worm-eaten.]

To the end of his discussion, Lamartine holds to his basic dictum, that *Paradise Lost* is poetic only in spots. In *Paradise Lost*, he concludes, Milton

n'a été poète que dans les pages où il a céléberé l'amour du premier homme pour la première femme, parce qu'alors il n'inventait pas, il se souvenait; il ne cherchait pas son inspiration dans sa théologie, mais dans son cœur. Aussi ces pages resteront-elles à jamais dans la mémoire des hommes. (*Vies* 3:21)

[was a poet only in those pages where he celebrated the love of the first man for the first woman, because then he was not making things up, he was remembering; he was not seeking inspiration in his theology but in his heart. As a result, these pages will remain in people's memory forever.]

In his consideration of Milton, one of the most serious issues Lamartine raises has to do with Milton and regicide, a problem to which the critic returns again and again. Passionately, Lamartine wanted to absolve Milton. Wishing to believe that the poet's attitude did not remain static, he eventually convinced himself, then set out to convince his readers. Arguing emotionally and intuitively, he asserts that Milton not only changed his mind but, in *Paradise Lost*, sought to make amends. Having stated the idea, Lamartine comes back to it, declaring that under the Restoration Milton used to get together now and then with friends from the good old days. Inevitably, Charles I would be mentioned. When that happened, the critic imagines, a shadow would cross the poet's handsome features. To be sure, still a republican, Milton deplored that the people had abandoned their government and that the army had betrayed it. But, his conscience troubling him, there was something he deplored even more. He was tormented that the blood of an innocent, hapless individual had been brutally spilled in the name of a political ideal. "Ce remords, le seul de sa vie, empoisonnait tout pour lui dans le passé, même sa noble aspiration à la république." "Heureuses les théories qui s'évanouissent ou qui s'ajournent sans laisser une trace de sang sur la main," exclaims the critic. On Milton's hand there *was* blood. "Parmi tous les songes de sa belle vieillesse, il y avait une tête coupée qui saignait du haut d'un échafaud sur la tête de deux enfants." If Cromwell, drawing his last breath, had been able to admit his own remorse over the event, why not Milton? Lamartine has his answer, such as it is. "S'il ne le confessa pas publiquement alors, c'est que Charles II régnait et que ce repentir, honorable à avouer devant Dieu, aurait paru à Milton un lâche désaveu et une vile supplication devant les hommes." Lamartine had already lauded the poet's unwillingness to recant his principles when the monarchy was restored. Still, the idea that Milton could have gone to his grave an impenitent regicide horrifies him, and he takes the stance that the poet's views, at some point, underwent a complete overhaul. "Tout dans ses derniers ouvrages" indicated his "tristesse" and his "repentir," the critic insists (*Vies* 3:30). Lamartine advances no real textual support to buttress the assertion, but what he appears to mean is that, in castigating the rebel angels for revolting against the King of Heaven in *Paradise Lost*, Milton was passing retrospective judgment upon his own conduct in justifying the beheading of an erstwhile King of England.

Eikonoklastes, Lamartine had stated in his essay on Cromwell, was a blot on the poet's memory, "une tache de sang sur sa gloire." The blot was not eradicated until, in old age, the poet celebrated, "dans un poème divin, la première innocence de la terre, les révoltes des enfers, les factions du ciel et le triomphe de l'éternelle justice sur l'esprit du mal" (*Vies* 2:374). Having taken a harsh view of *The Tenure of Kings and Magistrates* and *Eikonoklastes*, Lamartine now adopts a simple rationale. Milton, a pious man and a moral one, could not have lived with the knowledge that he had once called for and then vindicated an act that, however one looked at it, was murder. A man of his stamp would have had to repent. In *Paradise Lost*, Lamartine thought he saw the evidence that Milton had done so. The epic was the poet's atonement. Had Lamartine taken a better look at *De Doctrina Christiana*, he might not have been so sure. Milton tinkered with his manuscript to the end of his life, but without ever deleting a passage that seems to indicate that his attitude toward kings and kingship did not change very much over the years. "Some maintain," he wrote toward the end of the work, "that magistrates must be obeyed... when they are tyrannical and when their commands are wicked. There is, however, no divine authority for such an opinion." While it might be prudent to obey a despot in order to guarantee one's personal safety, one should only do this in "lawful matters." Even so, such obedience ought to be tentative, while waiting for events to deliver one from the constraints of necessity (*YPW* 6:800, 801).

Finding fault with Lamartine's treatment of Milton is not hard to do, obviously. It is a poetic treatment, filled with striking imagery. Lamartine's Milton is something of a French romantic hero, superior to other people and misunderstood by them, delighting in nature and loving to write in its midst. For all the importance Lamartine attached to the historical approach, he went about his documentation in a slipshod manner. He did not know the number or gender of Charles I's progeny. From the Civil Wars' initial skirmishes, he thought Cromwell was in complete control of things and that Milton was a minister in the new government. He was not sure how many brothers or children Milton had. Uncritically, he accepted too many anecdotes as authentic, and he jumped to impetuous conclusions.[18] Nor was he consistent. Having accused Milton of imitating illustrious predecessors, instead of following up the charge, he exonerates him later on.[19] One could wish, moreover, that the critic had had something to say about *Areopagitica, Paradise Regained* and *Samson Agonistes*. He may not have been aware that they existed. In his Cromwell essay, he deplored the strictures placed on printing once the soldiers and zealots had taken over in Puritan England (*Vies* 2:374). Here was an opportunity to point out that Milton had raised his voice in support of an unshackled press, but Lamartine did not point it out. A passing allusion to the poet's "derniers vers et les plus belles de ses œuvres," while it could have been made with *Paradise Regained* and *Samson Agonistes* in mind, undoubtedly refers to *Paradise Lost* instead (*Vies* 3:28).

In concluding his consideration of Milton, Lamartine suggested, curiously, that epic poetry had run its course and was no longer a viable literary genre. With *Paradise Lost* Milton produced an epic that was not quite in the classical mold, but neither was it suited to the reader of today. Tasso had written the last real epic, the critic asserted (*Vies* 3:32). Now, producing one would be almost unthinkable. Lamartine held that modern times were not attuned to epic literature, at least not to epic literature as he and his contemporaries knew it. An epic would have to be something quite different from the classics they were accustomed to, he held. Necessarily, such a work would be "l'épopée intime du cœur humain. Un vaste poème qui prendrait l'homme à son berceau, qui le conduirait à la tombe à travers les vicissitudes, tour à tour heureuses ou misérables, de l'existence ordinaire des hommes...." The work would be "l'épopée du sentiment"—in other words, feeling rather than deeds. There would be little plot, little divine intervention. "Le poète qui tenterait de... chanter aux hommes de nos jours n'aurait pas besoin d'autre surnaturel que la création, d'autre merveilleux que l'infini, d'autre fable que la vérité, d'autre lyre que son propre cœur" (*Vies* 3:33). The new epic, then, would be something that the author of *Paradise Lost* could not have conceived of.

7
J. B. Sanson de Pongerville

J. B. Sanson de Pongerville (1792–1870) was a poet, translator and editor whose labors won him a seat in the Académie Française, to which, like Lamartine, he was elected in 1830. It did not make him rich, but eventually sinecure librarianships at the Bibliothèque Ste-Geneviève and the Bibliothèque Nationale, perhaps created, came along to enable him to exist as a man of letters. His chief title to fame was his translation of Lucretius's *De Rerum Natura*, initially in verse (1823) and then in prose (1829). He also translated Ovid's *Metamorphoses* (1827) and Virgil's *Aeneid* (1843). In addition, he wrote occasional verse. His *Paradise Lost* translation, in prose, dates from 1838. For it and its later editions, he wrote a preface that eventually, with a few modifications, became the Milton article in the *Nouvelle Biographie générale* (1861). The essay reached a rather extensive, discriminating audience and thus deserves our attention here. Since it is somewhat disorganized, its various threads have been disentangled and, in the discussion that follows, these ideas are presented in a more cohesive arrangement than originally given. Entitled "Sur Milton, son époque et ses ouvrages," it is peppered with irritating little mistakes counterbalanced by measured, sometimes original remarks and judgments.

Most of Pongerville's mistakes have to do with biographical details. One learns, for example, that Milton grew up in the midst of civil turmoil. In addition to a love of study that led to precocious erudition, the youthful Milton demonstrated an eager interest in polemics. Peevish and cantankerous, "Il se fit remarquer surtout par un désir irrésistible de prendre part aux controverses que les partis politiques cachaient alors sous les formes de questions religieuses." This is a bit premature. Moreover, Milton, "avec un caractère mobile, une imagination ardente, tenta diverses routes avant de suivre celle où l'appelait sa véritable vocation." The critic's meaning is not clear. The *Nouvelle Biographie générale* tells us that the poet considered the ministry, presumably an allusion to a remark in *The Reason of Church Government*. Whatever the case, at 30, Milton had returned to his first love, literature, and had added to this a perfect command of foreign languages, ancient and modern. Thus equipped, he set out for France and Italy, where he was admired on every hand. In turn, he was "enthousiasmé par les lieux où il trouvait à chaque pas de grands talents et de grands souvenirs." His friendship with Manso, Marquis of Villa, is brought in. We are told that "il se procura l'insigne honneur de visiter Galilée dans les fers." In the *Nouvelle Biographie générale* Pongerville corrects what he had said in his preface, and we learn that "il eut des entretiens philosophiques avec Galilée, alors reclus et non pas enchaîné, comme on l'a faussement répété" ("Sur Milton," 4; *Nouv. Biog.*, 571). Milton's first publications date from this trip, for it was in Italy that he published some of his Latin poetry. While abroad he determined to write a monumental work.[1] All of this Pongerville expands somewhat in the *Nouvelle Biographie générale*. Obviously, what he knew about Milton's early life was superficial.

Pongerville mentions possible sources for *Paradise Lost* that the young traveler may have encountered. Whatever he saw, read or heard about, however, the visitor assimilated and made his own (*Nouv. Biog.*, 571). Andreini's *Adamo* is alluded to, with an incorrect title. St. Avitus of Vienne is mentioned as well. Pongerville was one of the few French critics of his time to point out that the novice poet could also have run into Du Bartas's *La Semaine*. Even more startling is a reference to Anne D'Urfé's *Hymne des anges*. Since Milton critics have not noticed the *Hymne des anges* and since it has not been listed among the works the poet could have read, it warrants a digression on our part. While Pongerville makes no effort to demonstrate this, it is significant that he believed that, while in France, Milton could have heard of it as he moved about in social and intellectual circles. "Pendant son séjour en France, il dut entendre parler de *L'Hymne des anges, ou la révolte des esprits célestes contre Dieu*, d'Anne D'Urfé, frère de l'auteur de *L'Astrée*" (*Nouv. Biog.*, 571). Surprisingly, Pongerville does not comment or develop. A few years later, Edme Rathéry would mention the same work, but again without discussing it.[2] Calling attention to no specific passage or passages, neither suggests any particular parallels. It would have been easy enough to do. It seems very possible that Milton had read the *Hymne des anges* when he wrote *Paradise Lost*.[3]

Overshadowed by his brother Honoré,[4] who wrote one of literature's classic pastoral novels, Anne D'Urfé (1555–1621) has hardly left a trace in French letters. Had the English remained at home, not many in England would have known about him. Not all of his work was published, to be sure, but even so, posterity has given him less than he deserves. Catholic soldier and courtier, a member of the bar, he was a devout Christian. He and his wife proved incompatible and petitioned to have their marriage annulled (1598). This done (1599), the poet took religious orders (1603) and held several ecclesiastical prebends. His writings include various sonnets and an imitation of Tasso's *Gerusalemme liberata*. Like Du Bartas, he was interested in the Book of Judith and left a *Judic*.[5] His *Livre des hymnes* was published in 1608. The *Hymne des anges*, probably written around 1580 or 1585 and reworked later, constitutes its third segment, the *Troisième Livre des hymnes*.[6] Composed in the classical French verse form, rhyming alexandrine couplets, it begins with a dedication to Marie de Medici. After an invocation, the rest of the poem deals with God, the Son, Heaven and the angels.

Aside from the major emphasis, which in the French poem is on the angels, there are several notable differences between the *Hymne des anges,* which has 1,004 lines, and *Paradise Lost.* Acknowledging that God and the Son are of the same substance, D'Urfé was a strict trinitarian (*Hymne,* 166, 164). He also believed in episcopal and papal authority.[7] He respected

> Le Pape et les Prelats qui ont l'auctorité
> Sur le spirituel..
> (*Hymne,* 563–64)

Moreover, he held that one should revere and serve monarchs, "les hommes qui règnent,"

> .... Les Roys, et les Princes
> Qui commandent ça bas regissant les Provinces.
> (*Hymne,* 566, 561–62)

And, of course, unlike *Paradise Lost,* the *Hymne des anges* is not an epic.

Neverthheless, between the two poets there are numerous similarities. At the outset, D'Urfé does not propose to justify the ways of God to humans, since his intention is to describe and laud the angels:

> ... J'y veux celebrer ces Esprits admirables
> Qui possèdent au Ciel les Sieges desirables.
> (*Hymne,* 9–10)

Although his primary goal is different, he will manage nonetheless to describe Heaven, recount the struggle that took place there, tell of humankind's first disobedience, mention the fall and indicate the redemption. Having stated what he intends to do, the poet invokes his muse:

> Muse qui desdaignez cette fresle Couronne
> Des lauriers tant aimez par le fils de Latonne,

Mais qui portez au lieu pour orner vostre front
D'Astres resplendissans un beau cercle tout rond
Dive, où me guidez-vous? dites, Vierge Sacree......
(Hymne, 13–30)

While she is not called by name, we know that the muse is Urania because of her crown of stars.

D'Urfé talks about angels at great length. As in *Paradise Lost*, they are pure in essence:

L'Ange, comme i'ay dit, est d'une essence pure.
(Hymne, 833)

D'Urfé gives their names, their places in the celestial hierarchy, and their functions and duties:

Apres les Seraphins, le lieu plus honorable
Est pour les Cherubins ....
(Hymne, 505–06)

and so on. There are Thrones, Dominions, Princedoms, Powers, Virtues, Archangels and Angels. Milton's Raphael, Michael, Gabriel and one or two others are named. One of their occupations is to praise God.

Lors mille millions de voix furent ouïes
Rendant à l'Eternel loüanges infinies,
Entonnant ces propos melodieusement,
Honneur et gloire à Dieu soit eternellement.
(Hymne, 389–92)

To Powers is assigned the task of keeping an eye on Satan and preventing his mischief:

Parce qu'ils ont pouuoir sur la force du Diable
Qu'ils firent en Enfer autrefois trebucher
Et que leur propre office est aussi d'empescher
Les maux qu'à tous moments ce Demon aduersaire
Nostre ennemi mortel est poussé de nous faire.
(Hymne, 379–83)

With these angels on guard, Satan can do no harm unless God permits it. These and the other angels, as we have seen, have ranks and appropriately graduated positions in Heaven:

> .... Un chacun a la place
> Que Dieu leur ordonna, ou plus haute, ou plus basse:
> Car ainsi que i'ay dit, ils ne sont tous esgaux,
> D'autant que les plus grans ont leurs sieges plus hauts.
> (*Hymne*, 449-52)

Ruling over this throng is God. D'Urfé calls him God, the Almighty, the King of the Universe, the King of Kings, the Eternal. Among His attributes are an absence of need and a desire to communicate His goodness and glory to others (*Hymne*, 47-50). As in *Paradise Lost*, He speaks and holds council meetings (*Hymne*, 31-39). In the *Hymne des anges* Jesus is called Christ, Jesus Christ, the Son, the Man-God, the Word. He will triumph over the Cross, Death and Hell (*Hymne*, 1004).

As *Paradise Lost* does, D'Urfé's poem contains numerous references to ancient mythology. Allusions to biblical characters and situations abound as well. Like Milton, D'Urfé was interested in the story of Raphael and Tobias, for example (*Hymne*, 607-13; *PL* 5.222). Referring to Powers, he declares that Raphael was a member of that order:

> Ie tiens que de cet Ordre est l'Ange Raphaël,
> Qui, conduisant Tobie allant vers Gabaël,
> Le sauva du poisson et luy fit prendre à femme
> Serre de Raguel, liant l'esprit infame
> Meurtrier de ses maris aux deserts montueux
> D'Egypte, et redonna la clarté de ses yeux
> A son pere ancien..
> (*Hymne*, 607-13)

To Milton, Raphael was

> ...... the sociable Spirit, that deign'd
> To travel with Tobias, and secured
> His marriage with the seven-times-wedded Maid.
> (*PL* 5:221-23)

Cosmography has a less important place in the *Hymne des anges* than in *Paradise Lost*, but "le mouuement tant admiré des Cieux" is mentioned (*Hymne*, 811–12).

In D'Urfé's Heaven as in Milton's, trouble is brewing. Satan is a handsome, superb spirit, the most brilliant of the heavenly host. He is also proud, disdainful, ambitious. "Un Esprit si beau" cannot accept any creature's being greater than he:

> Mais le plus grand de tous que Dieu fit nonpareil
> En exquise beauté fut possédé d'orgueil,
> Qui le fit embraser d'ambition extreme....
> (*Hymne*, 143–50)

Finally, war breaks out. God commissions St. Michael to deal with the rebels (*Hymne*, 227–46). Michael and Satan line up their forces. With Michael representing good and Satan evil, there are speeches opposing the mighty captains.

> Ie ne viens en ce lieu le cœur rempli d'audace,
> Me fiant à ma force; ains par commandement
> De ce grand Eternel qui regne au Firmament,
> Lequel te fera voir par ce dard que ie porte,
> A ta confusion, combien sa dextre est forte,

Michael begins (*Hymne*, 322–26). Though arrogant, Satan is an able, convincing speaker. Proud of his status and cause, he takes an almost heroic stance as he urges his opponent to switch sides:

> Je me cognois heureux d'estre ce que ie suis
> A present en grandeur, et ce que ie poursuis
> Est pour l'honneur de tous; et toy comme bon frere,
> Deurois nous assister encor en cette affaire,
> Et pour ton interest; car nul n'est apres moy
> Qui doive meriter cet honneur tant que toy.
> (*Hymne*, 307–20)

Satan is cunning and appeals to his opponent's self-interest. The battle is terrible:

> Sous leurs pas furieux le Ciel d'airain trembla,
> Paradis en fremit, l'univers se troubla.
> (*Hymne*, 221–23)

The din is incredible. Lightning and thunderbolts rock the universe. With His thunderbolts, it is as if God has decided to let the universe return to chaos. But worse, perhaps, is to come. Cannon is called up. In Heaven, declares the poet, all one could hear was

> .... tonnerres grondans, avec vn bruit hideux
> Cannoner coup sur coup, et les esclairs sans cesse
> S'entresuiuant l'vn l'autre avec grande vitesse.
> (*Hymne*, 344–46)

The poet does not say who invented the cannon. In any case, Satan and his rebels are at last vanquished, "overturned" and cast out. Amid moans and cries, they find themselves not on a burning lake but rather

> .... versez sur les charbons ardents
> Parmi les cris, les pleurs, et grincemens de dents,
> (*Hymne*, 419–20)

burning coals instead of a "fiery gulf." Like Milton, D'Urfé insists upon the "feu violant qui brusle incessamment" and the "chaisnes effroyables" in the dismal place. Despite the fire, there is

> No light, but rather darkness visible
> (*PL* 1:63)

in *Paradise Lost*. D'Urfé's image is almost the same. French translators have always rendered "darkness visible" as "ténèbres visibles." After their expulsion, D'Urfé's stunned devils roll about in "ténèbres palpables." Here, instead of a purely visual image, we have the tangible combined with the visual. Nevertheless, for the most famous image in *Paradise Lost*, this might well be the inspiration or source (*Hymne*, 421). In *Milton's Biblical and Classical Imagery*, John M. Steadman finds no antecedent.[8] In the last book of *Paradise Lost*, Milton actually refers to "palpable darkness" (*PL* 12.188).

Though it is not the poem's main thrust, in the *Hymne des anges* it is known that human beings will sin and have to leave their ideal abode. The Son, however, will take on human attributes and redeem humankind in time (*Hymne,* 167, 1003–004). D'Urfé brings his poem to a somewhat abrupt close, telling his muse that, tired and hoarse, he is unable to continue.

Redescendons en terre et reprenons haleine.
(*Hymne,* 981)

Perhaps another, "auec meilleure veine,"

Vn iour acheuera ce que i'ay commencé.
(*Hymne,* 984)

That poet, it would seem, would be John Milton. It is curious that, while naming the *Hymne des anges* as a possible source for Milton's epic, Pongerville failed to pluck it out and call attention to some of these parallels. Probably, when he wrote his Milton essay, he no longer remembered such details.

While not a truly great work, the *Hymne des anges* is a highly creditable one, deserving its place in the splendid outpouring of intensely-felt religious poetry written in France as the sixteenth century was drawing to a close and the seventeenth century was beginning. It is a poem that probably left its mark on *Paradise Lost.* As pointed out above, it was dedicated to Marie de Medici, mother of Queen Henrietta Maria. It was published the year Milton was born, 1608. One of the author's brothers was a Protestant who moved to England during the siege of La Rochelle in 1628. This brother took his son with him and founded an English branch of the family. D'Urfé would have been saddened had he lived to see the career of his grandnephew, Thomas D'Urfey (1653–1723). Poet and dramatist, this grandnephew delighted Restoration audiences with his ribald comedies. Among his other works are satires on Catholicism.

Pongerville writes that, after his travels abroad, "riche de sa récolte littéraire," Milton came home and began turning out works of a most disparate kind. Again the critic is wrong in some of what he has to say. "De petits poèmes, des élégies, des intermèdes, des traités théologiques, des vers latins, un commencement d'*Histoire d'Angleterre*, et des pamphlets politiques" were written. Essentially, though, the poet neglected his true calling. "L'écrivain se fit entièrement homme de parti, et son génie, descendu dans une triste arène, s'éclipsa." For the moment, at least. Becoming a schoolmaster, he "commença comme finit le tyran de Syracuse" ("Sur Milton," 4; *Nouv. Biog.*, 571). Needless to say, Pongerville's chronology is less than perfect here.

Milton's writings at this time won their author "un certain renom," though less than he really deserved. Already he had shown genuine talent. Just as some of his poetry bore witness to what he would be able to do later, Pongerville notes, much the same can be said for his early prose, especially *Areopagitica*. One suspects, however, that the critic has not bothered much with the prose works. Nothing is said about the divorce tracts, and, as we shall see, there is a certain haziness concerning the *Defensios*. After mentioning "les traités sur les principes religieux," the critic comes out with a remarkable generalization, true only if hedged by enough qualifiers. Milton, he tells us, "ne fut point inspiré par l'esprit de secte; on sait que tous les cultes étaient respectables à ses yeux. Le chantre des mystères célestes demeura toujours tolérant envers les autres...." This bit of nonsense disappeared from the essay prior to its republication in the *Nouvelle Biographie générale* ("Sur Milton," 5).

As pointed out above, Pongerville had chronology problems. Like many another critic, he believed that once the monarchy had come to its bloody end, Cromwell grabbed the reins of power immediately. Thus, as Pongerville saw it, from January 1649 onward, Milton was working for this new master. In spite of his own views concerning order and morality, Pongerville admired the dictator and his legacy, but he considered the man a criminal. Trying to come up with a satisfactory explanation for why Milton would have served such an individual, he was unable to find much. Overlooking what he had said about the poet's family being honorable but obscure and unconcerned about the fact that, a little later in the essay, he would be calling Cromwell a despot, he notes that the two men had things in common. Both, although "aristocrats," were republicans and both were radical innovators. Milton believed in virtue and merit and thought that the man on horseback possessed both. In this he was to be deceived. On the other hand, while their reasons were different, both desired the general prosperity. Cromwell needed the nation to be prosperous and therefore content in order to achieve his own ends, which were supreme power. Milton wanted it because it was inherent in his democratic ideal. He thought the soldier would bring it about. This, at least, did happen. Even though Milton was naive and got taken in, it is pathetic to see him, "asservi aux pieds du despotisme," renounce his independence and unwittingly betray that freedom that he prized so much. Milton, it appears, did not understand that, as far as government is concerned, the Civil Wars only replaced one tyrant with another, the new one much more powerful, much more terrible than his predecessor. Pongerville is wrong in asserting that Milton was Cromwell's private secretary, friend and even confidant. Personally, the critic states, Milton "n'a souillé sa vie d'aucun acte cruel, d'aucune de ces rigueurs que les gouvernements appellent des nécessités."

Pongerville does not bring up *The Tenure of Kings and Magistrates* or *Eikonoklastes*. On the other hand, he does inform his readers that the poet destined to write *Paradise Lost*, in the interests of a bad cause, answered Saumaise's *Defensio Regia*, a "sage plaidoyer." Milton's reply was *Pro Populo Anglicano Defensio*, where the poet "fit à la fois un mauvais ouvrage et une mauvaise action." With it he made himself a servile accomplice. "Il y a des complaisances impardonnables et des mots qui sont des crimes." Nonetheless, the author redeemed his "abaissement coupable" with the frank advice he dared give the Lord Protector in the *Defensio Secunda*. Pongerville translates some of it but seems unaware that he is quoting from the second rather than the first *Defensio*.[9] In the *Nouvelle Biographie générale* he notes that, in this work, the author, in addition to giving his readers some biographical material, "rend compte de sa mission politique" (*Nouv. Biog.*, 573).

Eventually the Protectorate fell, and after a troubled interim the Restoration took its place. "A l'approche du changement, Milton, qui venait de résigner ses hautes fonctions, eut le fatal courage de combattre par de virulents écrits le nouvel ordre de choses, au moment où le prétendant marchait déjà vers le trône paternel. . . . " Milton hid. Several times arrest warrants were issued, then withdrawn. Davenant, grateful for a similar intervention in the past, may have interceded and saved his life, Pongerville speculates. Milton, never sure that he was out of danger, lived in a certain amount of dread that can be seen in his work, the critic believes. "Lui-même, descendu de la haute sphère de son imagination, éprouvait l'inquiétude de se voir arraché à ses doux travaux. Dans ses chants, il invoque l'oubli de ses puissants adversaires et demande des consolations à la muse divine qui le visite. . . . Il a connu la crainte, car il n'était pas sans reproche" ("Sur Milton," 8; Nouv. Biog., 573-74). Apparently forgetting what he had said earlier about Milton's not having sullied himself by any cruel act, Pongerville tells us that the poet was not innocent. Still, with his disappointments and afflictions, he expiated much of his wrongdoing. His perseverance, as he labored in the midst of it all to produce his masterpiece, commands admiration. Milton was a pathetic genius, "accablé à la fois par tous les maux," enduring it all "afin de doter son pays de l'un des plus beaux monuments de l'esprit humain" ("Sur Milton," 9).

His utopian illusions gone, Milton revived and set to work. Two of his daughters, loving and diligent, had to read to him in languages they could not comprehend and then write as he dictated. Beneath his obscure roof he lived poor, sick, scorned and abandoned. The solace others refused him he found within himself. He had his imagination, says Pongerville. Blind, he could no longer behold with mortal eyes the great book of nature, but his inner vision extended beyond the world's limits. Like the angels whose rapid flight he depicts, he had his own wings that allowed him to soar above vast uncharted spaces. They permitted him to be present when the Heavenly Father deliberated in council, when the War in Heaven was being fought, when the rebel angels were cast out. As he captivates with his sublime inventions, one is aware that, behind it all, a thinker is at work. "Il fallait l'alliance de la philosophie et de la poésie pour produire cette grande personnification des deux principes rivaux qui agitent et renouvellent le monde. L'un destructeur, l'autre réparateur, par des luttes constantes et des triomphes alternatifs, ils maintiennent l'équilibre éternel." Pongerville will return to good and evil, thought and poetry.

Clearly, in *Paradise Lost* Milton was working within two traditions, classical antiquity and the Bible. Coping with two modes of thought, both of which placed constraints upon him, he emulated the one and gave new expression to the other. Pongerville further asserts that the restrictions did not prevent Milton's poetic imagination from reaching incredible heights:

> Poète et penseur, disciple des poètes et des penseurs de l'antiquité, Milton emprunte à la mythologie moderne, aux traditions sacrées, les scènes sublimes de son drame divin. Il trouve le secret de satisfaire la philosophie par la profondeur de ses vues, la religion par ses formes, et l'une et l'autre par sa morale. Son œuvre est un brillant miroir qui réfléchit et embellit, sans les dénaturer, les scènes bibliques. Il parle au cœur du croyant sincère, comme à l'esprit du rigoreux philosophe. ("Sur Milton," 10)

> [A poet and thinker, a disciple of the poets and thinkers of antiquity, Milton borrows from modern mythology, from sacred tradition, the sublime scenes of his divine drama. He discovers the secret of satisfying philosophy by the depth of his insights, religion by his form, and both by his ethic. His work is a brilliant mirror that reflects and embellishes the biblical scenes without distorting them. He addresses the heart of the sincere believer, just as he does the mind of the stern philosopher.]

His God is the ancient Pan, the universal Jehovah. Step by step, the poet follows this God in the intricate creative process. Having made them, "Dieu ... allume un soleil nouveau pour ses nouveaux enfants. Il les place dans l'Eden, environnés de tant de délices que l'enfer s'en émeut de jalousie; le dieu des anges rebelles juge l'homme assez puissant pour lui déclarer la guerre; il le combat en rival, et l'homme ne

succombe que pour se relever" ("Sur Milton," 11).

Pongerville believes that *Paradise Lost* did not appeal to the Restoration public in part because of its subject matter. People did not take to huge scenes based on dogma. Mythology was much more to their liking because, emphasizing their weaknesses and virtues, it showed Gods to which humankind could easily relate. Moreover, from the standpoint of contemporary taste, Milton's language and style were basically too stark and rough, even when appearing ornate; the language seemed cold and distant. Even for readers schooled in epic literature, *Paradise Lost* was something too new, too unusual for them to handle:

> L'œuvre de Milton ne met pas en relief ses grands tableaux par la magie du style abondant, coloré, harmonieux et flexible de l'*Iliade* et de l'*Odyssée*. Il ne peint point, comme Virgile, la nature réelle dans sa noble simplicité, ni les joies et les douleurs humaines; en un mot, le poète anglais est dépouvu de cette mélodie éloquente qui est la musique de l'âme et dont toutes les âmes sont émues. Son idiome est rude, incomplet dans son apparente richesse; Milton est contraint pour interpréter sa pensée de rechercher des expressions vieillies, d'emprunter des tours, des locutions helléniques et hébraïques. Il viole même la syntaxe de sa propre langue. (*Nouv. Biog.*, 575)
>
> [Milton's work does not make its great scenes stand out through the magic of the luxuriant, highly colored, harmonious, flexible style of the *Iliad* and *Odyssey*. Unlike Virgil, the poet paints neither real nature in its noble simplicity nor human happiness and sorrow; in a word, the English poet is devoid of that eloquent melodiousness which is the music of the soul and by which all souls are touched. His idiom is rough, unfinished in its apparent richness; to express his thoughts Milton is forced to seek out archaic ways of putting ideas across, to borrow Greek and Hebrew expressions and locutions. He even does violence to the syntax of his own language.]

To Pongerville, Milton was writing in "le langage d'une civilisation incomplète." Unavoidably, "une rudesse native" shows up in the epic now and then ("Sur Milton," 12). Obviously, Milton's language is a point on which Pongerville and Véricour held very different opinions.

As an epic poet, Pongerville feels, Milton stands essentially

alone, even though matters of detail lend themselves to comparisons between him and his predecessors:

> Entre son œuvre et les autres épopées il ne peut se produire de jugement comparatif. Sa témérité originale lui donne une place à part. Son plan tient un peu de la variété désordonnée du chaos, qu'il a si bien décrit. Milton se distingue surtout par une conception vaste et hardie; mais, dans de nombreux détails, il imite les poètes de tous les temps et s'approprie leurs richesses par droit de génie. Il se permet tout, s'abandonne à l'essor de sa verve, et, les bornes de l'humaine raison une fois franchies, le vol du poète s'élève sans cesse et traverse les déserts de l'infini; l'impossible n'existe plus dans les régions dont il s'empare. (*Nouv. Biog.*, 575)

[Between his work and the other epics there can be no comparative judgment. His bold originality assigns him a place unto himself. His outline is somewhat like the turbulent diversity of chaos, which he has described so well. Milton stands out above all because of his vast, daring overall concept; but, in numerous details, he imitates the poets of all the ages and expropriates their riches by right of genius. He allows himself everything, letting his verve take flight, and, once the boundaries of human reason have been transcended, the poet soars endlessly and crosses the deserts of the infinite; the impossible ceases to exist in the region he claims as his own.]

Milton, remaining basically a loner, took from the other epic poets only bits and pieces, nothing really important. One could wish that this critic had expanded his intriguing idea.

Pongerville also admires Milton's supernatural beings, which are "grands comme la nature dont ils personnifient les forces éternelles." Homer's gods pale in comparison. Because both wrote sublime epics, Milton has, of course, been compared to Homer. Perhaps, however, there is another ancient writer with whom the English poet could be better compared. Here Pongerville remembers that he has translated *De Rerum Natura*, in which some readers have claimed to see an epic. "La mâle vigueur, l'indépendance, l'énergie de Milton, ses hardiesses, ses imperfections, et de nombreuses parties de son œuvre lui donnent peut-être une plus grande ressemblance avec Lucrèce." Superficially, the two poets are not alike. Lucretius toppled ancient beliefs,

whereas Milton, in magnificent poetry, proclaimed those of a later era. On the other hand, both writers, deep thinkers as well as great poets, reached pretty much the same conclusions. "Tous deux ont retracé les merveilles de l'univers, la formation du monde et des êtres, le berceau de la société humaine. Ils arrivent ensemble à la personnification des grands principes, agents mystérieux du monde, rivaux implacables, qui, par d'incessants combats, toujours comprimés à propos, rétablissent l'équilibre dans le grand tout." As philosophers and as poets, Lucretius and Milton both explain the enormous contradictions in nature, which nevertheless seem not to emanate from an identical source. As moralists, they explain with equal wisdom the aberrations of the human heart, a chasm no less impenetrable than the secrets of nature. The Roman philosopher paints things as his mind conceives them. Milton paints them as they are revealed to him and are then embellished by his powerful imagination. Finally, both poets write in an idiom that is still imperfect, with the result that their poetry is less harmonious and inviting than it is bold and vigorous. Whether striding ahead to their destinations or meandering along the way, both are equally adventurous, innovative, admirable ("Sur Milton," 11–12).

Despite his enthusiasm, Pongerville has been hinting that, linguistically at least, *Paradise Lost* has its flaws. He lists several, and some indeed are verbal. Frequently form and tone are not suited to each other, the critic thinks. Often the most exquisite ornamentation bears little relationship to the subject. Unfortunately, he gives no examples. He notes that sometimes delightful images are followed by childish peculiarities, or coming on the heels of a vibrant poetic expression one will discover the "âpre langage d'une civilisation incomplète." Noble concepts and language can also degenerate into sheer triviality. Moreover, on occasion, the author is quite simply guilty of bad taste. And overall, Pongerville holds, the epic lacks proportion. But if there are disproportion and even disorder in *Paradise Lost*, one must remember that, however much he may have towered above them, Milton was the product of disordered times. To those

times the poet owed much of his artistic accomplishment, but they were awesome (*Nouv. Biog.*, 576; "Sur Milton'" 12).

Milton doit peut-être sa brusque et vigoureuse originalité à la rudesse fougueuse de ses compatriotes; peut-être sa verve énergique est-elle l'écho du fracas des luttes intestines. Témoin des grandes catastrophes, il apprit à les peindre. Il semble, en effet, avoir introduit les débats politiques dans le Pandemonium. Le poète a trouvé sur la terre les exemples de la révolte des cieux. Il avait vu, il avait lui-même encouragé l'effervescence d'un peuple qui, au nom de la liberté, se détournait brusquement de la voie de l'ordre pour se précipiter au milieu de ruines sanglantes vers un but qui recula longtemps devant ses téméraires exigences. (*Nouv. Biog.*, 576; "Sur Milton," 13)

[Milton may owe his abrupt, vigorous originality to the rough, impetuous mettle of his compatriots; perhaps his energetic ardor is the echo of noisy internal struggles. Having witnessed enormous catastrophies, he learned to depict them. He seems, actually, to have introduced political debates into Pandemonium. On earth the poet found the models for the revolt in Heaven. He had seen, indeed encouraged the ferment of a nation that, in the name of freedom, suddenly swerved from the path of order to rush headlong, amid bloody ruins, toward an objective that long resisted its bold demands.]

In other words, his contemporaries' frenetic pursuit of an elusive political ideal left its mark all too clearly on the author of *Paradise Lost*. For some of his episodes, Pongerville believes, all Milton had to do was remember.

Pongerville was not very interested in Milton after *Paradise Lost*. *Samson Agonistes* is not even mentioned as such. While *Paradise Lost* did not leave the poet exhausted, according to the critic, it used up the treasures he had stored away. Having written his great epic, he composed "quelques poèmes, acheva un dictionnaire latin, et créa le *Paradis retrouvé*. Vaine fécondité, les richesses de son génie s'étaient entassées dans sa première épopée, il ne lui était plus permis de se montrer prodigue. Son goût, vieilli, donnait toutefois la préférence à sa dernière œuvre: on sait que les fruits de la vieillesse sont les plus chers à la faiblesse d'un père; mais cette prédiction ne trompe que lui-même." Milton's

other works do not matter, then. When one has written *Paradise Lost*, nothing can add to or diminish one's stature ("Sur Milton," 14). Milton died knowing that he had given his country the masterpiece he had promised it and suspecting that one day it would be discovered and appreciated. He could by no means be sure that this would happen, though. As for French readers, it would be revealed to them when Voltaire, "l'arbitre universel de la raison et du goût," called their attention to it ("Sur Milton," 14). Pongerville does not add that the arbiter's initial enthusiasm shrank considerably over the years.

The preceding analysis makes one suspect that Pongerville did not know much about Milton, apart from *Paradise Lost*. Fuzzy about biographical details, he also blundered now and then when referring to the political backdrop against which the poet lived and wrote. All he really knew was that the situation was unsettled and even violent. Regrettably, he was not always sure which Milton prose work he was discussing at a given moment. Aware that Milton had applauded the king's trial and execution, he took a harsh view of the poet's attitude, only to exonerate him a little too easily, a little too abruptly, on the basis of his infirmities and genius. "S'il n'est aucun pouvoir qui efface le crime, l'infortune peut absoudre les erreurs. Quelle inflexible rigueur ne se désarmerait pas à l'aspect du génie accablé..." ("Sur Milton," 9)? It is worth noting that Pongerville, like Véricour, saw allusions to recent events in *Paradise Lost*, particularly in the devils' conclave, which recalled England's Parliament at the time of the Civil Wars and Commonwealth. As to whether Milton was Cromwell's dupe or not, one can only speculate, of course. One could wish that Pongerville had cited passages in *Paradise Lost* that, to his way of thinking, corroborated his view that the poet never ceased fearing that his enemies might one day apprehend and punish him. In any case, the critic was certainly wrong when he insisted upon the poet's solitude in his later years. In asserting that people abandoned him, Pongerville forgot that much of what we know about those years comes from those who knew him during that time.

It is unfortunate that Pongerville had little to say about Milton's poetry other than *Paradise Lost*. Nevertheless, his essay was written, after all, as an introduction to the epic. For it, his admiration was almost boundless. He could exclaim with conviction that, in it, "le poète, dans son saint enthousiasme, s'empare de l'univers entier" ("Sur Milton," 9). Among the outstanding features of Pongerville's treatment is the critic's preferring to compare Milton to Lucretius rather than Homer. This was a new departure in nineteenth century French Miltonism. Since Pongerville's day, the place the Latin poet occupied in Milton's thought and writing, not just in *Paradise Lost*, has been explored in somewhat greater depth.[10] Pongerville was almost alone in noting Milton's possible debt to Anne D'Urfé's *Hymne des anges*, which we have explored as an important insight. Aside from this, Pongerville's most salient point undoubtedly has to do with Milton's language in *Paradise Lost*, which almost preoccupied the critic. Compared with Homer and Virgil, he felt, the English poet was at a linguistic disadvantage. "Son idiome, né du mélange de langages antipathiques, n'était point fixé," the critic contends. The sometimes strident notes in Milton's poetry result from the fact that the author was writing in an inchoate language that, still crude, was far from having received the final coat of polish it needed, Pongerville says. He stops just short of calling it a "barbarian" tongue. ("Sur Milton," 12, 13).

8
Jules Barbey d'Aurevilly

Jules Barbey d'Aurevilly (1808-1889) cut an odd figure indeed in the nineteenth century world of letters. He was an aristocrat and a dandy, an uncompromising monarchist and an equally intransigent Roman Catholic. Not much in his background, habits and outlook should have attracted him to John Milton. Emile Zola wrote that, as a critic, he was "un des plus curieux de notre littérature contemporaine."[1] From Zola's vantage point, it could not have been otherwise, as Zola and Barbey represented opposing literary persuasions. Zola was the leader of the naturalists. Barbey, though still writing, was almost an anachronism. An impenitent holdover from romanticism, he saw no reason to change with the times. While he liked Taine, he scoffed at his deterministic theories, which, to the naturalists, were articles of faith. Barbey, committed to his own tenets, was uncompromising. Milieu, he asserted dogmatically, does not account for creative genius.[2]

A *conteur* and novelist, Barbey is best known for the six novelettes that make up *Les Diaboliques* (1874). As with numerous other writers of his day, his financial mainstay was journalism, his articles appearing in *Le Pays, Le Réveil*,

Le Figaro, Le Nain Jaune, Le Constitutionnel and elsewhere. When not devoted to polemics of one kind or another, the articles generally dealt with literature. Eventually, most of his articles were collected, appearing in the various volumes known as *Les Œuvres et les hommes*. When Edmond de Guerle's *Milton, sa vie et ses œuvres*, came out, it triggered such an article. However, what Barbey wrote, far from being a simple book review, was an original production. Entitled "Milton," the article appeared in *Le Constitutionnel* on 22 September 1868. The year he died, Barbey included it in the volume of *Les Œuvres et les hommes* he called *Les Poètes* (1889).

De Guerle's book was a pretext. For Barbey, *Paradise Lost* and its author had long been a major interest. Barbey never mentions *Paradise Regained* and *Samson Agonistes*, which he may or may not have known, but he knew Milton's other poetry, and he had some knowledge of the prose. Still, it was *Paradise Lost* that kindled his enthusiasm. It had become so much a part of him that, here and there in his letters, allusions to and even appropriate quotations from the work appear. Once, for instance, lamenting that he was going to have to spend a month without seeing a woman he loved, he reminded himself that he would have to keep his mind busy during her absence. Quoting in French, he told a correspondent that

> The mind is its own place, and in itself
> Can make a Heav'n of Hell, a Hell of Heav'n.
> (*PL* 1.244–45)

The epic had permeated his thought.[3] Writing on other authors, he had a marked tendency to compare them with Milton. Once he declared that Gœthe could never have written *Paradise Lost* because he was too "ocular," his perceptions too visual. Milton's blind eyes served a different purpose. For the epic poet, they were "trous d'ombre... par lesquels passait sa pensée."[4] We shall have occasion to return to Barbey's view of Milton's relationship to other authors.

About Milton's life, Barbey's notions were sketchy at best. The critic was somewhat interested in the poet's childhood, however. What he had to say about it gave him an opportunity to blast some of his own adversaries, in this case the literary determinists. In his opinionated way, he affirmed that Milton was not at all the inevitable product of the environment into which he was born and in which he grew up—far from it. He was a creature apart. If anything, the environment should have kept him from becoming a poet. Although he may have had noble ancestry, "Il était né bourgeoisement, et ce n'est pas dans la bourgeoisie que les poètes doivent naître.... Les poètes sont faits pour être roulés dans la pourpre de la splendeur ou dans les haillons de la misère." Ordinary creature comfort is not their element. Curiously, Milton was reared in much the same manner and surroundings as someone who, later, was to be his bitter foe, Claude de Saumaise. For example, Barbey cites the education the two were given. In Milton's case as in his opponent's, "on en fit un pédant monstrueux." Milton's father had his own ideas about education. The education he gave his son meant going against nature, and it took its toll. Nevertheless, Milton's poetic vocation was so strong that it survived.[5] "Ad Patrem" is never mentioned, though the critic may have had it in mind. Presumably referring to the prose tracts, the critic declares elsewhere that "Milton fut un affreux pédant, un Saumaise insupportable et illisible, voilà ce qu'il *devint;* mais ce qu'il *était* de nature, c'était le poète du *Paradis perdu*."[6] In his Milton article, Barbey observes that the poet never rebelled against his upbringing and that, even though it was an encumbrance, he came to relish the attitudes and habits it instilled in him ("Milton," 209, 211). Picking up an ink bottle, he became a schoolmaster and a quarrelsome theologian.

Milton remained untouched by another environmental or conditioning factor, those his duties as a government functionary entailed. Barbey believes the atmosphere in which Milton moved during the Civil Wars, Commonwealth and Protectorate, like his upbringing, should have killed his poetic genius. Here, too, nature prevailed. That it did so can be attributed to his having been "si profondément, si absolument poète que la prose[7] de ses jours ne tua pas la poésie de sa pensée, qu'elle aurait dû dix fois étouffer" ("Milton," 211). Money, or the lack of it, did not affect the poet, either. More than any other mortal, he was impervious to "les influences extérieures" of materialism. Probably Barbey means that Milton made no effort to enrich himself while serving the Commonwealth and Protectorate and that he is supposed to have declined to write for the Restoration, which would have made it worth his while at a time when his means were scanty indeed ("Milton," 206).

Without going into detail, Barbey broaches Milton's travels abroad. All the English, he remarks, have the seabird's urge to roam. Milton was no exception. In Barbey's essay, there is nothing to indicate that the journey might have had an educational purpose. Barbey does not mention the brief stint in France, nor does he attach much importance to the experience of having been in Italy. Alluding to Mme de Staël's *Corinne*, he asserts that, unlike that novel's hero Oswald, this British traveler did not find love there. His Puritan heart, even if he had done so, would not have known how to cope with such a tender emotion. As far as can be determined, he never experienced romantic love. And yet, a handsome youth, he had been able to inspire it. After all, there is that anecdote about the Italian girl visiting Cambridge University. Seeing him asleep on the grass, she paused, slipped some verse into his hand, and fled. Quoting some of the lines, Barbey would seem to be taking Amédée Pichot's charming novelette as an account of something that really happened.[8] If Milton inspired love, though, he could not and did not return it. Barbey had shown his readers a schoolboy prematurely turning into a pedant. Not much later, again prematurely, he turned into a Puritan as well. Cutting off his magnificent hair, "Milton, ce beau jeune homme qui ensorcelait les femmes," became a dour sectarian. This, too, should have been contrary to his nature, but he did it anyway and learned to calm his passions, if they can be called that. Love was something Milton did not need, Barbey holds, possibly something he did not want. He married, but marriage brought him no spiritual rewards. "Marié trois fois successivement, il fut malheureux par sa première femme, qui l'abandonna, et les deux autres ne lui constituèrent que le vulgaire bonheur du pot au feu et des chemises reprisées." Only by indirection does the critic suggest that, if these domestic relationships were arid, it was because the poet made them so. Nothing is said about a "late espoused saint."

The poet was no luckier with his children, in whom he failed to inspire love. In a study on Edgar Allen Poe, Barbey observes that in later life Milton at least had his daughters to comfort him. Quickly, he corrects himself. "Il est vrai que dernièrement on a dit, contrairement à la vieille légende, qu'elles furent de petites parricides de tous les jours au logis . . . , dans tous les menus détails de l'intimité domestique."[9] Whether the critic knew how many daughters there were is uncertain. In any event, Barbey says, Milton managed to alienate them. No doubt they felt abused. Forcing them to read languages they did not understand must have seemed barbarian to them. How could they have loved a father whose religion made him so austere, so forbidding? In that religion there was no unction, nothing but "une horrible sainteté, qui n'a rien ni de saint François de Sales ni de Fénelon" ("Milton," 209–10). Here as elsewhere, one sees the critic's recurrent theme, that the poet's environment, emotionally sterile, had nothing to do with what, as an artist, he created.

According to Barbey's interpretation, Milton never realized what his real vocation was. He seems to have believed that he came into the world to serve the Commonwealth and Cromwell, to whom he was "sombrement dévoué." Politically, he was ambitious. This was his compensation for being a genius, which by itself might not have led to any rewards. "Homme politique universellement respecté dans une société ardemment et fougueusement politique, il avait été le secrétaire intime du grand homme qui gouvernait alors l'Angleterre, . . . la main au bout du rude bras de Cromwell" (*Littérature étrangère*, 394–95). He got involved in religious and political bickering. England was being torn asunder by controversies of all kinds. Sublimating his true nature— which somehow survived it all—Milton leaped in, raising questions and taking positions that, for him, were manifestations of his own brand of virtue, even heroism. Having eluded human love, he espoused the passions of his time, giving himself over to polemics. To do this, he had to put his creative drives on hold, but this he knew how to handle, since he had learned to subdue even more tender inclinations. Still, he was sacrificing his real persona to an artificial one. "Lui, l'ancien chantre du *Comus* et du 'Penseroso,' il ne courbait pas seulement son génie poétique, dont il devait être sûr, devant un génie théologique qu'il n'avait pas, mais il alla jusqu'à vouloir écraser l'un par l'autre." The poet in him did not succumb, but the severe, doctrinaire publicist did his best to kill him ("Milton," 212).

Barbey d'Aurevilly was a polemicist himself, more urbane than Milton but just as energetic, just as redoubtable. In the nineteenth century he denounced his antagonists in the name of religious and political conservatism. Two centuries earlier, John Milton had done it in the name of puritanical republicanism. That Barbey felt little empathy for the positions his predecesssor had taken goes without saying. In scorning the masses, though, he agreed with Milton. An ardent monarchist, Barbey did not approve of democratic systems. The masses, with their little minds getting even smaller whenever they congregate, made him think of the shrinking devils in Pandemonium. "Je ne suis point partisan des masses," he acknowledges.[10] This could have come straight out of *The Ready and Easy Way to Establish a Free Commonwealth*. Revolution, since it was a rejection of authority, bothered the critic in much the same way the masses did. Inevitably it gets out of hand and leads to "un combat à outrance," he had observed in an article in *La Mode* on 7 July 1850. This is not to say that a rebel, especially a rebel leader, cannot be great. The leader may be wrong but can command admiration nonetheless. "Satan est grand," for instance (*Littérature étrangère*, 327–28).

This does not vitiate the critic's basic contention that Milton's polemical work can be dismissed. In Barbey's opinion, the treatises, the diatribes, the rebuttals do not count. Nothing in them helps elucidate *Paradise Lost*. And were it not for *Paradise Lost*, the dour roundhead, Cromwell's secretary, Saumaise's wrangling, determined opponent, the republican saint would have been forgotten. But *Paradise Lost* in some measure valorizes them because, with his epic, the "puritain en habit gris," the "vieux théologien aveugle ... près de sa porte ouverte, aux derniers rayons du soir, se fixe en immortalité" ("Milton," 213). Whatever worth the pamphlets have derives from their authorship, nothing else. *De Doctrina Christiana* would not have assured Milton a place in the history of literature. As with the pamphlets, its sole importance lies in the fact that this "large manuscrit latin" was compiled by the author of *Paradise Lost*. Since it is "un manuscrit, oublié et authentique, d'un grand homme," one needs to know that it exists, but in itself it has little value. The work "ne nous intéresse un peu que parce qu'elle est de l'auteur du *Paradis perdu*." Whether Milton was "orthodoxe ou hétérodoxe, trinitaire ou unitaire," is of little consequence ("Milton," 202, 213). The book's possible application to problems arising out of *Paradise Lost* apparently does not occur to the critic. Comparing Milton to Dante and Lamartine at one point, Barbey insists that, in all three cases, the men's greatness rests not upon their historical or political writing but rather upon their poetry. Dante is not remembered for *De Monarchia*, nor will Lamartine be remembered for the *Histoire des Girondins*. Milton, likewise, will not be remembered for his prose.[11] Presumably, the poet's ideas as expressed in the prose work contribute no more to understanding *Paradise Lost* than does the environment in which it was conceived and written. Milton's controversies, which gave rise to the prose, simply do not show up in the epic. *Paradise Lost*, then, is Milton's great achievement, virtually his only one.

Barbey should have balked at Milton's Protestant bias in the poem, and he almost did so. If republican or democratic visionaries were not to his liking, neither were Protestants. "Un protestant ne peut jamais être poète," he went so far as to claim in 1865.[12] Protestantism has little about it, in essence, that is poetic. But Milton was a Protestant, and he was also a poet, an extraordinary one. Attempting to reconcile his categorical pronouncement with his deep admiration for the heretic poet, Barbey hit upon an ingenious way out of the dilemma. In Milton's work, he claims, it is not Protestantism that stands out. What dominates the poem rather is an Old Testament Jewish way of looking at things (*Les Philosophes et les écrivains religieux*, 271). Barbey's position is only partially true, but it allows a conservative critic to rationalize his intense admiration for an author, most of whose beliefs and causes were radically at odds with his own.

In keeping with his insistence that Milton was first and foremost a poet but that everything he did, apart from his verse writing itself, should have stifled his talent, Barbey notes what seems to him a curious feature of Milton's artistic career: the protracted interruption, after which the poet picked up where he had left off. That Milton was able to do this was because, no matter what else he did, he was essentially a poet and nothing could destroy that. Barbey notes that Milton began writing poetry at a rather early age. Then came a tumultuous hiatus, followed by a return, rather late in life, to poetic creativity. In the critic's words,

> La vocation poétique de Milton fut révélée par ses premières œuvres de jeunesse, mais elle fut arrêtée et suspendue par toute une vie de travaux et de préoccupations contraires. Et cependant elle éclata, à la fin, quand personne n'y pensait plus, par cette détonation foudroyante du *Paradis perdu* qui remplissait, quelques années après la mort du poète, tous les échos de l'Angleterre. Les poètes poussent partout, quand ils sont vigoureux, mais aucun poète sous le tournant du soleil ne l'a mieux prouvé que Milton, et on peut l'étudier comme un véritable phénomène de végétation poétique, ce chêne de rocher que rien, rien n'a pu empêcher de devenir, à l'âge où les hommes les plus forts se cassent, le rouvre du *Paradis perdu*. ("Milton," 208)

> [Milton's true vocation was revealed in the poet's earliest works, but it was arrested and suspended by a whole lifetime of contrary preoccupations and labors. And yet it burst forth at last, when no one was thinking about it anymore, with the thunderous explosion of *Paradise Lost*, which, a few years after the poet's death, reverberated throughout England. Poets spring up anywhere, when they are vigorous, but no poet under the sun proved it better than Milton, who can be studied as a true phenomenon of poetic vegetation, this rock oak that nothing, nothing could keep from

becoming, at an age when the strongest men bend and break, the even sturdier oak of *Paradise Lost*.]

Bursting into bloom so close to the end of the poet's life, his great epic could be compared to a "rose née sur une tombe entr'ouverte" ("Milton," 212).

As French critics have always done, Barbey d'Aurevilly finds Satan compelling. He does not like the other devils, but, as we have seen, he admires Satan, the rebel angel par excellence. Barbey believes it would be a mistake, however, to think that Milton, though a rebel himself, was depicting his own impulses and attitudes in this magnificent, recalcitrant character. Despair drove Satan to be what he was; Milton felt no despair. In his debates and controversies he had been in his element. "Satan, cet insurgé du ciel qu'il peignit si bien, ce révolté et ce désespéré sublime, ce n'est pas Milton. Ce n'est pas dans son âme... qu'il en a trouvé les accents" ("Milton," 211). Satan, with all his brilliance, was something the poet invented. It was a spectacular invention, one that made Milton "le chantre de la révolte."[13] Similarly, the poet invented Eve, "la céleste et fragile mère du genre humain dans sa fleur," who could have owed nothing to the poet's own amorous or domestic experience ("Milton," 210).

Barbey d'Aurevilly's examination of Milton is highly personal. Though less flexible, it reflects a viewpoint much like that of Hilaire Belloc in more recent times. It is by no means balanced, but then it does not aspire to be. Disapproving of the education Milton was given, the critic makes no attempt to relate it to the poet's own pedagogical notions. He disdains Milton's learning, which he looks upon as cumbersome, a millstone around an artist's neck. It does not occur to him, obviously, that, without the erudition, the *Paradise Lost* he admires so much would not be what it is. Similarly, Barbey's dismissing Milton's political works as unreadable ephemera is troublesome. That Milton was a dogmatic theologian in some of his tracts does not mean that he ceased to be one when he wrote *Paradise Lost*. Some of the doctrine propounded elsewhere necessarily found its way into the epic or at least colored it. One must also take exception with one of the critic's main points, that Milton's life, public and private, did not leave its mark on *Paradise Lost*. Moreover, to Barbey, Milton became an austere zealot much earlier than most French critics of his generation seemed to think. That Milton deliberately cut off his marvelous hair is an odd touch. He "rasa ses magnifiques cheveux bouclés," the critic believes. Just as deliberately, the poet throttled his ability to experience love. Long before *Paradise Lost* came into being, its author had made himself impervious to such an emotion. "Rigidifié et durci par le puritanisme, on ne lui connut jamais d'amour. Ses passions furent toujours austères, quand il en eut, et il les dompta" ("Milton," 210). As Barbey sees it, Milton's writing convincingly about love merely denotes a powerful imagination at work. Barbey does not talk about the divorce tracts, not even to compare or contrast them with attitudes toward love and marriage in *Paradise Lost*.

Reading Barbey's comments, one is surprised that *Paradise Regained* and *Samson Agonistes* draw no attention. Almost as surprising is the critic's apparent view that Milton ceased writing poetry during the Civil Wars and Commonwealth. No sonnets are mentioned, not even those addressed to public figures, and the possibility that *Paradise Lost* may have been started at this time is not explored. Barbey is convinced that during the political interlude Milton renounced his poetic vocation, even tried to smother it. If he returned to it in later life, it was because he had not succeeded in killing it and because, having lost his government position when the republican adventure collapsed, there was nothing left for him to do but write poetry. Fortunately so, the critic holds, since, in returning to his true calling, he endowed world literature with a masterpiece that is little short of miraculous. Barbey's enthusiasm was shared by another Catholic writer of the period, Léon Bloy, who calls *Paradise Lost* one of "les spectacles les plus splendides pour l'intelligence humaine," one of "ces impérissables merveilles d'équilibre et de statique intellectuelle dans la plus bouillonnante inspiration qui fut jamais."[14]

Barbey's Milton criticism stands out for several reasons. To Barbey, Milton was the author of *Paradise Lost* and little else. Discarding the prose, religious and political, that this "controversiste infatigable" turned out would be no loss. Though a skilled polemicist himself, the critic did not have even a connoisseur's interest in his predecessor's work. Not without surprise, one notes his belief that Milton harbored political ambitions. Barbey's most adamant pronouncements, no doubt, are those having to do with whether the poet's life and surroundings influenced his great epic. Barbey emphatically denied that there was a connection. Milton's comfortable childhood, his education, his travels, his polemic battles left no traces on *Paradise Lost*. Another of Barbey's surprises is the contention that, during his career as a pamphlet writer, Milton consciously sought to destroy his poetic gift, a curious viewpoint. Barbey held that *Paradise Lost* should be read for what it is, an exquisite artistic creation, and for its originality as well, for Milton was "l'originalité victorieuse et immaculée, indestructible et immortelle" ("Milton," 207). At the end of his life, Milton could not know how future generations would assess his work. He only knew that his contemporaries shunned him. In this respect, Barbey compares him to Lamartine, likewise poor and deserted in his old age. Lamartine was saddened by his poverty, but it made him like Homer and Milton (*Les Critiques ou les juges jugés*, 355). Milton's fate also reminded the critic of Ernest Hello, a French Christian novelist. Like Milton, the novelist has remained alone and unnoticed in an era that does not believe. Barbey hopes that the modern writer can accept his contemporaries' neglect, as did the "grand poète du *Paradis perdu*, qui prit son mâle parti de l'obscurité" (*Les Critiques ou les juges jugés*, 403).

9
Alexandre Rodolphe Vinet

Alexandre Rodolphe Vinet (1797–1847) was born in Crassier, in Switzerland. The family had been French Protestant and had settled in Switzerland two generations earlier. As one writer has observed, Alexandre Vinet was French not only by language but also by viewpoint. According to this source, to the land of his forebears he owed "le sentiment exquis des qualités propres à la langue française, la mesure, la finesse, la justesse, et cette implacable logique de l'esprit qui va jusqu'aux dernières conséquences d'un principe."[1] It was an attribute he shared with John Milton. Vinet studied and taught theology, but he is best remembered for his literary criticism, a domain in which his insights were introspective and deep. Though dating from the romantic period, his critical studies reveal his placid, unswerving moderation in writing about literature. Vinet was Professor of Practical Theology at the University of Lausanne, where on occasion he also lectured on French literature.

On the surface of it, what Alexandre Vinet had to say about John Milton and *Paradise Lost* was written as a response to Chateaubriand's *Paradise Lost* translation, which came out in 1836. Vinet's discussion was published in *Le*

Semeur in three parts, on 30 November 1836, 25 January 1837 and 15 April 1837. The translation was a pretext, and the extended review turned out to be a series of articles on Milton. Remarking that the translator, presumably in the *Essai sur la littérature anglaise*, had brought to life the period in which the poet lived and wrote, Vinet declared at the outset that it would be impossible for him not to talk about the author of *Paradise Lost*.[2] He confined his remarks to the epic, which he proposed to examine from both the literary and religious standpoints. We need to keep in mind that our guide was both a theologian and a literary critic and was eminently qualified to do this. In his first two articles, dealing with *Paradise Lost* as literature and then as a profession of faith, there is considerable overlapping, and the two aspects will be considered together. The third article, which need not concern us here, evaluates the translation as such. Obviously Vinet knew English quite well. Going into the intricacies involved, he awarded the translator, with some reservations, rather high marks for his achievement. Vinet early on reminded his readers that the poet had been translated many times but that "bien peu de personnes" had read his great epic. Not all periods have been able to appreciate it. Not even the best critics have succeeded in making it come to life and keeping it alive, despite the efforts of Charles Delalot, "homme d'un goût exquis, dont la critique était à la fois de la philosophie et du sentiment, passionné à la fois pour le beau antique et pour le beau chrétien." But Delalot had been premature; the public had not understood his message. What Chateaubriand's translation did was make the real John Milton and his epic accessible to French readers (Vinet, 440–42).

Vinet took note of the fact that the young writers of his day aspired to go back to what he terms the "primitive." It did not occur to them, he says, that the period in which they live has made them much too old for such an undertaking. "Ils ne sentent pas les soixante siècles qui pèsent sur eux." Lamartine had tried it with a certain success in "La poésie sacrée." Vinet does not summarize the poem, which deals largely with the world and the creation of humankind, the disobedience, the punishment and the promised redemption. In Lamartine's words,

> Sept fois de Jéhovah la parole féconde
> Se fit entendre au monde.
> Et sept fois le néant à sa voix répondit;
> Et Dieu dit: Faisons l'homme à ma vivante image.
> Il dit, l'homme naquit; à ce dernier ouvrage
> Le Verbe créateur s'arrête et s'applaudit![3]

Man and woman disappoint their maker. Since God is "clément dans sa rigueur," fallen humankind can now only lament and hope. Despite his talent, which is very real, Lamartine still does not make his readers feel that they are looking at the newborn world and its first inhabitants, man and woman. The poem cannot be compared to the art that went into *Paradise Lost*,

> à cette divination qui retrouve les premières bases de tout ce que nous éprouvons, à cette puissance qui, nous séparant de tous les siècles que nous avons vécus, nous reporte d'un élan jusqu'à notre point de départ, à cette éloquence qui nous rend les vraies voix, les sons primitifs de notre nature, l'accent majestueux et ingénu de l'homme, alors que pour la première fois il rencontra son auteur dans l'univers et soi-même dans sa conscience....
>
> [to that divination that reveals the basic sources of all that we experience, to that power which, isolating us from all the centuries we have spent on earth, carries us straight back to our point of departure, to that eloquence that gives us back the true voices, the primitive sounds of our nature, man's candid, majestic speech when, for the first time, he encountered his author in the universe and himself in his consciousness....]

In this kind of thing, Milton is superior even to Homer (Vinet, 443). Nothing is more appealing than poetry that combines cumulative modern knowledge with a feeling for human existence as it must have been at the dawn of time. The inherent contrast lends charm to literature. Milton was a master of this, Vinet declares, but his successors have not been able to emulate him (Vinet, 444).

Pursuing his comparison of *Paradise Lost* with modern poetry as he conceived it, Vinet asserts that the latter has become enamored of shadow, phantom, abstraction. In it one sees "les réalités compactes se résoudre en brouillard perméable, les existences en rêve, et les idées s'emparer de la place des choses." Vinet can understand and appreciate this, but he considers it a misconception, "la poésie prise à l'envers." The result is a desolate universe. To its dark pantheism he much prefers Milton's sublime light and genuine religion (Vinet, 447). Milton's approach had been totally different from modern practice. In *Paradise Lost*, concepts, however nebulous and abstract, took on attributes that allow one to perceive them as realities:

> L'âme cherchait à se faire jour par des images; l'invisible, à leur aide, se rendait visible, l'abstrait palpable, et, sur les traces du langage humain, qui n'est tout entier qu'un vaste poème dans ce même sens, la poésie matérialisait tout dans le seul dessein de rendre tout sensible, de même que, dans une sphère infiniment plus haute, la religion s'était faite anthropomorphiste pour être humaine et la divinité même s'incarnait afin de nous sauver. (Vinet, 446)

> [The spirit strove to reveal itself through images; the invisible, using these, made itself visible, the abstract tangible, and, coming on the heels of human speech, which is nothing but a vast poem in this very sense, poetry gave physical form to everything for the sole purpose of making everything perceivable through the senses, just as in an infinitely loftier sphere religion had become anthropomorphic in order to be human and the godhead itself became incarnate so as to redeem us.]

Poetic art is not likely to retrace its steps, but its modern practitioners nonetheless need to bear in mind that art has some features that do not change with time. "L'art a quelques conditions immuables, parce qu'il y a dans l'homme lui-même, vraie moule de l'art, des caractères également immuables" (Vinet, 448). For *Paradise Lost* Milton chose basic human characters and situations. Later poets, attempting this in their own work, have missed the mark. "Comparés à Milton, ils n'ont attaqué leur sujet qu'obliquement et par des faces plus ou moins étroites. Des traits énergiques et purs dessinent chez eux, par quelque côté important, le sexe et l'âge, la grandeur et la misère, la joie et la douleur, quelquefois l'homme, séparé de toutes ces circonstances et considéré dans sa seule opposition avec tout ce qui n'est pas lui." Sometimes they manage to show us a man and a woman and, with luck, they may even show us universal humankind. They would be unable to show us Adam and Eve (Vinet, 444, 446). Such skill is probably extinct. Milton's achievement would be impossible in the nineteenth century, Vinet believes.

But there is more to the achievement than this. The poet found his topic, his characters and the action in "la région du mystère," "au sein même de l'infini," and thus set himself an incredible task. First of all, he situated his narrative in an absolute world devoid of reference points. Next he chose only two human beings as actors, recruiting the rest of his characters from the heavenly sanctuary and the infernal abyss. Then he made his plot revolve around a dogma, one of the most baffling in all of religion. From this a modern writer would have extracted either a theological tract or a metaphysical elegy. Not so John Milton. With these elements he created "une épopée plus vivante, plus riche en vraies individualités que toutes les épopées, un drame plus rempli de mouvement que tous les drames, en un mot le poème à la fois le plus *plastique*... et le plus intime." Vinet argues that Milton could do this because his was the most extraordinary mind that ever applied itself to the writing of poetry (Vinet, 448–49). Not even reason deterred him. Like John Bunyan, writing *Pilgrim's Progress* at the same time, he was above such considerations, and this his era understood. Bunyan did not disdain now and then to introduce an incoherent allegory. Milton, wishing to give his poem color and substance and wishing at the same time to make his ideas as concrete as possible, used everything that has happened since the world's creation to bring that first moment in time to life. If to do this he had to use anachronisms, he used them. In short, he had to "animer les idées de ce premier jour par des allusions logiquement impossibles," and he had to "emprunter des images à la mythologie même." The alternative would have been to "demeurer abstraite et incorporel."

To put across his basic truth, Milton in some cases had to fly in the face of logic. Up to a point, criticism is perhaps justified in holding him responsible for this, Vinet concedes. On the other hand, the poem could not have been written if Milton had not done so. Clearly, the problem does not bother Alexandre Vinet. As he phrases it, "Il s'agissait pour le poème *d'être ou de ne pas être."* Without the anticipations and even anachronisms, there would be no *Paradise Lost.* These flaws, if that is what they are, do not account for the poem's beauty, needless to say. However, they did give the poet a freedom of action that he needed and that he would not have had otherwise, permitting him to "faire éclater, dans les différentes parties de sa composition, ce génie vraiment poétique, cet esprit de création et de vie qui le distingue si éminemment" (Vinet, 449–50).

Style, Vinet holds, consists of description, characterization and speech. The critic proposes to look at all three in *Paradise Lost*. Milton excelled in each. Most people would consider description the least important, but be that as it may, Milton is such a master in this area that his place in literature would be assured even had he been less successful in bringing his characters to life. Milton describes people and places both from without and within, much depending upon contrast. In his descriptions there is order, precision and decisiveness. To use Milton's own expression, he even makes "darkness visible" (Vinet, 450–51). Things that readers would find it hard to conceive of are made accessible to the senses through allusions and comparisons within the domain of human experience. When Milton leads his readers "dans des lieux ou dans des situations dont la nature actuelle et la vie humaine ne peuvent nous donner l'idée, il rapproche de nous ces objets par d'heureuses allusions aux objets qui nous sont connus, par des comparisons" (Vinet, 451). Even Hell and the devils' activities become plausible when linked to the wonders of nature, destined to "éclairer, à humaniser, pour ainsi dire, l'objet infernal et à procurer à l'âme épouvantée une douce diversion." And Vinet cites the demons' reactions after one of their conclaves, with allusions to rain, snow, "radiant sun," and happy birds and sheep (*PL* 2.486–95). Along with this, Milton takes care not to scatter his readers' impressions or disconcert their faculties. The elusive and the material, the image and the idea are kept distinct. Readers can turn their attention to the one and then the other, but they are not expected to contend with both at the same time. The "terrible" allegory of Sin and Death is no exception. It addresses the problem of concept and representation "avec la dernière audace et le résout avec la dernière puissance. Depuis le jour où Homère composa d'un triple carreau la foudre de Jupiter, jamais allégorie religieuse n'avait rien tenté de si grand ni rien exécuté de si parfait" (Vinet, 451–52).

Returning elsewhere to his idea of the concrete as opposed to the abstract, Vinet describes Milton's poetry as *positive*. To explain his attitude, he adds that "la poésie de Milton affirme; elle exprime des êtres; elle individualise, elle incarne ses idées; elle est pleine de courage, elle a foi en elle-même." Modern poets would do well to follow their predecessor's example. Whether they do or not, *Paradise Lost* survives to raise the banner of the true and the beautiful, "l'enseigne du vrai et du beau," in order to encourage and console the believer who has to make his way in the confused world in which we now live (Vinet, 458–59).

From this Vinet goes on to characterization. Here Milton, again, was more than equal to the task. All of the characters in the epic are unusual; some are even colossal. As in the case of his descriptions, however, the poet presented them in a manner that ordinary human beings could understand. Adam and Eve, the celestial and demonic creatures are more "human," so to speak, than are the characters in the *Iliad* and *Gerusalemme liberata*. What the characters are supposed to do in the poem does not determine what they are like. None can be said merely to represent an idea; each stands out as a personality. This gives the poem dramatic interest. All a reader expects in the poem is philosophical and religious interest. We must not forget, however, that a true epic needs to be dramatic. The dramatic element, very real in *Paradise Lost*, adds another dimension, making the poem an epic.

For the characters to be real, they must speak, of course. To reveal their motivations and passions, they have to do this often. Thus, speeches are necessary. Milton realized this and acted accordingly. If he is eloquent when speaking in his own name, Vinet feels, he is much more so when he lets his characters express themselves in their own words. As they talk, they tell us unerringly who and what they are. The poet "fait parler ses personnages avec une suprême convenance; et, dans le moindre de leurs discours, il a mis ce qui constitue essentiellement l'éloquence et ce qui fait la première vertu du style, *le mouvement*." Eloquence is the product of "soul" and "movement," the critic goes on to say (Vinet, 453–55). Vinet follows with something of a digression on these, at the end of which he concludes that Milton's verse is written with "soul," that it is limpid and natural, with pauses built in to make its pace uneven and interesting.

> Milton est beau de bien des manières; son expression est tour à tour majestueuse, profonde, gracieuse, naïve, mais ses paroles ne sont pas plus belles que les intervalles de ses paroles; ce n'est pas dans ses phrases seulement, c'est entre ses phrases que je l'admire; et la plus sublime de ses images n'est pas plus sublime que tel passage, telle transition, tel détour de sa parole dans les discours dont il a semé son poème. (Vinet, 455–58)

> [Milton is admirable in many ways; his manner of expressing himself is in turn majestic, profound, charming, simple, but his words are no more admirable than the pauses between those words; it is not merely in his sentences that I admire him; and the most sublime of his images is no more sublime than this, that or the other passage, transition, or new direction in his discourse seen in the various speeches he has planted in his poem.]

Thus even the speeches in *Paradise Lost* reveal the poet's mastery of style and here, as elsewhere, command admiration.

What about God's speeches? Pushing his source material to its limits, Milton was perhaps too anthropomorphic, according to some. In *Paradise Lost,* Vinet admits, God talks too much. Milton has been compared in this respect to Friedrich Klopstock, who was more discreet; Klopstock's God makes fewer speeches. When He does speak, not many words are spoken, but these are solemn and worldshaking. Often the divine will is communicated through a kind of superangel. Milton is more direct, more practical. His God talks and talks often, but the poet's respect and even awe are much in evidence at all times. If having the Father speak is bold, the poet's reverence is never in doubt. God does not sound like a mortal, notes the critic. What He says, in any case, comes straight out of the Bible, now and then somewhat modernized.

> La forme peut sembler plus moderne, l'exposition du dogme plus systématique qu'elles n'apparaissent dans la Bible; mais le fond est biblique au dernier degré. Rien d'anxieux d'ailleurs, rien de péniblement littéral dans cette orthodoxie chrétienne professée de si haut; l'expression, toujours large, pleine, libre, respire la souveraineté de Celui dont la pensée est la substance même de la vérité et dont la parole est vraie par cela seul qu'elle est sa parole.
>
> [The form may seem more modern, the expounding of dogma more systematic than they appear in the Bible; but the basic material is as biblical as it can be. However, there is nothing unsettling, nothing painfully literal in this Christian orthodoxy so loudly professed; the expression, always broad, ample, free, testifies to the sovereignty of the One whose thought is the very substance of truth and whose word is true for the very reason that it is His word.]

To Vinet this is demonstrated, for instance, in the Father's speech just before the Son volunteers to redeem humankind (Vinet, 464–69; *PL* 3.168–202).

Making the Son speak was fraught with even greater dangers, the critic believes. The Son, after all, was at once deity and mortal, a being whom we both worship and view as a brother. Putting words into the mouth of such an entity would seem an impossible task. Yet Vinet feels that Milton achieved it without discarding verisimilitude or piety. The Son is made to utter words that "on ne peut même transcrire sans un indicible saisissement." An example would be those proposing to go to earth to reconcile human beings with their creator (Vinet, 469–71; *PL* 3.227–71). Consonant with such speeches are the things said *about* this divine intercessor and this "sublime tendresse." Again Milton's devout intent cannot be called into question. "La contempler, la dépeindre semble être le délice du poète, l'objet de son travail, le prix de ses peines." Vinet quotes the poet's comment after the Son has announced to Adam and Eve their punishment (*PL* 10.209–23).

After God and the Son, the critic examines how the poet conceived and presented the devils. If such a thing could be envisioned, the devils might be described as "l'homme dans la perfection du péché." In *Paradise Lost* they are "les diverses images de l'humanité pécheresse, se glorifiant dans sa chute, se faisant un empire de son péché." Milton could only make his devils human, each representing a particular human vice depicted in its most quintessential state. In Adam and Eve sin was to be shown as incipient. The demons, on the other hand, had to represent evil that has matured and developed, not only knowing what it is but reveling in it. With the devils, Milton was detailing nascent human sin after it has taken over people's lives. Thus the poet gave "au péché dans les démons les mêmes caractères et les mêmes conséquences qu'au péché dans la vie humaine." Despite what each represents, the devils have their own individualities. We must bear in mind that they are people, after all. Reading *Paradise Lost,* "nous croyons avoir vu des démons et nous avons vu des hommes." Milton's devils make us realize what the world would be like if sin ruled it unchecked. The devils try to convert others to sin, but then, so does the human person. "Le mal, comme le bien, est expansif." Sin's very nature entails a need to proselytize. Vinet does award the devils a plus in one respect, however. In *Paradise Lost* they stand out as the only characters who express any curiosity regarding "les mystères de l'existence et les secrets incommunicables de la divinité" (*PL* 2.555–69). Vinet appears to forget Adam's desire

.... to know
Of things above his world, and of their being
Who dwell in Heav'n ....
(Vinet, 473–74).

And what about Satan, the devils' leader? He is the only demon in which one senses a pleasure other than evil, an emotion other than sin. Unlike his cohorts, he has multiple dimensions, Vinet points out. Unlike them, he is dramatic, poetic. None of the others is capable of hating as he does. His hatred dominates him much more than his pride. But if he hates, it is because he is still capable of feeling, such as remorse and even pity. "Il reste dans l'âme de Satan un coin lumineux. . . . Quelque chose en lui se révolte contre sa déchéance; il a un profond souvenir, un regret amer du ciel." This nostalgia, turning into fury, makes him stand out among the others and drives him onward (Vinet, 473—75).

Vinet also takes a look at how the poet characterized Adam and Eve. Their characterization, as with the devils, is bound up with the notion of sin. To begin with, sin is possible only because of an individual's awareness of self. This awareness, with the desires it gives rise to, sets in motion the conditions that lead the individual to break human and divine laws. Milton realized this, and his account of the first sin is based on it. In conceiving his plan, he was careful, however, to avoid philosophical abstractions. Instead he showed us two sinners, quite distinct from each other but nevertheless representing the universal human race "dans toute la généralité de son être, dans toute la suite de ses générations, dans toute la majesté de sa collective infortune." Showing the fall as he did, the poet has made all readers contemplate their inner lives and indeed their moral existences, causing them to visualize while in this world a richer life and, for the world to come, an even richer one. In *Paradise Lost*, the first humans were unknowing and innocent before their downfall (Vinet, 476–79). After the fall, they were given the means to see what they could attain if, repentant, they persevered,

la vertu naissant avec le péché; la lutte succédant à la paix; la tranquille possession du royaume faisant place à ce nouvel ordre où la possession, selon la parole évangélique, n'est promise qu'à la violence... des soupirs, des prières, et des sacrifices; enfin la bénigne chaleur de la miséricorde fécondant au sein de notre nature la semence amère du repentir, et l'homme, humble conquérant de son héritage, d'un meilleur Eden que celui qu'il a perdu; le tableau sommaire de l'humanité, de la société, telles que le péché les a faites et telles que la vérité les remue et les modifie: voilà les vérités que développe et qu'anime, profond tour à tour, sublime et délicat, mais vrai et sérieux toujours, le biblique génie de notre grand poète. (Vinet, 479–80)

[virtue being born with sin; struggle coming on the heels of peace; the calm possession of the kingdom giving way to this new order in which possession, according to the divine word, is promised only to the violence... of sighs, prayer, and sacrifice; finally the blessed warmth of mercy fertilizing the bitter seed of repentance in our bosoms; and man, the humble conqueror of his inheritance, of a better Eden than the one he lost; the summary picture of humanity, of society, as sin has made them and as truth reworks and modifies them: these are the truths, in turn deep, sublime, and delicate but always true and serious, that the biblical mind of our great poet brings to life and develops.]

All who read *Paradise Lost* see and hear themselves in the conversations of the unhappy but fortunate couple, says Vinet. Trembling at their dangers, terrified at their fall, sharing their heartrending despair, we realize that their problems and choices are our own. Watching them, we conclude that their repentance, hope and consolation can be ours. This done, we can ask with Adam:

What better can we do, than to the place
Repairing where he judg'd us, prostrate fall
Before him reverent, and there confess
Humbly our faults, and pardon beg, with tears
Watering the ground, and with our sighs the air
Frequenting, sent from hearts contrite, in sign
Of sorrow unfeign'd, and humiliation meek.
(*PL* 10.1086–092)

What Milton preaches here is a positive religion, devoid of the ideas with which modern skepticism has sullied both humankind and religion. Here are the real foundations of social order in their primitive candor, Vinet continues. Along with everything else, men and women's mutual obligations, so distorted in the world of today, are carefully spelled out. All in all, the mind and spirit are revived when they contemplate "ces vérités graves et douces, qu'on ne peut s'empêcher, dès la première vue, de reconnaître et de saluer." If they could, societies today would do well to emulate the simple, chaste existence described in *Paradise Lost* before Adam and Eve discovered sin (Vinet, 481–82).

No one, the critic asserts, has ever doubted that *Paradise Lost* was intended as deeply serious. That Milton wrote his narrative in verse does not mean that he was seeking to ornament what he had to say. That was what Tasso did in *Gerusalemme liberata*. For Milton the poetry was inseparable from the message. "Elle est l'expression naturelle et intime de la vérité qu'il veut raconter." Thus the question does not arise here as to which is the more important, plan or form. Poet and Christian, both inspire one another in this poem. In it, art and faith are one and the same and, far from getting in each other's way, "se donnent la main dans la plus parfaite intelligence. Aucune épopée, aucun drame, ne présente au même degré cet imposant caractère." That the poet should have addressed himself to the Holy Spirit is as it should be (Vinet, 460–61). A little later Vinet would return to the Holy Spirit in another context.

Few epic poets have had less to invent than Milton, yet few have been more original, this critic argues. Taking his basic material from the Book of Genesis, Milton did with it what no other writer could have done. His originality arises from his having taken a simple truth, along with all of its conditions and consequences, and treating it with a poet's creative freedom, including "cette haute logique du génie toujours sanctionnée et jamais prévue par le bon sens." Changing nothing in the well-known narrative paradoxically enhanced his originality, just as tampering with it would have cast him adrift. In order for the poetic elements inherent in "la substance de ce grand récit" to take shape, Milton had to accept and believe it wholeheartedly. He did, and he produced a great poem. Still, he had to organize his material and bring it to life (Vinet, 461–62).

Vinet describes this as an enormous undertaking. In the hands of wise men, he says, the result would have been metaphysical. In audacious hands it would have been tasteless and farfetched. To make *Paradise Lost* credible, Milton had to proceed exactly as he did. To alter or suppress any circumstance or episode whatsoever in the poem would undermnine its coherence. For example, if God's presence as a character were eliminated, there would be no poem. Likewise, if one substituted human errors and passions for Satan and his cohorts' gigantic drives and ambitions, the drama would be gone, "un drame immense, où ces passions mêmes que vous voudriez mettre en scène trouvent l'expression la plus vive dont elles soient susceptibles et que l'art leur ait jamais donnée." Similarly, Milton gives a religious, poetic account of woman's creation, her relationship with man, and her position in the world. If that were discarded, about all that would remain to justify her existence would be social necessity. If one eliminated the tree of the knowledge of evil, what would take its place? Whatever one invented, how could it be made to harmonize with the rest of the poem, assuming any of the poem still remained at this point? For revelation and the supernatural, what could be substituted? The absurd, the bizarre and the incoherent? Even if these pitfalls, with luck, could be avoided, the critic believes poetry would have been dispensed with as well (Vinet, 462–463).

Just as *Paradise Lost* has been criticized for its structure and content, the doctrinal views it expounds or seems to expound have come under fire. Vinet proposes to address one or two of these. Believing that Milton was "orthodox," Vinet cites his proof. There are those who have asserted that Milton looked upon Jesus as neither divine nor coeternal with the Father. The critic acknowledges that Milton complicated the matter, exposing himself to such an accusation. *Paradise Lost* tells its readers several times, to be sure, that Jesus was *begotten* or *created*, which implies that this took place after the beginning of things. Vinet counters by pointing out that, while still in Heaven, Jesus is said to be not only the Son of God but the Son of Man as well. This would appear to indicate that the Incarnation had already taken place and that the Son has always been with the Father, existing even before the mission on earth. In any event, Milton views Jesus as the "filial" divinity, which, however one looks at it, is divinity all the same. Presumably Vinet has in mind the poet's several allusions to the "filial godhead" (*PL* 3.269, 6.722, 7.175). Vinet could have added that in book 3, God "ordains" His Son's incarnation after the latter has volunteered to ransom humankind. Vinet could have cited other passages as well.

As this critic points out, it has also been claimed that Milton was an antitrinitarian. It is true that *Paradise Lost* is silent on the third person of the Trinity. In book 3, when the Father and the Son are being worshiped, the Holy Spirit is not even mentioned, and one notices the omission. On the other hand, the Holy Spirit is named and invoked in book 1 (*PL* 1.17). Likewise, the one time the Holy Spirit is mentioned in the first chapter of the Book of Genesis, Milton faithfully reproduces it in book 7 (*PL* 7.165, 235). Moreover, the Holy Spirit's deeds are acknowledged, invoked, recalled in the poem a hundred times. Finally, in book 12 Adam and Eve are told that

> The Spirit of God, prómis'd alike and giv'n
> To all believers..
> (*PL* 12. 519–20)

will be with them. Vinet is sure that John Milton was no heretic (Vinet, 463–64).

He was sure, too, that *Paradise Lost* was an admirable, imposing, realistic piece of literature. Concluding his discussion, he asked what general impression the poem could be expected to leave its readers. With Boileau, some no doubt would hold that "le diable toujours hurlant contre les cieux" is an inappropriate topic to start with. In any case, they are disappointed because it is a sad poem, based on a somber event. For those who feel no need to be consoled, it is indeed a sad poem, and there is no denying this. For others—and the critic declared himself one of them—*Paradise Lost*, the "amère saveur du dénouement" notwithstanding, awakens the soul with "des chants d'espérance" and even joy. This effect is not due "à quelques parties riantes, à quelques recoins éclairés de cet immense tableau," but rather to something quite different. The ultimate joy that emanates from the epic is the consolation the poem brings to the reader who is prepared to accept its real message (Vinet, 482-83). Again, individuals who cannot see beyond their own sin, of which they are at once the authors and the victims and which they deny, *Paradise Lost* is disheartening. Such individuals see nothing but the dark side of the poem. But to the reader who understands what human beings and existence really are, *Paradise Lost* offers something totally different. "Celui qui trouve, dans le *Paradis perdu* comme dans la Bible, un but donné à sa vie, une lumière versée dans ses ténèbres et dans les ténèbres du genre humain, celui qui, s'estimant déchu, se sent glorieusement relevé, celui-là ressent à la lecture du *Paradis perdu* une joie grave et sainte, mais délicieuse, car le paradis perdu est pour lui le paradis retrouvé" (Vinet, 484-85). Vinet explains that we think of literature as being comic or serious, but as a rule even the works we consider funny are not really amusing. They merely reflect a society endeavoring to cope with its gigantic malaise. Milton offers wholesome relief; his masterpiece is serious, calm, serene (Vinet, 485-88).

> Ce poème, fondé sur la pensée chrétienne que la joie ne peut naître pour l'homme que du sein des larmes, nous présente le bonheur aux seules conditions possibles; et s'il nous défie d'en obtenir d'autres, s'il se rattache et nous ramène à de terribles souvenirs, ces souvenirs rehaussent la joie chrétienne en la rendant plus grave; et quoi qu'il en soit, ces souvenirs sont des faits, des réalités, qui ne s'effaceront pas devant nos illusions, des faits dont la trace subsiste dans la vie et dans les consciences, dont les conséquences se retrouvent sans cesse et qui opprimeront de leur poids les hommes du monde jusqu'à ce que la main qui a soulevé de dessus tant d'âmes

ce terrible fardeau, s'abaisse aussi sur eux pour les en délivrer. (Vinet, 488)

[This poem, based on the Christian idea that for mankind joy can only be born of tears, shows us happiness under the only circumstances possible; and if it defies us to find others, if it is bound up with terrible memories and leads us back to them, these memories heighten Christian joy by making it more sober; and, whatever the case, these memories are facts, realities, that will not vanish in the face of our illusions, facts that linger in our lives and consciousness, with inevitable results that show up at every turn and will weigh earthlings down until the hand that lifted this terrible burden from so many souls also reaches down to deliver them from it.]

Alexandre Vinet's articles deal only with *Paradise Lost*. By date of birth, the critic belonged to the romantic generation but was able, like Philarète Chasles on occasion, to look at romanticism with a detached eye. He never got carried away by nebulous concepts, always remaining objective in his approach to literature. He was also profoundly religious. His admiration for *Paradise Lost* was almost unbounded, but he had good reasons for liking the poem as much as he did. Quite simply, he regarded Milton as the greatest poet who ever lived, including Homer and Tasso. The speeches in *Paradise Lost* that have worried or irritated so many critics did not disturb this one, who considered them necessary to the characterization. Unlike any number of other commentators, Vinet viewed the poem as extraordinarily credible, its various conceptualizations and episodes indispensable to the whole.

Raising the question of the poet's religious orthodoxy, Vinet examined a few matters and then, to his own satisfaction at least, brushed aside the charge of heresy. In discussing religion in the poem, he did not look into the pamphlets, however. Nor did he talk about the times in which the poet lived, perhaps believing with Barbey d'Aurevilly that, when all is said and done, those issues contribute little to our understanding of *Paradise Lost*. For Vinet, *Paradise Lost* was not just a book for the English seventeenth century. Rather, it contains a durable lesson for all believers, whatever their nationality, whatever their era.

Along with the Bible, it is a guide. Using it helps readers cope with a world given over to wrong values, promoting their moral enrichment in this life and their salvation in the next one.

10

Alfred Mézières

Among French Milton critics, Alfred Mézières (1826–1915) marked a new approach. By the time Mézières came on the scene, romanticism was pretty much dead—except for Barbey d'Aurevilly, its almost sole active practitioner. Realism had taken hold. From this point on, literary criticism would discard sentiment and close its eyes to pathetic, misunderstood heroes, and its judgments would be more sober, more balanced than in the past. The historical approach, gone about with greater care than before, would take on added importance, and some critics would show a more serious interest in sources. Visiting Cambridge University, Mézières probably would not have tried to get a branch of the famous mulberry tree, as the sentimental Amédée Pichot did. In passing, he specifically warned his readers about the Pichot anecdote. Mézières thought romanticism had been a sterile movement, as we shall see. Avoiding it in his own evaluations, he neither praised extravagantly nor condemned out of hand, at least not often.

The son of a university professor, he decided to be one himself. He attended the Ecole Normale Supérieure and took his doctorate in 1853. The following year, having been appointed to the University of Nancy, he taught "foreign literature." Today he would be referred to as a comparative literature specialist. Called to the Sorbonne in 1861, he continued to teach comparative literature. He took active military duty at the time of the Franco-Prusssian War and had the disheartening experience of seeing his native province, Alsatia, incorporated into the new German Empire. He did not live to see the French take it back at the end of World War I. Choosing to remain in France after the war, Mézières resumed teaching at the Sorbonne. Some of his articles appeared in the prestigious *Revue des Deux Mondes*. Among his books are one each on Dante, Petrarch and Gœthe. Shakespeare interested him a great deal, and he wrote *Shakespeare, ses œuvres et ses critiques* (1860), *Prédécesseurs et contemporains de Shakespeare* (1863) and *Contemporains et successeurs de Shakespeare* (1864). He would mention one or two of Shakespeare's predecessors and successors in discussing Milton. Mézières was elected to the Académie Française in 1874. As a somewhat liberal republican, he later went into politics, like Edmond Scherer. In 1881 he entered the Chamber of Deputies.

Across the English Channel and elsewhere, the middle years of the nineteenth century produced some important Milton studies. Thomas Keightley's *Life, Opinions, and Writings of John Milton* came out in 1855. Close on its heels came an annotated edition of the poet's works, published in 1859. W. D. Hamilton's *Original Papers* also came out in 1859, as did David Masson's *Life of John Milton*, or rather its initial volume. At the same time, Hyde Clarke's biographical discoveries were appearing in the *Athenæum* and *Notes and Queries*. 1860 saw the publication of Gustav Liebert's *Milton*. The following year, on 10 and 25 February, Alfred Mézières added an article of his own to these new studies. His "La Jeunesse de Milton" was published in two issues of the *Revue Nationale et Etrangère*.[1] The article is a methodical look, detached but interested, at the poet's youth and earliest work. Specialized and forthright, it deserves to be considered in a study of Milton and his nineteenth century French critics. The biographical content, accurate enough, takes up much of the article but need not particularly concern us here. Milton's father, Mézières felt, had a great deal to do with his son's intellectual development. Encouraged by the older John Milton, the son grew up in a cultivated atmosphere, one in which music and theatre were cherished pastimes. There was reading as well. Young Milton learned ancient and modern languages. Precocious and eager, he did not have to be pushed. At Cambridge University, he was already writing. Mézières mentions several prolusions and quotes part of one in translation. A few lines from the sonnet on Shakespeare are quoted also.

Whereas many authors' earliest works have little merit, Milton's compositions do, according to Mézières. He points out that some of these juvenilia are in Latin, others in English. The Latin ones are sensitive and elegant and show "quelques traces de son puissant génie." More importantly, they bear witness to their author's temperament and character. They are not really remarkable, however (Mézières, 362). From the English verse, it is clear that the budding writer had a thorough knowledge of classical Latin poetry. "C'est en maniant la langue de Virgile et d'Horace que le poète s'est accoutumé à donner à son style poétique la précision de la prose, sans relentir pour cela l'élan de l'imagination. Il a appris, à l'école des Latins, la sobriété, cette qualité admirable des classiques que ne connaissaient ni Spenser, ni Fletcher, ni Massinger" (Mézières, 363). As for the early works themselves, it will be clear that several poems interest the critic much more than others. The coverage stops, in effect, with *Comus* and "Lycidas."

Mézières has great regard for Milton as a poet but considers him almost antipathetic as a human being. Viewed from a distance, Milton could be admired in some respects, but as a person he was not very likable. This became clear even in his student days. He allowed no one to tell him what to read, what studies to pursue. Morally and intellectually, he had a high opinion of himself and a rather low one of the other students. "La comparaison qu'il faisait nécessairement de sa conduite avec celle de ses condisciples développait en lui le sentiment de sa supériorité morale et intellectuelle, qu'il n'était déjà que trop porté à concevoir, par orgueil naturel." Proud and aloof, he was also intolerant. "Dur pour lui-même, il l'était aussi pour les autres, et la vertu qu'il s'imposait, il voulait la voir pratiquer par tous les hommes. Sans aucune pitié pour la faiblesse humaine, il suivait, avec une inflexible persévérance, la route qu'il s'était tracée, et il ne cachait pas son mépris pour ceux qui en choisissaient une autre," Mézières writes. Permitting no one to question the principles that regulated his life, Milton was at once "mystique et absolu, et, tandis que son imagination s'élançait dans le monde un peu vague des spéculations idéales, sa raison soumettait la réalité à un rigoureux examen." Milton, even as a young man, was thus both a dreamer and a rationalist. These contradictions were paralleled by others. On the one hand, he had a poet's talent and temperament; on the other, he was uncompromisingly dogmatic. On the threshold of life, he was a paradox in himself (Mézières, 371). He could not have been very pleasant company. Ending his article before Mary Powell came into Milton's life, the critic does not speculate about what the poet would have been like as a husband.

And yet Milton was capable of humor. Some French critics have deplored his clumsy humor in the prose works and have been dismayed by the puns and jokes in *Paradise Lost*. Mézières is not concerned with that, but he does mention the two epitaphs on Thomas Hobson, which no one else did. It was a cruel humor, perhaps, but the critic does not mind. He may have been struck by the lines in which the poet declares of the late coach driver, described as "obedient to the moon," that "his wain was his increase." Mézières calls the poems a clever paradox (Mézières, 368).

Not too many of the critic's contemporaries were interested in the earlier minor poems. Those who were, however, generally called attention to one or two that this critic does not—"On May Morning," for example. Most critics mentioned the sonnets, even when not discussing them. One they liked was "How Soon Hath Time," which Mézières does not cite. Likewise, he is not concerned with the Italian poems, which is a little surprising. Villemain and Chateaubriand had praised them. Unfortunately, even about the shorter poems he admires, Mézières often does not comment at great length.

Mézières points out that Milton's poetic skill developed quickly. This is not to say that the critic liked all of the early poems. As we shall see, there were those that he did not, or about which he had reservations. Milton's youthful poems in his native language reveal a precocious natural gift, but it was a gift that had been sharpened and trained by university study (Mézières, 365). "On the Death of a Fair Infant," the work of an intellectual, is a case in point. It is more than an occasional poem, however. Mézières believes that it reveals genuine sadness and shows that the poet was already a mystic who cannot "se résigner à l'idée de la mort absolue." Mézières has mixed reactions to the "Nativity Ode." He does not share Arthur Hallam's view that it was the most beautiful piece of lyric poetry in the English language. The "énumération un peu déclamatoire des divinités païennes, que la naissance du Christ met en fuite," he does not care for. On the other hand, the poem shows that, at a very tender age, Milton had discovered "le véritable accent de l'ode." He was the first of his compatriots to do so. One of the poem's real achievements is that it unites two qualities difficult to reconcile, lyricism and precision. This is especially true at the beginning of the poem, the critic feels (Mézières, 367).

The "Epitaph on the Marchioness of Winchester," Mézières decides, was serious, even noble, but devoid of emotion. No real grief appears to inform the exquisite lines. Ben Jonson's elegy on the same occasion, though less ornate and brilliant, is more touching. Mézières does not quote Jonson's conclusion, in which the poet declares that, in dying, the Christian

.... bruiseth then
The serpent's head: gets above death and sin
And, sure of Heaven, rides triumphing in.
(ll. 98–100)

The lines would have provided an allusion to *Paradise Lost*. Sir William Davenant also wrote a short poem on Lady

Winchester's death, but it is not mentioned here.

Mézières likes "L'Allegro" and "Il Penseroso." He points out, however, that the poems were not generally known in France. This he considers understandable enough, since there had been no good translation. Translating the poems would be problematical, in any case, he says. Rather than on their ideas, these little compositions depend for their charm on their delicate, subtle poetic expression, which would be hard to convey in translation. Thus the poems have remained inaccessible to most French readers. In France, as a result, they have stirred up little interest. What attention they have aroused, asserts the critic, is due to the fact that they were written by the author of *Paradise Lost*. These twin poems have their charm, though. In them the author "s'inspire des anciens, tout en restant fidèle aux traditions nationales." Milton combines ancient myth and the medieval *merveilleux populaire*. These pieces, unlike so many of the poems written while he was at the university, are not occasional pieces, as no particular circumstance produced them. No one died, for instance. Milton chose their topics, and thus it can be expected that, in the poems, he had something personal to say. And the poems are indeed personal statements, representing the two inclinations the author detected within himself at this stage in his life. The personal element in "L'Allegro" tells one a great deal about the poet as a very young man. His pleasures, "plus honnêtes que gais," were quite sober. Neither he nor his hero, in seeking entertainment, ever ventured to look for mirth. The hero is "plutôt un homme de bonne humeur qu'un homme jovial" (Mézières, 509–14).

Of the two poems, Mézières finds "Il Penseroso" the more interesting and provocative. Without going into detail, he compares it to Lamartine's "L'Isolement." The comparison is somewhat apt. The first of Lamartine's *Méditations poétiques*, "L'Isolement" is a quiet poem, with a pensive, somewhat sad aura about it. As in "Il Penseroso," a certain mood is evoked and exploited, and objects in nature occupy a significant place. One stanza will suffice to show the tone, as the poem's narrator states:

Au sommet de ces monts couronnés de bois
  sombres,
Le crépuscule encor jette un dernier rayon;
Et le char vaporeux de la reine des ombres
Monte, et blanchit déjà les bords de l'horizon.
                                    (ll. 9-12)

The atmosphere is similar, and the moon, obviously, is part of the décor. After setting the scene, the hero goes on to meditate, in a vague sort of way, about eternity.

Mézières digresses at this point in order to make another of his *rapprochements*. Here he observes that, in melancholy, Milton and the French romantics had found a common inspiration that served them well. "La mélancolie, qui nous a paru si nouvelle quand elle a revêtu une expression poétique au commencement de ce siècle, servait déjà de texte aux imaginations anglaises deux siècles auparavant." Even before Milton, melancholy was an established motif in English literature. To illustrate, Mézières cites Romeo before he meets Juliet. And there was Robert Burton's *Anatomy of Melancholy*, of course. Mézières also mentions Beaumont and Fletcher's *The Nice Valour* (1615 or 1616), which contains the song (3.3):

  Hence all you vaine Delights
  As short as are the nights,
    Wherein you spend your folly,
  Ther's naught in this life sweet
  If men were wise to see't
    But only Melancholy,
    O sweetest melancholy,

and so on.[2] Wondering why melancholy, as a literary theme, should have taken root in England long before it did so in France, the critic chalks it up to England's "ciel triste" and the people's seriousness.

Returning to Milton and the French romantics, Mézières sees a kinship but also a basic dissimilarity. If there is a pervasive sadness in "Il Penseroso," the same atmosphere—the same subdued, meditative ambiance—shows up in romantic literature, both in France and elsewhere. Even the accessories are the same. In a remarkable paragraph, Mézières points up the similarites:

> En lisant certaines parties du "Penseroso," on croit lire l'œuvre d'un romantique moderne. Rien n'y manque de ce qui est devenu, pendant quelques années, le thème habituel de la poésie, en France, en Allemagne, et en Angleterre, ni le pâle clair de lune, ni le chant du rossignol, ni le murmure lointain de la mer, ni les sombres édifices du moyen âge. Milton réunit dans cette petite pièce tous les éléments matériels de la mise en scène poétique dont nous avons eu de si nombreuses éditions. (Mézières, 513)
>
> [On reading certain parts of "Il Penseroso," one gets the feeling that he is reading the work of a modern romantic. Nothing is missing in what has become, lately, the standard theme of French, German, and English poetry, whether it be the pale moonlight, the nightingale's singing, the distant murmur of the sea, or the gloomy medieval buildings. In this little piece Milton brings together all the physical elements of the poetic setting of which we have been given so many editions.]

While Mézières likes "Il Penseroso," his attitude toward the romantics is clearly distant and rather disapproving. The romantics did indeed have a penchant for such décor items as the sea, the moon, a nightingale's warbling, and dark medieval buildings, whether "some high lonely tower" or "the studious cloister" with its "storied windows richly dight." These trappings are present in "Il Penseroso," it is true, but with a difference. A romantic hero, characteristically, wanders about in a setting like this, alienated and moping, lost in sterile meditation and oblivious to the real world around him. Not so in "Il Penseroso," where such things, far from being an end in themselves, are mere ornamentation and where the narrator, an active individual, is given to serious thought and aspires to wisdom. The atmosphere, says Mézières, is healthier. The Puritan author, a rationalist, would not have let it be otherwise:

> Seulement, entre les mains d'un puritain, le romantisme n'aboutit pas à ces conclusions énervantes et stériles. Il ne s'absorbe pas dans la contemplation oisive des merveilles

de la nature ou des œuvres de l'art, il ne détourne pas l'âme de l'activité pour la nourrir de vagues rêveries. La mélancolie dont s'enveloppe le poète n'est que l'ornement de sa pensée, et n'en fait ni le fond ni l'essence. Le "Penseroso" ne passe pas sa vie à soupirer ou à errer dans la campagne, comme une ombre plaintive: il agit. L'énergie d'un caractère viril perce sous la langueur des images poétiques. (Mézières, 513)

[Yet, in the hands of a Puritan, romanticism does not lead to these enervating, sterile conclusions. It does not absorb itself in the idle contemplation of the wonders of nature or works of art, it does not turn the soul from activity in order to feed it on vague reveries. The melancholy in which the poet drapes himself is but the adornment of his thought and is neither its basis not its essence. "Il Penseroso" does not spend his life sighing or wandering around the countryside like a plaintive ghost, he acts. Beneath the lassitude of the poetic images one detects the energy of a virile character.]

Perhaps Mézières overstates, but he makes a good point. Influences there were, but there is a difference, a very real one, between Milton and the French romantic poets. Mézières believes that, in "Il Penseroso," Milton's sadness could have been induced, an innocent luxury the poet was permitting himself. Mézières also believes that Milton could only have written the piece as a young man. Later the poet was to know what real sadness could be. Both in content and the manner in which the material is treated, there is "une sorte de sentimentalité qui trahit la jeunesse de l'auteur. Milton plus âgé eût été moins mélancolique. Il faut être jeune pour sentir et aimer la mélancolie, cette souffrance vague de ceux qui n'ont point encore souffert. Plus tard, les maux réels qu'apporte la vie ne laissent plus à l'homme la faculté de se créer une tristesse imaginaire" (Mézières, 513).

To Mézières, "Lycidas" had its flaws. It was an occasional poem, a *pièce de circonstance,* with all that entails. For one thing, too many literary conventions are at work in it for the poem to convey a feeling of deep sorrow. It appeared in a commemorative collection in which the student authors did their best to "tirer le meilleur parti possible d'un lieu commun." They did not cope with the problem too well, and the poems are stilted. "Ce ne sont pas des amis qui pleurent un ami." Milton is not at his best, either. For

Mérzières, "Lycidas" is a curious, distasteful, inappropriate hodgepodge of classical myth and Christian dogma. Worse still, it is not moving, and a successful elegy has to touch the soul. The poet "a beau nous rappeler que celui qu'il regrettait est chrétien et Anglais, en faisant apparaître, au milieu des divinités païennes, le dieu du Cam qui passe à Cambridge et saint Pierre, gardien du paradis." Conceptually, the poem is a failure. True, "Lycidas" has moments worthy of *Paradise Lost*, especially when the poet forgets his models and introduces a personal note. "Chaque fois que Milton s'arrache à la pastorale pour exprimer ses sentiments personnels, il parle avec une singulière éloquence." But when he becomes satirical and attacks the established Church, the personal note becomes venomous and detracts from the poem instead of enhancing it. Milton does show that he can paint realistically, however. Yet, when all is said and done, "une poésie plus humaine nous toucherait davantage" (Mézières, 528–34).

In the nineteenth century, Mézières was one of the few French critics to say anything about *Arcades*. He not only knew about the masque, but he seems to have read it. In mentioning the poem, he asserts that, though brief, it reveals that its author was a master of the new genre. "*Les Arcadiens*, qui ne contiennent que neuf cent vers, ressemblent à un essai ou à un fragment plutôt qu'à une œuvre complète." Brief though it is, it shows the poet's astonishing intellect to great advantage. "*Les Arcadiens* ne sont que l'esquisse rapide d'un masque, et cependant, dès son début dans ce nouveau genre de poésie, Milton révèle la force de son génie." Unlike his contemporaries, whose masques as a rule were charming but shallow, Milton, with *Arcades*, arouses serious meditation on the part of his audience. He takes the audience with him as he soars away into the stratosphere of that Platonic world in which he was so much at home (Mézières, 517–18).

Unlike *Arcades*, *Comus* was not a trial composition but "un drame complet, développé, qui remplit toutes les conditions du genre. C'est l'œuvre la plus considérable et la plus belle de la jeunesse de Milton." The finest example of its genre, Mézières believes *Comus* deserves its reputation as the best masque ever written. Such predecessors as Ben Jonson, Shirley and Carew had been intent on spectacle. Milton, on the other hand, filled his entertainment with solid ideas, then wrapped it in poetic splendor. Of Milton's youthful poems, clearly this is the critic's favorite.

Unlike Thomas Warton, Mézières does not believe that *Comus* was based on an actual experience. The masque has too many literary sources for that. One of the sources the critic calls attention to is George Peele's *The Old Wives' Tale* (1595), which Warton had discussed. He also mentions Eric van de Putte's *Comus*, published at Louvain in 1608, Lyon in 1630 and Oxford in 1634. Finally, he thinks that John Fletcher's *The Faithful Shepherdess* (c. 1609) inspired the episode in which Sabrina is invoked to save Lady Alice. As Mézières puts it, Fletcher is more lush and observes the poetic niceties better, but Milton is more precise and more robust. Mézières would return to the idea in a later work. In Fletcher's play, when Perigot thinks he has killed Amoret, "ce meurtre donne lieu à une scène charmante que Milton, qui avait étudié les œuvres de Fletcher presque autant que celles de Spenser, a imitée, à la fin de *Comus*, dans l'épisode célèbre de Sabrina. On voit sur le théâtre le dieu d'un fleuve recueillir le corps de la jeune fille qui a été livré à la merci des flots. La divinité compatissante la rend à la vie et lui offre son amour." Amoret thanks the God of the River who saved her, and Milton remembered the lines in which she does so. "La langue de Milton, qui a reproduit, dans *Comus*, le mouvement et l'intention de ces derniers vers, est plus sobre que celle de Fletcher, mais elle n'a ni plus de grâce ni plus d'harmonie. Quand la poésie anglaise est sortie des mains de Shakespeare et de ses contemporains, elle n'avait plus d'autres qualités à acquérir que la sobriété et la mesure."[3] But while *Comus* has its sources, in it the poet also drew upon ancient myth as well as indigenous popular lore and tradition, as he did in some of his other early works. Whatever else it does, *Comus* demonstrates that, at this time at least, Milton's talent was not dramatic. The poet dispenses with action, substituting speeches. Where Shakespeare would have introduced some moving deed or an adventure, Milton plants a discourse. Milton's penchant for generalization likewise reveals a "nature plus philosophique que dramatique." And yet the philosophical content is not really new.

Perhaps the characters are what Mézières likes most in *Comus*. They are *not* characters, of course, but rather "opinions" that the poet sets up in opposition to each other, naturally making his own win out in the end. The characters thus stand for ideas. As Mézières says, "Partout, dans *Comus*, sous le masque des personnages, nous découvrons l'idée qu'ils expriment, et la lutte qui s'engage entre les personnes n'est que le symbole extérieur du combat que se livrent les tendances opposées de l'homme." Characters are used to point up abstract principles. Interestingly enough, the Attendant Spirit is given no name. Had he been called Ariel or Puck, for instance, we would find ourselves assigning him various characteristics whether we wanted to or not. As it is, being nameless, he retains the universal quality that ought to be associated with what he represents. "Un esprit céleste," his task is to "exprimer les sentiments qu'éprouvent pour la race humaine tous les génies de son espèce, sentiments de mépris pour les pécheurs, et de pitié sympathique pour le petit nombre des honnêtes gens." As for Comus, he is much more than a pagan god. He represents materialism and sensuousness, but the poet at least permits him to make his case. "Ce sont tous les instincts matériels de l'homme, ce sont les voluptés des sens auxquelles le poète donne une voix et qui plaident éloquemment leur cause en regard des aspirations plus pures des âmes vertueuses." The critic does not point out that, in *Paradise Lost*, Satan too is allowed to plead his cause and does it very well. In *Comus*, the Brothers, both of them, are virtuous, but they are not alike. One is strong, while the other, despite good intentions, is weak. "L'aîné des Egerton parle au nom des hommes pieux et confiants dans la justice de Dieu, tandis que le plus jeune représente au contraire le troupeau nombreux des âmes timides que le plus léger souffle du malheur abat et qui désespèrent de la protection de Dieu, avant même d'avoir essayé de résister à l'orage." The Lady is virtue incarnate, self-assured and inflexible. "Lady Alice est l'image fidèle de cette pureté morale, de cette chasteté fière qui remplit le cœur d'une jeune fille courageuse en prêtant à son esprit des lumières surhumaines" (Mézières, 522–23).

Thus Mézières concludes his observations on Milton's juvenilia. Though he did not discuss it, he knew the rest of the poet's work, however. Elsewhere he mentions, but not much more than that, several other works. The personal matter in *An Apology for Smectymnuus* is brought in at one point for what it tells us about the poet's youthful goals and the moral bases he considered necessary to attain them. As the critic observes, "La pureté morale lui parut le fondement nécessaire du génie. Le poète qui aspirait à prendre son vol vers les plus hautes régions de l'infini ne pouvait tremper ses ailes dans les voluptés de la terre sans en alourdir l'essor. Cette conviction le mit en garde contre toute sensualité. . . . Il s'interdit même les amusements permis, dans la crainte de perdre une partie de ses forces en les dissipant. Sa gravité naturelle lui rendit facile la tâche qu'il s'imposait." In *Hors de France* Mézières evokes *Areopagitica* in passing, calling it an "éloquent traité" and noting that censorship was not abolished until 1695. In the same book he remarks that, during the Restoration, the only road to wealth open to the gifted man of letters was the theatre. The failure of *Paradise Lost* proved this.[4] One could wish that Mézières had undertaken a detailed study of *Paradise Lost*. Unfortunately, he never did. In a lecture on 11 December 1863, he nonetheless alluded to it, declaring that it contained "les idées les plus hautes que puisse porter l'intelligence humaine."[5]

The critic's discussion of Milton's early poems, despite the surprising omissions, is a refreshing look at these poems by a critic schooled in comparative literature. Mézières knew a great deal about Milton's literary ancestors, and what he said about them is generally pertinent. The comparisons and contrasts are appropriate and enlightening. One of the critic's interesting points is the remark that, both in Milton's personality and in his work, there are curious oppositions. The poet was austere but not altogether humorless, for example. And oppositions underscore the whole of *Comus*, which is built upon them. Mézière's discussion of "Il Penseroso," with its view that the narrator is not a mere contemplative sort but a man of action, is unusual. Comparing this poem, taking stock of the resemblances and dissimilarities, with French romantic poetry is also illuminating. The *Comus* discussion is thoughtful. The point about the Attendant Spirit's having no name so as to retain the abstract universality of what he symbolizes demonstrates that the critic had an excellent sense of what the poem is about. That he saw so little to admire in "Lycidas," which he regarded as cold, comes as a disappointment. On the other hand, the fine tribute to *Paradise Lost* in one of his published lectures makes one wish that, in an article or book, he had turned his attention to this epic and to *Paradise Regained* and *Samson Agonistes*.

11

Hippolyte Taine

"Milton, prédestiné à la barbarie et à la grandeur par sa nature personnelle et par les mœurs environnantes," wrote Hippolyte Taine (1828–1893). Taine was an historian, philosopher, aesthetician, teacher and critic. He was elected to the Académie Française in 1878. In his own day as in ours, his critical approaches and conclusions—which commentators have tended to oversimplify—have been on the one hand questioned, misunderstood and decried, while on the other they have been hailed and warmly applauded. By some, they have also been objectively examined, discussed, evaluated and have had their desiderata pointed out. Whatever one's reactions to them, their importance to aesthetics and criticism cannot be denied.[1] Writing in an era colored by positivism and more and more oriented toward science and scientism, Taine evolved and applied a doctrine of artistic determinism propounded in the introduction to the *Histoire de la littérature anglaise* (1863 and 1864). In article form, the introduction appeared as "L'Histoire, son présent et son avenir," in the *Revue Germanique* on 1 December 1863, as the book's first three volumes were going to press. The doctrine is best summed up in the author's expression, "la race, le milieu, et le moment," which simply means that a work of art is the exact product of a particular intellect, with its paraphernalia of inherited racial and national determinants working at a particular time within particular social, political and cultural environmental conditions. This is not as awesome nor as predetermined as it sounds. Taine does make allowance for an artist's individual proclivities, education and inspiration, but he insists that these even so will be acted upon and to a great extent molded by the factors listed above. Thus Milton cannot be understood, far less appreciated, unless one understands what produced him.

Taine's extensive examination of Milton was the sixth chapter in the second volume of the *Histoire de la littérature anglaise*. It had been written in October 1856. It appeared initially as an article in the *Revue des Deux Mondes* on 15 June 1857 under the title "Milton, son génie et ses œuvres," substantially the same as the later version. Preparing to write it, Taine had been reading Milton's prose works as early as the previous July.[2] Taine's principles and method inform the entire discussion, the critic devoting ample space to the poet's background and career as well as to his works. Between the article and the book, Taine's theories sharpened perceptibly. In revising the article somewhat for the *Histoire de la littérature anglaise*, the author made the idea of determinism, though not a consideration that necessarily swept all before it, a somewhat more important factor than it had been in the original essay.

Taine invites his readers to visualize the poet growing up in a commercial neighborhood and in a family that was at once devout and cultivated. Here

> le chant, les lettres, la peinture, tous les ornements de la belle Renaissance viennent parer la gravité soutenue, l'honnêteté laborieuse, le christianisme profond de la Réforme. Tout le génie de Milton sort de là: il a porté l'éclat de la Renaissance dans le sérieux de la Réforme, les magnificences de Spenser dans les sévérités de Calvin, et s'est trouvé avec sa famille au confluent de deux civilisations qu'il a réunie.[3]

[singing, literature, painting, all the ornamentation of the high Renaissance come together to adorn the constant gravity, the hardworking respectability, the deep Christianity of the Reformation. Milton's entire outlook emanates from this: he transported the brilliance of the Renaissance into the seriousness of the Reformation, the magnificence of Spenser into the austerity of Calvin, and found himself, along with his family, at the juncture of two civilizations that he combined.]

The idea that Milton was both product and representative of two cultural eras was a pet concept with Taine, and he returns to it several times. Nowhere is it better stated than in the conclusion, where he tells us of Milton that,

Placé par le hasard entre deux âges, il participe à leurs deux natures, comme un fleuve qui, coulant entre deux terres différentes, se teint de leurs deux couleurs. Poète et protestant, il reçut de l'âge qui finissait le libre souffle poètique et de l'âge qui commençait la sévère religion politique. Il employa l'un au service de l'autre et déploya l'inspiration ancienne en des sujets nouveaux. Dans son œuvre on reconnaît deux Angleterres: l'une passionnée pour le beau, livrée aux émotions de la sensibilité effrénée et aux fantasmagories de l'imagination pure, sans autre règle que les sentiments naturels, sans autre religion que les croyances naturelles; volontiers païenne, souvent immorale; telle que la montrent Sidney, Shakespeare, Spenser, et toute la superbe moisson de poètes qui couvrit le sol pendant cinquante ans; l'autre munie d'une religion pratique, dépourvue d'inventioin métaphysique, toute politique, ayant le culte de la règle, attachée aux opinions mesurées, sensées, utiles, étroites, louant les vertus de famille, armée et roidie par une moralité rigide, précipitée dans la prose,[4] élevée jusqu'au plus haut degré de puissance, de richesse et de liberté. A ce titre, ce style et ces idées sont des monuments d'histoire; ils concentrent, rappellent, ou devancent le passé et l'avenir, et dans l'enceinte d'une seule œuvre on découvre les événements et les sentiments de plusieurs siècles et d'une nation. (*Histoire*, 434–35)

[Placed by chance between two eras, he has the characteristics of each, like a river that, flowing between two different kinds of soil, picks up the colors of both. A poet and a Protestant, he received free poetic inspiration from the era that was coming to an end and, from the era that was beginning, austere political religion. He used the one to serve the other and deployed old inspiration on new subjects. In his work are seen two Englands: the one passionately in love with the beautiful, given over to the emotions arising from boundless sensitivity and the phantasmagorias of pure imagination, with no other rule than natural feelings, no other religion than natural beliefs; consciously pagan, often immoral; as Sidney, Shakespeare, Spenser, and the whole superb crop of poets that covered the soil for 50 years reveal it; the other wrapped in a practical religion, devoid of metaphysical inventiveness, completely political, worshiping rules, bound by measured, sensible, utilitarian, narrow opinions, lauding the family virtues, armed and stiffened by rigid morality, engulfed in the prosaic, raised to the highest degree of power, wealth, and freedom. Viewed from this position, this style and these ideas are historical monuments; they concentrate, recall or anticipate the past and the future, and within a single work one beholds the events and feelings of several centuries and a nation.]

To these determinants must be added Milton's studies, his travels, his domestic tribulations, and the religious and political dissentions that were coming to a head when he returned from the Continent. Into these disputes, Taine remarks, Milton threw himself "tout entier, armé de logique, de colère, d'érudition, et cuirassé par la conviction et par la conscience" (Histoire, 341).

As Taine sees him, Milton was not a poetic individual prone to multiple and varied sensations. If "L'Allegro" and "Il Penseroso" seem to contradict this, Taine does not notice the contradiction. Instead Taine sees him as reserved but a man of action, stubborn and impervious to pressures. Milton and those like him "par défiance, par rigidité, avec un instinct de combattants et un prompt regard jeté sur la règle se replient naturellement sur eux-mêmes et, dans l'enceinte close où ils s'enferment, ne sentent plus les sollicitations ni les contradictions de leurs alentours" (Histoire, 336–37). What Taine means here is that once environment and other determinants have led them to reach a conclusion or take a position, obstinate individuals such as the poet maintain that conclusion or position to the end, no matter what others do to win them over. The conclusion is not reached, the position is not adopted in a vacuum remote from the environmental stimuli that would produce it. Here, as elsewhere, Taine does not allow for evolution in Milton's ideas, which is the basic flaw in this critic's approach. While never stating this, Taine seems to believe that Milton's views burst into existence as cohesive ideas, all of a piece, and that they remained static. He apparently does not think the poet's stand on God, the church, ministers, civil administration, love, marriage and sin changed or evolved with circumstances.

Taine's position that Milton, or anyone with his temperament, "ne tourne pas à tout événement et à toute passion, comme cet être changeant et maniable qu'on appelle un poète," is problematical in light of Milton's break with the Presbyterians, for example. In short, Taine discovers a unity in Milton's character and work that may not be there. Twice, at least, he seems to recognize this. Once, he records that Milton had been destined for holy orders and had then declined to take them. Later Taine would describe Milton as having been "puritain contre les évêques, indépendant contre les presbytériens," adding that "il fut toujours le maître de sa pensée et l'inventeur de sa croyance." Altering his career plans and his religious views, Milton was to this extent less monolithic in his thinking than Taine generally believed. Whatever the case, the poet had a basic dedication to a core principle. "Espérance et renoncement, tout chez lui partait de la même source, la volonté fixe d'agir noblement" (*Histoire*, 333, 336). As for that other Milton, the withdrawn visionary secluded in his mind's own place, Taine had alluded to him earlier in the chapter. "Contre les fluctuations du dehors, il trouvait son refuge en lui-même; et la cité idéale qu'il avait bâtie dans son âme demeurait inexpugnable à tous les assauts. Elle était trop belle, cette cité intérieure, pour qu'il voulût en sortir; elle était trop solide pour qu'on pût la détruire" (*Histoire*, 329).

Still earlier, Taine had posited what seemed to him to be the other essential characteristics that set Milton apart while at the same time explaining his art. To Taine, Milton did not have a "poetic" or "artistic" nature. He was too much the rationalist for that. There were even limits to his imaginative powers, but this is an idea that, later, the critic would water down somewhat. Reason, in any event, was dominant over sentiment and impulse. What stands out most are erudition, ruthless logic, and exuberance. As Taine phrases it,

> John Milton n'est point une de ces âmes fiévreuses, impuissantes contre elle-mêmes, que la verve saisit par secousses, que la sensibilité maladive précipite incessamment au fond de la douleur ou de la joie, que leur flexibilité prépare à représenter la diversité des caractères, que leur tumulte condamne à peindre le délire et les contrariétés des passions. La science immense, la logique serrée, et la passion grandiose, voilà son fond. Il a l'esprit lucide et l'imagination limitée. Il est incapable de trouble et il est incapable de métamorphoses. Il conçoit la plus haute des beautés idéales, mais il n'en conçoit qu'une. Il n'est pas né pour le drame, mais pour l'ode. Il ne crée pas des âmes, mais il construit des raisonnements et ressent des émotions.[5]
>
> [John Milton is not one of those feverish souls, powerless against themselves, that inspiration seizes by fits and starts, that unhealthy sensitivity constantly plunges into the depths of suffering or happiness, whose flexibility prepares them to portray the diversity of characters, whose tumultuousness condemns to paint the delirium and contradictions of the passions. Immense learning, tight logic, and grandiose passion, these are his basic components. He has a lucid mind and a limited imagination. He is incapable of turmoil and he is incapable of metamorphoses. He conceives the highest of ideal beauties, but he conceives only one. He was not born for the drama but rather for the ode. He does not create souls, but he builds rationalizations and experiences emotions.]

Taine's Milton was no romantic hero, obviously. Philarète Chasles would hardly recognize him in this incarnation. Many readers would not agree that Milton was "incapable de trouble" and that his imagination had its limits, but the statement is provocative. Provocative too, although we have already encountered it in Mézière's article, is the idea that Milton did not have a sense of drama and that, instead of creating characters, he presented his readers with ideas and rationalizations. Later Taine would assert that *Samson Agonistes* was a mere imitation, lofty in tone and content, perhaps, but cold and in no wise dramatic. *Paradise Lost* should have been a drama, the critic says, but Milton tried and realized his inability to cast it in such a mold (*Histoire*, 403).

For Taine, Milton's life, character and art can be explained by the poet's dedication to one aspiration, the sublime, which at once united and ordered the diverse elements in his nature and their expression in his work. Milton both lived it and strove to attain it in his writing. It was at once an outlook and a goal, a social as well as a personal and artistic ideal. That this ideal was impractical Taine does not deny.[6]

> Il se faisait illusion à lui-même, et vivait ainsi seul à seul avec le sublime.... Il demeurait en dehors du monde, aussi aveuglé contre les faits palpables que défendu contre les séductions sensibles, placé au-dessus des souillures et des leçons de l'expérience, aussi incapable de conduire les hommes que de leur céder.... Enfermé dans ses idées, il ne voit qu'elles, et s'éprend d'elles. (*Histoire*, 344–45)
>
> [He deluded himself, and thus lived alone with the sublime.... He remained isolated from the world, as blind to tangible facts as he was protected from sensuous enticements, above the lessons and dirt of experience, as incapable of leading people as he was of giving in to them.... Closeted with his ideas, he sees nothing but them and becomes enamored of them.]

On 8 July 1856 Taine wrote a friend that he was reading Milton's prose (*Corr.* 2:137). He comments that it took idle, secure, polished social intercourse to make men urbane. It is time wasted to look for anything like this in the "redoutable" pamphlets. Taine sees Milton's prose as falling into two categories, a given work sometimes belonging to both. On the one hand, it is violent, vitriolic, turgid, sophistic and pedantic, replete with authorities and couched in syllogisms. On the other, it can be—and often is—serene and so poetic as to transcend the bounds of prose. Milton was not far removed from scholasticism, as his prose demonstrates.[7] Beneath their secular armor, his discussions advance in a methodical but pedantic fashion. First the author states his thesis. Thus, at the beginning of his *Doctrine and Discipline of Divorce* Milton writes down in big letters the proposition that he will demonstrate: "That indisposition, unfitness, or contrariety of mind, arising from a cause in nature unchangeable, hindering, and ever likely to hinder the main benefits of conjugal society, which are solace and peace, is a greater reason of divorce than natural frigidity, especially if there be no children, and that there be mutual consent." Then come the arguments. Taine often uses military images in connection with his author, and he does so here. To win his case, Milton brings up, "légion par légion, l'armée disciplinée des arguments. Bataillons par bataillons, ils passent numérotés avec des étiquettes visibles. Il y en a une douzaine à la file, chacun avec son titre en caractères tranchés et la petite brigade de subdivisions qu'il commande." Milton relies for the most part on scriptural texts. "On les discute mot à mot, le substantif après l'adjectif, le verbe après le substantif, la préposition après le verbe; on cite des interprétations, des autorités, des exemples, qu'on range entre des palissades de divisions nouvelles." And yet the question is never reduced to a single issue. Point after point is established, but there is no order in the presentation. One is not won over but rather worn out. Chateaubriand, it will be recalled, had observed that *The Doctrine and Discipline of Divorce* does not prove what it sets out to prove.

Taine calls on readers to remember that Milton was addressing an audience reared in the cumbersome ceremonial of academic debate and thus accustomed to such wearisome turmoil (*Histoire*, 354–55). Above all, one must not expect wit. When Milton tries to be funny, the result is disastrous. "Il a l'air d'un piquier de Cromwell qui, entrant dans un salon pour danser, tomberait sur son nez de tout son poids et de tout le poids de son armure." Mired down in the classical allusions, the lamentable puns, intended to provoke laughter, are in atrocious taste. Milton tried to be comic in *Animadversions*, for example. The result? "Il y a peu de choses aussi stupides."[8] All of his polemical works demonstrate that Milton knew how to hate cordially. They also prove that he could do battle with concentrated rancor and ferocious bullheadedness. No one, Taine asserts, has ever equaled Milton's harsh, implacable invective (*Histoire*, 355–59).

Characteristic of Milton's prose are its "sublime" energy,

its "poignante" irony, its "invective ouverte et sérieuse" (*Histoire*, 375, 378). "Accablante" is the word Taine uses to describe the impression that *Eikonoklastes* creates:

> Phrase par phrase, durement, amèrement, le roi est réfuté et accusé jusqu'au bout, sans que l'accusation fléchisse une seule minute, sans qu'on accorde à l'accusé la moindre bonne intention, la moindre excuse, la moindre apparence de justice, sans que l'accusateur s'écarte et se repose un instant dans des idées générales. C'est un combat corps à corps où tout mot porte coup, prolongé, obstiné, sans élan, sans faiblesse, d'une inimitié âpre et fixe, où l'on ne songe qu'à blesser fort et à tuer sûrement.

> [Sentence by sentence, harshly, bitterly, the king is refuted and accused to the very end, without the prosecution letting up a single moment, without the defendent being granted the slightest good intention, the slightest extenuating circumstance, the slightest appearance of being in the right, without the prosecutor stepping aside to rest an instant in generalizations. It is a duel in which each word deals a blow, prolonged, obstinate, stolid, unflinching, with sharp, determined hatred in which the sole intent is to wound to the quick and kill without fail.]

Taine does not condone "tant de grossièreté et de balourdises," but he understands them in terms of the era they reflect. Modern polemics has become more polite, he believes, but at the same time it has become debilitated. "Si nous avons effacé chez nous la férocité et la sottise, nous avons diminué chez nous la force et la grandeur. La force et la grandeur éclatent chez Milton, étalées dans ses opinions et dans son style, sources de sa croyance et de son talent" (*Histoire*, 360–61).

No one more than Milton "n'a plus aimé, pratiqué, et loué l'usage libre et hardi de la raison. Il l'exerça jusqu'à la témérité et jusqu'au scandale." His reason craved free outlets, and his works denounced all unnatural or imposed restraints. This is what made him revolt against custom, that opponent of truth (*Histoire*, 362). *Areopagitica* and *Of Reformation*, championing both public and private freedom, contain some of the author's best prose. Despite zealot wrath and moments of brute doctrinal viciousness that crop up in the second, there are places in these two works, as well as in others, where one detects a Platonic tone or inspiration (*Histoire*, 373). Elsewhere, in connection with the two treatises, the critic would return to the theme.

Taine had an extremely sensitive ear for harmonious, carefully wrought periods, as anyone familiar with his *Essai sur Tite-Live* knows. If an author is sincere, what the author thinks dictates the style, this critic believes. "La puissance de logique et d'enthousiasme qui explique les opinions de Milton explique son génie. Le sectaire et l'écrivain sont un seul homme." This idea, central to his attitude toward his author, especially as a prose writer, is pursued and expanded. "En raisonnant, Milton s'exalte, et la phrase part comme une catapulte, doublant la force de son élan par l'énormité de son poids. Je n'oserais traduire devant un lecteur moderne les gigantesques périodes qui ouvrent le *Traité de la réforme*.[9] Nous n'avons plus ce souffle. . . . Je doute pourtant que la perçante phrase de Voltaire soit plus mortelle. . . . " And Taine cites a protracted sentence to prove his point. Were Michelangelo's prophets to speak, he adds, it would be like this (*Histoire*, 368–69). This is praise indeed. From his remarks about *The Doctrine and Discipline of Divorce*, we know that Taine did not always like such sentences, but it is clear that he recognized how powerful they could be. What is more interesting is his noting that, now and then, the formidable pamphleteer laid his ponderous rhetoric aside, giving his emotions free rein. When this occurred, his ideas, clothed in their most poetic garb, soared and gave his cause a purer, nobler voice. Here as elsewhere, however, the man and the writer remain inseparable, each explaining the other.

Despite his minor reservations, Taine singles out three prose works as being truly remarkable. Relatively devoid of useless, pedantic rhetoric, they show Milton's prose style at its best. These are *Areopagitica*, *Of Reformation* and *Animadversions on the Remonstrant*. Quoting liberally in French, Taine comments in glowing terms. Milton's brave words about censorship, like his other pamphlets, show a strict identity between the writer and his work. Penning *Areopagitica*, Milton had been wounded in his principles, and he let his oppressed ideal dictate a vehement rebuttal to the idea of limiting free expression. "Il éclate en images magnifiques, il déploie dans son style la force qu'il aperçoit autour de lui et en lui-même." The images are sustained by the same powerful logic that amplifies the periods. "Chacune de ses images s'étale en un petit poème, sorte d'allégorie solide, dont toutes les parties attachées entre elles concentrent leurs lumières sur l'idée unique qu'elles doivent embellir ou éclairer (*Histoire*, 366, 369, 370). Not only an impassioned citizen but also a poet, Milton substantiates his views with classical allusions, even introducing Juno. The lush ornamentation, Taine declares, contributes to the work's effectiveness: "la surabondance comme la rudesse ne fait que manifester ici la vigueur et l'élan lyrique que le caractère de Milton avait prédits." Passion follows as a matter of course. "L'exaltation l'apporte avec les images. Les audacieuses expressions, les excès de style, font entendre la voix vibrante de l'homme qui souffre, qui s'indigne, et qui veut." Milton's vehemence is labeled "sublime." To the critic's way of thinking, in this work "l'homme vaut la cause, et jamais une plus haute éloquence n'égala une plus haute vérité." Neither here nor elsewhere is the metaphoric intoxication an accident. The author is at all times in command. Like a priest conducting a magnificent worship service, he intentionally dazzles the eye in order to convince the heart (*Histoire*, 371, 374, 375).

Milton's first tract, *Of Reformation*, is one of those Taine singles out for special praise. Here, as Milton joins "les perspectives du ciel aux visions des ténèbres," a pamphlet becomes a hymn.

> Au milieu de ses syllogismes, Milton prie, soutenu par l'accent des prophètes, entouré par les souvenirs de la Bible, ravi des splendeurs de l'Apocalypse, mais retenu à la porte de l'hallucination par la science et la logique, au plus haut de l'air serein et sublime, sans monter dans la région brûlante où l'extase fond la raison, avec une majesté d'éloquente et une grandeur solennelle que rien ne surpasse, dont la perfection prouve qu'il est entré dans son domaine, et au-delà du prosateur promet le poète....

[Deep in his syllogisms, Milton prays, sustained by the tone of the prophets, surrounded by biblical recollections, enraptured amid the splendor of the Apocalypse, but restrained at the threshold of hallucination by erudition and logic, floating in the highest level of calm, sublime air without pushing on to that torried sphere in which ecstasy melts reason, with an eloquent majesty and solemn grandeur that nothing can surpass, so perfect that it proves the author is in his element and that beyond the prose writer there is a poet....]

By way of illustration, the critic calls to mind four eloquent passages from *Of Reformation* and another from *Animadversions*.[10] Taine considers these superlative. "En sondant toutes les littératures," he declares, "vous ne rencontrerez guère de poètes égaux à ce prosateur" (*Histoire*, 383).

But this is poetry. Was Milton a prose writer? Taine has doubts. Certainly Milton was not a prose writer in the usual sense, not if one expects prose to be lucid and rational, not if its function is to persuade or convince. Milton, despite his logic, was never able to produce the perfect prose work. He only wrote utilitarian pamphlets dictated by practical self-interest and hatred and tarnished by barbarian crudeness, awkward wit and ponderous dialectic. There were inspired moments, however, when, chained in metaphors, the poet let his zeal and inventiveness run riot. When this happened, "l'exalation religieuse et lyrique," "la grandeur épique des images soutenues et surabondantes," took over, revealing here and there "de beaux morceaux isolés, inspirés par la rencontre d'une grande idée et par l'essor momentané du génie." With all their flaws, these works have the merit of showing their author as he really was. The pamphleteer and the poet were the same man. "L'esprit systématique et lyrique se peint dans le pamphlet comme dans le poème; la faculté d'embrasser des ensembles et d'en être ébranlé reste égale en Milton dans ses deux carrières, et vous allez voir dans le *Paradis* et dans le *Comus* ce que vous avez prévu dans le *Traité de la réforme* et dans les *Remarques sur l'opposant*."[11] In the prose as much as elsewhere, Milton's rhetorical devices never cease to enchant the critic. Fundamentally utilitarian, these devices, Taine believes, were no accident. However profuse, however intricate, each was there for a purpose, even though it might appear to a be a microcosm in itself. "Chacune de ses images s'étale en un petit poème, sorte d'allégorie solide, dont toutes les parties attachées concentrent toutes leurs lumières sur l'idée unique qu'elles doivent embellir ou éclairer (*RDM*, 831–32).

As a poet, Milton extended the English Renaissance, but he did it in his own way. From his native predecessors he inherited myth and allegory, a marvelous feeling for nature, an inexhaustible admiration for forms, colors and textual splendor. He inherited and sometimes used their conceits as well, for example in the opening stanzas of the "Hymn on the Morning of Christ's Nativity" and in "Lycidas." But Milton was an innovator as well. He transformed his predecessors' diction, and, along with the diction, he altered the content, making poetry serve new ends. He was at once spontaneous and erudite, never hesitating to borrow from others to enrich his own work.[12] To illustrate his point, the critic cites examples from *Arcades*, *Comus*, "At a Solemn Music," "Lycidas." What set Milton apart from the Renaissance poets who had been his masters was that, unlike them, he sought grandeur in his verse. To achieve it he needed majestic, rolling lines; commodious, resounding stanzas; and immense, extended periods. "Ce n'était pas assez des images et de la poésie qui ne s'adresse qu'aux yeux; il fallait encore des sons, et cette poésie plus intime qui, purgée de représentations corporelles, va toucher l'âme: il était musicien et artiste" (*Histoire*, 387–88).

Taine likes Milton's early poems. Calling attention to the "chants tristes" heard in "On the Death of a Fair Infant" and "An Epitaph on the Marchioness of Winchester," he also praises the "graves et nobles vers" that characterize "On Time," "At a Solemn Music" and "How Soon Hath Time." Taine waxes romantic for a moment as he tells us that at Horton "les attentes, les rêveries, les premiers enchantements de la jeunesse," along with "contemplations souriantes et sereines," were what occupied the nascent poet's time (*Histoire*, 390). Milton wrote "L'Allegro." As though he had praised sensuous pleasure too much in it, he wrote its solemn companion piece, "Il Penseroso." In these poems as in the later ones, whatever the form or the language, the themes are the same: reverence, heroism, chaste love, moral stature. Not that the poet considered it his duty to celebrate these virtues; rather, it was his nature to do so. "Son besoin et sa faculté dominante le portaient aux conceptions nobles." This was true even in so highly decorative a genre as the masque, to which he gave his own special stamp.

Comus, a pæan to virtue, could well be Milton's masterpiece. In his *Revue des Deux Mondes* article, Taine had not hesitated to call it "sa plus belle œuvre."[13] As supermen, the characters are too noble to speak. They must sing. Thus the drama becomes, as it were, an opera on the ancient model, made up, like *Prometheus*, of solemn canticles. Spirited out of the real, sordid world and deposited in some ethereal sphere, the spectator listens not to persons but to feelings. Particularly noteworthy to Taine is the "ode" pronounced at the end by the Attendant Spirit, an ode in which "toutes les magnificences de la nature s'assemblent pour ajouter une séduction[14] à la vertu" and in which "la poésie conduit à la philosophie." To be sure, at times the poem lacks smoothness. Here and there, one stumbles across a cumbersome expression or a philosophical debate. But these disappear in the rich texture of the whole, which is none other than "la Renaissance riante transformée par la philosophie austère" and the "sublime adoré sur un autel de fleurs" (*Histoire*, 394–95, 399–400).

Virgilian in manner, "Lycidas" mourns the death of a beloved friend, but into it creep Puritan wrath and exasperation. Likewise, the sonnets deal with both private and public concerns. A given sonnet might lament a pious, deceased friend, honor a virtuous young woman, or praise a soldier or political leader. While one sonnet pleads the cause of the Piedmontese Protestants, another honors the poet's second wife who, dead after a year of marriage, appeared to her husband in a dream. These sonnets reveal "loyales amitiés, douleurs acceptées ou domptées, aspirations généreuses ou stoïques, que les revers ne firent qu'épurer" (*Histoire*, 401–02).

With the Restoration, Milton was cast aside. In inactive,

dissident civil life, he became a spiritual exile, without even hope to sustain him. By now an old man, he nevertheless turned to the noble dreams of his youth. Poetry beckoned, says Taine, and Milton answered. Earlier in point of time, he had situated his characters as far back in mythological antiquity as he could. Similarly, he would now place them in the utmost reaches of sacred history, creating an aesthetic distance that would help prevent their being judged by ordinary human standards. Thus Joy, Melancholy, Comus were replaced by Samson, Satan and the devils, Christ and the angels. Whatever Taine may have thought about Samson and Christ as characters, he said but little about *Samson Agonistes* and *Paradise Regained*. Samson, it is true, is "l'élu du Dieu fort, l'exterminateur des idolâtres," but the work in which he appears is a cold imitation. Likewise, if Christ is superhuman, He is a superhuman statue. *Paradise Regained* is noble, but it too is cold, "une épopée froide et noble."

What had happened? However poetic his prose could be on occasion, years of polemics had taken their toll on the author, politics and pious controversies dulling his poetic temperament. Writes Taine, "La virilité a pris la place de la jeunesse. La richesse est devenue moindre et la sévérité plus grande.... L'habitude de la dissertation a fini par abaisser l'essor lyrique; l'érudition accrue a fini par surcharger le génie original. Le poète ne chante plus en vers sublimes, il raconte ou harangue en vers graves. Il n'invente plus un genre personnel, il imite..." (*Histoire*, 403). In these serious reservations, the critic sums up what he considers amiss in *Samson Agonistes*, *Paradise Lost* and *Paradise Regained*.

There is much that Taine admires in *Paradise Lost*, but there is also much that he does not like. Not all of the latter was the poet's fault, however. True epic inspiration had died with Dante, the critic believes. When Milton sat down to write, that inspiration had not been revived. Protestantism may have remolded humanity, but it had not revitalized God. Incapable of producing a divine epic, at best it could only create a human one (*Histoire*, 403–07). But *Paradise Lost* had other problems as well.

"Un poème imparfait et sublime," the epic reveals first

of all the deleterious effects of the poet's impassioned involvement in his era's controversies. Milton had become too erudite, too imbued with his recent bitter religious and political preoccupations. Too disillusioned as well. While he was as sublime as ever, the charm was gone. Now he was all seriousness. No longer a lyric poet, he had become a narrative one (*Histoire*, 403). For a moment Taine abandons his scientism. Momentarily romantic, he takes the position that it is within the province of an epic to be essentially lyric. As he points out, for Milton to make his supernatural characters and events come alive, he needed an emotional element that strict narration cannot provide. God must be felt, not described. When His deeds, like those of an Oliver Cromwell, are merely recounted, the reader is unable to perceive Him. Since the whole poem revolves about this heavenly being, the epic suffers. With God, Milton has borrowed a tradition that he has embellished with "fictions" he has worked out carefully. Nevertheless, he remains a preacher, not a prophet; a decorator, not a poet. He has celebrated God the way most people pray to Him, "suivant une formule apprise, non par un tressaillement spontané."

Lacking the "antique exaltation des psalmistes" and the "ébranlement sublime par lequel l'esprit inspiré et désorganisé produit Dieu," Milton could not bring his divine narrative to life. Had his propelling force been emotional inspiration, we, his readers, would be swept along with him in his "déraison créatrice." Nothing like this happens, however. Since we are unable to respond to the poem on an emotional level, we approach it in a critical mood, quibbling over matters of detail as we read. We are bothered by questions of verisimilitude. For example, scrutinizing the characters as we would those in a novel or play, we demand that they be "real," well-rounded, consistent. Sometimes we wonder whether their actions are childish or odd. Adam and Eve must behave like primitive creatures, God and Satan like superhuman entities. Milton, with his excessive rationalism, could not make them behave in this manner. As a result, his characters "sont des harangues, et dans leurs sentiments on ne trouve que des monceaux de puérilités et de contradictions" (*Histoire*, 403–07).

Taine's mirth at the poet's characterization, or lack of it, is well known. In Adam and Eve, the critic expects to see robust, voluptuous, idle children, with eyes ablaze and minds utterly devoid of thought. Not so. To his astonishment and disappointment, he beholds a learned Puritan couple. Taine goes on to describe the two characters. Ere setting foot in Eden, these two had done a stint in England, where they had absorbed that nation's ideas about various things, including what is and what is not "respectable." It is hard to visualize them naked, he says. This pair would be sure to have invented modesty and trousers. While in England, they went up to Oxford University, where they took courses in law and courtroom procedure and earned doctorates in moral discourse and casuistry. Instead of conversing, they lecture each other, sometimes about politics. Adam, an ambitious, practical landowner, will one day take his seat in the House of Commons as a Whig. An excellent housekeeper and hostess, Eve will second his ambitions.[15] They practice on Raphael, who comes to visit. However ethereal, the visitor does more than human justice to the earthly repast served him. As is true with his host and hostess, he likes to make speeches and, during the visit, delivers orations on matters astronomical and political.

What bothers Taine most in Adam and Eve is that they never cease their "dissertations," not even in their most intimate moments. As the couple retires, for instance, Adam indoctrinates his wife.[16] "Ecoutez cet homme qui n'a pas encore goûté à l'arbre de la science," exclaims the critic. "Un bachelier, dans son discours de réception, ne prononcerait pas mieux et plus noblement un plus grand nombre de sentences vides." The speech is a "très utile et très excellente exhortation puritaine," he adds on a sarcastic note. "Voilà de la vertu et de la morale anglaises, et chaque famille, le soir, pourra la lire en guise de Bible à ses enfants." Adam is too learned, too much the debater to dawdle over mere horticulture. He must needs orate about more vital issues, and orate he does. To Eve, who has had a worrisome dream, he later gives a tedious, pedantic explanation, having first donned his academic cap.

>..................... But know that in the Soul
> Are many lesser Faculties that serve
> Reason as chief; among these Fancy next
> Her office holds; of all external things,
> Which the five watchful Senses represent,
> She forms imaginations, Aery shapes,
> Which Reason joining or disjoining, frames
> All what we affirm or what deny, and call
> Our knowledge or opinion; then retires
> Into her private Cell when Nature rests.
> Oft in in her absence mimic Fancy wakes
> To imitate her; but misjoining shapes,
> Wild work produces oft, and most in dreams,
> Ill matching words and deeds long past or late.
> (*PL* 5.100–13)

This is enough to put the poor woman back to sleep. Observing his unintentional effect, Adam adds,

>..............................Yet be not sad.
> Evil into the mind of God or Man
> May come and go, so unapprov'd, and leave
> No spot or blame behind..........................
> (*PL* 5.116–19)

Here, the critic notes merrily, one detects the "époux protestant confesseur de sa femme." But if the speeches have been a problem up to this point, there is worse to come. Eve's eating the apple unleashes still other blasts. "C'est à ce moment que les discours interminables fondent sur le lecteur, aussi nombreux et aussi froids que des douches de pluie en hiver." To avoid them, one would almost rather be cast into an arena to be devoured by wild animals (*Histoire*, 407–14).

To get away from them, Heaven is certainly not where one should go. It is not an attractive place to start with. As Milton presents it, one would not want to spend any time there, Taine is certain. Featured in it, with other horrors, are munitions dumps, an elaborate court ceremonial, and the tiresome lectures and academic debates. For not only

Earth but also Heaven and Hell resound with their terrible din. Actually, God is one of the most wearisome and emphatic of the orators. Like James I, He is at once a monarch and a schoolmaster, unlovable in both roles. How unlike the God of Dante and Gœthe is this trivial, ranting pedant. And as for celestial pastimes, they are not very amusing. Council meetings, debates, ceremonies, picnics and banquets, musical entertainments, dances: none seem to have much interest. Then there is the war, in which "les deux partis se taillent à coups d'épée, se jettent par terre à coups de canon, s'assomment de raisonnements politiques." Are all these the wondrous things that "eye hath not seen, nor ear heard, nor hath entered into the heart to conceive?" Simply stated, Taine concludes, when Milton wrote *Paradise Lost*, his creative powers had been exhausted. As a result, he was able neither to bring his characters to life nor, failing that, arouse his readers to an emotional pitch that would make them blind to the poem's drawbacks (*Histoire*, 414–23).

If Heaven and Earth are disappointments in *Paradise Lost*, Hell fares much better. "Ce qu'il y a de plus beau dans ce paradis, c'est l'enfer," Taine observes. Milton described Hell better than Dante did. Dante's Hell "n'est qu'un atelier de tortures." "Immense et vague," Milton's Hell, on the other hand, captures and thrills the imagination. No poetic creation can equal its impressive horror (*Histoire*, 425–27). From its leader on down, its denizens are just as remarkable as their habitat. Whereas Milton's heavenly and earthly characters are failures, this is not true of Satan. Like all French critics, Taine has unbounded admiration for the rebel leader. It is true that, like the other characters, Satan talks too much, that at times he sounds like a preacher or a drillmaster himself, but he is still a marvelous creation (*Histoire*, 420–21). "Dans cette histoire de Dieu, le premier rôle est au diable," Taine decides. Medieval literature had presented the devil as an absurd mountebank. With Milton, who was a rebel, he has become a hero. Noble and awesome, Satan is all the more superior because he is weaker than his opponents and has fewer resources at his disposal to fight them with. Their "fières et sombres passions politiques" still intact, the other rebels admire him, even though he has caused their ruin. "Plus ferme, plus entreprenant, plus politique que les autres," he deserves their admiration. Militarily he lost the war, but did he really lose it? Defiant, he refuses to accept the outcome. "Quoique défait, il l'emporte, puisqu'il a ravi au monarque d'en haut le tiers de ses anges et presque tous les fils de son Adam."

Taine continues on an enthusiastic note reminiscent of Villemain. At the same time, he is remembering his dictum that there is an inevitable correlation between literature on the one hand and, on the other, the national character.

> Cet héroïsme sombre, cette dure obstination, cette poignante ironie, ces bras orgueilleux et roidis qui serrent la douleur comme une maîtresse, cette concentration du courage invaincu qui, replié en lui-même, trouve tout en lui-même, cette puissance de passion et cet empire sur la passion sont des traits propres du caractère anglais comme de la littérature anglaise, et vous les retrouverez plus tard dans le Lara et dans le Conrad de Lord Byron. (*Histoire*, 425)
>
> [That somber heroism, that hard stubbornness, that poignant irony, those tough, proud arms embracing sorrow like a mistress, that mass of undaunted courage which, turned inward, discovers within itself all that it needs, that power to feel and control passion belong to the English temperament just as they belong to English literature, and you will see them again in Lord Byron's Lara and Conrad.]

Milton perceived dimensions inaccessible to most mortals, which helps explain why his vast landscapes are "sublime." Without going into detail, Taine compares these primitive landscapes, seascapes and immense, naked mountains, to the background of certain religious paintings. The landscapes accounted for much of what he had found attractive in "Lycidas," where the lush abundance looked like an exotic expanse of "fleurs orientales dont l'entassement et l'énormité écrasent tout le luxe de nos parterres européens" (*RDM*, 837). But if Milton could produce incredible landscapes, he could also create a radiant sunset and a spectacular nightfall. When the sun went down,

> Arraying with reflected Purple and Gold
> The Clouds that on his Western Throne attend:

> Now came still Ev'ning on, and Twilight gray
> Had in her sober Livery all things clad;
> Silence accompanied, for Beast and Bird,
> They to thir grassy Couch, these to thir Nests,
> Were slunk, all but the wakeful Nightingale;
> She all night long her amorous descant sung;
> Silence was pleas'd: now glow'd the Firmament
> With living Sapphires: *Hesperus* that led
> The starry Host, rode brightest, till the Moon
> Rising in clouded Majesty, at length
> Apparent Queen unveil'd her peerless light,
> And o'er the dark her Silver Mantle threw.
> (*PL* 4.596–609)

In lingering over this passage, the critic seems to have forgotten his assertion that, when he wrote *Paradise Lost*, Milton was no longer capable of lyricism. The same might be said of another passage the critic admires, the tender canticle to wedded love. "Dans cette louange protestante de la famille, de l'amour légal, 'des douceurs domestiques,' de la piété réglée et du *home*," he points out, "nous apercevons une nouvelle littérature et un autre temps" (*Histoire*, 431–33). Gone are the Elizabethans. A new era, with new values, has dawned.

Taking an overall look at his author, Taine returns in his peroration to one of his favorite ideas, that Milton's principal trait is the sublime, that "instinct des choses nobles" that he was born with and which underscores all that he was, did and wrote. That instinct, reinforced by meditation, vast learning and strict discipline, resulted in a codex of beliefs and precepts that no temptation could dissolve, no reverses shake. Activated by circumstances and events, these beliefs and precepts made the author both a warrior and a poet. Armed with them, "il traverse la vie en combattant, en poète, avec des actions courageuses et des rêves splendides, héroïque et rude, chimérique et passionné, généreux et serein, comme tout raisonneur retiré en lui-même, comme tout enthousiaste insensible à l'expérience et épris du beau" (*Histoire*, 433).

Further, chance did much to make him what he was. "Jeté par le hasard d'une révolution dans la politique et dans la théologie, il réclame pour les autres la liberté dont a besoin sa raison puissante et heurte les entraves publiques qui enchaînent son élan personnel," an allusion to the pamphlets the critic had discussed earlier. Milton had his personal attributes, and circumstances determined what direction they would take. With his intellect and zeal, Milton

> est plus capable que personne d'entasser la science; par sa force d'enthousiasme, il est plus capable que personne de sentir la haine. Ainsi armé, il se lance dans la controverse avec toute la lourdeur et toute la barbarie du temps; mais cette superbe logique étale son raisonnement avec une ampleur merveilleuse et soutient ses images avec une majesté inouïe; cette imagination exaltée, après avoir versé sur la prose un flot de figures magnifiques, l'emporte dans un torrent de passion jusqu'à l'ode furieuse ou sublime, sorte de chant d'archange adorateur ou vengeur. (*Histoire*, 433)
>
> [is more capable than anyone of piling up erudition; by the strength of his enthusiasm, he is more capable than anyone of feeling hatred. Thus armed, he leaps into the fray with all the unwieldy brutality of the times; but that superb logic marvelously deploys his reasoning and sustains his images with incredible majesty; that heated imagination, having emptied a flood of magnificent figures into the prose, carries it off in a torrent of passion until it becomes a furious or sublime ode, a kind of song intoned by an adoring or avenging archangel.]

Once more, though only in passing, the critic calls attention to the poetic character of some of the prose.

Summing up his ideas on the poetry, Taine notes that the poems written before the Civil Wars, the Republic and the Protectorate, as well as those published during the Restoration, have two things in common: the poet's enthusiasm and his quest for the sublime. "Dans l'une et dans l'autre, il cherche le sublime et inspire l'admiration, parce que le sublime est l'œuvre de la raison enthousiaste et que l'admiration est l'enthousiasme de la raison." In both periods, Milton achieved his goal "par l'entassement des magnificences, par l'ampleur soutenue du chant poétique, par la grandeur des allégories,[17] par la hauteur des sentiments, par

la peinture des objets infinis et des émotions héroïques." But there are striking differences between the younger poet and the older one. The younger one, free from constraint, was more lyrical. The later one was writing in the interests of causes that carried with them certain creative limitations. Generally speaking, the mature writer waxed poetic only sporadically. Of Milton and his two manners, the critic declares that

> Dans la première, lyrique et philosophe, possesseur d'une liberté poétique plus forte, il produit des odes et des chœurs presque parfaits. Dans la seconde, épique et protestant, enchaîné par une théologie stricte, privé du style qui rend le surnaturel visible, dépourvu de la sensibilité dramatique qui crée des âmes variées et vivantes, il accumle des dissertations froides, change l'homme et Dieu en machines orthodoxes et vulgaires, et ne retrouve son génie qu'en prêtant à Satan son âme républicaine, en multipliant les paysages grandioses et les apparitions colossales, en consacrant sa poésie à la louange de la religion et du devoir. (*Histoire*, 434)

> [In the first, which is lyrical and philosophical and reveals more poetic freedom, he produces almost perfect odes and choruses. In the second, which is epic and Protestant, hemmed in by strict theology, deprived of the style that makes the supernatural visible, devoid of the dramatic sensitivity that creates diversified living souls, he accumulates cold dissertations, changes God and man into common, orthodox machines, and only recovers his genius by lending Satan his republican soul, by painting numerous grandiose landscapes and colossal visions, by dedicating his poetry to the praise of religion and duty.]

As we have seen, Taine was not sure Milton was basically a "poet." Whatever shortcomings there are in *Paradise Lost*, they cannot be chalked up to the language the poet had at his disposal. It was a remarkable tool, well suited to what the poet had set out to do. Within limitations, the poet exploited its possibilities. As Taine was to say in his *Notes sur l'Angleterre*, "On n'a vraiment su parler à Dieu que dans le grand siècle littéraire de Shakespeare à Milton."[18]

It is easy to disagree with Taine. He was autocratic, for one thing. Often, carried away by an idea, he failed to notice that there were exceptions to his generalizations. One could wish, moreover, that he had allowed for some measure of evolution, even reversals, in his author's thought. He does not mention, for example, that the Church of England ritual, which the polemicist came to excoriate, had been beautifully evoked in "Il Penseroso." For most readers, the poet's masterpiece would not be *Comus*, although the critic came close to declaring that it was. Exasperated at the numerous, recurrent "dissertations" in *Paradise Lost*, he appears not to have been irritated by those in the masque. Once in a while he was a trifle inconsistent. Having told his readers that the prose works have occasional moments comparable to those in *Paradise Lost*, eventually he decided that the genuine poetic element was, on the whole, absent in the epic. Most readers would not concur that, when the polemical interlude was over, Milton's real poetic talent was gone.

Whatever reservations one may have about Taine, however, it must be conceded that there is great merit in his picture of John Milton as a literary midpoint between the exuberant artists of the sixteenth century and the subdued classicists of the age that would follow. An isolated intellect, Milton was nonetheless a man of his time. Taine tried to show that, acted upon by external events, this intellect developed in a certain way, almost in a predetermined one, as if matters could not have taken a different course. Through it all, however, the poet never swerved from his own basic constant, his dedication to the sublime. Taine's view of him, not always a sympathetic one, was nevertheless very honest, and generally the critic was as ready to admire and to praise as he was to censure. Walt Whitman considered his discussion "vivacious."[19]

Many critics have commented, some disapprovingly, on Taine's contention that the characters in *Paradise Lost* came straight out of the English social and political landscape as it existed at midpoint in the seventeenth century. The idea was not new. Taine no doubt said it better, but any number of his French predecessors had noted that *Paradise Lost* had Puritan England as its real inspiration and décor. Taine's humorous observations about Adam and Eve should not bother us too much. In *The Portable Milton*, Douglas Bush has suggested that today "Adam and Eve, realistically treated, would be a suburban husband and wife practicing nudism in the backyard." Still, a few of Taine's contemporaries were offended. Edmond de Guerle considered the remarks "une parodie qui serait mieux faite par un autre que lui."[20] Since then, writers have disagreed among themselves. While acknowledging Taine's brilliance, René Wellek has chided the critic for his cold intellectualism, his scientism. Even in "the brilliant chapter on Milton," he was little interested in his author's thought, Wellek charged.[21] To Enzo Caramaschi, Taine exaggerated, but exaggeration was necessary to make his points.[22] Even though Taine's school of literary criticism disturbed him, Ferdinand Brunetière, writing toward the end of the nineteenth century, declared that the *Histoire de la littérature anglaise* was "un des plus beaux livres de ce temps, quoi qu'on en puisse dire."[23]

12

Edmond Gabriel Héguin de Guerle

Where Milton is concerned, "Rien de ce qui fait partie du domaine poétique ne lui est...étranger. Il est rarement sorti de ses méditations sublimes; mais partout où il a passé, il a marqué sa route par des chefs-d'œuvre."[1] Such was Edmond Gabriel Héguin de Guerle's overall opinion. Along with Taine, de Guerle (1829–1894) was one of France's most distinguished Milton critics of the nineteenth century. Though coming from a background of intellectuals and writers, he was not an academic. Instead of choosing the university career that might have been expected, he went into business management, eventually moving on to become a government administrator. While in business, he headed the French office of a British firm, The Gresham Life Assurance Society. The job necessitated frequent trips to London.

From his father, de Guerle inherited a sound knowledge of the classics. He also knew French and English literature thoroughly. All of this was to enrich what he had to say about Milton, in whom, somewhere along the line, he picked up a special interest. Knowledgeable about what the French and English critics had already said, on occasion he alluded to their comments. His reactions and judgments are his own, however. The first volume or so of David Masson's *Life of Milton* had come out when de Guerle wrote his own *Milton, sa vie et ses œuvres*, published in 1868, the year a Paris street was named Rue Milton. Masson provided him with valuable material in treating the earlier part of his author's career, but after that he was on his own. Generally, he was very thorough and very accurate, and his comments are consistently based on a close reading of the works. In quoting Milton's English prose, he usually presented his material in French. This is also true for Milton's Latin and Italian poetry. As a rule, English verse is left in the original, although "On May Morning," "How Soon Hath Time," and several other works inspired splendid French prose renderings. Toward the end of his book, there is a remarkable translation of *Paradise Lost* 3.95–128.

As de Guerle saw it, Milton came along at a curious time in literary history. The Elizabethan Age, creative and heroic, had gone, and nothing had taken its place. Arriving on the scene when he did, Milton lacked the spontaneity that characterized the English Renaissance. For this he substituted learning. Poetry did not gush from him; it was controlled. Says de Guerle, "La poésie n'est pas pour lui une effusion naturelle de l'âme, mais la langue savante des sentiments forts et élevés. Il devait ... rester fidèle à l'idéal poétique que lui imposaient à la fois son éducatioin et le caractère particuelier de son génie" (de Guerle, 32).

The critic admires Milton's minor poems. He considers the Latin elegies a "forte et solide poésie." Various early and late sonnets, mostly in connection with personal or historic events, are mentioned and some are translated The later ones are "bien différents de ton et de sentiment de ceux qui avaient clos la première période de son activité poétique" (de Guerle, 173). *Arcades*, the poet's first attempt at dramatic allegory, is "une œuvre impérissable." *Comus*, where the poet "se trahit en traits irrécusables" and which overflows with exquisite poetry, is a demonstration of "la lutte morale contre le mal." Comus is an amorous demigod unable to speak the language of love. Instead, "il philosophe d'une manière plus immorale que séduisante sur les nécessités de la nature et les lois de l'amour" and thus resembles Molière's cunning but overweening hypocrite Tartuffe. Even without *Paradise Lost*, this poem would have assured its author an eminent place among his nation's great poets (de Guerle, 43, 36, 50–55). "On May Morning" the critic translates into harmonious French prose, struck by its marvelous attitude toward nature (de Guerle, 43–44). Among the things he likes most about "L'Allegro" and "Il Penseroso" is, again, the intimate feeling for nature that, amid the classical allusions, the two poems radiate. In both there is much more than a description of the pure, noble pleasures that come from gaity on the one hand and melancholy on the other. There is also "un tableau saisissant des deux faces de la destinée humaine, condamnée à osciller sans cesse de la joie à la tristesse." Displaying neither the simple but elegant charm of classical models nor the studied airiness of Italian pastoral literature, the poems are direct and immediate in their appeal (de Guerle, 41–47, 53).

Even in England, de Guerle admits, "Lycidas" has few admirers. Here, like Virgil and André Chénier, Milton combines his classical erudition with sincere emotion. The lament shows more freedom, more variety than the preceding works. "La facture poétique y atteint une telle perfection que le langage semble s'y dépouiller de son enveloppe grossière et résonne à nos oreilles comme un doux écho de Virgile et de Théocrite." Yet, in the middle of the poem, the reader is startled when the tone all at once changes. As the poet begins to thunder against the abuses in the church, one is reminded of the moment at which Beethoven's *Pastoral Symphony* takes an unexpected new direction, abrupt and strident. For Milton, "Il était temps qu'une distraction violente vînt mettre un intervalle entre les dernières rêveries de son imagination juvénile et les sombres tableaux que la guerre civile allait dérouler devant lui" (de Guerle, 57–58). Another poem marked the transition period. With "Epitaphium Damonis," "les plus beaux vers latins qu'ils ait écrits," the poet sought to "se recueillir et jeter comme un éternel adieu à ces pompes de l'art, de la nature, et de la pensée" before hurling himself into the controversies awaiting him (de Guerle, 79–80).

The second section of *Milton, sa vie et ses œuvres*, by far the longest, is mostly devoted to Milton's writings and public life from 1639 to 1660. "Milton pamphlétaire et prosateur" is its subtitle, and it is a methodical look, work by work, at Milton's prose during the period in question. The prose works interest de Guerle primarily from the standpoint of the cultural and political circumstances that produced them. For readers who might not know much about such matters, he provides historical background and commentary where needed. He is also interested in what the prose works tell us about the evolution of the author's thought. Sometimes he comments on specific pamphlets as rhetorical performances. Finally, the critic examines Milton's prose style, which he often finds poetic.

Returning from his travels, Milton could have looked forward to a promising future, the critic asserts. His modest reserve, his solitary, bookish inclinations and habits were such that writing ought to have been enough for him. He became a conscientious schoolmaster. As outlined in *Of Education*, the program he laid down was unrealistic. "Il voulait le bien et le poursuivait avec une ardeur qui méconnaissait la véritable nature des choses." Milton conceived of it as utilitarian. In reality, the course of studies he proposed would crush the human mind (de Guerle, 103–05).

Point by point, de Guerle summarizes *Of Reformation*, translating much of the magnificent prayer that concludes it. "Une semblable éloquence, dans laquelle l'élévation du langage n'enlevait rien à l'amertume et à l'énergie de l'invective, dut retentir comme un coup de tonnerre" (de Guerle, 115–21). Noting that at this time Milton was still in the Presbyterian camp, de Guerle sketches the pamphlet war that broke out at this time, situating Milton in it. In *Of Prelatical Episcopacy* and *The Reason of Church Government*, even though the brochures remain within the bounds of impassioned dialectic, "le ton s'agrit." Milton had not cut loose from scholasticism, but, in the midst of his erudition and passionate invective, he managed here to pour out "des torrents de poésie" (de Guerle, 127–28). Unfortunately, he did not stop there. As pamphlet answered pamphlet, Milton and his adversaries grew insulting. "De mesquines provocations" found their way into "cette controverse de principes." The *Animadversions* gave free rein to their author's scorn and sarcasm. Still, the work has remarkable poetic sections that the critic singles out and praises.[2]

As an oratorical achievement, de Guerle hailed the *Animadversions*. "L'Angleterre n'avait point encore entendu d'aussi libres accents," he writes. The majestic passage in section 4, beginning "In this age Britain's God..." and ending with an invitation to Christ to take possession of His church, he describes as a magnificent prosopopœia. Enthusiastically, de Guerle adds that "la rhétorique et la déclamation ont leur part dans cette éloquente apostrophe" but praises its "exubérante ardeur." "L'excès est dans l'esprit, il n'est point dans la forme. Toute la magnificence de la poésie biblique se présente à la fois à cette imagination obsédée de la lecture des prophètes." Milton, "en cherchant la vigueur du pamphlétaire...," "ébauche déjà la poésie du *Paradis perdu*" (de Guerle, 132, 136–37). The *Animadversions* are Milton's high water mark as a controversialist. After that, the poet and his antagonists came down from their serene heights and belabored one another with pedantry, insults, and quips. Milton proved as able as his opponents. "Les sarcasmes de Milton, lourdement assénés, tombèrent de tout leur poids sur ses adversaires" (de Guerle, 138).

When *A Modest Confutation* appeared, an enraged Milton replied. *An Apology for Smectymnuus*, a savage rebuttal, was warranted, in de Guerle's view. In it Milton answered insult with insult. "Il ne faut plus chercher ni argument ni dialectique," the critic observes. On the other hand, it is to this pamphlet that we owe much of what is known about the author's youth and intellectual development. Somewhat earlier and in another context, de Guerle had quoted the essential passage (de Guerle, 108). De Guerle thinks that all of Milton, the human weaknesses and the ideals, the reprehensible and the admirable, come alive in the passage, "son orgueil inséparable de sa grandeur d'âme, sa personnalité hautaine et son inaltérable honnêteté." To characterize the passage, the critic finds a suitable image, comparing the angry pamphleteer's confession to a remarkably frank statue. "On voit se dresser devant soi une statue d'un airain sonore coulée d'un seul jet, mais où l'on chercherait en vain la grâce des contours et l'agrément de l'expression" (de Guerle, 139).

Here, de Guerle pauses to assess Milton as a pamphleteer up to the *Apology*, making some generalizations regarding the author's style as it had evolved up to that point. Until then there had been little to make the writer stand out as far as his religious and political views were concerned. He was for Parliament and the Presbyterians, but so were many others. Milton's originality lay in the style with which he voiced his opinions. It was entirely his own. In commenting upon it, de Guerle produces numerous standards of comparison drawn from his own vast exposure to Greek, Latin, English and French prose stylists. Between Milton and his immediate French and English predecessors and contemporaries there were few similarities. "Cette phrase lumineuse et ondulante dont tous les mots semblent regorger de vigueur et d'énergie ne ressemble en rien au style nerveux, concis, aphoristique de Bacon. Elle est encore plus différente de l'éloquence onctueuse de Jeremy Taylor, de la diction originale et colorée de Burton, et de l'énergie toute biblique de Bunyan." Nor does it have "l'ampleur majestueuse de Bossuet." Here and there, the ancients provided a touch or two. While there are no Ciceronian periods, one hears Thucydides' virile but somewhat ponderous tread, "mais avec le goût et la simplicité de moins." And as one might expect, the Bible, with its "couleur vigoureuse et tranchée," made its contribution, too. With Milton, "Il semble qu'il y ait place pour tout dans son ample et vaste sein," de Guerle observes.

But even though Milton has assimilated his models, they hinder him and slow him down. At once cumbersome and impetuous, his progress is like that of "un ruisseau d'orage qui se perd dans une mer." Only the author's inspiration makes it all work. Yet there are spectacular moments. "Au miliieu de ce chaos puissant, on voit surgir de temps à autre des tableaux d'une grandeur saisissante...," writes de Guerle. Milton appears to have thought that prose could be as noble as verse. Translating as he goes, the critic singles out what he considers a case in point, Milton's description of Zeal in the *Apology for Smectymnuus*. Here Milton was imitating Virgil's portrayal of Fame. To de Guerle, he was also showing what he was capable of (de Guerle, 140–43; YPW 1:899–900). Frederick L. Taft was to point out much later that Zeal's chariot resembles that of the Son in *Paradise Lost* 6.750–59.[3]

From the early pamphlets, de Guerle goes on to discuss Milton's first marriage and the divorce tracts. The critic is harsh with Mary Powell, whom he characterizes, mentally and emotionally, as ordinary. He points out that, years later, Milton remembered her desertion and the reconciliation when, in *Samson Agonistes*, he had the chorus lament man's innate weakness for a woman he loves:

> Yet beauty, though injurious, hath strange power,
> After offense returning, to regain
> Love once possest, nor can be easily
> Repuls't, without much inward passion felt
> And secret sting of amorous remorse.
> (*SA* 1003–007)

When it became clear that Mary Powell would not return from her parents' home, Milton, hurt and angry, searched the Scriptures to help him prove that divorce is permissible. He went public with his private problem. He angered those he sought to persuade, however. The product of error and illusion, *The Doctrine and Discipline of Divorce* is a compilation "des opinions les plus étranges," even dangerous. Although there was little overt reaction, it scandalized everyone. No matter, says de Guerle. "Milton, seul contre tous, entassait argument sur argument pour soutenir une erreur qui sortait du plus profond de son cœur. Il y resta attaché jusqu'à son dernier jour..." (de Guerle, 150–53, 170).

Reminding his readers that, in *De Doctrina Christiana*, Milton would insist upon woman's natural inferiority to man and that he would sanction polygamy, de Guerle summarizes the arguments in *The Doctrine and Discipline of Divorce, The Judgment of Martin Bucer, Tetrachordon* and *Colasterion*, pointing out that similar ideas abound in *Samson Agonistes* (*SA* 1034 ff.; de Guerle, 148 n. 1). While admitting that they reveal talent and learning, the critic is severe with the divorce tracts, noting the author's extreme care in selecting authorities that appear to bear him out and a corresponding avoidance of those that do not (de Guerle, 162–63). De Guerle also minimizes the public's reaction to the pamphlets:

> Ce fut, en effet, la juste punition de Milton de n'avoir pu rencontrer dans cette campagne malheureuse d'adversaire digne de lui. Son véritable adversaire était celui qui se taisait, le bon sens public qui faisait avec raison justice de pareils emportements. Personne ne voulut prendre au sérieux cette violente sortie d'un mari outragé qui veut transformer une infortune personnelle, digne de pitié, en calamité publique et en iniquité sociale et religieuse. (de Guerle, 168)

> [Actually it was a fitting punishment for Milton that he encountered no worthy opponent in this deplorable campaign. His real opponent, the public's good sense, was one that remained silent, treating such outbursts as they deserved to be treated. Everyone dismissed this violent philippic on the part of an irate husband seeking to convert a personal misfortune that deserved pity into a public calamity and a social and religious iniquity.]

De Guerle notes that the divorce tracts did alarm the Presbyterians and made Milton's break with them inevitable (de Guerle, 153).

If, in the divorce tracts, the content was offensive, the style was another matter. The tracts were an "éloquent fatras." While there were fewer pages that could be described as "éloquentes et achevées" when compared with the religious pamphlets, the author's prose had, on the whole, made considerable strides. "On y sent partout l'écrivain devenu maître de sa forme, sentant la phrase s'assouplir sous sa main et se prêter à toutes les exigences d'une controverse à la fois savante et passionnée." Milton was less conscious in these pamphlets of classical models, de Guerle argues. "Aiguisée par la passion et la colère, sa plume avait pris une allure plus libre et plus dégagée. La phrase ne se traîne plus ici sur les modèles de l'antiquité, et si parfois le langage paraît encore vieilli et suranné, il est toujours énergique et expressif. Style, images, tours, tout y est plus personnel et plus original." There are also poetic moments, and a case in point is singled out.[4] Publishing the pamphlets would seem to have made reconciliation between Milton and his wife impossible. Nevertheless, in spite of the pamphlets and in spite of all that had happened between them, Milton forgave Mary Powell. "Ainsi pardonnent et punissent les poètes, et leur pardon comme leur noble vengeance traversent les siècles." Adam's forgiving Eve in *Paradise Lost* parallels what happened in the poet's own life. Elsewhere de Guerle had already translated several lines from Adam and Eve's reconciliation scene (de Guerle, 151; *PL* 10.937–45). He concludes his discussion of the divorce tracts by translating, in prose and with some omissions, the salute to wedded love in *Paradise Lost*, hoping that this, rather than the tracts, represents the poet's real attitude toward marriage (de Guerle, 170; *PL* 4.750–57). De Guerle chooses to believe that Milton's mind had been "égaré" in the divorce business and that the rest of his life constitutes a denial of a fleeting aberration. The critic had obviously forgotten his earlier statement that, to his ideas on divorce, the poet "resta attaché jusqu'a son dernier jour."

Milton's second marriage was happy but brief. In connection with it, de Guerle translates Sonnet 23. The critic is skeptical about the third marriage. Late unions, he believes, are never without problems. Whatever the case, Elizabeth Minshull seems to have been gentle and submissive, and to her husband she may well have been "l'épouse selon son cœur." Though perhaps not as disinterested as her spouse, she provided him, in his old age, a measure of domestic happiness that he needed. Little is known about her relations with his daughters, the critic notes. For all we know, Elizabeth may not have been as good a mother to them as she should have been. Living with Milton may not have been easy. The poet was authoritarian, even despotic, and tried to impose his views upon others, which could not have made for a pleasant household. This does not, of course, excuse his daughters' subsequent behavior toward their father.

De Guerle takes a dim view of Milton's political stance during the Republic and Protectorate. Punctuating it with extensive quotations in French, he summarizes *The Tenure of Kings and Magistrates*. In taking the reprehensible position he did, Milton showed that he was incapable of visualizing a midpoint between absolutism on the one hand and popular sovereignty on the other, and he pandered to the masses. Worse still is the cruel streak, shocking in a poet, that the work reveals. De Guerle's view is like that of Lamartine. "Mêlée aux orages de ce monde, la poésie doit avoir, pour ainsi dire, l'immobilité des croyances religieuses: elle ne doit prêter sa voix qu'à la justice, à la clémence, et à la pitié." Not even the violent times, then, excuse what this poet did. "L'éternité ne transige pas avec le temps." The best that can be said for Milton is that he made a terrible mistake, which must be attributed to human weakness. Still, "Il y a une chose sur laquelle les poètes n'ont pas le droit de se tromper, c'est sur la générosité et la pitié due à l'infortune" (de Guerle, 175–77, 184, 192).

Having made his initial mistake, Milton compounded it. Scarcely had he vindicated the king's trial and execution than he was called upon to answer *Eikon Basilike*. There was but little purpose to *Eikonoklastes*. Aside from national and international politics, which the critic does not go into, there could be no reason for this diatribe. The king was dead, and there was no longer any need to justify the act that had removed him from the scene. The real object, then, was to besmirch his memory. It was not an inspiring task, and de Guerle believes it resulted in the poet's least remarkable polemic work. Although "un pamphlet sérieux et plein de faits," it indicts its author (de Guerle, 192–99). When Claude de Saumaise published the *Defensio Regia*, Milton was ordered to reply. Given his failing eyesight, he could have eluded the order but chose not to do so. *Pro Populo Anglicano*

Defensio restated his views on popular sovereignty, emphasizing the monarch's role as the people's delegate. In this bitter pamphlet, Milton is as harsh as ever. "Le lourd marteau se soulève et retombe sans merci." The reader looks in vain for "quelques lignes tempérées des larmes de l'humaine commisération" (de Guerle, 199–206).

When Du Moulin's *Regii Sanguinis Clamor ad Cœlum* appeared, Milton answered with his *Defensio Secunda*, heaping trivial but ponderous abuse upon his presumed opponent. Nevertheless, the pamphlet is a valuable book, "une véritable autobiographie, racontée avec une noblesse dont la colère ne peut dépouiller l'âme de Milton" (de Guerle, 209). What is pathetic in *Defensio Secunda* is the author's apostrophe to Oliver Cromwell, most of which de Guerle translates. Milton's attitude toward the man, as de Guerle understands that attitude, disturbs the critic. Sonnet 16 and the long digression in *Defensio Secunda* "sont témoins vivants qui accusent la faiblesse ou l'erreur de Milton," he holds. By 1654 Milton should have been able to see that his hero was a despot. Seeing it or not, he stuck to his illusion that the Lord Protector was "le protestantisme armé et triomphant" on whose successes the European Reformation depended. Perhaps that was enough. For the poet, no personal gain was involved in the adulation, certainly (de Guerle, 187, 209–21). De Guerle mistakenly cites the adulation as having appeared in *Pro Se Defensio*, about which he has little to say except that it was the author's reply to Alexandre More's *Fides Publica*. *The Ready and Easy Way to Establish a Free Commonwealth* shows Milton in a better light as he tried, in a desperate hour, to make his innovative plea for enlightened government by the few. It is clear that freedom, as he saw it, was "un ensemble de nobles et vertueux sentiments dans lesquels venait se noyer cette précaire et chétive prérogative des faibles, qui devient à la longue le plus ferme et le seul appui des forts" (de Guerle, 236).

As we have seen, de Guerle deplored the positions Milton took in the controversies that rocked his era, chalking them up to weakness, illusion and sectarian passion. Assessing the pamphlets as a whole, the critic is balanced but ultimately

negative except where style is concerned. While acknowledging that, with his prose, Milton invented a powerful tool, de Guerle believes *Pilgrim's Progress* a better example of Puritan literature. As for the pamphlets' religious content, they lack the "doctrine substantielle et suivie" that makes Calvin's *Institution chrétienne* unforgettable. And yet the pamphlets should be read, though not when one is looking for "belles pensées exprimées dans un beau langage." Rather, they have to be examined in the context of the terrible times that gave rise to them. Even so, they have their moments. "Au milieu de cette argumentation à outrance et souvent désordonnée, surgissent des pensées nobles et vigoureuses, dont l'ampleur n'a jamais été dépassée" (de Guerle, 239–41).

Of all the pamphlets, there is one for which de Guerle has nothing but praise, however. *Areopagitica* stands out; enthusiastically, the critic summarizes it in detail and quotes long passages in French. "Un écrit qui consacrerait à lui seul la renommée de prosateur de Milton et dans lequel il a pu donner, au moins une fois, la juste mesure de son génie et de ses généreuses inspirations." With its "libre et virile énergie," de Guerle compares it to La Boétie's *Discours sur la servitude volontaire*. Its plea for truth also reminds him of one of Pascal's *Lettres provinciales*, the twelfth. Pascal concluded with observations similar to those of Milton. "C'est une étrange et longue guerre que celle où la violence essaie d'opprimer la vérité," wrote Pascal. "Tous les efforts de la violence ne peuvent affaiblir la vérité et ne servent qu'à la relever davantage.... La violence et la vérité ne peuvent rien l'une sur l'autre.... La violence n'a qu'un cours borné par l'ordre de Dieu, qui en conduit les effets à la gloire de la vérité qu'elle attaque, au lieu que la vérité subsiste éternelle et puissante comme Dieu même."[5] In *Areopagitica*, obsessed with neither his classical models nor his religious convictions, Milton "déploie toute l'énergie, toute la pompe naturelle de son génie. La phrase, nerveuse, concise, colorée, se presse, se condense, procède par interrogation, par apostrophe, au lieu de déborder... comme un fleuve qui a perdu ses rivages," as in the other pamphlets. "L'*Areopagitica* de Milton est le premier appel éloquent à la liberté qu'ait

entendu le monde moderne," the critic affirms. Though less eloquent, *Of True Religion* displays some of the same admirable qualities (de Guerle, 233). De Guerle has little to say about *The History of Britain* aside from the fact that Milton had already written four of its books when he became the Council of State's Latin Secretary. The work does not show its author as an innovative historian. Written in a relatively simple style, the work "s'élève parfois à une véritable éloquence" (de Guerle, 180, 222 n. 1).

After *De Doctrina Christiana*, de Guerle notes, Milton seems to have written nothing new. In 1674 he published his *Prolusiones Quædam Oratoriæ* and *Epistolarum Familiarum*, dating from earlier periods. *A Brief History of Muscovia* is posthumous. The author died quietly on 8 November 1674 and was buried at St. Giles, Cripplegate. Pointing out that Elizabeth Forster, his last known descendant, died on 9 May 1754, de Guerle notes that "Les hommes de génie semblent épuiser en une floraison gigantesque, comme certaines plantes des tropiques, toute la sève vitale de leur souches." Milton's children and grandchildren, all of them obscure, appear to establish such a rule. With the family now extinct, posterity, even if it were of a mind to do so, would be unable to find an individual to whom, belatedly, it might extend the recognition or gratitude contemporaries never gave the author of *Paradise Lost* (de Guerle, 394, 396).

De Guerle's religious outlook was conservative, traditional. The critic was openminded, however, and, of all his compatriots, he is undoubtedly the one who, in the nineteenth century, best copes with Milton's religious thought. Unfortunately, on one or two points he is not as consistent as he could have been. With a solid grounding in philosophy and theology, he could cite at will the church fathers, St. Theresa, Calvin, Pascal, Leibnitz, Bossuet, Fénelon, Bayle, Hume, Wesley, Fox and others, and thus he is able to compare or contrast their positions on a given doctrine with the one he attributes to Milton. Of Unitarianism and its approach to salvation, he remarks that "Channing ne parle pas mieux que Pascal de la grandeur de l'homme; mais il oublie sa misère." Elsewhere, the French romantics' social Catholicism that his era still wrote and talked about was on his mind. Probably this and Renan's *Vie de Jésus*, which had created such a storm on its publication in 1863, were what led him to observe that, in modern times, Jesus had been humanized. "Le sentimentalisme de notre temps ne s'est attaché qu'à Jésus vivant et marchant parmi les hommes," he writes. He regards this Jesus as a far cry from Milton's Son of God conversing with the Father in Heaven (de Guerle, 370–74).

Although he looked upon Milton's religious beliefs as fundamental to understanding almost the entire corpus of the author's work, it was only in the final section of *Milton, sa vie et ses œuvres*, that de Guerle attempted to analyze them. It might have helped had he done it sooner. De Guerle presumes that *De Doctrina Christiana* dates from Milton's last years and that it contained at least one allusion to *Paradise Regained*, which may account for why he reserves his discussion of Milton's religious views for the end of his book. For the most part, the discussion is based on *De Doctrina*, but additional material as well as examples and demonstrations are drawn from such works as *Tetrachordon, The Likeliest Means to Remove Hirelings out of the Church* and *Paradise Lost*. De Guerle's analysis has held up reasonably well in the light of subsequent studies.[6]

De Guerle theorizes that if Milton did not publish *De Doctrina* during his lifetime, he had a good reason for not doing so. With old age approaching, the poet craved peace of mind. "Milton jugea sans doute qu'il était inutile de troubler les dernières années de sa vieillesse et de réveiller des haines qui n'étaient pas assoupies en jetant au milieu de la réaction antipuritaine ... ce défi aux opinions triomphantes." As we know, Maurice Kelley long ago demonstrated that there was a better reason, a simpler one. Having begun the work much earlier, Milton kept making emendations in it until he died.[7] De Guerle believes that eventually Milton wanted the book, a religious testament containing the "opinions auxquelles s'était arrêté son esprit hardi et indépendant," to appear. With that end in mind, he must have entrusted it to Cyriack Skinner. De Guerle surmises that the Daniel Skinner who later tried to publish it in Holland was Cyriack's nephew (de Guerle, 323).

De Doctrina Christiana reveals its author's good qualities and also his bad ones. As de Guerle sees it, Milton had calmed down somewhat when he wrote it, and it shows that he had attained a new spiritual peace. The book has about it a certain "unction." Most of all, it is the complete, definitive expression of the poet's religious thought. Despite his contempt for theological systems, Milton produced a clear, coherent one with this treatise (de Guerle, 344, 347, 390). The book is authoritarian, as one would expect. While Milton seems to champion the view that individuals have a right to their personal convictions, in reality he was anything but tolerant. "Il était loin d'admettre, dans les matières religieuses, la liberté de penser," the critic writes (de Guerle, 325–26, 367). Milton's tolerance or lack of it is one of the two or three matters about which de Guerle is not wholly consistent. De Guerle also claims that Milton held the church fathers in rather low esteem, not adding that the poet was a bit selective about this (de Guerle, 123).

In examining Milton's religious thought, de Guerle does not propose to go into "le détail minutieux des points sur lesquels l'opinion de Milton se rapproche ou s'éloigne des doctrines professées par les diverses églises de son temps." Rather, he sets out to classify the general tendencies in his faith. Several things he does not investigate. Except to mention divorce, which he calls a "licence," he does not explore Milton's attitude toward interpersonal relationships. Nor does he look into such things as virtue and duty. Notably missing, also, is a consideration of good works. The characteristics to keep in mind, the critic believes, were Milton's absolute independence and his willingness to push a concept to its rational extremes, however problematic it might be to apply the conclusions (de Guerle, 383–84, 387). His "radicalisme chrétien" guaranteed that his creed would be nonconformist. Indeed, it was a very personal thing, natural and adventurous, its heterodox coloration revealing a few gnostic elements and verging now and then on pantheism and materialism. Worth delving into, Milton's religious individualism should not disturb anyone. Using a good image of his own, de Guerle observes that "Le christianisme est un édifice assez solide pour qu'une pierre qui s'en détache n'en entraîne pas la ruine." Given the age in which it was written, *De Doctrina Christiana* even so strikes a discordant note, altogether out of tune with its era (de Guerle, 326, 334–35, 339–40). If, for the most part, the ideas come from the Bible, they come from a highly interpretive, sometimes erroneous reading of that document. There are times, as in the case of man's share of responsibility for sin, when it got in the author's way. When it suited his purposes, Milton laid it aside and invoked what he considered common sense and reason instead. On occasion, he even went against it (de Guerle, 325, 355, 363, 374, 388). Above all, Milton was no mystic. "Jamais esprit ne fut plus éloigné que celui de Milton du mysticisme, qui voit passer ce monde comme une ombre néfaste, qui nous cache le soleil de notre véritable patrie. Tout ce qui vit, matière et esprit, prenait à ses yeux une forme concrète et palpable." This is another point on which de Guerle is not entirely consistent (de Guerle, 347–52, 389).

According to de Guerle's interpretation, Milton's scheme of things posited the existence of two Heavens. The one, which Moses talked about, is visible. The other, invisible, came into being prior to the world's creation. De Guerle defines Milton's Son of God as the "émanation première de la Divinité mais non coessentiel à la Divinité." The Holy Spirit is an "attribut de Dieu mais non personne divine." At the time of the Creation, matter already existed. Something had to exist that could be acted upon by the divine fiat. If God created the world, He did it through the Word (the Son) and the Holy Spirit. Angels came into being when the visible world was created. As for human beings, they are not composed of two distinct substances, the soul and the body, spirit and matter. The two cannot be separated. On the contrary, the human person is "quelque chose comme une inspiration de la vertu divine, façonnée pour l'exercice de la vie et de la raison et infusée dans un corps organique," making it quite literally a living soul (de Guerle, 333–38, 351).

One of the trickiest problems Milton had to deal with, according to de Guerle, was reconciling God's unlimited foreknowledge, providence and power with the human being's free will. *De Doctrina's* handling of this is simply a commentary upon *Paradise Lost* 3.95–128, where God explains to the Son that, having been created free, human beings will be the artisans of their own ruin.[8] While he managed to keep foreknowledge and predestination separate, the author nonetheless had a dilemma on his hands that he was unable to resolve. The best he could do was conclude that God wants all of us to be saved and, on occasion, may help certain individuals achieve this goal. Though loath to punish, He knows that there are those who will resist salvation, and these, as is proper, will be condemned. The "elect" will not be chosen arbitrarily but rather will be those individuals who have persevered in the faith. Being one of them is thus contingent upon our working at it. All of this might seem to restrict grace somewhat, of course. To compensate, God allows us to repent. He also permits us, even on our deathbeds, to take advantage of whatever grace is available to us.

In broaching Milton's views on salvation and redemption, de Guerle tries to establish that the poet's position on these two points was at odds with Unitarian teaching. Unitarians, the critic asserts, tend to dismiss grace in actual practice, thus making it all but impossible for individuals to accomplish their own salvation. De Guerle believes that, in *Paradise Lost*, the poet demonstrated his own position better than he did in *De Doctrina Christiana*. By admitting grace, the critic points out, Milton showed that there was a basic Calvinist doctrine that he did not accept. But another fundamental Calvinist tenet, predestination or whatever one wishes to call it, he *did* accept. As early as *The Doctrine and Discipiline of Divorce*, he had announced his adherence to the idea. Far from hindering or even ruling out salvation, Milton took the view that predestination worked in the interests of those who believe. Nothing specific is said in this context about the Arminian position. However, in connection with justification, the question of Arminianism comes up. Here the critic contends that Milton reconciled "dans une large tolérance les opinions si divergentes des communions chrétiennes," although there are some opinions that he repudiated. Deciding that human beings were responsible and that, once saved, they could fall back into sin and remain there, he laid himself open to the charge of Arminianism. As often happened, Milton was, in any event, making Scripture prove what he wanted it to prove (de Guerle, 367, 369, 371-82).

In 1861 Théodore Karcher noted in passing that Milton was a Unitarian.[9] Not everyone agreed. Much of de Guerle's discussion of Milton and his religious beliefs has to do with whether or not the poet should be considered a precursor of modern Unitarianism. Emphatically, de Guerle contends that he should not. Milton's being an antitrinitarian does not mean that he was, in fact, a Unitarian (de Guerle, 344). It was in 1826, the critic recalls, that William Ellery Channing, claiming to see a spiritual ancestor in *De Doctrina Christiana*, wrote his *Remarks on the Character and Writings of John Milton*. De Guerle, however, bases his comments upon some of Channing's more theoretical or speculative works, such as *Unitarian Christianity* (1819) and *Evidences of Christianity* (1821). As the critic points out, Channing admits that Unitarians disagreed with Milton on several vital points, including human nature, original sin and humankind's regeneration and redemption. But there was more, according to de Guerle. Milton's position was nowhere near the Unitarians' stand concerning the Son of God, the nature of His mediation, and the price He paid to redeem humankind, not to mention what the salvation He brought with Him consisted of. That Christ was divine Milton did not contest. De Guerle insists here upon a passage in *De Doctrina* in which Milton declared, "As for Christ's divine nature..., He was God with God, and although He was not supreme..., He must have existed before His incarnation, whatever subtleties may have been invented to provide an escape from this conclusion by those who argue that Christ was a mere man" (de Guerle, 382–83, 363–64; *YPW* 6:419). The Fall, according to de Guerle, is still another doctrine on which Milton and the Unitarians do not see eye to eye. *Paradise Lost* is built around this very doctrine, which Unitarians do not accept (de Guerle, 366).

Continuing, de Guerle points out that Unitarians reject the Calvinist stand on the human being's total depravity and condemnation, the perseverance of the saints, the inability to resist grace, and the matter of justification by faith. Milton rejected these also, but with a difference. Whereas Channing's Christianity is founded upon a series of dogmatic negations, with Milton this is not the case. Channing dismisses other people's doctrines and shoves them aside. Milton does this also, but then he proposes something to take their place. "Il n'abat que pour relever" (de Guerle, 383). De Guerle was more detailed, but Paul Chauvet would be just as positive several decades later in dismissing Milton's Unitarianism in his *La Religion de Milton*.

De Guerle says that this was not his plan, but, having decided that Milton's religious thought did not foreshadow Unitarianism, he turns his attention to a few doctrines on which the poet disagreed with various other Christian denominations. The Sacraments, for example: Milton considered several, baptism among them. The Scriptures seem to prescribe baptism by immersion, he held. As for infant baptism, he went on record as being opposed to it since it involves a profession of faith that babies are incapable of making. Communion he questioned also. Transubstantiation he condemned because it makes communion "un banquet de cannibales." Communion is no more than an outward sign, and if one believes what God has promised, the ritual is unnecessary. In any case, there is no reason why one should have to have a priest administer it. Here Milton's position is close to that of Zwingli (de Guerle, 384–85). Milton dismisses the Catholic Church's claim that it is the true church. On the contrary, the church is made up of all believers collectively. No minister, certainly no chief minister, can be said to represent it alone. Milton accepts deacons, priests and even bishops, but thinks the people should select and test them. Ordination is not necessary, however. If individuals can teach and minister and wish to do so, then they should do it, whether there have been prior ceremonies or not. Clergy, like the apostles, ought to earn their living doing something other than performing their ministerial duties. Nevertheless, if they are paid for those duties, people should not have to tithe or be taxed to provide the salaries (de Guerle, 386–87). Otherwise, civil authority, which has no business in ecclesiastical matters, would become involved. Excommunication ought to be used when called for, but it should be spiritual only. Church members as a unit should have the sole right to impose it (de Guerle, 118, 386–87).

Concluding his summary and analysis of Milton's religious ideas, de Guerle points out that the poet took Christ's second coming literally. Since he believed that the body and the soul are not distinct from one another, he held that both would be resurrected together. To be consistent, he did not hesitate to go against Scripture on the matter. Judgment would take place on earth. As for the damned, Milton was not sure how long their punishment would last, but he was certain that it would be meted out in a place somewhere below the visible world. The saved, on the other hand, would be rewarded in Heaven, though the rewards would not be the same for everyone (de Guerle, 388–90).

After elaborating upon his theology, de Guerle sees little need to go into the poet's actual religious practices. However, he does insist that, for Milton, religion was a highly personal thing. If, as has been claimed, the poet seldom attended church services in his later years, this is wholly consonant with his view that communion with God is a private matter. Thus the tolerance he extended to others he was entitled to himself. Once more the critic forgets that, earlier, he had called attention to Milton's impatience with the views and practices of other people. Curiously, he calls *Of True Religion* the *Traité de la tolérance*, overlooking its vehement, intolerant blasts at "popery." In a surprisingly harsh comment, de Guerle brings his discussion to a close with the remark that, had he spent more time worshiping with others, Milton might have learned to love his neighbor a bit more than he did (de Guerle, 391-92).

De Guerle's commentary on *Paradise Lost, Paradise Regained* and *Samson Agonistes* lacks organization and even absolute consistency but sparkles with intelligent observations. The critic points out that *Eikonoklastes* and *Pro Populo Anglicano Defensio* were publicly burned on 27 August 1660. A new edition of the *Cabinet Council*, attributed to Sir Walter Raleigh, appeared with a new title and without the editor's name at about the same time. De Guerle is incorrect in dating the publication of the Latin grammar from this period.[10] Already Milton was at work on *Paradise Lost*. Although with it he was realizing an old dream, his poem was appearing at the most inauspicious possible moment. Given the topic, it was two decades late. Given contemporary literary taste, it was at least two decades early. Given how the material is treated, it may have been as much as a century off. Milton was all too aware that it might be ignored.[11]

De Guerle was well versed in what previous critics had had to say about Milton and now and then refers to Dryden, Addison, Johnson, Coleridge and Taine, whose *Histoire de la littérature anglaise* had appeared several years earlier. We know, the critic states, that Milton originally considered writing a drama, and the epic's numerous speeches would seem to bear this out. Except for Satan's proud, passionate outbursts, however, the speeches are didactic rather than dramatic. Epics are supposed to have speeches, nevertheless. With "L'Allegro," *Comus* and *Samson Agonistes*, Milton proved that he could work within dramatic forms. In *Paradise Lost* he chose not to do so. "Il connaissait trop son art pour faire une épopée en croyant faire un drame" (de Guerle, 266-67). De Guerle observes that, in *Paradise Lost*, Milton was not the first to treat the subject. Including Andreini's *Adamo*, there are sources almost as numerous as those of the Nile River and perhaps even more obscure. The important source, needless to say, is the Bible.

De Guerle was not sure that his own era was capable of understanding the epic mentality. Epic poetry, he observes, has flourished in times when simple people invent incredible heroes and really believe in them or else when, no longer simple but having become highly sophisticated and "classical," they imagine rather than believe. For his own contemporaries, in either case, the age of epic poetry is quite over.

> Nous sommes bien loin de l'enfance naïve; nous avons même passé l'âge viril et classique.... L'ordre, les proportions, l'harmonie des formes, en un mot ce grand édifice construit entre ciel et terre qu'on appelle une épopée, tout cela est pour nous lettre close.... Nous avons arraché de notre lyre cette corde harmonieuse qui vibre à travers les âges.
>
> [We are far removed from our naive childhood; we have even passed the virile, classical age.... Order, proportion, harmony of form, in a word that huge structure between heaven and earth called an epic, all that is a closed letter for us.... From our lyre we have snatched that harmonious string which vibrates across the ages.]

Oriented toward personal concerns and correspondingly less interested in universals, de Guerle says, the modern era is attuned to lyric rather than epic poetry (de Guerle, 268–69). For other reasons, as the critic points out, Milton's immediate prospective audience was not prepared for *Paradise Lost,* either. Whatever the audience, the epic raises all kinds of problems, not all of which have solutions.

One of the most serious problems has to do with the religious mythology that provides an epic with much of its scaffolding. Should there be—indeed, *can* there be—such a thing as a Christian mythology? De Guerle has his doubts. God, the ultimate immaterial being, is hard enough for the human mind to conceive. Yet Milton dared give this being recognizable attributes as well as an essential thinking, speaking, acting role in his poem. We shall see that de Guerle has reservations as to how well Milton succeeded. Even so, the critic asks, do the other supernatural beings come off as well as this one does? At the hands of a Christian poet, can angels and demons be made plausible? For the ancient poets, the task was relatively simple, their divinities being little more than idealized, amplified human beings. A Catholic poet could have introduced saints into the narrative to help solve this dilemma. As a Protestant, Milton could not do this, so he created angels and devils instead. However, with his anthropomorphic leanings and his ill-defined notions concerning the distinction between matter and spirit, he vacillated between abstraction and the concrete. His celestial creatures and his demons show it. Made of some kind of nebulous cosmic matter capable of infinite transformations, they change form at will. "Tantôt les anges et les démons ont un corps essentiel et délimité, tantôt ils se subtilisent au point de pouvoir revêtir les formes les plus étranges." Thus Satan appears successively as a pure spirit, as a toad and as a serpent. It may be that Milton's basic uncertainties, reflected in the vague material out of which he created these entities, distort what they are supposed to represent theologically (de Guerle, 273-74, 282). De Guerle regards this as a problem but does not try to clarify it. He is much more concerned with the epic's immense scope. Narrating the Fall was vast enough, but Milton sought to do even more. He set out to probe human destiny beyond this life and, in so doing, he exceeded the narrow limits that the epic genre would seem to impose. What he achieved can only be measured in terms of its grandeur (de Guerle, 274-76).

To de Guerle, *Paradise Lost* is a poetic condensation of the ideas that dominated Milton's life. It must be read as an enormous didactic poem or else let alone. In addition to being a code of ethics, to be sure, the poem is a good many other things as well, such as a cosmology and a theodicy. But the epic is remarkable for a host of reasons. Structurally it is imperfect, but the critic does not care whether it has a beginning, a middle or an end. "Il y a tant d'œuvres qui ne pèchent contre aucune de ces règles et qui n'en sont pas meilleures pour cela." Like the structure, the topic leaves much to be desired. Still, if critics were to demolish the one and the other, *Paradise Lost* would still remain on its feet. With all its flaws, the poem "n'en demeure pas moins une œuvre majestueuse et sublime qui défie le temps et les critiques." It is the ultimate poem of Christian faith, "une magnifique illustration du mystère de la destinée humaine" (de Guerle, 276–78, 297–98, 306).

Early in his discussion of *Paradise Lost*, de Guerle embarks upon a protracted comparison between Dante and Milton, listing a number of areas in which he sees the two poets approaching their task from different backgrounds, perspectives and concepts. *The Divine Comedy*'s prestige continues to soar, while Milton, "avec un génie égal sinon supérieur, n'obtient qu'une admiration sans enthousiasme et pour ainsi dire raisonnée." For one thing, in *The Divine Comedy* human beings do the narrating, making the story more believable. Moreover, Dante was his own hero, which, to the reader, makes what happens more immediate. Thus Dante already has two advantages over the later poet. In the third place, there are the classical allusions. Milton was steeped in ancient literatures, of course, but this was a matter of education and culture. For Dante, on the other hand, these literatures were part and parcel of a living, continuous tradition. The reader detects this, and the classical allusions ring true. Milton's "souvenirs antiques viennent se jeter au travers de ses réminiscences bibliques" and seem jumbled. Then too Dante, despite his obscurités, is more universal than Milton. Undoubtedly this has something to do with the wide range of topics that vied for his attention. Revealing a wealth of interests absent in the later poet, Dante shows a "variété d'impressions qui fait passer sous nos yeux, en la notant d'un trait ineffaçable, la série la plus riche de sentiments et d'idées, avec leurs nuances les plus sombres et les plus lumineuses, les plus violentes et les plus tendres, les plus élevées et les plus humbles." As for the skill with which the two poets phrased their message,

> Chez Dante et Milton, le don de l'expression est égal, tout en procédant de sources fort différentes. Dante est incontestablement plus primesautier, plus riche, plus varié, plus parlant; il ne hasarde jamais une image, une comparaison qui ne soit une impression personnelle; il évoque les choses et les idées et les note d'un trait rapide qui traverse l'esprit comnme un éclair; personne n'a possédé au même point la magie pittoresque de l'expression. . . . Chez Milton, l'imagina-

tion est naturelle aussi; elle s'élève d'elle-même au grandiose et au sublime; mais l'expression est singulièrement étudiée. (de Guerle, 308)

[Both Dante and Milton have, to the same degree, the gift of expression, although it comes from very different sources. Dante is unquestionably more spontaneous, chatty, diverse, rich; he never risks an image, a comparison that is not a personal impression; he evokes things and ideas and puts them across with a quick word or so that shoots through the mind like a bolt of lightning; no one has ever equaled the picturesque magic with which he expresses himself.... Milton's imagination is likewise natural; unaided, it reaches the grandiose and the sublime, but how the poet expresses this is singularly studied.]

If Milton displays less variety than Dante, in his own domain, the sublime, he is the undisputed master. Here, "Il a su incarner des idées et les rendre sensibles sans les faire déchoir de leur transcendante sublimité." Perhaps Dante's more universal appeal is also bound up with the earlier poet's surer sense of the real. His Hell, Purgatory and Heaven are concrete, not abstract. Milton may have painted Hell better than his predecessor, says de Guerle, but he did not fare as well when he tried to ascend to the celestial spheres. Dante was also at home with the supernatural much more than Milton was. Even God was not the same to the two poets. For Dante, God was spiritual, elusive but personal, whereas Milton's God was the Bible's Jehovah, the stern Lord of Hosts. Elsewhere, as we shall see, the critic would attenuate this. Dante was a mystic and a dreamer, luring the reader on with his charm. Milton was a learned theologian, dogmatic and abrasive. Where Dante dreamed, inviting one to share his experience, Milton debated and argued. One attitude, at least, the two poets had in common. Both saw and depicted the dark, sorrowful, even violent side of the human condition. This is because both lived, though at different times, in eras when people viewed evil and its consequences with revulsion and even terror. Still, Dante has an "exquise délicatesse du sens moral qui, aiguisée par la vivacité de l'imagination, imprime puissamment dans l'âme cette idée saisissante du mal et de ses conséquences." In Milton this is less obvious (de Guerle, 278–92, 308–09).

De Guerle likes Adam, Eve, Satan, God and the Son. Without developing the idea, he notes that all of the characters in *Paradise Lost*, these as well as the others, are consistent from start to finish, all the more remarkable when one remembers that not one is an ordinary being. While he finds the description of Adam and Eve's habitat spectacular and moving, he does not hold with Taine's opinion that the first man and woman should have been made to look like two healthy children lolling about naked in their sunlit garden, as motionless and unthinking as the cows lying beside them in the grass. Presented in such a manner, they could not have maintained reader interest throughout *Paradise Lost*'s entire 12 books. As it is, de Guerle believes, Milton presented them the only way he could. Eve is natural and childlike, a woman in love. Nevertheless, like her husband, she is also flesh and blood. Both spouses are weak, yet both are noble. Their innocence is such that even the poet is hard pressed to understand it and endows them, still alone on earth, with the ideas and reactions of the social human being. Adam is the "victime d'une tendresse dont la déchéance a fait la passion." What took place after their sin evokes the critic's praise. Their consciences troubled by what they have done, they are not yet accustomed to remorse. Little by little the horror of their act dawns upon them, and they experience it. Their remorse, their mutual recriminations, their innocent love transformed into guilty passion—all of this the poet has rendered with consummate skill (de Guerle, 294, 297–98, 301–02, 304).

Even so, de Guerle does not consider Adam and Eve as the epic's main characters. As he states, "Je comprends difficilement comment, après avoir lu douze chants du *Paradis perdu*, on persiste à faire d'Adam et Eve les personnages dominants du poème." If the primitive couple were indeed the chief characters, the author would have had to introduce them at the outset or else violate the rules of his art. As it is, three books precede their initial appearance. Then, hardly have they made their entrance than Raphael takes over. When at last the drama reaches its moment of peak interest, when they have consummated their disobedience and doomed the whole of humankind with them, Michael comes along and foretells, in lengthy detail, the wretchedness and consolation that lie ahead. *Paradise Lost* would be a literary anomaly if, for more than half the poem, the two individuals who are supposed to be its hero and heroine were to sit on the sidelines and let others do the talking (de Guerle, 276–77). Obviously, Adam and Eve are not the heroes.

Could Satan, "le grand archange déchu," treacherous but sublime, be the hero, by chance? De Guerle points out that Dryden had thought so and notes the more recent enthusiasm of Coleridge and Taine. For the Middle Ages, Satan had been a pathetic sorcerer, roundly thrashed whenever he dared oppose the divine will. Milton rehabilitated, enobled him. Surrounding him with a romantic aura, he made him a precursor of Faust and Manfred, "un de ces êtres plus grands dans leur défaite par leur orgueil souverain que d'autres par leur victorieuse résignation." He was the poet's most memorable and possibly his best creation. De Guerle admires him, it is clear, but he stops short of calling him a hero (de Guerle, 52, 291, 295–96, 314).

The critic concludes that the real heroes of *Paradise Lost*, if there are heroes, are God and the Son. Without God, "vivant, parlant et agissant," there would be no poem. How can one describe God? Michelangelo and Raphael "n'avaient point hésité à donner à Dieu un corps matériel, espérant l'animer d'une parcelle de feu divin, qui sauverait l'audace de leur dessin." Falling back on a robust imagination, Milton likewise gave Him material form and, like Moses, made Him talk. While his God is a human God, Milton has introduced Him into the poem with reverence and awe, feeling that He should be present yet somehow invisible. Milton did not hesitate, however, to emphasize His most essential concrete attribute, the Son, "le médiateur entre la chair et l'esprit." With marvelous tact, the poet shows the "tendresse à la fois divine et humaine" that characterizes "cette victime qui s'offre à l'avance, pour expier le péché de la créature humaine." Thus boundless compassion motivates the Son in presenting to His Father "la prière que nos premiers parents adressent au Ciel dans leur inexprimable misère" (de Guerle, 286, 297, 299). Elsewhere and in a different context, de Guerle returns to God and the Son, pointing out that, having depicted the evils humankind is bringing upon it as a result of transgression, Milton could not allow his poem to close on such a note. A Christian epic could not end with a curse. Instead of waiting to show in another epic "toute la miséricorde de Dieu en face de toute la misère de l'homme," he called attention to "la compassion infinie que l'homme déchu inspire à Dieu." Its agent will be the Son, glimpsed amid the "douce mélancolie" of the last two books that bring *Paradise Lost* to a fitting conclusion, calm and grandiose (de Guerle, 305). If God and the Son are heroes, the heroism comes across as quiet, divine love.

French critics have always been struck by Milton's imagination. De Guerle is no exception. As he sees it, that imagination was exhuberant and untamed, taking the reader "tout d'un coup des régions les plus abstraites de la pensée aux sentiments les plus naturels et les plus vulgaires" (de Guerle, 309). It was an erudite imagination, drawing upon personal experience and even more upon literary recollections, all melting together in the blazing furnace of the author's mind like "un métal brillant et solide." Milton's blindness accounts for the learned imagination, of course. No longer able to see, the poet was dependent upon memory. His eyes, "fermés à la lumière, ne lui retraçaient plus que le souvenir des choses, et, dans le lointain, les réminiscences de l'esprit prenaient une importance égale aux impressions des sens" (de Guerle, 308).

The poet's kaleidoscopic imagination is paralleled in his unexpected language and style, both highly original. With words, Milton does whatever he wishes. For example, sometimes, like the Latin poets, he uses a simple verb where one would expect a complex one. At other times, like the Greeks, he combines two verbs with different meanings, creating a new one suggesting both of the others. Always, de Guerle contends, he aims at being precise. On the other hand, his style, though often conveying strength and grandeur, sometimes is nothing more than pedantic correctness. While admirable, it is a laborious style, filled with bookish reminiscences. Even when the poet is imitating, his imitations equal and sometimes surpass the originals. Still, because of the literary allusions, Milton's is an artificial style, even though a superb one. It is also independent, independent in that Milton recognized no other rule, no other grammar than his own. This independence gives rises to a stylistic diversity that is the reader's reward. One must let the poet do as he wishes, savoring his "ampleur majestueuse dans ces périodes où s'accumulent les phrases incidentes, les ellipses, les inversions, sans en rompre le cours" (de Guerle, 309-11). All of this adds up to making the poet "un artiste vraiment inimitable."

As they have done with the language and style, critics have tackled the structural underpinnings of *Paradise Lost* and found it wanting. However, the criticism is less warranted than one might think, according to de Guerle. Four great episodes, linked together, make up the plot. The War in Heaven, the Creation, the description of the Garden of Eden and the Fall could stand alone yet, linked to one another in the poem, do not threaten its overall unity. Even when he pauses to call the reader's attention to himself, the poet never loses track of where he is going, so not even this is a distraction. Having once entered the world the poet has created, "on y marche d'un pied ferme et sans rencontrer d'obstacle. Tout se lie et se convient," whether characters or events. Everything is "bien amené et bien suivi." Unity reigns throughout (de Guerle, 298).

De Guerle considers Milton's account of the Creation a masterpiece of didactic poetry. The Fall and its consequences, "la révolution que fait subir le péché de l'homme à la nature entière," may be "la partie la plus neuve et la plus inattendue du poème," its most original touch. But there is more. In *Paradise Lost* Milton attempted the impossible and almost succeeded, overshadowing all previous epics as he did so. Ambitiously going back to the very beginnings of humankind, he outdid Homer. "Remonter soixante siècles en arrière pour se replacer au berceau du genre humain, n'est-ce pas un dessein devant lequel pâlit celui qui a donné naissance à toutes les autres épopées?" More than that, Milton set out to make God come alive. In the Bible the Creator is revealed only in providential acts. He is not defined; no spiritual attributes are posited. Seeking to remedy this, Milton "épuise les ressources de la langue humaine pour arriver aux pieds du trône divin." However, when he tries to "représenter Dieu et son Fils siégeant dans les splendeurs de l'éternité," he fails. Too audacious a task, de Guerle asserts, it could not have succeeded. "Toute la pompe majestueuse de son style, toute la noblesse de sa puissante imagination n'arrive pas à figurer un Dieu supérieur à celui dont nous parlent nos nourrices. Ce n'était pas la peine de s'élever si haut pour retomber si bas." God, with all the implications we attach to this word, cannot be made to fit the dimensions of a poem, even an epic poem. Quite simply, "Dieu, tel que l'ont fait des siècles de christianisme et de philosophie, ne peut parler et vivre dans un poème, et la sublimité du génie de Milton ne peut nous fermer les yeux sur la vaine audace d'une pareille tentative." Milton aimed high, but he fell short of what he hoped to achieve. It was a magnificent failure (de Guerle, 298, 283–84, 286–87).

De Guerle has relatively little to say about *Paradise Regained* and *Samson Agonistes*. As to what inspired *Paradise Regained*, Ellwood is quoted in French. De Guerle observes that, even in England, the poem attracts few readers. It is, so to speak, the epilogue of *Paradise Lost*. As the crucial moment in salvation, Milton chose Christ's temptation in the wilderness because it is the only episode in Jesus' life in which Satan plays a direct role. Primitive man having succumbed to his wiles, this new Adam resists and taunts the Prince of Darkness, winning where the other had lost. It is a stark tale, with only two characters dueling in the wilds. As far as style is concerned, it is closer to the poet's earlier work than it is to *Paradise Lost*. With respect to outline and composition, it has little to recommend it, and it has more than its share of anachronisms. De Guerle suspects that the poet was thinking about his own childhood and polemical career when he had Christ declare that His early years had been spent in study and learning how to promote the public good. Almost exclusively didactic, the poem is relieved only by an occasional description (de Guerle, 9, 260–61, 311–14; *PR* 1.201–06).

Since *Paradise Lost*, Satan has aged. Not much remains of the divine spark that, in the earlier epic, made it possible to see him as a hero. Master of himself, however, he is a skilled Sophist and rhetorician. Pitted against a mere mortal, he could still win his debates. As it is, he knows that in the end he will lose out. Evil, with which he overcame the world, has now overcome him. He is even absentminded. In offering Him the whole world, Satan advises Jesus to make an alliance with the Parthians, thus neutralizing the Roman empire. For someone who rules the world, this would not be necessary (de Guerle, 313–14). As a character, Jesus is equally disappointing, the critic feels. In *Paradise Lost* He was all superhuman meekness and compassion. In *Paradise Regained* He is an even abler rhetorician than Satan. "Dans le *Paradis reconquis*, Milton, préoccupé de la nécessité de donner à Jésus l'avantage sur Satan, s'applique surtout à faire de lui un rhétoricien encore plus consommé, un logicien plus sévère que le démon. Il ne reste plus rien ici de ce Jésus des évangiles.... C'est un Christ érudit, élevé à l'école des sophistes grecs et qui n'éprouve rien des choses de ce monde qu'il vient remplacer par un nouveau royaume." If the learning and rhetoric had culminated in ardent preaching, it would be understandable. Unfortunately, this is not the case. "Jésus fait au démon un cours de morale stoïcienne à peine imprégnée de christianisme" (de Guerle, 314–15).

De Guerle likes *Samson Agonistes* somewhat better. Structurally simple, the drama is an application of the classical formula to a Biblical topic and is thus "une tentative suprême de conciliation entre les deux tendances qui se partageaient l'esprit de Milton." The critic is not sure, however, that it stuck as close to the rules as the poet intended. While it reminds one of *Prometheus* and *Œdipus at Colonus*, it is superior to its models. Even at first glance, one detects in it "une énergie et une majesté qui dépassent les plus beaux modèles de l'antiquité. L'inspiration biblique soutient le poète et ne le laisse pas faiblir." De Guerle notes that it has obvious flaws that he will not bother to mention or refute. Its chief problem is the "froideur" of its language and action. Little happens in it, and even the conclusion is narrated rather than acted out. Whatever its desiderata, it abounds, with its "énergie calme et soutenue," in splendid didactic and lyric verse. Renouncing "les riches couleurs et l'éclat" that one sees on every hand in *Paradise Lost*, the poet condemned himself to being somewhat arid and ponderous in this work. Even so, one is struck by his exalted spiritual commitment and by the noble, sustained dignity he maintained throughout the poem. "Le *Samson* est bien le testament poétique de Milton vieilli et attristé, de Milton à jamais séparé des illusions et des rêves dorés de sa jeunesse, mais invincible et fier et emportant dans la tombe l'indomptable pureté de sa conscience et la foi dans l'immortel avenir du droit et de la raison" (de Guerle, 266, 315–19).

De Guerle had probably read and assimilated everything Milton ever wrote. Virtually all of the works, short or long, are mentioned in *Milton, sa vie et ses œuvres*. While condemning the opinions expressed in most of the prose, this critic nevertheless called attention to the great passages to be found in certain works, such as *Of Reformation* and *Animadversions*. *Areopagitica* he praised without reservation. Almost all of the poems, whatever their language, are commented upon in some detail. The treatment of *Paradise Lost*, *Paradise Regained* and *Samson Agonistes* is both intelligent and lucid, though not particularly well organized. De Guerle made a serious contribution to his country's Milton criticism with his book. His biographical research was innovative, and his analysis of the poet's religious beliefs was well in advance of the times.

13
Edmond Scherer

O f Edmond Scherer (1815–1889) Henry James wrote that he was "a writer upon whom an ample fold of Sainte-Beuve's mantle has fallen."[1] In an era that boasted a wealth of unusually well-read critics, Scherer stood out as an extraordinarily cultivated one. Though born in Paris, his origins were Swiss Protestant. Hardly out of school himself, he became a professor of church history and then of exegesis at the Ecole Libre de Théologie, generally referred to as the Oratoire, in Geneva.[2] He left his post on 28 December 1849 (Gréard, 87) and turned to editing a theology magazine, which absorbed his energies for a decade. Deciding that this was not his true vocation, he moved to Versailles in 1860. In 1861 he became editor of *Le Temps*, a Paris newspaper aimed at the cultivated, liberal public.[3] It was in *Le Temps* that "Milton et le *Paradis perdu*" appeared in installments on 10, 17 and 24 November 1868. Later the article was reprinted in the author's *Etudes critiques de littérature* (1876) and then in a collection with a rather unlikely title, *Etudes sur la littérature contemporaine* (1882). De Guerle's book, given the date, no doubt inspired the original article.

Scherer's Protestant background was to be a help in his

289

understanding not only Milton the author of *Paradise Lost* but also Milton the controversialist. But in Geneva and elsewhere, Scherer's editorial work, much of it polemical, had taken its toll. Scherer emerged from it having rejected spiritual authority, free will, the religious supernatural and, finally, dogma itself. He became a relativist and a skeptic, maybe even an atheist. He was excommunicated in 1850 (Gréard, 87-88). Nevertheless, he retained a deep interest in religious matters and, with his antecedents, was in an excellent position to discuss them. His own thinking almost predisposed him to find *Paradise Lost* a compelling book. As early as 1855, deeply troubled by how original sin is transmitted, he wondered whether, if sin is a voluntary act, its taint can be passed on from one generation to the next. If one is tainted from the start, he reasoned, why should one bother to be moral? He devoted an article to the problem.[4]

Linguistically also Edmond Scherer was well prepared to write on Milton. His English was perfect. His mother, who had been a Miss Hubbard, was the daughter of an English banker in Paris. Scherer eventually married Mary Nesbitt. He had gone to England in 1831 and studied there a year or two. Later he would even write in English on occasion.[5] Articles on Laurence Sterne, Dickens, George Eliot, Disraeli and others demonstrate that he had a solid grounding in English literature. But while English was the one he preferred, he also knew other literatures remarkably well and was able to comment upon a given author in the context of the whole of western literature, including the ancient classics. This was a worthwhile attribute to have when discussing so learned an author as John Milton.

Objectivity, Scherer held, is indispensable to doing what literary criticism is supposed to do. He believed that method was a must. Even though the critic can allow his emotions to react to a particular author's charm, the critic's task is to understand a work rather than judge it. Sometimes, though not too often, Scherer violated his precept. His own method was more or less the historical one. While he had reservations about the other critic's approaches, the ones he subscribed to had much in common with those of Taine.[6] Genuine criticism, he declared, has to take into account the cultural milieu in which a writer grew up, must consider "la part du temps, du pays, de l'éducation, des idées dominantes, du courant général."[7] Just as important as a writer's individual mind and the "tour qu'a pris ce génie par les circonstances au milieu desquelles il s'est développé," however, are the writer's temperament, artistic endowments, "puissance créatrice." If such matters are weighed, instead of a mere reaction, the critic will have an educated opinion. Whatever views Scherer shared with Taine,[8] his program as outlined here could have come straight out of Sainte-Beuve's essay "Qu'est-ce qu'un classique?" which appeared in *Le Constitutionnel* on 21 October 1850.[9] Sainte-Beuve, the most famous French critic of the century, liked Scherer and held him in great esteem. As we have seen, Henry James saw Scherer as one of the older critic's successors.

Scherer had a good working knowledge of Milton's private and public life. Undoubtedly he knew the Masson volumes that had appeared. In addition, he knew where to locate the author's personal statements, so that his article is full of quotations from the early poems, *An Apology for Smectymnuus*, *The Reason of Church Government* and the *Defensio Secunda*. Collectively, he calls these statements the poet's "memoirs," presenting certain passages in excellent translation. Often, in notes, parallels in *Paradise Lost* are suggested. With considerable care, Scherer gives his readers a panorama of the poet's early life, his education, his travels, down to the moment when, returning from abroad, he leaped into the controversies that were to dominate his era for the next two decades.

For Scherer, John Milton was very much a man of his age. "Il appartenait à la fois à la Renaissance et au Puritanisme.... La Renaissance et le Puritanisme, deux puissants mouvements tout ensemble alliés et opposés." Just as the Renaissance, in the religious domain, gave rise to Protestantism, so Puritanism was Protestantism "à l'état aigu." For the Puritans, the Bible was a revelation from above, containing at once an ethical code, a religion and a political program. Whether they liked it or not, individuals and governments must be made to submit to its rules. People needed to have but one preoccupation: saving their immortal souls. To do this they had to "détruire les idoles, établir le vrai culte, conformer à la volonté divine un monde rebelle." In the process, they would establish the new Jerusalem, in which, unseen, Jehovah would dwell on earth among the elect. The Puritans did not compromise. To Scherer, they resemble the French Revolution's Jacobins, zealous iconoclasts determined to realize their abstract ideals, whatever the obstacles, whatever the resistance, whatever the cost.[10] In contrast with this, there was the Renaissance, with its abandon, its hedonism, its intellectual curiosity, its reverence for ancient culture, its love of music and the theatre, its exquisite taste. In Milton, both currents came together.

> Telles sont les inspirations diverses auxquelles il se livre à la fois et sans effort, poète élégant et polémiste passionné, humaniste accompli et sectaire étroit, admirateur de Pétrarque, de Shakespeare, et interprète subtil des textes bibliques, épris de l'antiquité païenne et du génie hébreu; et tout cela à la fois, sans effort, naturellement.[11]

> [Such are the various inspirations to which he yields simultaneously and effortlessly, this elegant poet and impassioned polemicist, this accomplished humanist and narrow sectarian, this admirer of Petrarch, of Shakespeare, and subtle exegete of biblical texts, in love with pagan antiquity and the Hebrew mind; and all of that at the same time, naturally, with no effort.]

Though Milton was a Puritan, Scherer warns, one must not see him as the "sombre fanatique" so many of his coreligionaries were. Still, he shared basic predispositions with these intransigent sectaries. Like them he was a "spiritualiste absolu" and saw everything in terms of abstract principle. Thus he was a peculiar phenomenon. If he appears to be a historical problem or a literary enigma, the explanation lies in his personality and artistic nature on the one hand and, on the other, in the period in which he lived. Milton was "un fils du Nord qui a passé par l'Italie: un dernier fruit de la Renaissance, mais un fruit plein d'une saveur étrange et nouvelle" ("Milton," 160, 169, 175–76).

Scherer's essay has little to say about Milton's early poetry.

The tribute to Shakespeare is mentioned, as are the "tendres élégies latines." Petrarchan "madrigals," commemorating "des peines de cœur réelles ou supposées," are likewise alluded to ("Milton," 169). Nevertheless, the critic points out that, having been born a poet and one of literature's most remarkable ones at that, Milton wrote "quelques morceaux qui auraient suffi à l'immortaliser," such as "L'Allegro" and "Il Penseroso" ("Milton," 177). There is nothing about *Comus*, nothing about "Lycidas," nothing about any other specific poems. Similarly, with respect to the later works, there was to be nothing about *Samson Agonistes*. *Paradise Regained* would be mentioned only to record Thomas B. Macaulay's "dogmatic" praise, which the critic appears not to have shared ("Milton," 153). On the other hand, there is much generalizing about the pamphlets.

A tried and tested controversialist who had not completely abandoned the arena himself, Edmond Scherer was in an excellent position to appraise Milton's skill as a verbal jouster. The poet's talent and learning made him a natural polemicist, Scherer believes. "De là une foule de pamphlets sur tous les sujets que les événements mettaient à l'ordre du jour. Il commença par des questions ecclésiastiques, attaquant les cérémonies, l'épiscopat, la tradition, et s'efforçant de ramener l'église à sa simplicité primitive." Soon the poet was beset with marital problems, attributable to his character. "Grave et vivant sur les hauteurs," given to meditation and toil, addicted to "notions tout orientales" as to woman's place in the social order, he must have been "un assez triste mari." Trying to make his personal problem a matter of general concern, "il se mit à écrire sur le mariage et le divorce comme il avait écrit auparavant sur l'épiscopat et les pompes du culte." To Scherer, Milton's last important controversy was the venomous duel with Claude de Saumaise. Scherer does not go into it except to note that, to the scandal of all monarchical governments, Milton maintained "froidement et doctement le droit des peuples de punir les tyrans" ("Milton," 174–75).

Scherer detects a pattern in Milton's polemical work. Often the pamphlets and books were "misérables discussions," but in them "l'auteur déploie les trésors de son érudition, entassant les témoignages de l'Ecriture, les passages des Pères, les citations des poètes, mettant à contribution l'antiquité sacrée et profane, discutant subtilement sur le sens de tel mot grec ou hébreu," all by way of proving a point. But here Milton was behaving like his adversaries, all men of their times. Another characteristic that made him a man of his era was the personal, at times violent tone his diatribes took. If his opponents were vicious, so was he. "More et Saumaise avaient attaqué ses mœurs, raillé sa petite taille, fait d'odieuses allusions à la perte de sa vue; Milton réplique en leur reprochant l'argent qu'ils ont reçu et les servantes qu'ils ont débauchées. Tout cela mêlé d'épigrammes grossières, de termes bassement injurieux. Luther et Calvin, ces virtuoses de l'insulte, n'avaient jamais fait mieux." Scherer seems to have believed that Alexandre More had a hand in writing the *Regii Sanguinis Clamor* ("Milton," 175, 178).

Scherer discusses one last piece of his author's prose. He suspects that the poet labored on it his whole life and that it might well have been his favorite work. This was *De Doctrina Christiana*, which would have had a special interest for this critic. In 1851 Scherer had written that Milton gave utterance to a state of Christian consciousness that was not in the period's mainstream, thus becoming an "isolé au milieu de son siècle" (*Mélanges*, 14). With this work, as he treated the main dogmas of Puritanism, free will, predestination and original sin, Milton showed that he was a "scolastique protestant." While in *De Doctrina Christiana* he demonstrated his natural independence by pushing his views on divorce to the point of championing polygamy and while he dared, with St. Paul and Arius, to present Christ as a kind of secondary or intermediary divinity, basically Milton was propounding a rather dull system of theology with close ties to the period in which it evolved, a theology "liée à la lettre des livres saints, sans grandeur, sans horizons, sans philosophie." The author "ne sort pas du texte écrit. Il tranche les questions les plus hautes par l'autorité d'un passage obscur ou isolé." Milton's Puritanism stands out in the book, says Scherer, but the work adds nothing to what we already know about religious thought in the English seventeenth century ("Milton," 178).

Milton was a born poet, though. In the midst of these works, his true nature could not be stifled. "Les écrits les plus arides de Milton s'illuminent . . . à chaque instant d'un éclair de poésie," the critic asserts. "Il y a des moments où, secouant la poussière des arguments, le poète éclate tout à coup et nous entraîne dans le torrent d'une éloquence incomparable. Ce n'est point la phrase oratoire, c'est l"élan poétique, un flot d'images qui se répand sur le thème aride, un coup d'aile qui nous enlève par delà les mesquines controverses. Les écrits polémiques de Milton sont remplis de ces beautés." Among them the critic lists the prayer that concludes *Of Reformation*, the encomiun of Zeal in *An Apology for Smectymnuus*, Cromwell's portrait in *Defensio Secunda*, and *Areopagitica* in its entirely. All of these "comptent parmi les plus mémorables pages de la littérature anglaise" ("Milton," 176–77). Clearly, Scherer knows Milton's prose. In short, he feels, Milton was at once a real poet and an austere, pedantic controversialist, "un génie nourri de la moëlle des lions . . . mais mordant aussi . . . à la poussière des maussades polémiques; et quand viendra le jour où il pourra réaliser enfin ses rêves de jeunesse et donner une épopée à son pays, il la composera de deux choses, d'or et d'argile, de sublimité et de scolastique, et il nous laissera le poème le plus extraordinaire tout à la fois et le plus insupportable qui existe" ("Milton," 178). Sweeping superlatives, these.

The epic, of course, was *Paradise Lost*. Before Milton completed it, he had seen his most cherished dreams, private and public, evaporate. After the labor that went into *Pro Populo Anglicano Defensio*, he lost his sight. Next Mary Powell died. The critic does not add that on the heels of this loss came the death of their infant son. Their three daughters' disputes with their stepmothers are mentioned, as is the domestic discord that kept the household in turmoil. Public problems may have caused the poet even greater anguish than these personal ones. A liberal, Scherer likes to think that Milton did not approve, even initially, of what could be called the coup d'état that made Cromwell Lord

Protector. After all, it had been a "première atteinte portée à l'idéal républicain qu'il avait caressé." Here Scherer makes a veiled allusion to Napoleon III's rise to power, then notes that, in Great Britain, the dictatorship died with Richard Cromwell's abdication. As the republic collapsed, Milton found himself isolated. Scherer does not evoke his last-ditch appeals to his compatriots as the inevitable was about to happen. With the Restoration, the poet was more isolated than ever. "Ses amis avaient disparu, ses rêves s'étaient éteints, la vieillesse se faisait sentir, mais il avait gardé sa foi." It was about all he had. At this point he either started or resumed work on *Paradise Lost*. "Grave, serein, tout entier à la contemplation des choses divines, mûrissant lentement l'œuvre de sa vie," Milton devoted himself to his epic. "Tournant ses regards vers la lumière céleste, il dictait des chants qu'il savait destinés à l'immortalité" ("Milton," 180). To Scherer, Milton was confident that posterity, if not his contemporaries, would recognize his masterpiece for what it was.

A Renaissance work, *Paradise Lost* is structured like the model epics, especially the *Aeneid*. Familiar with both, Scherer lists the parallels between the Latin and English poems:

> Exposition. Invocation. Après quoi l'auteur plonge in medias res. Satan et ses complices se trouvent échoués au fond des Enfers, comme Enée sur la côte de Carthage. Dès lors l'action s'engage. Elle restera très simple. Enée triomphe de Turnus, et Satan perd l'humanité dans la personne de nos premiers parents. Cette unité de l'action est exigé par les règles, mais il faut bien, d'un autre côté, que le poète nous apprenne ce qui a précédé et ce qui suivra.... On a donc recours à des récits. Enée raconte à Didon la prise de Troie; Raphäel raconte à Adam la révolte des anges et la création du monde. Nous voilà au courant; reste l'avenir. Le poète ne peut nous laisser sur la mort de Turnus ou sur la chute des premiers hommes, puisque le véritable intérêt des deux poèmes, c'est le rapport de l'histoire d'Enée avec les destinées du peuple romain et le rapport de la transgresssion d'Adam avec le sort de l'humanité entière. Patience! Un nouvel expédient va nous

tirer d'affaire! Enée descend aux Enfers et y trouve Anchise, qui lui montre toute la suite de ses descendants; l'archange Michel conduit Adam sur une colline et lui fait un cours complet d'histoire sainte, depuis la mort d'Abel jusqu'à la venue de Jésus-Christ et même jusqu'au Jugement Dernier. ("Milton," 180–82)

> [Exposition. Invocation. After which the author dives in in medias res. Satan and his accomplices have been cast into the depths of Hell, like Aeneas on the coast of Carthage. With that the action begins. It will remain quite simple. Aeneas wins out in his contest with Turnus, and Satan ruins humankind in the person of our first parents. This unity of action is dictated by the rules, but, on the other hand, the poet has to tell us what has already happened and what lies ahead. . . . So narration is resorted to. To Dido Aeneas relates the taking of Troy; Raphael tells Adam about the angels' revolt and the creation of the world. This brings us up to date, but we need to find out about the future. The poet cannot leave us with death of Turnus or the fall of the first two human beings, since the real interest of the two poems lies in the relationship between the story of Aeneas and the destiny of the Roman people and the relationship between Adam's sin and the fate of all humanity. Patience, a new expedient will solve our problems! Aeneas goes down to Hell and finds Anchises, who shows him all of his descendants; the archangel Michael takes Adam up on a hill and teaches him a whole course in sacred history from the death of Abel to the coming of Jesus Christ and even to the Last Judgment.]

So much for the epic's outline. Milton borrowed it. In doing so, he imitated Virgil, who in turn had imitated Homer. To this extent, *Paradise Lost* is a copy of a copy.

If the Renaissance's insistence upon imitation provided Milton his outline, Puritanism gave him his content. As in *De Doctrina Christiana*, he treated tenets dear to the hearts of the elect. This time he depicted the Fall, God's justice, God's sovereign decrees. Thus *Paradise Lost* is both an epic and a theodicy, the critic declares. In Milton the poet and the theocrat merged harmoniously. In *Paradise Lost*, poetry and religion did not. Like Lamartine and essentially for the same reason, Scherer has reservations about how well poetry and dogma can be expected to mix. In *Paradise Lost*,

> ces deux éléments, qui répondent aux deux hommes dont se compose Milton et aux deux tendances auxquelles obéit

son siècle, ces deux élements n'ont pu se fondre. Loin de là, ils répugnent l'un à l'autre, et il résulte de leur rapprochement une contradiction sourde qui s'étend à tout l'ouvrage, en altère la solidité et en compromet la valeur. ("Milton," 182)

[these two elements, which accord with the two men that went to make up Milton and the two tendencies that characterized his era, were never able to be fused. Far from it. They are antithetical, and bringing them together produces a dull contradiction that colors the whole work, alters its solidity and compromises its value.]

There is more, and Scherer's skepticism becomes evident at this point. In *Paradise Lost*, theology, instead of educating readers, creates hurdles for them. Choosing to elucidate certain biblical events, the poet selected some that even the hardiest believers recoil at taking as absolute truth. However, Milton related them as such and, worse still, was dogmatic about it. Theologically, Scherer sees pitfalls in the events themselves and also in the manner in which the poet presented them. For one thing, how is the reader supposed to take the Almighty's Son, begotten one fine day and named viceroy of the whole of creation? Then too, what evil angel is going to declare war on the ruler of the universe, whom he knows to be omnipotent? In doing that, Satan makes no sense, for to know God and nevertheless struggle against such an all-powerful force is to work at cross purposes with oneself. Today, Scherer says, the devil has become a comic character, and people do not believe in him anymore. Yet in *Paradise Lost* he is the hero, a curious hero who is at odds with himself. He is as implausible as the rest of this strange epic. Disturbing also is a talking snake that succeeds in ruining humankind by inducing someone to commit a sin that, after all, is rather trivial. But then, if these first humans were really innocent, how could they be led to eat something they had been commanded to avoid? And granted that they did it, how could their sin affect modern humanity? How could one possibly believe nowadays that we ourselves collaborated in this original sin? the critic asks. And if Milton does not convince us that we did, what happens to his poem? What is its interest, its value? It cannot be taken as the serious expression of a belief, since that belief escapes us. Nor can we construe it as the poetic expression of an outmoded theodicy because, to be poetic, the theodicy would have to be intelligible. With all the problems it creates for today's reader, *Paradise Lost* has somehow survived, doing so in spite of its subject matter ("Milton," 184–85). At times, Scherer seems to lose track of the audience Milton was writing for. These notions would not have bothered most of the poet's contemporaries. Those who, later, would find them disturbing had found other reasons to admire the work, and hence its survival.

For Scherer, *Paradise Lost* has another troublesome feature, not unrelated to what we have just seen. This is the poem's supernatural element. In the *Iliad* and the *Aeneid* there are divine beings, and whereas they work out in the old epics, they do not in the modern one. In heathen religions, there are gods presiding over every aspect of human existence and involved in every human act. That they should have their place in ancient literature is natural enough. Pagan myths, airy and capricious, were suited to it. Christianity, on the other hand, is serious and bristles with rigid dogma. To vast numbers of adherents, it is a living thing, an object of faith and hope. When a poet tampers with it, adorning it with "les créations de sa fantaisie," he can appear to be defiling it. Covering it with mythological trappings is inappropriate, perhaps dangerous. How to present the Christian supernatural is thus highly problematical, and Scherer concludes that Milton did not come up with a workable solution. The modern imagination cannot follow the poet if he goes too far in making God speak, in having the angels act. "De là l'embarras des poèmes qui ont voulu tirer de la théologie chrétienne le merveilleux dont ils avaient besoin. Ils ne satisfont ni à la poésie ni à la piété. Ils sont gênés par la peur d'aller trop loin, et, quelque timides qu'ils se montrent, ils ont encore un air de témérité." Tasso's *Gerusalemme liberata*, Voltaire's *Henriade*, Klopstock's *Messias* and Chateaubriand's *Les Martyrs* point to the inherent stumbling block. Only Dante avoided it, because, either having a feeling for such things or being a consummate artist, he put only sinners and the saved in his work ("Milton," 183–86). Choosing his subject as he did, Milton did not have to invent a supernatural, which minimized his problem up to a point. In *Paradise Lost* "tout y était placé d'emblée dans le domaine du surnaturel. Dieu et son fils, les diables et les anges . . . remplissaient . . . les premiers rôles. . . . Dès lors, nul besoin d'introduire arbitrairement la divinité. L'auteur du *Paradis perdu* n'avait qu'à rester dans les données de son sujet, qu'à prolonger un peu les lignes du récit sacré" ("Milton, 187).

Thus Milton did not have to invent an artificial *merveilleux*. Using what the Bible gave him, he still sacrificed action, however. The plot is too simple; there are too few real actors. "A proprement parler, il n' y a qu'un personnage en scène, Dieu le Père, puisque Dieu ne peut se montrer sans que tout le reste disparaisse ni parler sans que sa volonté s'accomplisse. Le Fils n'est qu'un dédoublement du Père. Les anges et archanges ne sont que ses messagers, moins que cela, la personnification de ses arrêts, les comparses d'un drame qui s'accomplirait aussi bien sans eux" ("Milton, 187). Milton saw the danger and did what he could to mitigate it. Unfortunately, the long speeches, which are nothing but sermons, merely point up the lack of drama. But *Paradise Lost* is an epic, and there had to be a struggle of some kind. In seeking to provide one, the poet hit upon a device that, instead of helping him, worked against him. In Scherer's view, the War in Heaven does not make sense. What the episode adds to the poem in terms of action, it causes it to lose in verisimilitude. The reader can take neither the war nor the warriors very seriously. A God who is resisted is not a God. Doing battle with omnipotence is not only brazen, it is stupid. Belial realized this and, in the devils' conclave, spoke against it. The reader can only wonder that his companions did not heed such obvious advice. Without this war, however, the poem would have been impossible. So, having decided what he would do, Milton coped as best he could with "la plus inadmissible des fictions." In the process, he shows us a King of Heaven fretful about possible dethronement. He depicts angels hurling mountains and firing cannon at one another. He makes us watch a battle hanging in the balance until the King's trusty lieutenant, armed with thunderbolts, arrives in a chariot hitched to four cherubs. Finally, the battle won, virtue has not altogether triumphed nor has vice been exterminated. Satan is no worse off than he was before, evil will remain, and humankind is damned ("Milton," 187–89).

We have seen that *Paradise Lost*, to Scherer, owes its outline to the *Aeneid*. Generally speaking, its content comes from the Bible. Thus for outline and plot, Milton obviously did not have to go very far. Did he have an "epic imagination" of his own?[12] By himself, just what did he invent? Not very much, Scherer decides toward the end of his essay. He holds that where Milton had had to create real characters and concoct real situations on his own, he did not fare too well. Left to his own devices, he created scenes that are laughable, though certainly he did not intend them to be funny. These scenes or episodes include the prince of rebel angels turning himself into a cormorant and a toad; the demons changing into dwarfs so as to fit comfortably in their council chamber; their punishment, which consists of being turned into snakes once a year; the Paradise of Fools; and Sin and Death. "Toutes ces fictions donnent une assez faible idée du génie inventif de Milton et permettent de supposer qu'il n'aurait point réussi dans un sujet où il aurait eu a créer des héros et à imaginer des situations" ("Milton," 189).

Scherer is aware that he could be accused of assessing *Paradise Lost* from a narrow nineteenth century vantage point, and he tries, not very successfully, to deflect the charge. Neither the *Iliad*, nor *The Divine Comedy*, nor any other work of art, he contends, could stand up under methodical, intensive scrutiny. *Paradise Lost* is a very special case. It is at one and the same time a poem and a didactic work, and, as a result, its form and content cannot be separated. "L'histoire qui en fait le fond n'a de sens et de valeur qu'à la condition de conserver sa portée dogmatique, et, en même temps, elle ne peut conserver cette signification sans tomber dans la théologie, c'est-à-dire dans un domaine étranger à l'art." For Scherer, who is returning to an idea he had expressed earlier, this was Milton's basic problem in *Paradise Lost*. But even with regard to content, he continues, the epic does not hold up under examination. As characters, Jehovah and Satan are incoherent, for example. What happens to Adam interests the reader but little. As for the poem's explanation of the problem of evil, it borders on the ludicrous. And finally, the action takes place in spheres to which modern individuals cannot relate. To create those spheres, the poet resorted to a cosmology about which he had his doubts but which he needed because he had to put his characters somewhere.[13] This strange cosmology is just one example of a more general antinomy that pervades and undermines the entire poem, where everything needs to be taken literally but where this simply cannot be done. From the reader's viewpoint, this poem does not deal with realities, however much the author may have tried to make it do so. "Le sujet du poème n'est rien s'il n'est réel, s'il ne nous touche comme le mot de nos destinées; et plus le poète cherche à saisir cette réalité, plus elle lui échappe" ("Milton, 183, 189–91).

Summing up, Scherer believes that Milton began *Paradise Lost* during the Civil Wars or the Commonwealth, knowing that it would be immortal. Basically the critic holds that the epic, brimming over with religious abstractions, "est un poème faux, un poème grotesque, un poème ennuyeux; il n'est pas un lecteur sur cent qui puisse lire, sans sourire, les livres neuvième et dixième ou lire, sans bâiller, les livres onzième et douzième. Cela ne se tient pas; c'est une pyramide en équilibre sur la pointe, le plus effrayant des problèmes résolus par le plus puéril des moyens" ("Milton," 192). Yet *Paradise Lost* is immortal somehow. Still, if it has survived, it is because of a few famous episodes, not the epic as a whole. Unlike *The Divine Comedy*, which must be pored over in its entirety to be appreciated, only fragments of *Paradise Lost* are worth reading. Those fragments are superb, however. The Garden of Eden, the description of morning, the characterization of Eve, the love the two primeval spouses feel for each other, and Satan's discourses are all part of humankind's poetic patrimony. Moreover, throughout *Paradise Lost* there are so many "incomparable" lines that one is almost ashamed to call random attention to some of them, "tant il semble arbitraire de choisir au milieu de telles richesses." And yet the critic singles out a few.[14] "La poésie de Milton est comme l'essence même de la poésie," he writes ("Milton," 192).

> L'auteur semble ne penser qu'en images, et ces images sont grandes et fières comme son âme, un mélange étonnant de sublime et de pittoresque. Il n'a pas seulement l'image et le mot, il a aussi la période, la large phrase musicale, un peu longue, un peu chargée d'ornements et contournée d'inversions, mais entraînant tout dans son ondulation superbe; il a enfin et surtout je ne sais quoi de serein et de vainqueur, l'égalité soutenue, la puissance indomptable. On dirait qu'il nous enveloppe d'un pan de sa robe et nous enlève avec lui dans les régions éternelles où il habite. ("Milton, 192–94)

> [The author seems to think only in images, and, like his soul, these images are proud and grand, an astonishing mixture of the sublime and the picturesque. Not only does he have the image and the word, he also has the period, the expansive musical phrase, somewhat long, somewhat strewn with ornamentation and twisted with inversions, but sweeping everything before it in its superb roll; finally and most of all, he has something serene and overpowering, sustained evenness, indomitable power. It is as though he were wrapping us in a fold of his robe and whisking us away with him into the eternal regions where he lives.]

Thus, after ripping the poem apart because of its subject matter, the critic, using some telling images of his own, extols *Paradise Lost* for its majestic style.

Scherer's article comes to a rather abrupt halt and has no real dénouement. To sum up how the critic reacted to his author, one may conclude that he saw Milton as a man of his time—essentially a poet, but a poet with religious and political commitments that for a time sent him in other directions and ended up, in his most important work, getting in his way. Some of Milton's early poems would have assured their author an important place in literature. Much of the prose, narrowly bound up with the period's controversies, is tedious, but in it there are nevertheless lyrical outbursts in which the poet momentarily drowns out the zealot's ranting. Scherer's belief that Milton worked on *De Doctrina Christiana* all or most of his life is notable. In addition, most French critics in the nineteenth century compared Milton to Homer. Scherer thought he had had a more important model. To write *Paradise Lost* Milton borrowed his outline from Virgil and took his plot, such as it is, from the Bible, constructing the work upon a scaffolding of Puritan dogma. Unfortunately, "la théologie n'a jamais passé pour favorable à la poésie." Milton's thesis in verse does not hold together because the two elements are incompatible. Viewed as a whole, *Paradise Lost* is a noble disaster, saved by splendid imagery, some truly memorable lines and a few great passages. There are magnificent details, but, generally speaking, in concept and execution the poem is a failure. Scherer insisted too much upon modern readers' inability to come to grips with the poet's plot and basic concepts, claiming that they have become alien to us. Even though dwelling upon the historical background that produced *Paradise Lost*, the critic did not really take into account the immediate audience for which the epic was written. These men and women had lived through the Puritan Revolution and the Commonwealth. Even though some would have considered them abominable, they could at least understand the poet's notions. Later generations, uninterested in the era's preoccupations and embroilments, have discovered other reasons for reading the work and recognizing it as great, enduring art.

In the *Quarterly Review*, Matthew Arnold summarized Scherer's main points, which he considered "natural, lucid and forcible," and gave the critic high marks for what he had to say about Milton. Arnold observed that "the note of blame fills much more place than the note of praise" but added that the criticism is nonetheless eminently rational. Scherer, he thought, was "disinterested, intelligent and sincere." Arnold agreed that Milton's best feature was his style and noted the critic's observation that *Paradise Lost*, however great an achievement, is vitiated by the poem's need to be taken literally and the reader's inability to do it.[15]

14

Gaspard Ernest Stroehlin

With some stretch of the imagination, Gaspard Ernest Stroehlin (1844–1907) may be considered French. He was Swiss French, actually. He had sat at the feet of Alexandre Vinet and cited Edmond Scherer. Deciding to become a Protestant minister, he went to France to study. There he submitted a doctoral thesis at the University of Strasbourg entitled *Essai sur le montanisme*, which examined a second century heresy.[1] His degree was conferred in 1870, the year the Franco-Prussian War broke out. Alsatia, where he had studied, would soon be overrun and annexed. Stroehlin deplored what happened but would not live to see the province returned to France. Even before taking his doctorate, he had begun writing and publishing. An *Etude sur William Ellery Channing* came out in Geneva in 1867. There was also a book on Jean Calvin and another on two French Protestant artists working in London in Milton's day. One of these was Jean Petitot (1607–1691), whom Charles I knighted. Stroehlin was a bibliophile and amassed an extensive Protestant Reformation library consisting of books published from the fifteenth to the seventeenth centuries. A three-volume catalog appeared during the years 1910 to 1912. In 1914 the collection was put up for sale in Leipzig.

Ernest Stroehlin had read widely in English literature, alluding on occasion to Bunyan, Defoe, Dickens and George Eliot. His article on Milton appeared in the *Encyclopédie des sciences religieuses* in 1880. He was in a position to recommend a number of previous studies, calling them his sources. Among the authorities he listed were Edward Phillips, Richard Bentley, Samuel Johnson, Thomas Warton, Thomas B. Macaulay, Joseph Hunter, Thomas Keightley and Edward Paxton Hood, along with William Ellery Channing. He also cited Hippolyte Taine. Curiously, he did not mention Edmond de Guerle. Like so many Swiss French, he knew German and was thus able to consult scholarship in that language. Of those writing in French, he was about the only critic to do so. He mentioned Heinrich von Treitschke's "Milton," which first appeared in the *Preussische Jahrbuch* in 1860, then was reprinted numerous times in several collections of the writer's essays.[2] Stroehlin also recommended Moriz Carrière's "Milton als Staatsmann und Dichter"[3] as well as Alfred Stern's *Milton und seine Zeit* (1877–79). For matters of specific detail, he suggested that readers have a look at Gustav Liebert's *Milton, Studien zur Geschichte des englischen Geistes* (1860) and Heinrich Schmidt's *Uber Miltons politische Schriften* (1882).[4] Even when citing works in English or German, Stroehlin had the exasperating habit of giving titles and even authors' first names in French. Among the German poets, he was aware that Lessing had admired Milton deeply, and he believed that *Paradise Lost* had "incited" Klopstock to write his *Messias.*

For the *Encyclopédie des sciences religieuses* readers, Stroehlin gave a sketch of John Milton's life, with a running commentary on the poetry and prose. By way of background, he states that Milton was born in London on 9 December 1608. The poet's family was wealthy gentry, owning a manor house on the banks of the Thames River in Oxfordshire. That the estate may have been confiscated at the time of the Wars of the Roses is not mentioned. Milton's father, disinherited because of his religion, had made his way to the capital and become a scrivener. The author of *Paradise*

Lost was reared in a Puritan milieu, its simple austerity enlivened only by music. Early on he applied himself diligently, already convinced that (*PR* 4.220–21)

.... the childhood shows the man
As morning shows the day..................

At St. Paul's School, Stroehlin reports, the young Milton soon turned to the study of classical antiquity, for which he had both a predilection and an aptitude. He continued this at Christ Church College at Cambridge University, where he received his bachelor's degree in 1628 and his master's in 1632. It was while in college, the critic believes, that Milton wrote his first Latin and English poems, including the "Ode on the Morning of Christ's Nativity." Already passionately devoted to the cause of religious freedom, which would concern him throughout his entire life, he declined, despite his father's urging, to prepare for the ministry, since he considered it odious to submit to the Anglican Church's Thirty-Nine Articles. Stroehlin fails to note that, in order to qualify for his degrees, he had already had to subscribe to the articles on two occasions. The happy equilibrium of his faculties, the purity of his morals, and the loftiness of his thoughts allowed him, even at this young age, to prove to himself that youth does indeed announce the mature adult, just as dawn announces the day.[5]

Having taken his university degrees, Milton retired to his father's home at Hammersmith and then Horton, in Buckinghamshire. There he spent five quiet, happy years during which exercise and hunting alternated with study and meditation. Although recognizing and admiring Shakespeare's genius, he did not choose the bard as his guide. For form at least, his model was rather Ben Jonson. But even here he showed a great deal of independence. *Comus* is a masque, but in it the poet broke with "le cadre habituel de ces sortes de divertissements" (Stroehlin, 169). Instead, he "célébrait le triomphe de la chasteté sur le dieu des festins et son cortège d'esprits nocturnes." To this same period belong *Arcades*, "Lycidas," "L'Allegro" and "Il Penseroso." "Lycidas" is characterized as "une touchante élégie, qui lui fut dictée par la mort de l'un de ses amis." "L'Allegro" and "Il Penseroso," which the critic dates from 1635, are poems in which "aux beautés de la nature, aux charmes de la forêt, aux fêtes champêtres et même aux joies plus intimes du foyer domestique, il oppose la félicité supérieure du penseur solitaire qui oublie les vanités mondaines dans le feu de ses recherches et s'élève par son commerce toujours plus approndi avec les chefs-d'œuvre de l'esprit humain jusqu'aux plus hauts sommets de la vision prophétique" (Stroehlin, 169). These are poems, in other words, in which the immediate simple pleasures, perceived through the senses, are contrasted with those of the mind. No attention is directed to the Latin compositions. By 1638, the critic thinks, Milton was already famous.

At this juncture, Milton decided to go abroad. His mother had died. His own health, somewhat undermined, seemed to call for travel. He headed for the Continent. In Paris he saw much of Hugo Grotius. For two years he resided in Italy, where the academies made him welcome. Stroehlin seems to have been thinking of *Areopagitica* and *Pro Populo Anglicano Defensio* when he noted that the young traveler visited Galileo and listened as the Marquis of Villa Manso recited Tasso's "novissima verba." Even in Rome, Milton did not conceal how much hatred the Jesuits and the Inquisition inspired in him. Already he had conceived "le généreux dessein de doter sa patrie d'un poème épique." His sense of the aesthetic prodded him to push on to Greece, in his "désir de puiser directement à la source du beau et de se pénétrer sur les lieux mêmes de l'idéal hellénique." However, it was at this time that the conflict between Charles I and the Long Parliament reached a crisis. As soon as he learned what was happening, he curtailed his trip. "Il n'hésita pas à sacrifier les rêves de l'artiste aux devoirs du patriote." He returned home (Stroehlin, 170).

It was not personal ambition that led him to get involved in public affairs. For some time after his return, he lived in quiet seclusion in London, his attention divided between literary activities and his chores as a schoolmaster. Eventually, though, he came to believe that he had to take action. Protestantism was in danger. On the one hand, there was the arrogance and unbending intolerance of Archbishop Laud and those who shared his views. On the other, there was the royal family, not only allowing but even encouraging Roman Catholic proselytizing. Alarmed, Milton decided to take up his pen in the interests of the good cause. On the controversies and pamphlets that ensued, the critic expends a good bit of his own ink. Milton was a great prose writer, in his opinion.

In 1641 five pamphlets appeared one after the other, all distinguished by "la même vigueur d'argumentation et la même verve de langage." These were *Of Reformation, Of Prelatical Episcopacy, The Reason of Church Government, Animadversions upon the Remonstrant's Defense* and *An Apology against A Modest Confutation.* The last two were written to support a few of his Presbyterian friends who, calling themselves "Smectymnuus," had blasted Bishop Joseph Hall. Needless to point out, the critic has misdated some of the pamphlets. In these works, Milton revealed himself as a true son of the Puritans. His goal was to lead the church back to an apostolic ideal, endowing it once more with its primitive flavor and strength. To achieve this, he proposed to do away with prebends and even bishops. Religious groups would elect their own leaders and spiritual guides. There would be no more ecclesiastical jurisdiction of any kind. These radical theories were not new, of course. Long before this, they had been espoused and proclaimed by John Knox and the exiles who, during the Mary Tudor persecutions, had sought refuge in Geneva. But in *Of Reformation*, Stroehlin asserts, the modern writer gave them new vitality, developing them with "une ampleur de pensées, une générosité de sentiments, une richesse d'images véritablement merveilleuses." Milton was not only a great poet, he was also a master of bold, virile, though not flawless prose. Amid the linguistic excesses and the sometimes arid scholasticism, two fundamental Protestant concepts stand out, brilliantly illuminated. These are, first of all, that salvation necessarily depends upon each individual's personal faith. Secondly, a nation's political greatness springs ultimately from its moral purity. For Milton, freedom of conscience was so imperious a need that he did not hesitate to detach himself from those Presbyterians he had once championed when, having seized power, they proved guilty of the same abuses they had so bitterly condemned in the adversaries they had now replaced. Stroehlin could have added that Milton not only repudiated his alliance with these people, but he even hounded them in several later pamphlets. So precious was that freedom of conscience that the poet went so far as to demand it of a victorious Oliver Cromwell (Stroehlin, 170).

At least as far as church government is concerned, not many scholars of today would endorse the critic's statement, not explained, that Milton was "en pleine communion d'idées religieuses" with the Lord Protector. Whatever the case, in 1659, after Cromwell's death, Milton penned one of his most vehement pamphlets, *Considerations Touching the Likeliest Means to Remove Hirelings out of the Church*. In this work, the author heaps upon the still flourishing ecclesiastical patronage system his most scathing sarcasm. Likewise, falling back upon the doctrine of universal priesthood, he calls for the abolition of all distinctions between minister and believer. He also insists upon the total separation of church and state, convinced that his country's troubles were due to the fact that both were ruled by the same authority. He holds that the church was too respectable, too venerable to wrap itself like a vine around the throne of the state.[6] That freedom of conscience he so needed for himself, Milton was noble enough to demand for all religious persuasions, including those his contemporaries looked upon as heretical and even dangerous to social order, such as atheists and Socinians. Excluded from his universal tolerance there was, to be sure, the Church of Rome, which he suspected of pursuing, beneath a pious cloak, a whole program of despotic aims. The Puritan Milton looked upon Roman Catholicism as the whore in the Book of Revelation.

Milton could be not only personal but speculative in his religious tracts, Stroehlin notes. His speculative side reflected a personal reading of a verse in St. Paul's Second Epistle to the Corinthians, in which the apostle declared that "where the spirit of the Lord is, there is liberty."⁷ For the pamphleteer it was a clear, abundant source of inspiration, and throughout his life he drew from it the most unexpected, the most daring consequences. His later years were spent elaborating a theological system, *De Doctrina Christiana*. Here, relying upon subjective truth alone, he airily and peremptorily discarded several basic orthodox teachings, such as trinitarianism and predestination, which he viewed as contrary to Scripture. The book, not published until the early part of the nineteenth century, caused a furor in the established Church, which was appalled to discover Arianism, Arminianism and other equally "pernicious" heresies in the poet of *Paradise Lost*. University people, on the other hand, greeted the book with happy surprise, seeing in its author not the rigid Calvinist they had always taken him to be but rather one of their own precursors (Stroehlin, 171). Presumably Stroehlin is referring here to the Oxford Movement. Milton would have endorsed the movement's commitment to revitalizing the church through a return to the beliefs and practices of the early church, of course, and he would have hailed the position that government has no business in religious affairs. However, he would most certainly have repudiated some of the movement's other ideals, especially those having to do with doctrine and ritual.

Another example of Milton's personal approach to religion involves his attitude toward divorce, as the critic points out. It was an incident in his own life that caused him to examine this matter, which was to inspire in him "la plus douloureuse vivacité." Married in 1643 to Mary Powell, daughter of an "opulent cavalier," he found himself deserted a month later because his young bride found his religious and political views repugnant. When all his attempts at reconciliation produced no results, he addressed his grievances to Parliament in the form of a treatise. This was *The Doctrine and Discipline of Divorce*, soon followed by *Tetrachordon* and *Colasterion*. *The Judgment of Martin Bucer* is not mentioned. Instead of considering it a judicial problem, the author chose to examine divorce from the biblical standpoint, leaving it up to husbands to decide whether it was appropriate in a given case. Though private disappointment and anguish excuse it, says Stroehlin, Milton's rationale was "bizarre."

More to the critic's liking are the ideas expressed in *Of Education*, dedicated to the German Samuel Hartlib. Here, in opposition to the pedantic approach then used in the universities, was the author's own classical studies program. This was in 1644, the same year that witnessed the publication of *Areopagitica*, filled with numerous memorable passages. Stroehlin quotes one: "Who kills a man kills a reasonable creature..., but he who destroys a good book kills reason itself" (*YPW* 2:492). Condensed and paraphrased, Stroehlin gives some of the rest of the passage. Milton's noble words bore fruit in the great debates that echoed throughout the reign of George III, he declares. In France, Mirabeau translated *Areopagitica*, claiming in the preface that England's greatness was due less to its political system than to the respect for public opinion that its poet had so valiantly championed. After *Areopagitica* the poet meditated in quiet seclusion for four years, as he wrote *The History of Britain*.

At this point, says the critic, Milton's public life began. The Independents having come to power, they named the poet their Secretary of State, a position he held with distinction throughout the Republic and the Commonwealth. In it he seconded the Lord Protector's scheme of a grand Protestant alliance to check Hapsburg despotism. Stroehlin declares that one can still derive pleasure from reading the elegant, noble *Letters of State*, in which the Lutherans and Calvinists are called upon to put an end to their fratricidal squabbles and the Elector of Brandenburg is urged to make peace with Sweden. Milton could be proud, too, that he had contributed to the King of Spain's receiving a few blows where it hurt most, such as in his trade with the Indies. Nor must we forget a sonnet in which the poet served his master's ends by calling upon the European powers to come to the aid of the persecuted Waldensians. Such a deed gives an idea of his role in the Lord Protector's government, this critic believes.

At home as abroad, Milton bestirred himself with unrestrained ardor. The Cavaliers, following the death sentence handed down against Charles I, appealed to public compassion, obscuring their monarch's faults in the halo of his martyrdom. A book attributed through pious fraud to the king but actually by John Gauden, whom Stroehlin calls the Bishop of Exeter, depicted King Charles's sufferings and resignation. The royalists distributed the book in such numbers that it quickly went through 47 editions. From the standpoint of natural law, Milton had already justified Parliament's decision in *The Tenure of Kings and Magistrates*. Now he answered *Eikon Basilike* with *Eikonoklastes*, declaring that the monarch's private virtues could in no way excuse his countless prevarications, his despotism, his cruelty. For Milton this marked the outset of a battle with the rest of Europe involving the disciples of republicanism on the one hand and the apostles of divine right on the other. Against Claude de Saumaise, Milton wrote *Pro Populo Anglicano Defensio*, in which he outlined the Puritans' political ideal with austere, even somber eloquence. If the examples taken from history and the Judaic concept of an eye for an eye have fallen into the oblivion they deserve, the book's dominant idea has become the common patrimony of all free people, Stroehlin says, and he quotes a sentence or two in French. Milton's immense labor on behalf of his compatriots, insulted and condemned by their opponents at home and abroad, led to total blindness. However, as a true disciple of classical antiquity, the poet consoled himself in believing that he had done his duty, even though it had cost him his eyes. To Cyriack Skinner he wrote that he realized he had

>..........................lost them overplied
>In liberty's defense, my noble task,
>Of which all Europe talks from side to side.
>(Sonnet 22, ll.10–12)

Elsewhere he asserted, with the critic's applause, that it had been his mission to plant a seed abroad, more noble than the one Triptolemus had sowed in Greece. That seed was a freedom ethic worthy of humankind.[8]

But all this came to an end with the collapse of the Commonwealth. Under the Restoration, calamities of all kinds came the poet's way. *Pro Populo Anglicano Defensio*, which had already been burned in Toulouse and Paris, was torn to shreds in London by the public executioner on 16 June 1660. A warrant for the author's arrest was issued, and only the active intervention of friends in high places saved him from imprisonment. His financial means had been seriously weakened by the Civil Wars, and now his house burned down in the Great Fire. Milton, poor and in bad health, was reduced to solitude as he contemplated the destruction of all that he had held dear. Without naming the passage, the critic quotes, more or less, the poet's statement to Peter Heimbach in which he observed, less bitterly than one might expect, that his *patriotism* had almost *expatriated* him.[9] Oddly, Stroehlin has Elizabeth Minshull share her stepdaughters' reputed aversion for their father. Without comment, he reproaches the women for their "sécheresse" and "froideur." Deborah, "sa dernière fille," was the exception. By reading the classical poets to her father and playing the harp, she "apportait quelque adoucissement à ses maux." Here, the critic tells us, he has in mind Michael von Munkacsy's *Milton Dictating Paradise Lost to his Daughters*, a painting shown at the Exposition Universelle in 1878. Again, there are no details (Stroehlin, 173). Stroehlin could have added that the painting won the artist a medal when exhibited at the Paris Salon the same year. Sold in 1932, it is now in the Metropolitan Museum in New York.[10] Stroehlin notes that the poet died at Bunhill, near London, on 8 November 1674. His remains, after being interred at the Church of St. Giles, were moved to Westminster Abbey in 1737 (Stroehlin, 174).

With Milton's deplorable emotional and material situation coincided the full flowering of the poet's artistic genius. In contrast with his immediate surroundings, he conceived of a better world, but one that humankind eventually forfeited through disobedience. "Les scènes du monde idéal se déroulèrent devant son esprit dans toute leur magnificence," the critic declares. Envisaging this world in his blindness, the poet would have been within his rights in comparing himself to the nightingale, which needs darkness to pour out its wondrous music. Stroehlin appears to believe that Milton spent his entire life writing *Paradise Lost* and that it was finished by 1665. The critic does not mention a subsequent rearrangement of the cantos, dividing the original 10 into 12. "L'œuvre de sa vie entière, l'épopée en douze chants du *Paradis perdu*, fut définitivement achevée en 1665 (Stroehlin, 174). For Stroehlin *Paradise Lost* was to the Protestant Reformation what the *Divine Comedy* had been to the Catholic Middle Ages. Stroehlin does not analyze the poem, sending his readers instead to Taine's *Histoire de la littérature anglaise*. However, he does call attention to the "conception de l'ensemble," which was comparable to that of the *Divine Comedy*. Singling out the poem's most impressive passages, he cites the blind poet's hymn to light, the description of the Garden of Eden, Adam and Eve's love, the Son of God's sudden appearance leading the heavenly hosts, and Satan's magnificent speeches and breathtaking flight across inchoate space. Despite its qualities, he notes, *Paradise Lost* did not catch on. It took Joseph Addison's praise to make his compatriots realize that its author was one of their national glories. *Paradise Regained*, a work of his old age, was something else again. Stroehlin believes that its theological dissertations, too numerous and too pedantic, deprive it of any kind of literary warmth or charm. We recall, however, that the critic had cited it when he mentioned the poet's education. One last time, Milton assembled his forces for a great undertaking. It was for a drama, *Samson Agonistes*. Artistically, the critic declares, this was his most perfect work. The lack of movement is compensated for by the sublime despair of the lyrical outpourings. Handel based his great oratorio on it.

Stroehlin was slipshod about matters of detail; his dates, as often as not, are wrong. One suspects that he had not looked at his "sources" very carefully. It is regrettable, too, that there is no discussion of certain minor poems. On the other hand, Stroehlin's "Milton" has some very positive features. The organization is quite good, for example. Notable also is that, unlike so many *Paradise Lost* readers who were culturally French, Stroehlin must not have been repelled by Sin and Death, which he did not even bring up. Like Chateaubriand and Geoffroy, he thought he detected a relationship between Milton's prose works and the ideas ushered in with the French Revolution. In addition, among critics writing in French, Stroehlin was unique in linking Milton with the Oxford Movement. He was also one of the few to take notice of the diplomatic correspondence, although he was wrong in thinking Milton was a Secretary of State. As a minister, Stroehlin was best in what he had to say about the poet's religious position, for which he had a good feeling. He was more interested in how it was explained in the pamphlets, however, than in how it showed up in *Paradise Lost*. He was incorrect in assuming that *De Doctrina Christiana* dates from the author's last years. Among his contemporaries, Stroehlin was not alone in considering *Paradise Regained* an inferior work, of course. On the other hand, one notes his very real admiration for *Samson Agonistes* as both poetry and drama.

15

Augustin Filon

Augustin Filon (1841–1916) was the son of a university professor and seemed headed for a university career of his own when chance decided otherwise. Victor Duruy, one of his former teachers and now Grand Master of the University, summoned him in 1867 and asked if he would like to be tutor to the Prince Imperial. Filon accepted. When the Second Empire fell and his pupil took the road to exile in Great Britain, so did Filon, who remained at the prince's side even at the Royal Military Academy in Woolwich. The prince's education completed, Filon continued to live most of the time in the peaceful English countryside to which he had grown accustomed, returning to France from time to time. Both French and English literature attracted him, and he wrote about both. His *Histoire de la littérature anglaise* appeared in 1883 and ran through a number of editions over the next several decades.

According to Filon, Queen Henrietta Maria's arrival in England touched off a curious phenomenon in literature. A few poets began to write in the French manner, characterized by "la gaieté, qui est déjà propre au caractère français, le badinage sur les choses graves, une sorte d'amour impertinent, éphémère et égoïste, qui s'appelle la galanterie." Its exponents were John Suckling, Edmund Waller, Robert Herrick, Abraham Cowley and John Denham. Nothing could have been less in keeping with the English temperament.[1] The trend was not to last. Along came the Puritans, and with them came literary and political upheaval. Where did John Milton fit into this? Filon believes that Milton was an isolated, exceptional figure, with no ancestors and no posterity. Because of his natural bent and his studies, he was a poet. So intertwined were his poetic nature and his religious ideas and causes that, as a poet, he would not have achieved what he did had it all been kept distinct. After Shakespeare, his is the greatest name in English literature (Filon, 240).

On the biographical side, what Filon has to say about Milton's life is generally correct, though not without occasional inaccuracies and noticeable omissions. However, he does warn his readers against some of the anecdotes, touching but generally not true, that have grown up. A case in point is the one about Leonora Baroni, who, before running away, slipped some verse into the hand of a young John Milton as he lay sleeping once, during his student days, near the university. Filon was referring, of course, to Amédée Pichot's novelette. Filon quotes the lines and, unlike predecessors mentioning the story, identifies the poet as Battista Guarini. Such things are legend, not reality, Filon observes.

Milton's early career, quickly sketched, takes into account the poet's university studies, his travels abroad, his return by way of Geneva, which Filon refers to as the Puritans' Rome. The stint as a schoolmaster is touched upon, as well as the schoolmaster's first marriage. Sentimental tradition, according to the critic, has accustomed readers to feel sorry for the poet, "trompé dans son amour par une épouse indigne de lui, qui le méprise et l'abandonne." The truth is that, used to merriment and gracious living, Mary Powell was bored. Moreover, her husband was indeed the "hard and choleric" man that he is supposed to have been. That she went home and did not come back is understandable enough, Filon surmises. We can be sure that what her husband wrote about divorce at this time made no impression upon her, but what she heard about his courting someone else was quite another matter. This news, plus her family's concern over what was happening to the royal cause, put things in a different light. Perhaps she wept, as she is said to have done. Whatever the case, "elle accusa sa mère, et, sur ce terrain, la réconciliation était infaillible." Filon implies that the experience netted only one divorce tract. A "vengeance de pédant," the pamphlet seemed to proclaim that all one needed to make divorce legal was to show that it was warranted. Milton's other two mariages are also noted. Filon evokes Katherine Woodcock's death in a splendid image, observing that the bereaved husband "embauma sa femme dans un sonnet sans défauts" (Filon, 241–42, 244).

Shortly after going to work for the Council of State, Milton went blind writing *Pro Populo Anglicano Defensio*, justifying regicide. Echoing Macaulay, Filon asserts that Charles I had made mistakes but that his execution not only made him sympathetic, it exonerated him. Forgetting his highhanded deeds, the popular mind remembered only his personal virtues, which were undeniable. Milton tried to combat this. Though the works are not mentioned, the critic is thinking here about *The Tenure of Kings and Magistrates* or *Eikonoklastes* rather than *Pro Populo Anglicano Defensio*. Filon did not check his chronology in this instance. Apparently it did not occur to him, in any event, that Milton would not have addressed English readers in Latin. Whatever the case, he holds that Milton should not be blamed too much for the position he took on regicide. He lived in an era accustomed to seeing royal heads fall. In addition, he was too obscure, then as well as even later, to have carried much weight with the public. After all, Bulstrode Whitelocke referred to him as "one Mr. Milton," who translated all or part of a treaty between the Commonwealth and Sweden.[2] Nothing is said in the *Histoire de la littérature anglaise* about *Eikonoklastes* as such.

Several other pamphlets, their titles again not listed, are alluded to. Of *The Ready and Easy Way to Establish a Free Commonwealth*, Filon declares the author a visionary. "Il avait sa chimère, son système politique, qu'il ne cessa de caresser. Il rêvait une assemblée unique, permanente, renouvelable par tiers, nommée par le suffrage à plusieurs degrés. Le pays n'eût été qu'une fédération. . . ." Elsewhere Filon has in mind *The Reason of Church Government*, *A Treatise of Civil Power in Ecclesiastical Causes* and, in particular, *Considerations Touching the Likeliest Means to Remove Hirelings out of the Church* when he points out that Milton wanted church and state to be and remain separate. The church should neither own property nor pay its clergy. "Pourquoi le ministre n'aurait-il pas vécu du travail de son cerveau ou du travail de ses mains? Pourquoi n'aurait-il pas été avocat ou boulanger?" Such, in broad outline, are what the critic conceives to be the main features of Milton's utopia. Filon calls attention to them but declines to weigh their merit. However, he adds that these notions deserve their place in the museum of constitutions that were never given a chance (Filon, 242–44). *Pro Se Defensio* and the other tracts and broadsides are not dealt with.

Nineteen years after the *Histoire de la littérature anglaise*, Filon published an article on Oliver Cromwell in the *Revue des Deux Mondes*. Surprisingly little is said in it about Milton. Asserting that, at the time of the Civil Wars, most intellectuals were in Parliament, Filon thought it surprising that, along with Thomas Hobbes, Milton was not. In connection with the Lord Protector's lackadaisical education, Milton's testimony is invoked to establish that the dictator's Latin was "vicious and scanty." Neither in the article nor in the book is anything said about Milton's attitude toward his master. Nothing is said either about his service to him or the veiled advice he gave him in *Defensio Secunda*.[3]

In his book, Filon briefly evokes the poet's final years. The Restoration had spared him. Although there were one or two minor incidents, his chastisement was proportionate to the relatively modest role he had played during the Republic. Considered too unimportant to mount the scaffold, he was ignored and forgotten. It was a kind of persecution to which literary people are unusually sensitive. The last 14 years of his life, except for one short absence, were spent not in some peaceful country retreat like the ones he had known in his youth, but in a dismal section of a city ravaged by fire and then pestilence. It was a dreary setting, one in which his daughters sold his books to buy themselves ribbons, helped his servant women rob him, and openly wished him dead. In 1674, he eventually obliged them (Filon, 244). For some reason, says Filon, artists have idealized the poet's later years and distorted them, thus contributing to a legend. Like Lamartine, the critic had seen paintings, though no specific ones are named. In those he saw, there appear to have been two daughters rather than three.

> La vieillesse de Milton a exercé et égaré les peintres. Qui ne se rappelle le poète aveugle, dont les yeux errent sans se fixer, pâle d'inspiration, la main étendue, dictant à ses filles les vers immortels du *Paradis perdu*? Les deux filles, en robe blanche, sont rayonnantes de grâce et d'idéalité; l'une tient une harpe et en tire quelques accords qui rhythment en quelque sorte la pensée de Milton; l'autre, la plume à la main, recueille avec émotion et respect ce qui tombe de la bouche harmonieuse du poète.
>
> [Milton's old age has both kindled painters' imagination and led it astray. Who does not recall the blind poet, his eyes constantly moving, pale with inspiration, his hand extended, dictating to his daughters the immortal lines of *Paradise Lost*? The two girls, idealized in their white dresses, radiate charm; one is seated at a harp on which she is plucking chords to accompany Milton's thought; the other, quill in hand, is collecting with respect and emotion what falls from the poet's harmonious mouth.]

This is not the way it was (Filon, 241). Filon is thinking of George Romney's *Milton and his Two Daughters* (1792), which depicts the sentimental scene he describes.

Having disposed of Milton's life and prose works, Filon examines the poetry. Mistakenly, he believes "On the Death of a Fair Infant" to be the earliest of the poems to have survived. He considers it devoid of feeling, unlikely to console a grieving mother. "Cette élégie, toute classique, ne contient pas un atome de sensibilité et n'était guère propre à remplir son objet supposé: consoler une mère qui a perdu son enfant (Filon, 245). On the other hand, poems such as "L'Allegro" and "Il Penseroso," "Lycidas" and *Comus* are brilliant. As for "L'Allegro" and "Il Penseroso," they are

très courts et forment pendants. L'un est un hymne à la gaieté, l'autre un hymne à la mélancolie. Le poète invoque la gaieté, personnifiée dans une déesse. Il décrit le cortège symbolique qui l'accompagne. Puis, il passe en revue les plaisirs qui entretiennent la gaité, les pensées dont elle se nourrit, les lieux où elle réside. Les vers sont légers, allègres, ailés, et tout concourt à l'expression d'un délicieux état d'âme. L'hymne à la mélancolie est fait sur le même plan, et de même qu'un souffle heureux vivifie le premier poème, une langueur exquise, une divine tristesse voile le second.

[very short and form a pair. One is a hymn to joy, the other a hymn to melancholy. The poet invokes joy, personified in a goddess. He describes the symbolic retinue accompanying her. Then he reviews the pleasures that make for joy, the thoughts that bear it up, the places where it is to be found. The verse is light, airy, brisk, and everything concurs to express a delightful state of mind. The hymn to melancholy follows the same pattern, and just as a happy breath of air animates the first poem, so an exquisite lassitude, a divine sadness wraps the second in a veil.]

Most nineteenth century French critics seem to have preferred "Il Penseroso," but Filon has more to say about "L'Allegro." In "Lycidas" Milton is mourning Edward King, drowned in the Irish Sea. The form, while borrowed from Propertius and Virgil, the poet made his own. "L'originalité de Milton est déjà assez forte, assez sincère, pour ne pas emprunter d'images à ses maîtres antiques" (Filon, 245).

Filon does not mention *Arcades*. However, he likes *Comus* very much and tells his readers how it came to be written. In addition, he tells them that it is based, as far as form is concerned, on the Italian masques, and he defines the genre as "une sorte d'opéra où la poésie tient plus de place que la musique et dont le sujet est à la fois idyllique et allégorique; les personnages sont des bergers et des êtres fantastiques" (Filon, 245). Filon summarizes the plot in some detail, showing good and evil spirits changing themselves into peasants and the heroine resisting Comus's entreaties and threats with "les maximes d'une sagesse ingénue." Sabrina, goddess of the deep, had once cast herself into the Severn River to save her honor. Now she saves others who are in distress on its banks. When invoked in the present case, she helps set matters right. His own work done, the Attendant Spirit takes his flight to

.... those happy climes that lie
Where day never shuts his eye.
(ll. 977–78)

More or less paraphrasing the Spirit's final words, the critic seems to consider them the moral of the entertainment. "Aimez la vertu et vous y viendrez, à votre tour, goûter les félicités infinies qui sont le partage des âmes pures" (Filon, 245–46). Filon does not point out that the masque contains elements that Milton would later use in *Paradise Lost*. Aside from those discussed here, nothing is said about any of the other early poems. Except for the one on the poet's deceased wife, Filon does not comment on the other sonnets, personal or otherwise.

At this point, Filon turns his attention to *Paradise Lost*. He begins by disagreeing with Macaulay, who had been amazed that genuine poetry could be written in the middle and later years of the seventeenth century, contending that the era was unsuited to poetry because it was too civilized. Highly civilized periods, essentially analytical, are concerned with science and philosophy, Macaulay thought. While they may turn out verse, they produce little that could be called poetry. Real poetry is born when a people is less advanced and hence more alive to a world that it still finds new and wondrous. Its language, as yet rough and imperfect, lends itself to spontaneous, natural impressions and reactions, whereas the polished diction that comes later does not.[4] Macaulay's paradox, if it is a paradox, caught the attention of the critic, who rejects it. Milton's language, Filon holds, was not the one his contemporaries spoke and wrote. It was in a class by itself. The idiom into which he translated his own sensations "différait de celui que parlaient autour de lui les hommes de son temps. A force de lire la Bible, de s'en nourrir, de la respirer, d'y vivre, il s'était fait une langue à la fois imagée et simple, grandiose et naïve," having nothing in common with that of the people about him. If Milton's era was not conducive to poetry, it was for a different reason, Filon thinks. Too embroiled in controversies, people simply were not poetically inclined (Filon, 246–48).

Milton's being able to write *Paradise Lost* when he did, however, means that the author did more than just triumph over the unpoetic atmosphere in which he lived, Filon continues. For all practical purposes, Milton had stopped writing poetry two decades earlier. Since "L'Allegro," "Il Penseroso" and *Comus*, more than 20 years had elapsed during which he had worn himself out in bureaucratic toil and partisan polemics. Now he was a different man. His inner being had grown somber, but it had also acquired new depth. Age, poverty, disappointment, a tarnished reputation as a prose writer, political proscription and a religious faith that, over the years, had become more austere and more ardent, all contributed to make him turn his back on ordinary pursuits and go back to poetry. In that it alienated him from the outer world, even his blindness was a help. Condemned not to see what others see, he became a seer, beholding things that the rest of humankind would never be able to contemplate. Along with this and in spite of the thankless labors he had been engaged in during the preceding years, he had retained his imagination, which was still

> pleine de fraîcheur, de grâce, d'innocence, presque enfantine, admirablement propre à sentir et à rendre l'ivresse des matinées d'été, la pénétrante et sereine majesté du soir, le balancement des grands arbres, le frémissement de l'herbe, l'odeur de la mer ou des fleurs. (Filon, 247–48)

> [full of freshness, charm, innocence, almost childlike, admirably suited to experiencing and conveying the intoxication of summer mornings, the serene, penetrating majesty of evening, the swaying of tall trees, the rustling of grass, the smell of flowers or the sea.]

His sense of color, or whatever he remembered about it, underwent a change.

> Le prisme oculaire n'opérant plus, les différentes couleurs n'arrivaient que comme des souvenirs affaiblis au cerveau de Milton. Il ne connaissait plus que l'alternative de la lumière et des ténèbres. Aussi tous les objets, tous les êtres

apparaissaient-ils à sa pensée, noyés dans l'ombre épaisse ou plongés dans une lumière ardente comme l'or en fusion. (Filon, 248)

[The ocular prism no longer functioning, different colors were now no more than a clouded memory in Milton's brain. All he knew were the alternatives of light and darkness. Thus all objects, all beings he perceived drowned in thick shadow or blazing in light so intense that it was like molten gold.]

Macaulay, Filon recalls, had observed that, in an enlightened and literary society, a man aspiring to be a great poet must first become a little child. Filon concurs, adding that Milton became that child. Like Homer, he was a child "par la fraîcheur de ses impressions, par la profondeur de ses croyances." Moreover, he had his experience. "Il porte le poids de trente années d'études et de vingt années de combats" (Macaulay, 90; Filon, 248).

Writing for readers who might not have a detailed knowledge of *Paradise Lost*, Filon summarized the epic, calling attention to most of its great speeches and episodes. Little commentary interrupts the résumé. It is pointed out that Beelzebub, ranking high among the demons, has his master's ear. During their leader's visit to the earth, the devils are shown exploring their new surroundings and getting accustomed to them. Like all French commentators, Filon is struck by Sin and Death, but, unlike so many of them, he is not revolted. He translates a few lines at the end of Satan's monologue during the flight toward the Garden of Eden:

.... Ainsi, adieu l'espérance, et avec
L'espérance, adieu la crainte, adieu le remords.
Puisque le bien est perdu pour moi, mal, sois mon bien.
(*PL* 4.109–11)

In passing, Filon notes the wasteland in which the poet has placed the world's vanities, including monks, "aux dépens desquels il se permet un sourire qui déride cette grave épopée." Adam and Eve's habitation is described as "délicieuse." When Adam presses Raphael to explain the cosmos, the angel, warning him not to delve into nature's secrets, nevertheless allows him to realize that two explanations are possible. As to which is the correct one, the angel remains vague. And with good reason, Filon points out. When Milton was writing, scientists had not made up their minds as to which system was the more authoritative. But "on peut voir que Milton incline vers celui de Copernic," Filon decides.

After this, when Adam relates his experiences to his guest, it is with a view to detaining him a little longer. Eve, listening to the serpent's apparently logical persuasions, resists and then gives in. Milton has made her tempter an able speaker. "Jamais plus spécieux discours, plus serré, plus riche d'arguments, n'a retenti depuis dans des oreilles crédules." Having tasted the forbidden fruit and knowing that she must die, Eve wants her husband to die with her. Selfishness and vanity have come into the world. After the couple's harsh words and troubled sleep, even though their punishment has not been meted out to them at this point, it is clear that "la déchéance de l'homme est complète." To obtain Adam's forgiveness, Eve humbles herself, sacrificing her woman's pride. The rest is summed up quickly, and readers see the couple driven, somewhat consoled, from their garden and striding toward whatever awaits them beyond it. The last nine lines are quoted in translation (Filon, 248–59).

Filon believes that *Paradise Lost* had its weaknesses, and he enumerates some. Milton's listing all of the demons, for example. In epic literature this is commonplace and trite. As for the Sin and Death episodes, they tire even the most dedicated, enthusiastic reader. Likewise, the War in Heaven interests us but little. "Un combat entre des êtres immortels n'est qu'une rixe où les plus effroyables coups produisent l'effet de simples gourmades" (Filon, 260). Whereas Hector's dead body arouses pity, Satan's getting bruised does not. The debates in the infernal assembly, debates in which all opinions, including those of the cabinet, are aired and in which oratorical niceties and parliamentary formalities are carefully observed, are too human, too reasonable not to be out of place amid the supernatural incidents that go into an epic. But if the devils' political maneuvering bores the reader, celestial theology risks making the reader smile. When the Heavenly Father tries to make the angels comprehend that divine foreknowledge does not in any way exclude human beings' free will, He sounds like an elderly pedant holding forth in his classroom. Raphael, though he claims otherwise, nevertheless teaches Adam astronomy by resorting to hypotheses. The last two books are nothing but a history course taught by the Archangel Michael. The poet's artistry, the proper placing of the scenes and their development in terms of each other can create an illusion in the eleventh book, but in the twelfth the hurried speech, the familiar demonstrative gestures show us a lecturer who, pressed for time, is covering the centuries as fast as he can, endeavoring to cram it all in somehow. Milton tried to say too much. A repository of vast erudition, he could not set his learning aside, so it crops up whenever he can work it in. Along with whatever else it is, *Paradise Lost* is thus a textbook on gardening, cooking, geography, astronomy, physics, medicine, military strategy, philosophy and theology, with a bit of casuistry thrown in for good measure. Milton was giving his poem that encyclopedic quality that the Greeks admired in the *Iliad* and the *Odyssey*. Unfortunately, says Filon, Milton's learning was that of the period in which he lived, and some of it had not evolved as much as it was going to do. Thus the poet stuck some cumbersome utterances into the mouths of his heavenly characters that time would show to be errors.

One of Milton's worst mistakes was to abuse anachronism, according to this critic. Treating a topic that was at once within and beyond time, the poet should have avoided all historical allusions and comparisons that presuppose a knowledge of what happened after the events with which he was dealing. Vulcan, Bacchus, Alexander the Great and Charlemagne have no business in *Paradise Lost*. When the poem's basic action takes place, civilization had not begun its slow march forward. Indeed, there is no such thing as civilization. Yet the reader encounters it at every turn, from its earliest stages up to the moment the epic was written. Similarly, the Bible's Adam came into a world that was all but empty, one in which things did not even have their nomenclature. However, in *Paradise Lost* primitive man is accomplished, the product—and an outstanding product at that—of 30 centuries of progress. His helpmate has likewise sprung into being as the perfect woman. Presenting humankind like this is the poem's striking anachronism. It is true that the poet had little or no choice in the matter, Filon concedes, and perhaps this anachronism justifies all of the others.

Compared to Dante's, Milton's Hell is disappointing. In describing it, the poet has used all the splendor, all the pomp, all the grandeur his art can muster, but the result leaves much to be desired. As for Heaven, God falls short of what the reader hopes for. Not that Milton felt constrained or intimidated when talking about the Creator. He was too much the rationalist for that. "Ame paisible sous le bouillonnement superficiel des passions sectaires, esprit réglé, digne en tout du siècle le plus sensé qui fut jamais, Milton ne se trouble ni ne s'affole en présence de l'infini" (Filon, 261). His God is an anthropomorphic creation, nonetheless.

> Il a conservé les formes de l'humanité. Il ouvre la bouche: nous reconnaissons notre pauvre langage, notre misérable raison humaine, qui pèse le pour et le contre, qui hésite, qui s'attendrit, qui se déjuge. Lorsqu'il fait reconnaître son fils, le Messie, comme associé à sa puissance souveraine, ne diriez-vous pas un vieil empereur d'Allemagne qui se sent mourir et qui se hâte de couronner son héritier roi des Romains?
>
> [He has retained human form. His mouth opens and we recognize our pitiful speech, our pathetic human reason weighing both sides of a question, hesitating, feeling pity, changing our minds. When He has His son, the Messiah, acknowledged as partaking of His sovereign power, would you not say that this is some elderly German emperor who feels death approaching and hurries to crown his heir King of the Romans?]

Already we have seen Filon taking note of parliamentary institutions in Hell. Comparing God's Heaven to the Holy Roman Empire is another touch indicating that the critic's memory is serving him well. Filon remembers that Taine had likened *Paradise Lost,* or at least its two opposing courts, to Stuart and Commonwealth England (Filon, 260–62).

These criticisms recorded, Filon calls upon his readers to admire *Paradise Lost* without hesitation. In particular, he likes the ninth book, which he calls a "modèle du drame épique, un des morceaux les plus parfaits qui existent dans aucune langue. Rarement le sentiment religieux s'est exprimé avec plus d'ampleur et d'une façon plus pénétrante" (Filon, 262). Filon compares it to cathedral music, only more solemn, more poignant. Milton's depiction of human love and the natural décor in which it is shown warrant special comment and praise, he thinks. There is nothing common about this love. The poet has managed to give it both charm and grandeur. To do so, he has sometimes mingled the epic with the idyllic.

> Quant à la description du premier amour humain et du décor charmant où cet amour se déploie, rien de plus délicat et de plus frais n'a été rêvé. L'épopée se fait ici plus gracieuse que l'idylle, sans rien perdre de sa dignité. Imaginez toutes les conditions qui se réunissent à certaines minutes privilégiées de notre existence et nous donnent un sentiment passager de bonheur, lorsque, les poumons pleins de l'air léger des cimes ou la joue rafraîchie par la brise de mer, la conscience libre et l'esprit en repos, nous jouissons à la fois de la beauté du ciel et de la présence des êtres chers: c'est ce genre de félicité que Milton fait régner, dans toute sa plénitude, sous les ombrages de l'Eden. Sa conception de l'amour confond la langueur voluptueuse du harem, la galanterie chevaleresque de l'âge féodal, la paisible tendresse d'un foyer anglais. (Filon, 262–63)

> [As for the description of the first human love and the charming décor in which this love unfolds, nothing more pristine, nothing more delicate has ever been conceived. Here epic has more charm than idyll, without losing its dignity. Imagine all the circumstances that converge at certain special moments in our existence to give us a transient feeling of happiness, when, our lungs full of the light air of the mountain peaks or our cheeks freshened by the sea breeze, our minds and consciousness free and at rest, we enjoy at one and the same time the beauty of the sky and the presence of those we love: that is the kind of happiness Milton deploys, in all its plenitude, beneath the bowers of Eden. His concept of

love mingles the voluptuous lassitude of the harem, the chivalrous courtliness of the feudal era, the placid tenderness of an English hearth.]

Filon marvels that this could have come from the pen of a writer who was old, blind, disillusioned and infirm. He concludes his *Paradise Lost* discussion by quoting, a little inaccurately, Chateaubriand's observation that, in *Paradise Lost*, the reader beholds the fire that is part of youth, the maturity that comes with age, and the seriousness that is born of misfortune, all blending to endow the epic, at one and the same time, with the incomparable charm of youth and old age, anxiety and peace, joy and sadness, love and reason. Without expanding the idea, the critic asserts that the poem's greatest attraction lies indeed in this system of perpetual contrasts.[5]

In *Paradise Lost* it was predicted that the son of woman would crush the serpent's head. In other words, Christ, insulted and tempted by the demon, would resist and triumph. Mary's Son, using simple, human materials and resources, would annihilate the power of Hell. This is what happens in *Paradise Regained*. Filon does not award this second epic very high marks. It is generally felt, both in "éclat" and "coloris," that the poem is inferior to *Paradise Lost*, the critic informs his readers. It is a long, drawn out conversation. It lacks the dramatic interest of Eve's dialogue with the serpent in *Paradise Lost* since Christ, unlike Eve, cannot succumb to His temptor's blandishments. But the poem has other defects. Geography and ancient history, pedantically flaunted, take up a third of it, while the rest is given over to theology. The Son of God quotes Socrates, Fabricius, Cincinnatus and a host of others and tells Satan in so many words that He knows His Roman history as well as the next one. Were it not for *Samson Agonistes*, one might think that Milton's poetic powers had abandoned him (Filon, 264).

Samson Agonistes ranks high in Filon's judgment. In his *Revue des Deux Mondes* article on Cromwell, he calls it "sublime" (*RDM*, 420). For Milton it was the "œuvre suprême de sa vieillesse." As with *Paradise Lost*, the plot is summarized. Filon applauds its simple outline, dismissing

Johnson's caveat that it has no action. When Manoa exults on learning that his pathetic but noble son has killed his enemies, the critic appropriately compares his proud paternal outburst to the one Milton's contemporary, Pierre Corneille, put into the mouth of one of his own characters. Old Horace, told that his son has killed three adversaries in mortal combat and thus guaranteed Rome's survival as an independent state, exclaims:

> Ô mon fils! ô ma joie! ô l'honneur de nos jours!
> Ô d'un état penchant l'inespéré secours,
> *(Horace* 4.2)

and so on.[6] Another parallel with classical French drama was to follow. Before that, however, Filon turns his attention to the ancients. Milton, he claims, had imitated neither Euripides nor Sophocles in writing *Samson.* If he had a model, it was Aeschylus. Aeschylus was writing at a time when drama, which had only partially broken away from lyric poetry to become a separate genre, still retained some of its lyricism. *Prometheus Bound* has no more action in it than *Samson Agonistes.* There is even less in *The Persians.* With *Samson Agonistes* Milton took early Greek dramatic form and suffused it with biblical poetry. The work has no analogue in modern literature unless it is Racine's *Esther,* also taken from the Old Testament. Like *Samson, Esther* is more lyrical than dramatic, but even so it has more drama in it than the other poem does, and the tone is different. *Esther* is the sweet, primrose side of the Bible. *Samson* is its dark, passionate one (Filon, 264–65).

We have seen that Filon believed Milton to have been too unimportant to sway public opinion at the time of the Commonwealth and Protectorate. In his conclusion he returns to the theme, pointing out that the poet remained obscure long after his death. During the 11 years following its initial publication, *Paradise Lost* sold only 3,000 copies. How could it have been otherwise in Charles II's England? With pleasure taking the place of religious, political and even literary ideals, the Restoration reserved its plaudits for the Earl of Rochester and those with similar tastes. Earlier, Filon had observed that Milton's life was like that of quite a few men of genius. The poet "a vécu obscurément, partie dans l'ombre d'une fonction subalterne, partie dans la retraite où son humilité l'abritait contre la persécution. Ses contemporains l'ont coudoyé sans le voir. Puis, sa gloire a grandi lentement" (Filon, 240). Posthumously, he was given the recognition he had earned, and "les arts, la poésie, l'imaginatioin populaire se sont évertués à couvrir de fleurs sa mémoire" (Filon, 265–67).

To Filon, Milton was the poet of *Paradise Lost* and *Samson Agonistes* and not much else. *Paradise Regained* left him cold. Except for "L'Allegro," "Il Penseroso" and *Comus*, he saw little in the minor poems and almost nothing in the prose. *Areopagitica* is not mentioned, far less the Latin grammar, *The History of Britain* and the like. Although he was writing for the general public—cultivated but nonetheless general—Filon took a great deal for granted on his readers' part, perhaps too much. Still, his achievements as a Milton critic are solid enough. He was very methodical and set down in an orderly fashion what his compatriots have traditionally found amiss in *Paradise Lost*. Then, having said it, he laid bare his enthusiastic admiration. His keen interest in *Samson Agonistes*, setting him apart from the critical mainstream, deserves special notice.

16
A Backward Glance

As pointed out in the introduction, the French Milton critics studied in this volume were cultivated, urbane individuals, writing for people like themselves. Although not necessarily addressing what they had to say to other scholars, several—like Villemain, Véricour, Mézières, Taine, Scherer, Filon, and eventually Geffroy and Chasles—were professional educators. Several were not. A few were Académie Française members. Religious views, or the lack of them, do not appear to have colored most critics' judgment, or at least not very much. One or two were Protestants. Presumably, others represented various shades of Roman Catholicism. Only Barbey d'Aurevilly was militant about his Catholicism. Most lived by their pens to some extent, several writing mainly for periodicals. One was a businessman, later to be a government administrator. All were widely read and wrote for men and women with similar backgrounds, interests and tastes.

Critics and readers remembered their Boileau but most, wanting to examine Milton for themselves, were generally able to ignore the *Art poétique*'s strictures. Unlike French readers of the preceding century, they were no longer intimidated by Addison, although the critics mentioned him now and then. Addison's view that *Paradise Lost* conformed to Aristotle's rules and was thus a true epic did not impress Villemain and Taine at all, and de Guerle went so far as to declare that whether the poem had a beginning, a middle or an end was of no concern to him.

Biographical accuracy, especially in matters of detail, cannot be taken for granted on the part of the earlier critics and one of the later ones, even making allowances for the relatively scant material that would have been at their disposal. Pongerville and Lamartine were particularly lackadaisical about this kind of thing. These two critics, along with Chateaubriand, believed that John Milton was a nobleman, for instance. Barbey d'Aurevilly held that, while he was reared in a bourgeois environment, he had noble ancestry. All four critics were aristocrats themselves, at least by birth. Several writers were on unsure ground when dealing with the Civil Wars, the Republic and the Protectorate, believing that Oliver Cromwell took charge of things from the moment hostilities broke out. Again, Pongerville and Lamartine were under this delusion. Villemain and Chasles, who wrote lives of the dictator and should have known better, believed this, too. Of the earlier critics, Chateaubriand was the best documented with regard to the poet's life and career.

David Masson's *Life of John Milton* began appearing in 1859, about the time French realism took root. From that point on, there was greater attention to biographical detail. Barbey d'Aurevilly would be almost alone in thinking such matters unimportant. Romantic writers tended to make Milton one of their own, presenting him as a pathetic idealist, misunderstood in his youth and living on into an age that neglected and even mistreated him. Filon conceded that he may have been neglected but added that he was not persecuted. Mézières, Taine and de Guerle reacted against sentimentalizing him. Taine, insisting on his rationalism, did not even consider him fundamentally poetic, whether as an individual or as an artist. In commenting on the prose, Taine was not altogether consistent on the point. Barbey d'Aurevilly and Mézières suspected that he was not a very lovable person, and Filon assumed that Mary Powell had good reasons for leaving him. Villemain and Chateaubriand admitted that he was irascible. Taine is credited with having applied determinism to literature, or at least literary criticism. He did, and he did it very well, but in the preceding chapters we have seen that, well before the advent of determinism as a literary doctrine, all of our critics, with one exception, have held that the mature John Milton would have been someone other than the man he was had he not seen what he had seen, been where he had been and done what he had done. *Paradise Lost* and, when the critics examined it, *Samson Agonistes* have been generally seen as reflecting personal experience, whatever else they may do. A few writers commented on the poet's physical appearance. Chateaubriand, Pichot, Chasles and Lamartine mentioned his striking good looks, both in his youth and in his old age. Chateaubriand and Barbey d'Aurevilly knew that at one time he had had magnificent hair.

To the French critics of the era that concerns us here, Milton was, naturally enough, the poet of *Paradise Lost*. Many, however, were interested in the minor poems and were even enthusiastic about them. The Latin elegies attracted some attention, as did several poems in Italian. Since he wrote a book rather than an article or a chapter, Edmond de Guerle often commented on the minor poems in the greatest detail, but not always. Chateaubriand admired these poems also and had a great deal to say about them. Philarète Chasles, Raymond de Véricour, Barbey d'Aurevilly, Alfred Mézières and Augustin Filon liked the early poems, and so did Edmond Scherer and Ernest Stroehlin, although they said little about them. Various sonnets elicited praise. "At a Solemn Music," "On Time," "On the Morning of Christ's Nativity" and "Lycidas" had their partisans, also. "On May Morning," with its attitude toward nature, appealed to de Guerle. Generally, "L'Allegro" and "Il Penseroso" were singled out for special comment. While he had reservations, Chateaubriand considered them imaginative and noble. De Guerle liked their classical allusions and their contrast of two basic human outlooks. To Mézières, "Il Penseroso" suggested a comparison with romantic poetry. *Arcades*, as a rule, was passed over, although Chateaubriand, Véricour, Mézières, Taine, de Guerle and Stroehlin mentioned it. *Comus* was another matter, and several critics reacted to it warmly. Filon talked about it in some detail, and Mézières and Stroehlin praised it. Véricour was almost ecstatic, and Taine came close to ranking it as the poet's best work. Scherer did not comment.

The later poems, *Paradise Regained* and *Samson Agonistes*, disappointed a number of critics. Scherer said little about *Paradise Regained*, nothing about *Samson*. Chateaubriand called *Paradise Regained* an "œuvre de lassitude, quoique calme et belle." Stroehlin called it a failure. Jesus stands out in the epic as a learned, able rhetorician, but the poem contains no divine message, de Guerle complained. Taine considered it cold. Véricour liked it but with reservations. As for *Samson Agonistes*, Pongerville did not allude to it. Taine thought it imitative and undramatic. While admitting that it was somewhat cold and plotless, de Guerle saw it as a good example of what classical drama is supposed to be. Chateaubriand championed it. "*Samson* respire la force et la simplicité antique," he believed. Véricour was a warm admirer and called it a "beau drame lyrique" but suspected that it may have been its idealistic old author's admission that he was a beaten man. To Chasles, on the other hand, it shows the poet more determined than ever not to give in to his adversaries. Filon, who had been disappointed with *Paradise Regained*, awarded it high marks because it proved that the poet had not lost his touch after all. Stroehlin considered *Samson* the poet's most perfect work.

Although there were a few constants, Milton's role in the controversies that rocked his world set off a multitude of diverse reactions on the part of his nineteenth century French critics. Except for Barbey d'Aurevilly, most agreed that this middle period was vital to the poet's development. Villemain and Chateaubriand noted with pleasure that Milton had called for Greek independence. At a much later date, they had done the same thing. Stroehlin admired *Of Education*. Auguste Geffroy thought the program it outlined was rigorous, but he approved. Taine considered it unrealistic and even quixotic. To those who commented, *Areopagitica* was Milton's greatest prose work. Véricour and Chateaubriand were among the critics who called attention to it. Chateaubriand appears to have considered it the poet's most telling prose achievement. The divorce tracts aroused a certain amount of comment. Geffroy discussed *The Doctrine and Discipline of Divorce* at some length. De Guerle noted with what care the author chose and avoided authorities on the issue. Stroehlin, Chateaubriand and Scherer took a close look at the ideas. Mindful of the personal element involved, Scherer believed that whatever marital problems the author had were due to his character. Chateaubriand decided that he did not prove his points as well as he might have.

About Milton's prose works in general, most commentators agreed that the author was pedantic. Taine thought him humorless. Scherer had little good to say about the pamphlets as literature but observed that they contain occasional flashes of almost pure poetry. Geffroy, Taine and de Guerle endorsed the idea that the prose works have their poetic moments. As a rule with some exceptions, the bulk of the later prose evoked little critical response. Chateaubriand, however, examined most of the prose in some detail, awarding its author both praise and blame. To this critic, some of Milton's causes were noble, others reprehensible. In both cases, the prose was well suited to its purpose. To Véricour and Taine, Plato had been Milton's guide in much of it. Geffroy thought the embattled publicist sincere but noted how well he made his authorities serve his purposes. Villemain's opinion was that he had been exploited but that he came to share the fanaticism of those around him. To Chasles he had little in common with those whose causes he championed. Véricour thought him disinterested, observing, however, that he had been dedicated to an impractical ideal. Filon characterized his political ideas as utopian. Taine, like Chasles, stressed the unity of his convictions. Both regarded him as a highly skilled polemicist, and so did Geffroy. To Taine he was eminently logical, but Villemain considered his reasoning absurd. Véricour, Chateaubriand, Geffroy and Stroehlin insisted on the pamphlets' modern ring, seeing their author as a precursor of later social and political thought. De Guerle looked upon *Animadversions* as the high point in the poet's career as a polemicist. After that, there was too much bitterness, too much invective. With Chateaubriand, Geffroy paid more attention to the later pamphlets than did most commentators.

Several critics had problems with the political attitudes Milton assumed toward the end of the Civil Wars and during the Commonwealth and Protectorate. Filon viewed those attitudes as wrong but could understand why the author held them. That he should have served Oliver Cromwell— whom Villemain, Chasles and Pongerville considered an impostor, a rascal and a criminal—was an obstacle to several critics. To Scherer's way of thinking, Milton could not, as a republican, have approved of such a person. Véricour and Lamartine concluded that, by supporting the dictator, the poet hoped to advance causes that were dear to him. Pongerville inclined to this view, reminding readers that Milton had dared give the Lord Protector advice in the *Defensio Secunda*. Nevertheless, Filon believed that Cromwell made his secretary uneasy. Chateaubriand deplored Milton's attachment to the individual but wondered whether the poet saw him as God's agent. Lamartine tended to hold this view also. Stroehlin thought Milton and Cromwell saw eye to eye on religious matters.

Chateaubriand, Lamartine, Geffroy and Scherer compared the Puritan Revolution to the French Revolution. Morally, Chateaubriand believed the Puritans were better than the Girondins. To Scherer, the English Puritans were like the later French Jacobins. Lamartine considered it a pointless crime to have executed Charles I and Louis XVI. As for Milton's guilt or innocence, Villemain, de Guerle and Pongerville considered the poet reprehensible. Chasles thought this too harsh, and Geffroy and Filon explained his actions by saying that he lived in a cruel era. Eventually Pongerville exonerated him. Geffroy liked to think that Milton was not really bloodthirsty. Lamartine imagined that he repented. Though condemning his stand on the king's death, Chateaubriand pointed out that, in *The Tenure of Kings and Magistrates*, Milton at least cited Scripture, which his own country's revolutionaries had not done. *Eikonoklastes* Chateaubriand considered methodical and clear but heartless. Véricour declared that it was not aimed at any individual but rather at all despots. Lamartine blamed it energetically, calling it a blot on the poet's memory. Whatever their stand, most critics were in accord that the period left its mark on *Paradise Lost*. Véricour, Pongerville and others viewed Milton as the product of the troubled times in which he lived, and they saw those times mirrored in the epic. Chateaubriand asserted that the devils were the men of the Civil Wars and Commonwealth. Chasles agreed, believing that the poet had known and watched the violent preachers and politicians of the period and put them into his poem. As for Milton's religious beliefs, these were studied in particular by Chateaubriand and de Guerle.

At least from the standpoint of the author's reputation, several critics felt that *Paradise Lost* came at a bad time. To Filon, the era's atmosphere was not conducive to poetry. Pongerville held that the Restoration was too shallow to appreciate a work such as *Paradise Lost*. Mézières agreed. De Guerle believed that while readers' taste indeed left much to be desired at the time, the subject matter alone would have been enough to doom the work. Scherer's viewpoint was similar, and so was Taine's. Lamartine put it in plainer terms, claiming that the age of epics, at least as we know them, was simply over. Modern times cannot understand the epic mentality. De Guerle tended to agree.

To Chasles, *Paradise Lost* was not an optimistic poem but rather a monument to the poet's deep disillusionment. Despite that disillusionment, however, Filon thought the poem remarkably fresh and alive. Even when comparing it to other epics, critics such as Barbey d'Aurevilly could extol its "originalité victorieuse." Mézières called it an intellectual monument. Vinet saw it as a manual for those seeking to make their lives on earth worthwhile as they strive for salvation. Most critics were impressed with the powerful imagination at work in its structure and execution. Vinet considered it the greatest poem ever written. But some of the critics saw what appeared to them to be serious flaws in the poem. While Pongerville praised its "conception vaste et hardie," de Guerle felt that the poem, notwithstanding an overall cohesiveness, had unmistakable structural defects and called it a magnificent failure. Scherer insisted upon what he considered its basic contradiction, its need to be taken literally and the reader's inability to accept it as absolute truth. Lamartine, citing its speeches and lectures, asserted that it was poetic only in spots.

Most of the French critics we have dealt with had a good command of English and were qualified to comment on *Paradise Lost* from a linguistic standpoint. Many did so. To Pongerville the epic had been written in a "harsh" idiom. Villemain, Véricour and Filon considered it basically English but held that it had been "modified" by other languages and the Bible. Villemain, Chasles and de Guerle called attention to the Greek, Latin and Hebrew elements it contains. While words derived from Latin usually dominated the poet's vocabulary, Chasles nevertheless pointed out that most of those in the first line and a half of *Paradise Lost* are Germanic in origin. Pichot, Villemain and Chasles were aware that an Italian influence had been at work in the poem as well. How Milton handled language pleased his critics. Pichot commented in his short tale that, whatever innate drawbacks his basic linguistic medium had, the poet had surmounted them. Chasles admired his diction, and Villemain praised his rhetoric. Pongerville considered his style less rich, less ornate than it appeared.

Few of these critics were curious about Milton's sources. Except for the Bible, Vinet did not discuss them, nor did Stroehlin. Chasles was not interested. De Guerle did not think them important. Véricour and Chateaubriand mentioned the usual ones, plus one or two others. Having borrowed here and there in no way diminishes Milton's achievement in *Paradise Lost*, Chateaubriand asserted. To Pongerville, Milton's real debts were to the Bible and to classical literature in general. Understandably enough, the critics appeared to see only a thin line between actual sources and the models with which the poet was familiar and to which, in order to remain within a certain literary tradition, he was expected in some measure to conform. Comparisons with the other epic poets were thus inevitable. Of all our critics, Véricour is the one who undertook the most exhaustive comparison with the other epic poems, ancient and modern. But there were comparisons with particular poets also. Though not as an epic poet, Vinet compared Lamartine to Milton. Pongerville, Chateaubriand and de Guerle compared Milton to Homer. With Scherer, Pongerville also compared him to Virgil. Chateaubriand thought *Paradise Lost* essentially Homeric. To Scherer it was Virgilian, although the critic admitted that Virgil had imitated Homer. In some ways, Véricour found it superior to both the *Iliad* and the *Aeneid*. There are comparisons with Tasso as well, from Chateaubriand, for one. Several critics, including Véricour, Taine, de Guerle and Filon, compared Milton with Dante. Perhaps the best of these *rapprochements* are the subtle one that Philarètes Chasles elaborated and the thoughtful commentary by de Guerle. Pongerville detected resemblences to Lucretius. Chasles and Véricour insisted on Milton's debt to Plato. Without going into much detail, several times critics compared Milton's art to that of certain painters and sculptors. It reminded Barbey d'Aurevilly of Correggio. Pichot, Chateaubriand, Chasles, de Guerle and Taine evoked Michelangelo. Vigny, Chateaubriand and de Guerle mentioned Raphael as well. Between Raphael's landscapes and those in *Paradise Lost*, Taine, who criticized art as well as literature, detected certain similarities. Chasles saw a likeness with Claude Lorrain. According to Pichot, Bartolommeo Bandinelli, the sculptor, may have left his mark on Adam and Eve.

Nineteenth century French critics, especially the earlier ones, considered *Paradise Lost* "sublime." Villemain, Pongerville, Véricour, but also Taine come to mind in this regard. As for its style, Villemain described it as bold, innovative, majestic. Moreover, it was poetic. Vinet liked the descriptions. De Guerle considered the style admirable but nonetheless contrived. To Taine it was at once resplendent and utilitarian. In Pongerville's opinion, it was marvelous, although there were times when form and tone were not suited to each other, as when the poet descended to the "trivial." Scherer believed that Milton knew his epic would eventually catch on.

As we have seen in the preceding chapters, there are specific things in *Paradise Lost* to which our critics have reacted negatively. In Hell, the demons' shrinking, hissing and jesting have always bothered French readers. Homeric inspiration helped Chateaubriand at least account for this behavior. But Véricour thought the angels left something to be desired as well. What they do, for one thing, is not at all times commensurate with their spiritual nature. If the devils' antics, or at least some of them, have irritated French readers, traditionally they have been even more disturbed by Sin and Death. These monsters, along with the incest involved, have always struck them as gratuitously repulsive. In the nineteenth century, their distaste and even horror, far from diminishing, remained as vivid as it had been to their grandparents. Vinet and Stroehlin were not bothered, but Scherer was revolted. Filon, while not revolted, did not like the episodes depicting the creatures. Véricour alone called them an "image grandiose." To some critics, the Paradise of Fools has been irksome. And Filon, for one, saw no good reason for Milton's anachronisms. Chasles and several other critics commented on the poet's attitude toward women.

Except for Vinet, who felt that they were necessary, the speeches and debates have annoyed almost everybody. If the discourses are so numerous and so lengthy, Scherer suspected that the reason was to conceal the near absence of plot in the epic. Still, the speeches, or at least some of them, found favor with one or two critics. Villemain admired those delivered in Hell, and Scherer and de Guerle considered the lord of the place a very accomplished speaker indeed. Lamartine praised the speeches between Adam and Eve, but Véricour disapproved when the speeches became recriminations. Just as there are too many speeches, there is too much narration, too little plot to suit various commentators. Taine, while insisting that the poem contains a disproportionate amount of narrative, also claimed that it was not lyrical.

Chasles and Filon disagreed, however. And everywhere, critics complained, there is the author's obtrusive, cumbersome erudition, encountered at every turn. Chateaubriand, Véricour and de Guerle, among others, called attention to it.

Milton's Heaven did not appeal to critics as much as could have been expected, even though it had partisans such as Véricour. Those there were who thought the poet could have presented it more advantageously and compared him with other epic poets who, in their opinion, did so. Even Chateaubriand had misgivings. One thing amiss in Milton's Heaven, according to some, was God. Lamartine and Filon considered Him too anthropomorphic, though Vinet disagreed. To Scherer, He was peevish and querulous. He came across to Villemain, Taine and Filon as a dogmatic preacher, and not a very endearing one. Véricour and de Guerle went against the current and liked Him. That cannon should have been called up during the War in Heaven annoyed some critics. Lamartine was one of those who complained. Chateaubriand said that there had been a time when it shocked him too but that, to his mind, it had come to seem natural enough for demons to have invented what the poet considered our most violent weapon.

Finally, de Guerle and Scherer questioned the structural concept of *Paradise Lost*, giving sensible reasons for doing so. Several critics believed, moreover, that the later books add nothing to the epic. To Villemain, Scherer and Filon, *Paradise Lost* really ends with the tenth book. The last two books, merely tacked on, are useless. Scherer did not really care for books 9 and 10, for that matter. Again, Véricour was a dissenter, claiming that the final two books add something essential to the epic.

If there were things the critics found objectionable in *Paradise Lost*, there was much, of course, that delighted them. Stroehlin listed what he considered the great scenes. Where de Guerle had a doubt or two as to whether the poem was as cohesive as it might have been, Véricour insisted that it had been made of whole cloth from beginning to end. The various episodes and even the digressions, while entertaining the reader, do nothing to vitiate the epic's basic unity. Whereas some of their activities irritated a few critics, the devils were on the whole appreciated. Villemain and Véricour liked them. So did Filon, though he believed that naming them all was pointless. Vinet noted their intellectual curiosity and pointed out that they incarnated individual sins or vices that would later charaterize human beings, after their fall. Satan, their leader, was a peerless creation, universally admired. Cultivated readers generally shared the opinion of Charles Baudelaire, who had had a look at Delacroix's painting. Satan, Baudelaire felt, was "le plus parfait type de beauté virile."[1] As Milton presented him, he charmed everyone. For Villemain, he was a masterpiece. Chateaubriand considered him awesome and superb. Barbey d'Aurevilly, Taine and Filon praised him. Vinet noted that he was complex. Chasles saw him as a consummate intellectual. To Véricour he was a genius. Chateaubriand looked upon him, along with whatever else he may have been, as an advocate of aristocratic, parliamentary government. To Scherer he was the poem's hero. De Guerle thought him brilliant and memorable but decided that he was not the hero. De Guerle noted, too, that between *Paradise Lost* and *Paradise Regained*, Satan aged somewhat and lost much of his drive. The War in Heaven, where he is so prominent and so vital, impressed most critics. Several, on the other hand, did not like it. Villemain and Scherer withheld their plaudits, observing that the war was useless. It makes no sense to take on omnipotence, they held. Filon agreed. We have seen that one or two critics objected to the use of artillery.

Several critics, though not all, commented on the variety they discovered in *Paradise Lost*. For them the décors, the characters, the events, even the rhetorical devices, never static, keep the poem moving and prevent dullness. Milton's descriptions enchanted some critics, Vinet among them. Scherer singled out the poet's description of morning; Taine praised the landscapes. The Garden of Eden, with its ideal décor, pleased everyone, though Villemain claimed that it was strewn with too many bookish reminiscences. The critics were almost unanimous in their delight at Adam and Eve's chaste love in this natural, luxuriant setting. Villemain,

Chateaubriand, Véricour, Scherer and Vinet marveled at it. Several writers, such as Lamartine, were touched at the couple's mutual forgiveness after their fall. Vinet felt that modern husbands and wives should emulate them. Filon thought them a little too civilized to be our primitive parents, and in this he echoed Taine, who held, in addition, that Milton could not create characters and that he peopled his poem with ideas. Otherwise, the characterization of the first couple, who impressed critics as very human, drew favorable comment. Chateaubriand and Scherer found Eve particularly touching. Except for the reconciliation episode, Lamartine assumed that the model had been Elizabeth Minshull. If to some critics Satan was more or less their declared hero, Adam and Eve were the hero and heroine to others. For de Guerle, however, they were not the main characters. If there are heroes in *Paradise Lost*, according to this critic, they are God and the Son. Even so, God is too immense to be conceptualized in a poem, even this one. Jesus' character, he adds, does not come across as well in *Paradise Regained* as it does in *Paradise Lost*.

From the above, it is obvious that in the nineteenth century French reactions to Milton were as diverse as the critics themselves. Despite a few common likes and dislikes, the critics did not agree, and there is no reason why it should have been otherwise. To his examination of the author's prose and poetry, especially *Paradise Lost*, each critic brought his own background, attitudes and interests. Concerning *Paradise Lost*, all had some reservation or other to articulate. But even Scherer, who insisted that it had been erected upon an unworkable premise, admired the poem. From the critics' dissimilar perspectives emerges a complex picture of how French intellectuals of the period looked at John Milton, the man and the writer. In the following century, the interest would continue. But by that time, critics would be addressing a different public, one no longer made up essentially of well-rounded, cosmopolitan laypersons but rather of students and professional academics. Milton would have found a new audience.

Notes

Notes to Introduction

1. Joseph de Maistre, *Cinquième Paradoxe* in *Œuvres complètes* (Lyon: Librairie Générale Catholique et Classique, 1893), 7:335–36.

2. J. J. Jusserand, *A French Ambassador at the Court of Charles the Second* (London: T. Fisher Unwin, 1892), 206. See also J. Milton French, The *Life Records of John Milton* (New Brunswick: Rutgers University Press, 1956), 4:393.

3. Edme Rathéry, "Des relations sociales et intellectuelles entre la France et l'Angleterre depuis la conquête des Normands jusqu'à la Révolution Française," *Revue Contemporaine* (1855), 22:78. *Nouvelle Biographie générale* (Paris: Firmin Didot, 1855), 11:74. See also Mary Gaither, "Pierre Costar on Milton," *Notes and Queries* (1962), 9:378.

4. Much later at Ferney, Voltaire's estate in Switzerland, the English traveler Martin Sherlock noticed a copy of Milton that his host still had in his library in 1776. See Sherlock's letter describing his visit. Edme Rathéry, "Des relations sociales et intellectuelles entre la France et l'Angleterre depuis la conquête des Normands jusqu'à la Révolution Française," *Revue Contemporaine* (1855), 22:290. Martin Sherlock, *Letters from an English Traveler* (London: Nichols, Cadell, et al., 1780), 154. Garland Publishing, 1971.

5. Ernest Desclozeaux, "Sonnets de Milton," *Le Globe* (1826), 363. The article, unsigned, gives "O Nightingale," "How Soon

Hath Time," "On the Late Massacre in Piedmont" and "On his Blindness" in prose translation.

6. Amédée Pichot, "Milton," Le Perroquet de Walter Scott (Brussels: Wahlen, 1834), 2:165. (Hereafter references to this work will be in the text, parenthetically designated as "Milton," plus page numbers.) Pichot likewise called for a good biography.

7. Jean Gillet, Le Paradis perdu dans la littérature française de Voltaire à Chateaubriand (Paris: Klincksieck, 1975), 488–92.

8. For a discussion of these works, see R.A. Sayer, The French Biblical Epic in the Seventeenth Century (Oxford: Clarendon Press, 1955).

9. From 1838 to 1877. It was here that Philarète Chasles published his first Milton article, although the article appeared three years before Pichot became editor.

10. Amédée Pichot, Le Perroquet de Walter Scott (Brussels: Wahlen, 1834), 2:165.

11. Battista Guarini, "Madrigale XI," Opere , ed. Luigi Fassò (Turin: Editrice Torinese, 1950), 449. I have quoted from this more or less critical edition. Pichot took a few liberties and omitted two lines as indicated.

12. Amédée Pichot, "Milton," Les Poètes amoureux (Paris: Michel Lévy, 1858), 29. Originally the tale appeared in Pichot's Le Perroquet de Walter Scott (Paris: Dumont, 1834).

13. Adolphe d'Avril, Le Mystère de Roncevaux (Paris: Maison de la Bonne Presse, 1893), 18.

14. Amédée Pichot, Voyage historique et littéraire en Angleterre et en Ecosse (Paris: Ladvocat et Gosselin, 1825), 1:81.

15. "Milton," 9–10, 9–30; YPW, vol. 1, part 1, 612, 622–26.

16. Late in May 1640, she married Giulio Castellani, a member of Cardinal Francesco Barberini's household. Georges Dethan, Mazarin, un homme de paix à l'âge baroque (Paris: Imprimerie Nationale, 1981), 74.

17. François René de Chateaubriand, Essai sur la littérature anglaise in Œuvres complètes (Paris: Garnier, 1860), 11:639.

18. Sonnet 74 and Sonnet 75. The first sonnet appeared originally in a newspaper in 1789, according to the poet, and recorded what was considered "a well known fact." The second poem added that Milton did not succeed in finding his elusive admirer.

19. See Henry John Todd, Some Account of the Life of Milton in Todd's The Poetical Works of John Milton (London: J. Johnson et al., 1801), 1:xxi–xxii.

20. Alfred de Vigny, Œuvres complètes (Paris: Gallimard, 1986), 1:24.

21. Alfred de Vigny, Cinq-Mars in Œuvres complètes (Paris: Gallimard, 1948) 2:264–69.

22. Robert Couffignal, "Le Paradis perdu de Victor Hugo à

Pierre Jean Jouve," *Le* Paradis perdu *1667–1967*, ed. Jacques Blondel (Paris: Minard, 1967), 251–74.

23. Victor Hugo, *Littérature et philosophie mêlées* (Paris: Klincksieck, 1976), 2:89–91. Originally Hugo wrote these words with Vigny's "Eloa" in mind. By 1834, when he published them, he had come to dislike Vigny and applied them to *Paradise Lost* instead.

24. Auguste de Villiers de l'Isle-Adam, "Les Filles de Milton," *Œuvres complètes* (Paris: Gallimard, 1986), 2:701–07. Villiers died in 1889. The story appeared in *L'Echo de Paris* on 17 February 1891. In a collection of the author's short stories, it came out in book form in 1893.

25. Gustave Planche, "La Poésie et la critique en 1852," *Nouveaux Portraits littéraires*, (Paris: Amyot, 1854), 2:405.

26. Ernest Renan, *Œuvres complètes* (Paris: Calmann Lévy, 1947–61), 1:210; 2:325.

27. Edgar Monod, *Milton théologien* (Montauban: Macabiau-Vidallet, 1882), 26. Presumably Monod was referring to Sonnet 16 and the stern remark in *Defensio Secunda* about leaving church matters to the church itself. *YPW*, vol. 4, part 1, 678.

28. M.H. Bailly, "Origines et caractère du Satan de Milton," *Bulletin de la Société Académique de Brest* (1881), 7:61, 62, 65. Bailly taught English at the Lycée de Brest.

29. A 7 September 1850 letter to Georges Mancel in *Correspondance générale* (Paris and Toulouse: Didier and Privat, 1958), 8:186. "La littérature anglaise m'a toujours tenté, je la sais peu et je lis mal l'anglais, quoique j'essaie bien souvent d'y mordre...." Sainte-Beuve's English was good enough to permit the critic to adapt or imitate Wordsworth, Keats and Kirke White.

30. Charles Augustin Sainte-Beuve, *Œuvres* (Paris: Gallimard, 1960–66], 1:36, 445, 718; 2:354–55; *Correspondance générale* (Paris and Toulouse: Stock, Privat, Didier, 1935–83), 15:137 and 19:16; *Cahiers* (Paris: Gallimard, 1973), 95; *Causeries du lundi* (Paris: Garnier Frères, 1853–56), 1:302–03 and 3:48. The Senate speech, delivered on 19 May 1868, is included in *Premiers lundis* (Paris: Calmann Lévy, 1886) 3:96–97. With only one or two variants, the translation is Chateaubriand's. See *PL* 2.557–61 and François René de Chateaubriand, *Œuvres complètes* (Paris: Garnier, 1860), 11:77.

31. Charles Nodier, *Cours de belles-lettres tenu à Dole de juillet 1808 à avril 1809* (Geneva: Droz, 1988), 121. Nodier never published the lectures.

32. Nodier, *Mélanges de littérature et de critique* (Paris: Raymond, 1820), 1:235–36.

33. Matthew Arnold, "A French Critic on Milton," *Quarterly Review* 143 (1877), 186–204.

Notes to Chapter 1/Villemain

1. Gustave Planche, "Villemain," *Etudes littéraires* (Paris: Lévy, 1855), 137–40.
2. Abel François Villemain, "Essai historique sur Milton," *Discours et mélanges littéraires* (Paris: Ladvocat, 1823), 312–13. Hereafter references to this work will be in the text, parenthetically designated as Villemain, plus page numbers.
3. Villemain, 314. Villemain provides an elegant French translation of the four lines. Chateaubriand liked it so much that he included it in his discussion of Milton in the *Essai sur la littérature anglaise* in *Œuvres complètes* (Paris: Garnier Frères, 1860), 11:636.
4. Abel François Villemain, *Cours de littérature française du moyen âge* (Paris: Pichon et Didier, 1830), 252–53.
5. Villemain, 321. Villemain has a lengthy footnote on the plight of the Greeks. Among other things, he points out that Francis Bacon, in *De Bello Sacro*, had called for a crusade against their oppressors. Villemain's contribution to their cause was the preface to his *Lascaris ou les Grecs au quinzième siècle* and his *Essai sur l'état des Grecs depuis la conquête musulmane*, both dating from 1825.
6. Villemain, 320. See Villemain's *Histoire de Cromwell* (Paris: Maradan, 1819), 1:233.
7. In French translation and with minor deletions. Villemain does not say from which work he is summarizing and quoting. Milton's plea that Cromwell restore freedom of the press is also recalled.
8. In assigning such works to Milton's later years, Villemain was relying upon dates of publication, of course. Although he was willing to believe that work on *Paradise Lost* could have started much earlier than 1667, apparently it did not occur to him that the *Artis Logicae* might have been conceived and even written during Milton's career as a schoolmaster.
9. Taine was to be even more severe toward Addison, whom he looked upon as a mediocre critic. Overstating, Taine asserted that Addison's view, in essence, was that Milton conformed to Aristotle's rules and therefore was acceptable. Villemain had touched upon this also, observing that "Addison a tort de vouloir admirer Milton par les règles d'Aristote."
In the quotation from Villemain, the critic is referring to *PL* 10.267, 277–78, where Death tells Sin that, as he follows her toward the earth, he will make his way,

>..................... such a scent I draw
>Of carnage, prey innumerable, and taste
>The savor of Death from all things there that live.

Turning his nostrils upward, he soon detects the "scent of living carcasses" that will die the next day and thus be ready for him.
  10. "Les fleurs de la poésie antique en font toute la parure." Villemain, 338.
  11. In poetry, words carried over in runover lines.
  12. Samuel Johnson in *The Rambler*.
  13. Philarète Chasles, "Milton, ses œuvres, sa vie, et ses opinions," *Revue Britannique*, July 1835, 54–55. Villemain was soon to becomes Chasles's patron and do much to advance his career.
  14. Alfred Michiels, "Du poème épique," *Histoire des idées littéraires en France au XIXe siècle* (Paris: Coquebert, 1842), 2:166. The correct title of Vincent de Beauvais's work is *Speculum majus*.

Notes to Chapter 2/Chateaubriand

  1. Rémy de Gourmont, "Commémorations: Chateaubriand," *Epilogues, réflexions sur la vie* (Paris: Mercure de France, 1921), 1:58–59. The note was first published in June 1898 in the *Mercure de France* (1898) 26:819–21.
  2. François René de Chateaubriand, *Les Quatre Stuarts* in *Œuvres complètes* (Paris: Garnier Frères, 1859–61), 10:399. Referred to hereafter, in the text and in parentheses, as *Quatre Stuarts*.
  3. François René de Chateaubriand, *Essai sur la littérature anglaise* in *Œuvres complètes* 11:793. Cited hereafter, parenthetically in the text, as *Essai*.
  4. François René de Chateaubriand, *Mémoires d'outre-tombe* (Paris: Flammarion, 1950), 1:509. Cited hereafter as *MOT*, parenthetically in the text, with page numbers.
  5. *MOT* 1:397, 225. Chateaubriand's posthumous memoirs had not been published when the *Essai sur la littérature anglaise* was written, but, along with some other material, the author lifted the remark about Mirabeau from his memoirs and inserted it in the *Essai*. *Essai*, 700.
  6. Napoleon did not allow the speech to be read at the induction ceremony, which was canceled. The *Discours* was not published until 1814, after Napoleon's initial fall.
  7. François René de Chateaubriand, *Itinéraire de Paris à Jérusalem* in *Œuvres complètes* 5:323; *PL* 1.10–12.
  8. *Œuvres complètes* 4:68. As in *Paradise Lost*, there are invocations in Chateaubriand's epic. God and the Son get involved in human affairs, there are celestial creatures and demons' assemblies, Satan makes speeches, and so on.
  9. "Lorsqu'au commencement de ma vie l'Angleterre m'offrit un refuge, je traduisis quelques vers de Milton pour subvenir aux besoins de l'exil." *Essai*, 793. Jean Gabriel Peltier, an exiled royalist

journalist and editor, helped his compatriot obtain this kind of work. *MOT* 1:439. When quoting Milton's Latin, Italian or English, Chateaubriand may or may not give the original, though he usually does. Almost always the translation is his own and is extraordinarily good. However, he sometimes changed his mind. *Paradise Lost* material translated for the *Génie du christianisme* was reworded for the complete translation of the epic published in 1836. Similarly, passages quoted in the *Essai sur la littérature anglaise* do not necessarily reproduce the translation's exact phrasing. Now and then in the *Essai*'s Milton section, Chateaubriand uses quotation marks but is summarizing rather than translating ("Elegia Septima").

10. Chateaubriand, thinking of a line from "L'Allegro,"

The frolic Wind that breathes the Spring,

was making it serve his purposes ("L'Allegro," 18), although a little later in the poem summer is mentioned. Chateaubriand and the other French romantics were obsessed with autumn and the sadness with which they invested it. Chateaubriand could have been doing some wishful thinking here, but on the other hand he could have found a few dates that allowed him to jump to plausible conclusions. After Milton's move to High Holborn, William Riley Parker observes that "In the autumn and winter of 1647 there was time again for writing...." Parker, 1:313.

11. *Essai*, 665. Since he refers to Homer, "Pluto's helmet," and "Latmus Hill," Chateaubriand was using the first draft of the "Letter to a Friend." For a text, see the Columbia University edition of *The Works of John Milton*, (New York: Columbia University Press, 1936), 12:320–22.

12. *Essai*, 633; *YPW* 1:823. As was his custom, even when using quotation marks, Chateaubriand condenses as he translates.

13. For the four lines quoted from "Mansus," Chateaubriand uses Villemain's translation.

14. Recently named Secretary to the French Embassy, Chateaubriand arrived in Rome for the first time on 27 June 1803. Initially the *Lettre à M. de Fontanes* appeared as an article in the *Mercure de France*, of which Fontanes was the editor, on 3 March 1804. Later it was published in new editions of the *Génie du christianisme*.

15. Milton had looked at it with "un regard aussi sec et aussi aride que sa foi." *MOT* 3:436. Likewise disappointed that Milton said so little about his stay in Rome was J. J. Ampère, Chateaubriand's friend. Ampère suspected, however, that the Paradise of Fools, "grotesque épisode du *Paradis perdu*, semble, en quelques endroits, un rancuneux souvenir des superstitions romaines." Ampère took Pichot's little tale seriously but believed that the

episode took place in Italy. "Tout puritain qu'était déjà Milton, il était jeune et beau dans ce voyage d'Italie, où de charmantes inconnues le regardaient dormir et improvisaient des vers sur ses yeux fermés par le sommeil." J. J. Ampère, "Portraits de Rome à différents âges: seconde partie (1600–1830)," Revue des Deux Mondes (1835), 3:135–36.

16. Essai, 635–36; MOT 3:425. Milton's encounter with Leonora Baroni probably took place at the Palazzo Barberini, as the traditional account would have it. Although it has been claimed that women could not penetrate this sanctum, Leonora, a special favorite of Cardinal Antonio Barberini, was often received there. In any event, Cardinal Antonio made it his business to hear her whenever and wherever he could and might well have taken the young English traveler to other places where she was performing. In 1640 she married Giulio Castellani, Cardinal Francesco Barberini's secretary, her career continuing as brilliantly as ever. In Rome Jules Mazarin, then Giulio Mazarini, had known her at the Palazzo Barberini, where the two cardinals were his patrons. Mazarin went to France in 1640 and entered French government service. When Richelieu died, he replaced him as French Prime Minister, a position he held until his own death in 1661. He had remained in touch with Leonora Baroni, whom he sent for around 1644 or 1645. In Paris she appeared at court and helped introduce Italian opera. Mme de Motteville was Anne of Austria's friend and lady in waiting. Her *Mémoires sur Anne d'Autriche et sa cour* state that the prime minister imported "des comédiens qui chantoient leur comédies en musique." A court performance was held on Mardi Gras 1646. Another, apparently even more elaborate, took place on 2 March 1647. Mme de Motteville preferred conventional theatre and at first did not like opera very much. Many contemporaries seem to have agreed. Less successful in Paris than she had been in Rome, Leonora did not stay. Chateaubriand was mistaken about Mme de Motteville's memoirs. While performances are mentioned, there are no allusions to particular singers. See Françoise de Motteville, *Mémoires* (Paris: Charpentier, 1886), 1:262, 312. Undoubtedly Chateaubriand was thinking of a contemporary's recollections. In those of the Marquis de Montglat, Leonora is identified and readers are told that Mazarin had had her brought from Rome "pour chanter devant la Reine." Alexandre Petitot and Louis de Monmerqué eds., *Collection des mémoires relatifs à l'histoire de France* (Paris: Foucault, 1826), 50:59. Probably Charles, Prince of Wales,was present at some of these court performances. Thus the superb artist who had captivated the regicide John Milton probably entertained the exiled Stuart prince, son of his foe. Some information about Leonora Baroni and Mazarin can be found in Georges Dethan, *Mazarin, un homme de paix*

à *l'âge baroque* (Paris: Imprimerie Nationale, 1981), 59-62, 97, 99. In 1844 Chateaubriand would mention Leonora again in the *Vie de Rancé*, (Paris: Didier, 1955), 1:173.

17. Chateaubriand again condensed as he quoted, even though using quotation marks. Thus, in the passage cited in *The Reason of Church Government*, what he presents as being one paragraph actually involves material that, in the introduction to the second book, is rather widely scattered. See *YPW* 1:810, 812, 820-21. In addition, by rearranging a few words, Chateaubriand has taken one or two other liberties with Milton's text.

18. *Essai*, 666; *YPW* 2:366-67. Erroneously, Chateaubriand gives 1650 as the date of publication.

19. *Essai*, 639, 665; *MOT* 1:125-26. While complimenting the author on his "beau portrait de Milton," Chateaubriand rejects Amédée Pichot's "touchante nouvelle historique," in which Leonora Baroni is the heroine, as literal truth.

20. Chateaubriand opposed divorce. See "Du divorce," *Œuvres complètes* 8:528-30. The fragment is supposed to have been a passage the author decided to omit in the *Génie du christianisme*.

21. Chateaubriand devoted several chapters to the freedom of the press in one of his earliest and most famous political pamphlets, *De la monarchie selon la charte* (1816). Among the other pamphlets are *De la censure que l'on vient de rétablir* (1822); *De l'abolition de la censure* (1824); *Du rétablissement de la censure* (1827); *Les Amis de la liberté de la presse* (1827); *Lettre à M. de Chateaubriand relative au projet de loi sur la police de la presse* (1827); etc. The pamphlet that got Chateaubriand in trouble was *Mémoire sur la captivité de Mme la duchesse de Berry*, which appeared 29 December 1832. It caused a furor. On 4 January 1833, between 1,200 and 1,300 young people congregated in the street where the author lived and gave him an ovation. Six Legitimist newspapers reporting the incident were closed down and their editors arrested. Chateaubriand was tried 27 February. The prosecution made incredible blunders, and he was acquitted.

22. Actually, Milton's move was probably motivated by a need for less spacious quarters. Milton's father and Richard Powell had died, and Mrs. Powell took most of her family to live at Wheatley. Milton appears to have changed residence in the autumn, not in April. In all likelihood Chateaubriand's mistake arose from a hurried misreading of Edward Phillips's life of his uncle. There the word "march" no doubt led the critic to believe that, soon after that "march," Milton moved into his new quarters. "It was not long after the march of Fairfax and Cromwell through the city of London with the whole army to quell the insurrections Brown and Massy, now malcontents also, were endeavoring to raise in the city . . . , ere he left his great house in Barbican. . . ."

See Helen Darbishire ed., *The Early Lives of Milton* (London: Constable, 1932), 68. Fairfax and Cromwell did not militarily occupy London in the spring of 1647. Fairfax occupied it on 6 August 1647 and 2 December 1648.

23. Whether correct or not, Chateaubriand was speaking from experience. In 1822 he had been French Ambassador to the Court of St. James. His diplomatic relations with Great Britain continued after he became Minister of Foreign Affairs, a post he held from 1 January 1823 to 6 June 1824. With George IV he seems to have spoken French. *MOT* 3:110.

24. Chateaubriand is in error here. King Charles and Queen Henrietta Maria worried endlessly that their letters might fall into the wrong hands, and there were some close calls. Probably the reference is to the letters captured at the Battle of Naseby. Published in *The King's Cabinet Opened*, the letters were suitably "annotated."

25. *Vie de Rancé*, 2:265.

26. Chateaubriand mistakenly calls him "François" More.

27. An energetic member of the Greek Committee in Paris, Chateaubriand made his most spirited statement in his *Note sur la Grèce* (1825). It went through several editions and, in its final form, was published in 1826 with the *Itinéraire de Paris à Jérusalem*. In the Chambre des Pairs, Chateaubriand spoke in favor of the Greeks notably on 13 March 1826. After independence had been won, King Otto decorated him for his efforts.

28. Chateaubriand knew what he was talking about. When he was elected to the Académie Française in 1811, Napoleon refused to allow him to read or publish his acceptance speech. Some of the emperor's objections had to do with a digression in which the recipient appealed to him for more freedom, including freedom of speech. For a time Chateaubriand was in rather serious trouble.

29. *Essai*, 657–60. Fascinated by Richard Cromwell's brief reign followed by complete obscurity, Chateaubriand returned to it elsewhere. "Caprices de la fortune," he called it. See *Les Quatre Stuarts* in *Œuvres complètes* 10:426.

30. Chateaubriand relates, in *Les Quatre Stuarts*, two anecdotes having to do with Cromwell's burial. According to one, "Cromwell, prévoyant les outrages qu'on pourrait faire à ses restes, avait ordonné qu'on précipitât son corps dans la Tamise ou qu'on l'enterrât sur le champ de bataille de Naseby, à neuf pieds de profondeur." One Barkshead, Lieutenant of the Tower, is supposed to have had his son carry out this second order. On the other hand, it has been said that "les corps de Charles Ier et de Cromwell, échangés, avaient été transportés de l'un à l'autre tombeau; de sorte que Charles II, dans sa vengeance, aurait pendu au gibet

le corps de son propre père au lieu de celui de l'assassin de son père." He adds that Cromwell was buried in Westminster Abbey but that his remains, exhumed in 1661, did not stay there long. As for King Charles's body, Chateaubriand reminds readers that it had been discovered in recent times in Windsor Castle, thus proving that "le meurtrier n'était pas allé dormir dans la couche du meurtri et que, satisfait de lui avoir ravi la couronne, il lui laissa son cercueil." *Les Quatre Stuarts* in *Œuvres complètes* 10:422. As we shall see, Auguste Geffroy would revive the story of the bodies being switched. Chateaubriand likewise rejects the anecdote about Milton's announcing his death and having a funeral service performed. Nevertheless, he points out that Charles II is said to have laughed at the ruse. *Essai*, 664. Chateaubriand does not accept the tale about an accidental meeting between Charles II and Milton in St. James Park. The story is familiar and is encountered in the work of several French critics. When the king suggested to the poet that his blindness was divine punishment for his part in the late king's death, the poet is said to have replied that if Heaven punishes us on earth for our misdeeds, Charles I must have done terrible things. *Essai*, 665. We know from "Milton et Davenant," a poem he wrote at that time, that Chateaubriand was interested in Milton at least as of the 1790s. In view of this early interest, it is a little surprising that he did not pick up on a grim episode that is supposed to have taken place shortly before his arrival in England as an émigré. This is the business about the exhumation and desecration of Milton's corpse in St. Giles, Cripplegate, in August 1790. The silence is all the more noticeable in that Chateaubriand dwells upon the exhumations that took place in France in September 1793, when the royal corpses were taken out of their vaults and profaned at St. Denis, a topic the author returns to over and over again in his writings. For a grisly account of what is said to have happened to Milton's remains, see John Ashton, "Milton's Bones," *Eighteenth-Century Waifs* (London: Hurst and Blackett, 1887), 55–82.

31. *Essai*, 666; *YPW*, vol. 5, part 1, 129–30; 402–03. Chateaubriand interprets here a bit more freely than Milton's text warrants. He also places the Norman Conquest at the end of book 1 rather than at the close of book 6.

32. François René de Chateaubriand, *Discours de réception* (Paris: Chaumerot, 1815), 4–5. This was the Académie Francaise acceptance speech that Napoleon forbade.

33. *Petit Bulletin de la Société Chateaubriand* (1952), 4:14.

34. François René de Chateaubriand, *Génie du christianisme* in *Essai sur les révolutions/Génie du christianisme* (Paris: Gallimard, 1978), 628. Hereafter noted parenthetically in the text as *Génie*.

35. Chateaubriand is bland as to the composition period. Once he tells his readers that "Milton, vers la fin du Protectorat, avait commencé sérieusement à écrire le *Paradis perdu*." Elsewhere, stating that the poem was written "sous la République et le Protectorat," he seems to be suggesting that it may have been finished by 1659 or 1660.

36. More or less, Paul Claudel, the great French poet and dramatist, was to agree three quarters of a century later. "Milton était un Arien, ou... au plus un Gnostique." Letter to André Gide, 28 September 1912. Paul Claudel and André Gide, *Correspondance 1899–1926* (Paris: Nouvelle Revue Française, 1949), 204.

37. Chateaubriand is thinking of *PL* 7.455–79, with such lines as:

> .... out of the ground up rose
> As from his Lair the wild Beast where he wons
> In Forest wild, in Thicket, Brake, or Den;

and

> The grassy Clods now Calv'd, now half appear'd
> The Tawny Lion, pawing to get free
> His hinder parts, then springs as broke from Bonds....

38. Chateaubriand has in mind *PL* 5.859–60, where Satan tells Abdiel:

> We know no time when we were not as now;
> Know none before us, self-begot, self-rais'd....

39. Jean Gillet, *Le* Paradis perdu *dans la littérature française de Voltaire à Chateaubriand* (Paris: Klincksieck, 1975), 625. See *PL* 12.539–51.

40. Versed as he was in the French classics, it is a bit surprising here that Chateaubriand makes no analogy with Milton's French contemporary, Pascal. In his *Pensées* Pascal gave his concept of the infinite. To demonstrate it, he proposed that, after contemplating what one can actually perceive visually, one should let his imagination take over for a moment. "Elle se lassera plutôt de concevoir que la nature de fournir. Tout ce monde visible n'est qu'un trait imperceptible dans l'ample sein de la nature. Nulle idée n'en approche. Nous avons beau enfler nos conceptions au delà des espaces imaginables, nous n'enfantons que des atomes, au prix de la réalité des choses. C'est une sphère infinie dont le centre est partout, la circonférence nulle part. Enfin c'est le plus grand caractère sensible de la toute-puissance de Dieu, que notre imagination se perde dans cette pensée.... Qu'est-ce que l'homme dans l'infini...? Qu'il recherche dans ce qu'il connaît les choses les plus délicates. Qu'un ciron lui offre dans la petitesse de son corps des parties incomparablement plus petites.... Je veux lui

faire voir là-dedans un abîme nouveau. Je lui veux peindre non seulement l'univers visible, mais l'immensité qu'on peut concevoir de la nature, dans l'enceinte de ce raccourci d'atome. Qu'il y voie une infinité d'univers...." Blaise Pascal, *Pensées*, ed. Louis Lafuma (Paris: Delmas, 1961), 101. In Lafuma's arrangement, this is *Pensée* 199.

41. *Essai*, 689–91. In the *Génie du christianisme* Chateaubriand develops at some length the unhappy couple's contrition and decision to appeal to God's mercy. In connection with the Son's intercession, he compares Milton advantageously with Homer. "Ces accents montent au séjour céleste, et le Fils se charge lui-même de les présenter à son Père. On admire avec raison dans l'*Iliade* les Prières Boîteuses, qui suivent l'Injure pour réparer les maux qu'elle a faits. Cependant Milton lutte ici sans trop de désavantage contre cette fameuse allégorie.... Toutes ces beautés réunies ont en soi quelque chose de si moral, de si solennel, de si attendrissant qu'elles ne sont peut-être point effacées par les Prières du chantre d'Ilion." *Génie*, 636.

42. On the publication of the *Essai sur la littérature anglaise* and the *Paradise Lost* translation, Planche wrote a series of articles on Chateaubriand. The articles appeared in the *Chronique de Paris* on 7, 21 and 28 August 1836 and were later published in Planche's *Portraits littéraires* (Paris: Charpentier, 1853), 2:153–83. There is almost nothing on Milton in the articles.

Notes to Chapter 3/Chasles

1. Claude Pichois, *Philarète Chasles et la vie littéraire au temps du romantisme* (Paris: José Corti, 1965), 1:510, 488–90; 2:356.

2. Jules Barbey d'Aurevilly, *Les Œuvres et les hommes. Les Critiques ou les juges jugés.* (Paris: L. Frinzine et Cie, 1885), 112–13.

3. There can be no doubt that Chasles wrote the article himself. The *Retrospective Review* existed for most of the 1820s and even had one or two articles on Milton. Chasles's *Revue Britannique* article was not one of them. Like Chasles's other Milton commentaries, this one has its author's characteristic disorganization. It also contains the same material, though sometimes expanded, that one encounters in the signed studies. Clearly intended for Gallic rather than English readers, it mentions French authors, critics, translators and utopian movements that, in some cases, would have had little or no meaning for an English audience. The article even concludes with a French translation of "On the Late Massacre in Piedmont," which English readers would not have needed.

4. *Journal des Débats,* 21 October 1836, 3. Using as his point of departure Chateaubriand's *Essai sur la littérature anglaise* and translation of *Paradise Lost,* Chasles wrote five Milton articles in 1836 for the *Journal des Débats,* the articles appearing on 14 July, 14 and 28 September, and 21 and 28 October. A sixth article, dealing with *Comus, Samson Agonistes* and the minor poems, appeared in the *Journal* in 1839. For convenience, these articles will hereafter be referred to parenthetically in the text as *JD* 1, 2, 3, 4, 5 and 6. Similarly, the *Revue Britannique* article will be designated as *RB* and the two *Dictionnaire de la conversation et de la lecture* articles as *DC* 1837 and *DC* 1863. Eventually and with only negligible changes, the 28 August 1839 *Journal des Débats* article was included in a book with the unlikely title, *Etudes sur l'Allemagne au dix-neuvième siècle* (Paris: Amyot, 1861), 306-09, 313-16. The comparison between *Comus*'s Lady and Spenser's Una is somewhat more developed than in the original article.

5. Raymond de Véricour and Auguste Geffroy were to borrow Chasles's translation for their own works. Véricour also borrowed Chasles's translation of Milton's letter to John Bradshaw recommending Andrew Marvell. Véricour, *Milton et la poésie épique* (Paris: Delaunay, 1838), 125, 91.

6. Philarète Chasles, *Olivier Cromwell* (Paris: Amyot, 1847), 38. Milton, he adds, was a Cromwell associate, "mélancolique comme Cromwell et puritain comme lui." *Olivier Cromwell,* 37.

7. Once Chasles goes so far as to claim that Milton was a republican only in theory. *DC* 1837, 178.

8. Chasles was not consistent as to the importance he attached to these influences. Elsewhere in the same article he listed as follows "les éléments chimiques de cette vaste formation: la Grèce d'abord, puis la Bible, puis l'Italie" (*JD* 2:4).

9. In one of his articles Chasles called attention to other debts Milton owed to Greek, debts involving style as well as thought. "Sa première éducation de penseur s'était faite à l'école de Platon, son maître et son modèle. Cette première étude ne s'effaça jamais; et il est remarquable combien, pour la force du style, le doux éclat des images, la méthode du raisonnement, et l'application de la méditation rêveuse à la vie réelle, Milton est demeuré l'élève fidèle de son premier maître. A tout moment vous retrouvez chez lui la forme grecque: la belle période qui se déroule; l'adjectif composé de deux nuances qui s'éclairent l'une par l'autre. Dans ce *Paradis perdu,* que les Anglais s'étonnent d'admirer en le trouvant si peu anglais, non seulement la syntaxe devient hellénique, mais la déduction des idées, le développement de la narration, les grandes images lumineuses qui brillent dans le récit comme des phares sur la mer semblent empruntés à la source

grecque. Ce n'est pas tout. A côté de cet idéal de la forme, que Milton a emprunté aux Grecs, vient se placer une seconde influence: c'est l'idéal hébraïque inspiré par la Bible. Corrigé par le génie des Hellènes, celui des Juifs a produit chez Milton à peu près le même résultat que chez notre Racine." *DC* 1837, 179.

10. Chasles was especially critical of Jacques Delille's verse translation, first published in 1805. Citing passages he disliked, the critic complained about the translation in several of his articles (*RB*, 50–51, 53–54; *JD* 3:4). In the *Journal des Débats* Chasles quipped that Delille's misfortune was that he had been "proclamé poète par une société sans poésie."

11. *DC* 1837, 174; *DC* 1863, 188. Chasles was aware of the recent discoveries and mentioned them toward the end of his *Revue Britannique* article as "documents trouvés dans les archives du gouvernement" "dans ces derniers temps." He also mentioned, and in the same article, Milton's letter recommending Andrew Marvell to John Bradshaw, "une lettre publiée pour la première fois en 1826." *RB*, 60–63. See n. 5 above.

12. *DC* 1837, 176–77. Making one minor error in transcribing it, Chasles reprints, as far as it goes, the excerpt Chateaubriand translated for the *Essai sur la littérature anglaise*. After that Chasles finishes off the monologue with his own translation. In the quoted material, Milton's lines have been slightly rearranged (*SA* ll. 16–114). Incredibly and without indicating what he has done, Chasles then prolongs the hero's lament by tacking on the last half of the invocation to light in *Paradise Lost* 3.33–55, again using Chateaubriand's *Essai* translation (Chateaubriand had rendered the passage a little differently in his book translation of *Paradise Lost*). With this additional material added to it, Samson's speech reads smoothly enough, but of course the critic had no business doing what he did. As pointed out in the introduction, the French romantics had a rather debonair attitude toward quoting. Even so, this is a bit extreme. Milton was speaking in the first person in the invocation. Taking quite literally Chateaubriand's remark in the *Essai* that "le poète s'est peint dans la personne de l'Israélite aveugle," Chasles felt free to lift part of the invocation and attach it to the end of Samson's monologue. See Chateaubriand, *Œuvres complètes* (Paris: Garnier Frères, 1859–61), 11:675–76, 698.

Notes to Chapter 4/Véricour

1. Raymond de Véricour, *Milton et la poésie épique* (Paris: Delaunay, 1838). (Hereafter referred to parenthetically in the text as Véricour, with page numbers.) The heading of the *Monthly Review*'s critique suggests that an English version of Véricour's

work also appeared or was going to appear in 1838, published in London by Baillière. Baillière, who specialized in medical textbooks, was a Paris publisher with a London branch. He was associated with Delaunay in bringing out Véricour's work, but there seems not to have been an edition in English. I find no trace of such an edition and do not believe that it was ever published.

2. Raymond de Véricour, *The Life and Times of Dante* (London: J.F. Hope, 1858), 255.

3. Véricour was aware that Old French epic manuscripts were being discovered, and he hoped that the future would reveal that some were authentic masterpieces. Véricour, 26.

4. "All the modern epic poets, with the exception of Dante, have more or less copied or imitated the *Iliad*; Milton, Klopstock and Tasso have, it is true, selected Christian subjects but, in the development of them, have adhered to the pagan form." *Life and Times of Dante*, 326–27.

Notes to Chapter 5/Geffroy

1. Auguste Geffroy, *Etude sur les pamphlets politiques et religieux de Milton* (Paris: Dezobry, Magdeleine, et Cie, 1848). Hereafter, references to this work appear parenthetically in the text as Geffroy, with page numbers. The other thesis was *De Polybiano circa Timæum Tarromenitam Judicio* (Paris: Bonaventure et Ducessois, 1848).

2. Geffroy, 51–52. Geffroy erroneously presents the passage as coming from the *Apology for Smectymnuus*. In reality, he is quoting and translating from *The Reason of Church Government*. See YPW 1:808–21. The material is highly condensed and the translation somewhat free.

3. Geffroy gives 13 June. Geffroy, 81.

4. Geffroy, 232. In his preface to the YPW edition of *Areopagitica*, Ernest Sirluck mistakenly affirms that Geffroy claimed the manuscript to be in the British Museum.

5. This version of *Areopagitica*, called *Sur la liberté de la presse*, appeared in London in 1788. There was a Paris edition in 1792, after Mirabeau's death. Villemain claims Mirabeau had nothing to do with the translation, but he almost certainly did. In a note Geffroy adds that Mirabeau also defended a free press in *De la monarchie prussienne* (1788). Geffroy, 97 n. 1. The work has been attributed to Jacob von Mauvillon and J. C. Thibault de Laveaux. Only in his bibliography does Geffroy mention a *Théorie de la royauté d'après Milton*. This was J. B. Salaville's condensation and translation of *Pro Populo Anglicano Defensio*, which appeared in 1789. In 1792, when Louis XVI's fate was being

discussed, there was another edition. The translation is sometimes attributed to Mirabeau.

6. Bishop Hall's protest was in *Cases of Conscience*. It did not appear, however, until 1649.

7. Geffroy, 120-28. Fénelon came to have reservations about divine right. See his *Lettre à Louis XIV*, in which a monarch's obligations to his people are stressed. Geffroy will mention the *Lettre à Louis XIV* a little later, but it is surprising that he does not do it here.

8. Uncritically, Geffroy accepts the legend that Saumaise was hired and paid. "Ce fut à lui ... que Charles II s'adressa pour faire détester à toute l'Europe le meurtre commis par les Anglais. Pour cent jacobus, avec son habituelle rapidité de travail, Saumaise eut bientôt écrit contre la République un gros volume latin de cinq cents pages que lui-même traduisit immédiatement en français." Geffroy, 145.

9. Geffroy, 161-62. Geffroy's chronology is somewhat shaky in this. The critic believed that *Pro Se Defensio* was initially published in 1654, for example. Apparently he also believed that Milton's rejoinder was a separate publication. Geffroy, 237.

10. The *Declaration* was approved for publication 26 October 1655. Problems with Spain had arisen over the murder of Anthony Ascham, whom the English Republic had sent as its diplomatic representative to Madrid several years before. Ascham arrived in June 1650. With his interpreter, he was murdered the day after his arrival by six English royalists. Spain tried the assassins but punished only one, letting the others escape. Parliament ranted and protested to no avail. With the *Declaration*, a statement of grievances against the Spanish, Cromwell was renewing the wrangle. He needed a pretext for seizing Jamaica and attacking Hispaniola, which he had done a few months earlier. The *Declaration* was the closest he came to formally declaring war against Spain. There is no clear evidence that Milton drafted the *Declaration*, and attributing it to him appears never to have come up prior to 1738. A text can be consulted in the Columbia University Milton. See *The Works of John Milton* (New York: Columbia University Press, 1937), 13:509-63.

11. Paraphrasing and translating, Geffroy recalls Milton's advice to Cromwell in Sonnet 16 and, in *Defensio Secunda*, the apostrophe concerning the distinction that should be maintained between church and state. Geffroy, 174-75. With regard to the *Defensio Secunda* material, Geffroy does not state what work he is summarizing and quoting.

12. Geffroy, 184-87. Geffroy calls it "une curieuse lettre, publiée pour la première fois par Fletcher." Listed in his bibliography is an 1844 reprint of Robert Fletcher's edition of Milton's prose

works. Geffroy was obviously unaware that the letter had been published much earlier. In 1753 it had appeared in Richard Baron's revision of the Thomas Birch edition of the prose. Baron republished the document three years later in his own edition of *Eikonoklastes*. Geffroy's negligence is all the more surprising in view of the fact that the Baron *Eikonoklastes* figures in his bibliography. Geffroy, 246. Like Baron, Geffroy gives Wall's first name as John rather than Moses.

13. "La prose se modela sur celle de Scarron..., et la poésie, parmi tous les genres, adopta de préférence le grotesque." Geffroy, 201. Geffroy does not account for Restoration drama, so markedly different from French theatre of the day.

14. See *YPW* 7:493; Columbia Milton 12:81.

15. Earlier, Geffroy had contrasted Milton with Bossuet concerning divine right. Here he could have made another comparison. Bossuet, Bishop of Meaux, had written an *Histoire des variations des églises protestantes*, arguing against Protestantism on the grounds that it was not a unified religion.

16. Henry John Todd, ed., *The Poetical Works of John Milton*, (London: Gilbert and Rivington, 1852), 1:185–88, 220.

17. Theoretically, this could have happened. After the execution, King Charles's head is said to have been sewn back on by Dr. Thomas Trapham. With his taste for such things, it is a litle surprising that Geffroy did not pick up on the grisly accounts of the exhumation and desecration of Milton's corpse, said to have taken place in August 1790. For a harrowing recital, see John Ashton, "Milton's Bones," *Eighteenth-Century Waifs* (London: Hurst and Blackett, 1887), 55–82.

18. As used to be the custom in France, doctoral candidates presented two theses. One of these, the minor thesis, had to be in Latin. Geffroy had composed his second study in that language.

Notes to Chapter 6/Lamartine

1. William Fortescue, *Alphonse de Lamartine: A Political Biography* (London: Croom Helm, 1983), 282.

2. Alphonse de Lamartine, *Vies de quelques hommes illustres* in *Œuvres complètes*, (Paris: Chez l'Auteur, 1860–63), 36:6. References to Lamartine's 3-volume work are hereafter given parenthetically in the text as *Vies* 1, 2 or 3, along with appropriate page numbers.

3. *Vies* 2:332. In passing, Lamartine compares Milton to Chateaubriand and Mme de Staël at the beginning of the French Revolution. Careless about dates, no doubt he had two works of Chateaubriand in mind, one during the Revolution and one later.

These would have been the *Essai sur les révolutions* (1797) and *De Buonaparte et des Bourbons* (1814). As for Mme de Staël, he probably was thinking of the posthumous *Considérations sur la Révolution Française* (1817), although there had been several less remarkable pamphlets earlier.

4. After the French Revolution of 1830, those ministers of the deposed Charles X who had not escaped were put on trial. Some of the fallen regime's enemies howled for the death penalty. Lamartine disagreed. His poem, "Contre la peine de mort," appeared 15 December 1830. Later, one of the Second Republic's significant legislative acts abolished the death penalty for political offenses.

5. Alphonse de Lamartine, *Œuvres complètes* (Paris: Chez l'Auteur, 1860–63), 12:106; 15:172.

6. Tradition has it that Prince Charles, not Louis XIV, commissioned the *Defensio Regia*. Milton accused Saumaise of having been hired to write it, but Saumaise denied the charge. The matter is still unresolved. As Don M. Wolfe observed, "It is not yet proved that Charles paid a hundred pounds for the writing and printing of the *Regia*." See introduction to *YPW*, vol. 4, part 1, 102.

7. Even when using quotation marks, Lamartine had a maddening habit of condensing his material or even paraphrasing it. In this case his remarks come, more or less, from two sentences in *Defensio Secunda*. See *YPW*, vol. 4, part 1, 550, 555–56.

8. *Vies* 3:14–15. Lamartine has summarized, paraphrased and quoted *YPW* 7:422–28.

9. David Masson, *The Life of John Milton* (New York: Peter Smith, 1946), 5:674.

10. This story, as dubious as some of the others concerning Milton, is evoked in J. Milton French, ed., *The Life Records of John Milton* (New Brunswick: Rutgers University Press, 1956), 4:317. Lamartine could have seen a colorful version of it in *Select Reviews and Spirit of the Foreign Magazines* (1809), 2:69.

11. *Vies* 3:16–17. Milton's having been made such an offer rests upon doubtful authority. Lamartine alleges that the poet's "seconde femme le sollicitait à cette bassesse." By the time this could have happened, needless to point out, Katherine Woodcock had been dead for several years and the Restoration had not taken place. There is no evidence that Milton's third wife ever urged her husband to write for the new king, although she is said to have remarked that he had been approached about doing so.

12. In 1855 Lamartine would publish *Histoire de la Russie*.

13. *Vies* 3:35. See Marcia R. Pointon, *Milton and English Art* (Toronto: University of Toronto Press, 1970), 252. The author thinks the scene could be St. Giles rather than Hampstead Heath. Aside from the fact that he extolled nature and would have liked to visualize the poet in a natural setting, Lamartine remembered

that "le dernier ami qui le visita avant sa fin raconte qu'il habitait une petite maison retirée et silencieuse... près des prairies qui se confondent avec la ville." *Vies* 3:31. A little before this, Lamartine had poetically imagined Milton walking there "dans la saison du soleil et des fleurs." "Quand il se fiait au bras de sa femme ou d'une de ses filles, il marchait droit et ferme dans les sentiers des collines voisines de Londres, écoutant avec délices tous les bruits de la campagne, et surtout le chant des oiseaux." *Vies* 3:29–30. This poetic image of a Milton abandoning himself to nature is in keeping, of course, with Lamartine's assertion that various paintings used to exist showing him in precisely such a décor.

14. *Vies* 3:7. Characteristically, Lamartine is a bit confused. He thinks Milton made his prediction in "une lettre confidentielle" in the early years following his return from abroad. Although he uses quotation marks, Lamartine is actually paraphrasing a passage in *The Reason of Church Government*. See *YPW* 1:811–12.

15. *Œuvres complètes* 6:17.

16. Eric Partridge, *The French Romantics' Knowledge of English Literature* (Paris: Champion, 1924), 160.

17. "Je lave mes mains et mon front dans ses eaux; je répète les vers de Milton, pour invoquer, à mon tour, ses inspirations." *Œuvres complètes* 6:458. The allusion is to *PL* 1.11.

18. Once, confronted with two rival anecdotes, Lamartine decided not to choose between them. Speaking of *Paradise Lost*, "Selon les uns, le poème resta dix ans enseveli dans la boutique de l'imprimeur sans être ni mentionné ni lu. Selon les autres, il obtint une renommée circonscrite, mais rapide, et fit luire un crépuscule de gloire sur les dernières années du poète." *Vies* 3:22. Lamartine did not investigate and remained unaware that, before the ten years mentioned in one of the anecdotes had expired, Milton had prepared and published a second edition.

19. "Milton est le moins original des trois grands poètes chrétiens, car il imite d'abord Homère, puis Virgile, puis Dante et le Tasse. Mais son vrai modèle est Dante...." "Quant à sa poésie..., elle est souvent imitée, mais le plagiat de Milton est digne de l'antiquité qu'il copie." *Vies* 3:4, 21, 34.

Notes to Chapter 7/Pongerville

1. J. B. Sanson de Pongerville, "Sur Milton, son époque et ses ouvrages," *Paradis perdu* (Paris: Charpentier, 1843), 1, 3–4. Hereafter references to this work are given parenthetically in the text as "Sur Milton," with page numbers. See also "Milton (John)," *Nouvelle Biographie générale* (Paris: Firmin Didot Frères, 1861),

35:570–71. References to this work are given hereafter parenthetically in the text as *Nouv. Biog.*, with page numbers.

2. Edme Rathéry, "Des relations sociales et intellectuelles entre la France et l'Angleterre depuis la conquête des Normands jusqu'à la Révolution Française," *Revue Contemporaine* (1855), 22:78.

3. Anne D'Urfé's *Hymne des anges* is not mentioned or discussed in Watson Kirkconnell, *The Celestial Cycle* (Toronto: University of Toronto Press, 1952), although the work contains translations of the major *Paradise Lost* analogues. While it considers a number of Milton's sources, Grant McColley's *Paradise Lost* (Chicago: Packard, 1940) does not mention it either, nor does Stella Revard, *The War in Heaven* (Ithaca: Cornell University Press, 1980). *The Milton Encyclopedia* is silent on the matter, and so is Jackson Boswell's *Milton's Library* (New York: Garland, 1975). William Riley Parker, *Milton* (Oxford: Clarendon Press, 1968), does not include the *Hymne des anges* as one of the books Milton sent home from the Continent.

4. Three volumes of Honoré D'Urfé's *L'Astrée* came out in 1607, 1610 and 1619. A posthumous fourth volume appeared in 1627, as did a fifth one generally attributed to D'Urfé's secretary, Balthazar Baro.

5. Yves Le Hir ed., *Œuvres morales et spirituelles inédites* by Anne D'Urfé (Geneva: Droz, 1977), 13.

6. The subtitle Pongerville gives does not appear in the printed text. The *Livres des hymnes* contains five hymns, all published together and each constituting one "volume" or "book" of the whole work. The title page, *Le Premier Livre des hymnes de messire Anne D'Urfé* (Lyon: Pierre Rigaud, 1608), is misleading in that it suggests that there were volumes to come other than those in this one book. Though discarding the ampersand, I have generally kept D'Urfé's spelling, capitalization and punctuation but have corrected one or two printing errors.

7. Du Croset, one of those who wrote laudatory poems preceding the *Hymne des anges*, hoped that the Pope would name D'Urfé to an archbishopric. Du Croset's poem suggests that the matter was discussed. See "Stances sur l'*Hymne des anges*," *Hymne*, 84. For whatever reason, the archbishopric was never conferred.

8. The closest Mr. Steadman comes to this is not a French adjective but a Latin verb. In quoting from Richard Rolle de Hampole's *The Pricke of Conscience (Stimulus Conscientiæ)*, he includes the lines:

Palpabunt tenebras in meridie
sicut in media nocte.

See *Milton's Biblical and Classical Imagery* (Pittsburgh: Duquesne University Press, 1984), 126.

9. "Sur Milton," 5-7, 9; Nouv. Biog., 571-73. Throughout this discussion of Milton's polemical works, the critic has blundered more than once. In the presentation above, his references, at least, have been straightened out.
10. See William B. Hunter, Jr., "Lucretius, Titus," A Milton Encyclopedia (Lewisburg: Bucknell University Press, 1979), 5:38-39. See also the notes to Merritt Y. Hughes ed., John Milton. Complete Poems and Major Prose (New York: The Odyssey Press, 1959), passim.

Notes to Chapter 8/Barbey d'Aurevilly

1. Emile Zola, "La Critique contemporaine," Documents littéraires (Paris: Charpentier, 1894), 353. Originally this was an article published in a Russian periodical in February 1877.
2. In an article on Lamartine, Barbey noted that the naturalists thought of their movement as a "républicanisme littéraire." Jules Barbey d'Aurevilly, "Lamartine," Les Poètes (Paris: Alphonse Lemerre, 1889), 150. Calling the movement a "républicanisme" shows the extent to which Barbey, a monarchist, scorned it.
3. Jules Barbey d'Aurevilly, Correspondance générale (Paris: Les Belles Lettres, 1985), 5:236.
4. Jules Barbey d'Aurevilly, Gœthe et Diderot (Paris: Alphonse Lemerre, 1913), 63, 46-47.
5. Barbey d'Aurevilly, "Milton," Les Poètes (Paris: Alphonse Lemerre, 1889), 203. Hereafter referred to, parenthetically in the text, as "Milton," with page numbers.
6. Jules Barbey d'Aurevilly, Polémiques d'hier (Paris: Savine, 1889), 91.
7. Here Barbey is playing with a possible meaning of prose. In the critic's context, it means "the prosaic." Once, in connection with Milton, Taine would use the word in the same manner.
8. Jules Barbey d'Aurevilly, Littérature étrangère (Paris: Alphonse Lemerre, 1891), 18. See also "Milton," 209.
9. Article reprinted in Littérature étrangère. See 394.
10. Jules Barbey d'Aurevilly, Théâtre contemporain, (Paris: Stock, 1908-1909), 2:222-23. The statement dates from 1869.
11. Jules Barbey d'Aurevilly, Les Critiques ou les juges jugés (Paris: Frinzine, 1885), 345-46. Barbey's prediction that the Histoire des Girondins would sink into oblivion turned out to be incorrect. The work continues to be highly esteemed. As for Milton's prose, Barbey was so uninterested in it that he made a serious mistake evoking it here. What he said was that Lamartine's reputation owed nothing to his prose writing, "pas plus que le livre de La Monarchie du Dante et Le Mare Clausum de Milton n'ont fait

celles du poète de *La Divine Comédie* et de l'auteur du *Paradis perdu*. L'épée du Gibelin et la plume du secrétaire de Cromwell pèsent assez peu, maintenant...." Needless to say, Milton never wrote a *Mare Clausum*. There was such a pamphlet, however, and it was by an English Milton contemporary. Signed "E. S.," it is the work of Elkanah Settle, and it appeared in London on 23 May 1666. The publisher's name presumably accounts for Barbey's slip. The publisher was a certain J. *Million*. Forgotten today, Settle's *Empress of Morocco*, performed at court, briefly set its author up as a rival to Dryden.

12. Jules Barbey d'Aurevilly, *Les Philosophes et les écrivains religieux* (Paris: Quantin, 1887), 271.

13. Jules Barbey d'Aurevilly, *Voyageurs et romanciers* (Paris: Alphonse Lemerre, 1908), 168.

14. Léon Bloy, *Œuvres* (Paris: Mercure de France, 1975), 15:92. See also 15:41, 70; 2:180; 6:334.

Notes to Chapter 9/Vinet

1. Philippe Godet, *Histoire littéraire de la Suisse française* (Neufchatel and Paris: Delachaux et Niestlé and Fischbacher, 1890), 479-99.

2. Alexandre Vinet, *Etudes sur la littérature française au XIXe siècle* (Lausanne and Paris: Georges Bridel and Fischbacher, 1908), 1:439. Hereafter referred to parenthetically in the text as Vinet, with appropriate page numbers.

3. Alphonse de Lamartine, "La Poésie sacrée," *Méditations* (Paris: Garnier Frères, 1968), 117. There is no reason to believe that the poem owes much, if anything, to *Paradise Lost*, though a relationship is, of course, possible. Actually the French romantics were more interested in the Middle Ages than they were in biblical antiquity. It is curious, incidentally, that Vinet should consider Lamartine one of literature's "jeunes gens." Born in 1790, Lamartine was 46 at this time, seven years older than the critic.

Notes to Chapter 10/Mézières

1. Alfred Mézières, "La Jeunesse de Milton," *Revue Nationale et Étrangère* (1861), 2:346-73, 509-37. Hereafter referred to parenthetically in the text as Mézières, with appropriate page numbers.

2. Mézières, 511-12. The lines are not quoted in the article. Mézières attributes the play to Fletcher, but the authorship is disputed.

3. Alfred Mézières, *Contemporains et successeurs de Shakespeare* (Paris: Charpentier, 1864), 203–04, 207.
4. Alfred Mézières, *Hors de France* (Paris: Hachette, 1883), 146, 157.
5. Alfred Mézières, *Cours de littérature étrangère. Discours d'ouverture* (Paris: Dupont, 1864), 9.

Notes to Chapter 11/Taine

1. An excellent modern study is Sholom J. Kahn, *Science and Aesthetic Judgment. A Study in Taine's Critical Method* (New York: Columbia University Press, 1953), reissued by the Greenwood Press in 1970. Colin Evans, *Taine, essai de biographie intérieure* (Paris: Nizet, 1975) argues that Taine's method was not rigid and that it even had its inconsistencies. Jean Thomas Nordmann's thesis, *Taine et la critique scientifique*, stresses the unity of the critic's thought (University of Paris IV, 1989).
2. Revising the article for inclusion in the *Histoire de la littérature anglaise* he considered a major undertaking, although the emendations, however significant, were not that spectacular. On 22 February 1863, in a letter to his friend Edouard de Suckau but without mentioning that it was a question of revising something he had already written, he noted that he still had "un grand bout d'article à faire sur Milton." Hippolyte Taine, *Correspondance* (Paris: Hachette, 1908), 2:268. This work is hereafter referred to parentheticallly in the text as *Corr.*, with appropriate volume and page numbers.
3. "Milton," *Histoire de la littérature anglaise* (Paris: Hachette, 1863), 2:331. This work is hereafter referred to parenthetically in the text as *Histoire*, with appropriate page numbers. I have chosen to quote Taine's Milton chapter in French, as it was written, because that is how the other critics treated in the present study are quoted. In any case, the Van Laun translation, inaccurate to start with, is in the incredibly stilted manner so dear to translators of the middle Victorian era and bears little resemblance to the swift, vigorous style that characterizes Taine.
4. In context, "the prosaic." Taine is playing on words, contrasting the dour Puritan era with the magnificent poetic age that preceded it.
5. *Histoire*, 328–29. Taine had been more detailed and, except for omitting "passion" as one of the poet's main characteristics, had probably expressed the idea better in his article "Milton, son génie et ses œuvres." There, after mentioning "le délire et les contrariétés des passions," the critic went on to state that "la science immense et la logique grandiose, voilà son fond. L'antiquité sacrée et profane, les langues, l'histoire et les littératures modernes,

les sciences nouvelles, l'horrible fardeau de la législation et de la théologie, il a tout porté sans fléchir. Sous ce poids, il s'est trouvé plus fort. Les faits accumulés par l'érudition étaient groupés en lui par la logique. Raisonneur infatigable, il a construit des édifices de démonstrations dont les rudes assises et les solides attaches témoignent d'une énergie qui n'est plus. Sur cette base s'éleva sa poésie. Apercevant des choses mieux ordonnées et plus nombreuses que les autres hommes, il apercevait des choses plus grandes. Tant d'idées et d'images régulièrment disposées formaient un horizon immense qu'il embrassait d'un coup d'œil. Cette vue magnifique l'exaltait; il éprouvait la sensation du sublime; son âme débordait, et l'ample fleuve de la poésie lyrique coulait hors de lui, impétueux, uni, splendide comme une nappe d'or." *Revue des Deux Mondes* (1857), 9:818–19. (References to this work are hereafter given parenthetically in the text as *RDM*, with appropriate page numbers.) The sentence "La science immense et la logique grandiose, voilà son fond," was to antagonize Edmond Scherer. See Edmond Scherer, "M. Taine ou la critique positiviste," *Mélanges de critique religieuse* (Paris: Cherbuliez, 1860), 464. An addendum was to be tacked on later, but Scherer's basic article had appeared in 1858, a year after Taine's statement.

6. To Taine, Milton's quixotic idealism was nowhere better demonstrated than in *Of Education*, a treatise in which the author proposed an exhaustive and impossible curriculum that, in a short while, was supposed to produce a virtuous, learned elite. Taine reminded his readers that Milton had been a schoolmaster and had thus had to contend with classroom practicalities. "Pour garder de pareilles illusions après de pareilles expériences, il fallait être insensible à l'expérience et prédestiné aux illusions." *Histoire*, 346.

7. Elsewhere in this chapter Taine was to write, in connection with Milton's polemics and the era that gave rise to them, that "la critique n'est point née; l'autorité pèse encore par toute la moitié de son poids sur les esprits les mieux affranchis et les plus téméraires." *Histoire*, 356. This included Milton, who thus resembled all his learned but pedantic contemporaries. Milton's "scholastique pesante" was to be mentioned again in Taine's discussion of *Eikonoklastes*. *Histoire*, 361.

8. *Histoire*, 355. Later on (*Histoire*, 378 n. 1) Taine declares that "Quand il est simplement comique, il arrive comme Swift et Hogarth à la bizarrerie rude et drôlatique: 'A bishop's foot that hath all his toes maugre the gout, and a linen sock over it, is the aptest emblem of the prelat himself. Who, being a pluralist, may under one surplice, which is also linen, hide four benefices, besides the metropolitan toe....'" An *Apology against a Pamphlet* in *YPW* 1:894. Taine makes one or two slight mistakes in quoting the passage.

9. *Of Reformation.*

10. In *Of Reformation* Taine cites the passages beginning "The table of communion, now become a table of separation...," *YPW* 1:547–48; "They... shall be thrown down eternally into the darkest and deepest gulf of hell...," *YPW* 1:616–17; "When I recall to mind at last, after so many dark ages...," *YPW* 1:524, and "Thou therefore that sits't in light and glory unapproachable...," *YPW* 1:613–14. From *Animadversions* is singled out "O thou the ever-begotten light...," *YPW* 1:705–07. These passages are in *Histoire*, 378–82. Taine's French renderings are very moving.

11. *Histoire*, 383. *Remarques sur l'opposant* is Taine's French title for *Animadversions upon the Remonstrant's Defence.* Here *Paradis* refers to *Paradise Lost.*

12. Milton wrote "avec l'aide des livres, apercevant les objets autant à travers les écrits précédents qu'en eux-mêmes, ajoutant à ses images les images des autres, reprenant et refondant leurs inventions comme un artiste qui resserre et multiplie les bosselures et les orfèvreries entrelacées déjà sur un diadème par la main de vingt ciseleurs. Il se formait ainsi un style composite et éclatant, moins naturel que celui de ses précurseurs, moins propre aux effusions, moins voisin de la vive sensation primesautière, mais plus solide, plus régulier, plus capable de concentrer en une large nappe de clarté tous leurs scintillements et toutes leurs lueurs." *Histoire*, 384–85.

13. *Histoire*, 390–94; *RDM*, 839. Unfortunately, the idea is not developed.

14. Highly attractive quality.

15. When Eve, in a "compliment philosophique," tells Adam that feminine beauty is eclipsed by the male's virile grace and wisdom, Taine becomes derisive. How Milton must have wished that one of his own three wives, like a schoolgirl reciting a lesson, had declaimed "cette solide maxime!" *Histoire*, 407.

16.

.... Fair Consort, th' hour
Of night, and all things now retir'd to rest
Mind us of like repose....................,

and so on. Taine cites *PL* 4.610–22.

17. For Taine, this achievement alone commanded enormous respect, since he looked upon allegory as the most artificial of literary productions. Using it successfully he would have considered a true accomplishment. Taine's remark about its being artificial occurs in connection with *Pilgrim's Progress*. "L'allégorie, le plus artificiel des genres, est naturelle à Bunyan." *Histoire*, 313.

18. *Notes sur l'Angleterre* (Paris: Hachette, 1885), 381. The work originally appeared in 1872.

Notes to pp. 255–70   371

19. See Roger Asselineau, "Un Inédit de Walt Whitman, 'Taine's *History of English Literature*'," *Etudes Anglaises* (1957), 10:134.
20. Edmond de Guerle, *Milton, sa vie et ses œuvres* (Paris: Michel Lévy, 1868), 93.
21. René Wellek, "Hipppolyte Taine's Literary Theory and Criticism," *Criticism* (l959), 1:135. See A *History of Modern Criticism* (New Haven: Yale University Press, 1966), 4:54.
22. "Taine est de ceux qui estiment qu'il faut dépasser son but pour l'atteindre." Enzo Caramaschi, "Taine esthéticien," *Critiques scientistes et critiques impressionnistes* (Pisa: Libreria Goliardica, 1963), 4.
23. Ferdinand Brunetière, "Une Nouvelle Histoire de la littérature anglaise," *Revue des Deux Mondes* (1883), 50:693.

Notes to Chapter 12/de Guerle

1. Edmond Gabriel Héguin de Guerle, *Milton, sa vie et ses œuvres* (Paris: Michel Lévy, 1868). This work is hereafter referred to parenthetically in the text as de Guerle, with appropriate page numbers.
2. "The Romans had a time once every year.... Who could be angry therefore but those who are guilty, with these freespoken and plaine harted men that are the eyes of their country and the prospective glasses of their prince." YPW 1:669–70. "In this age, Britain's God hath reform'd his church.... The voice of thy bride calls thee, and all creatures sigh to be renew'd." YPW 1:704–07.
3. YPW 1:900 n. 2. See *Aeneid* 4.174–97.
4. In French translation and without identifying it, de Guerle cites a passage from *The Doctrine and Discipline of Divorce* 1.6. "That love, if he be not twinborn, yet hath a brother wondrous like him.... He kindles and repairs the almost faded ammunition of his deity by the reflection of a coequal and homogeneal fire." YPW 2:254–255; de Guerle, 169–70. Concerning this passage de Guerle compared Milton to Plato.
5. De Guerle, 222, 230–31. Blaise Pascal, *Œuvres* (Paris: Hachette, 1914), 5:386–87. This *Provinciale* dates from 1656. In defending truth, Pascal agreed with Milton, but there is nothing to suggest that he borrowed from him. As for Milton, it is known that he owned the *Lettres provinciales*, but he could not have used it in writing *Areopagitica* since the French work did not appear until more than a decade later.
6. Important recent scholarship on Milton's theology includes William Empson, *Milton's God* (London: Chatto and Windus, 1965); Georgia B. Christopher, *Milton and the Science of the Saints* (Princeton: Princeton University Press, 1982); Dennis R. Danielson, *Milton's Good God* (New York: Cambridge University Press, 1982);

James H. Sims and Leland Ryken eds., *Milton and Scriptural Tradition* (Columbia: University of Missouri Press, 1984); and Philip J. Gallagher, *Milton, the Bible, and Misogyny* (Columbia: University of Missouri Press, 1990).

7. Professor Kelley's conclusions were made public in *This Great Argument* (Princeton: Princeton University Press, 1941). In 1973 they were restated and developed in Mr. Kelley's edition of *De Doctrina Christiana* in *YPW*, vol. 6.

8. De Guerle liked this passage and discussed it elsewhere in his treatment of *Paradise Lost* per se.

9. Théodore Karcher, "Les Sectes religieuses de l'Angleterre," *Revue Nationale et Etrangère* (1861), 2:499. Karcher did not elaborate.

10. De Guerle reproduces an error that goes back to Anthony Wood's *Athenæ Oxonienses*. Samuel Simmons published the *Accedence Commenc't Grammar* in 1669. Masson's volume dealing with this period in Milton's life had not come out when de Guerle was writing, which may explain the mistake.

11. De Guerle quotes, in French, *PL* 9.13–47.

Notes to Chapter 13/Scherer

1. Henry James, "Honoré de Balzac," *French Poets and Novelists* (London: MacMillan and Company, 1919), 67.

2. Octave Gréard, *Edmond Scherer* (Paris: Hachette, 1891), 67, 69. Scherer's doctoral thesis was called *La Dogmatique de l'église réformée*. The degree was conferred 10 August 1843. Gréard, 45, 65.

3. Founded in 1861, *Le Temps* remained one of Paris's best newspapers until the end of the century and beyond. Scherer was its literary critic until 1886 or 1887, when he was succeeded by Anatole France.

4. He studied the matter in his article "Du Péché." See Gréard, 119. With an addendum, the article is reproduced in *Mélanges de critique religieuse* (Paris: Cherbuliez, 1860), 65–107. In his article the author defined sin as "la résistance à l'obligation contenue dans le sentiment du bien" but added that "le péché ne consiste pas seulement à omettre le bien, mais aussi à commettre le mal" (67). Dante is cited in the article but not Milton.

5. Scherer wrote for several English and American periodicals, including the *New York World*, the *Manchester Guardian*, the *Daily News*, *Lippincott's Magazine*, the *Fortnightly Review*.

6. Scherer reviewed Taine's book. See Edmond Scherer, "Histoire de la littérature anglaise par M. Taine," *Etudes critiques de littérature* (Paris: Calmann Lévy, 1876), 111–35.

7. Edmund Scherer, "Milton et le *Paradis perdu*," *Etudes*

critiques de littérature, 154. Hereafter parenthetically referred to in the text as "Milton," with page numbers.

8. In an article dating from 1858, Scherer took exception with Taine and, in doing so, claimed that art and science are not really incompatible. On the basis of the R*evue des Deux Mondes* article, he accused Taine of having tried to reduce Milton to one or two characteristics. "'La science immense et la logique grandiose, voilà le fond du poète'. Fondé sur la logique et sur la science, Milton eut la force. Mais la force, c'est la fermeté, la fierté, la sérénité; Milton eut toutes ces qualités et fut un héros. Cependant, la force de conviction qui soutient l'homme contre les séductions peut l'aveugler sur les faits, et dans un héros on trouve souvent un théoricien: Milton fut donc théoricien. Etant donc théoricien, il fut généreux; en effet, ce qui détruit le dévouement, c'est l'expérience, car l'expérience sait ce que vaut la vertu, tandis que le théoricien, ne tenant pas compte de l'expérience, croit à la vertu et peut rester généreux." Presumably Scherer has in mind Milton's republican theories. A virtuous man himself, Milton did not allow for other republicans' being less virtuous. Experience should have taught him better. Edmond Scherer, "M. Taine ou la critique positiviste," *Mélanges de critique religieuse* (Paris: Cherbuliez, 1860), 464, 483. This is a reprint of the earlier article, with an addendum.

9. See Charles Augustin Sainte-Beuve, "Qu'est-ce qu'un classique?" *Causeries du lundi*, (Paris: Garnier Frères, 1858), 3:38–55.

10. "Milton," 155–59. "Chez les jacobins et les puritains, même conception abstraite des choses, même tyrannie de l'idée, même besoin de réaliser les visions entrevues. De part et d'autre, idéalisme et radicalisme, ces tendances jumelles. De part et d'autre, foi égale à l'absolu, cette source de tout fanatisme. De part et d'autre, invocation de la liberté; mais de part et d'autre aussi la liberté comme moyen plutôt que comme but, et la vérité mise au-dessus de la liberté." "Milton," 159.

11. Scherer stressed this duality. "S'il y avait du théologien dans ce poète, il y avait aussi du poète dans ce théologien; les deux inspirations s'unissaient en lui le plus étroitement et le plus naturellement du monde." On the other hand, in the light of what comes later in the essay, one can assume that, to the critic, the mix did not produce ideal results. When Milton, "dans une grande épopée, satisfera à la fois aux deux passions de sa vie, l'art et la foi," he achieved a less than perfect blending of the two, Scherer writes. "Milton," 161.

12. Scherer is thinking of the famous remark Voltaire attributed to Nicolas de Malézieux, that the French "n'ont pas la tête épique." Scherer, applying the remark to Milton, suggests that the English poet may not have had an epic mentality either.

13. Although he found it decidedly wanting, Scherer was intrigued by Milton's cosmology. Summarizing and commenting upon it, he declared that "Milton n'a pas même su où placer son drame. Il est obligé de se faire un système du monde tout exprès et auquel il ne croit lui-même qu'à demi. La science de son temps le gêne.... Il faut... modifier la cosmologie sacrée, l'accommoder aux lumières du jour. Rien de plus curieux que de lire le *Paradis perdu* à ce point de vue et d'y noter les modifications imposées par la science à la tradition. Milton regarde l'espace infini comme divisé en deux régions: celle de la lumière ou de la création et celle de la nuit ou du chaos. Sur la terre, dans la contrée d'Eden, le Paradis Terrestre, qu'une échelle met en communication avec la demeure du Très-Haut. Le chaos environne tout ce monde créé; mais au bord du chaos, dans le demi-jour, est le Limbe de la Vanité, et, au delà du chaos, dans les profondeurs de l'espace incréé, se trouve l'Enfer, avec une porte et avec un pont construit par le Péché et la Mort, au moyen duquel on va de la terre à l'abîme." Scherer looked upon this as a "conception vague, moitié littérale, moitié symbolique," even to Milton ("Milton," 190–91). Scherer could have added that Raphael's unwillingness to go into great detail about it may have sprung from Milton's uneasiness with this shaky cosmology. *PL* 8.66–178.

14. "Milton," 192–93. "Darkness visible" and "imparadis't in one another's arms" appealed to him, as did the lines in which the moon (*PL* 1.784).

Sits arbitress, and nearer to the Earth
Wheels her pale course..............

The sun "on his wide watrie Glass," causing evaporation, evoked admiration (*PL* 11.844) and so did (*PL* 11.713)

The brazen Throat of Warr had ceast to roar.

15. Matthew Arnold, "A French Critic on Milton," *Quarterly Review* (1877), 143:186–204. The article was anonymous but was included two years later in Arnold's *Essays Religious and Mixed*. For a modern edition, see *Complete Prose Works* (Ann Arbor: University of Michigan Press, 1972), 8:165–87. Arnold and Scherer knew and admired each other's work. Arnold's own Milton essay dates from 1888.

Notes to Chapter 14/Stroehlin

1. Gaspard Ernest Stroehlin, *Essai sur le montanisme* (Strasbourg: Silbermann, 1870). Montanus and his disciples preached that Christ's second coming was imminent and urged stringent

asceticism in preparation for the event. The movement's adherents were very rigorous in observing the precept. The movement was still going in the fifth century. Tertullian, whom Milton cites from time to time, went through a Montanist period. See Kurt Aland, "Montanism" and "Montanus," *Encyclopedia of Religion* (New York: MacMillan, 1987), 10:81–83.

2. An energetic German nationalist, Treitschke wrote on literature, politics, history and religion. One of his books was on Martin Luther.

3. *Jahrbuch der Illustrierten Deutschen Monatshefte* (1870), 29:293–314. Carrière also translated Sonnet 16, to Oliver Cromwell. For this information my thanks are due to Professor John T. Shawcross. Carrière included the translation in his *Oliver Cromwell*, published in *Lebensbilder*.

4. The work also appeared in English as *Milton Considered as a Political Writer* and was published in Halle (Ploetz, 1882).

5. Ernest Stroehlin, "Milton," *Encyclopédie des sciences religieuses* (Paris: Sandoz et Fischbacher, 1880), 175. Hereafter, references to this work are given parenthetically in the text as Stroehlin, with appropriate page numbers.

6. Stroehlin uses quotation marks but does not identify his reference. Actually he is paraphrasing *Of Reformation*, YPW 1:554. "I am not of opinion to think the church a vine in this respect, because, as they take it, she cannot subsist without clasping about the elm of worldly strength and felicity, as if the heavenly city could not support itself without the props and buttresses of secular authority."

7. Stroehlin, 171; 2 Corinthians 3.17.

8. Stroehlin, 173. In Greek mythology Triptolemus is credited with having invented agriculture. Stroehlin's reference is to *Defensio Secunda*, YPW, vol. 4, part 1, 555–56. "It seems to me that... I am bringing... home to every nation liberty...; and as is recorded of Triptolemus of old...."

9. "Mon amour filial pour mon pays a fini par me laisser sans patrie...." YPW 8:4.

10. Emmanuel Bénézit, *Dictionnaire des peintres, sculpteurs, dessinateurs, et graveurs* (Paris: Librairie Gründ, 1976), 7:609.

Notes to Chapter 15/Filon

1. Augustin Filon, *Histoire de la littérature anglaise* (Paris: Hachette, 1922), 214. Hereafter references to this work are given parenthetically in the text as Filon, with appropriate page numbers.

2. Ultimately, the Swedish treaty dates from 1656. Filon's

allusion is to Whitelocke's *Memorials of the English Affairs* (London: Ponder, 1682), 633. Whitelocke's *Journal of the Swedish Embassy* suggests that the ambassador actually may have known Milton rather well.

3. Augustin Filon, "Olivier Cromwell et le gouvernement des 'saints,'" *Revue des Deux Mondes* (1902), 12:423, 431. (References to this article are hereafter given parenthetically in the text as *RDM*, with appropriate page numbers.) Presumably, it slipped Filon's mind that Hobbes lived in France during the Civil Wars.

4. Thomas B. Macaulay, *Critical and Historical Essays* (Boston and New York: Houghton, Mifflin and Company, 1900), 1:86–91. Macaulay's position may owe something to Victor Hugo's pronouncement regarding the three periods in humankind's literary development, periods outlined in the famous introduction to the writer's play *Cromwell*. The dramatist claimed that primitive man expressed his wonder at the universe with the ode. Later on, his horizons expanding, he created the epic. In modern times, advancing still more, he has created what the theorist called the *drame*. Victor Hugo, "Préface," *Cromwell* in *Théâtre* (Paris: Gallimard, 1985), 1:411–23.

5. Filon, 263. François René de Chateaubriand, *Essai sur la littérature anglaise* in *Œuvres complètes* (Paris: Garnier Frères, 1859–61), 11:698.

6. Though not published until January 1641, Corneille's play dates from 1640. Filon refers to the passage but does not quote it.

Note to Chapter 16/A Backward Glance

1. Delacroix's ceiling fresco in the Chapelle des Saints Anges at the Church of St-Sulpice shows St. Michael's triumph over Satan. Delacroix's paintings completed, the chapel was reopened to the public on 21 August 1861. Baudelaire was one of the admiring spectators.

Select Bibliography

Barbey d'Aurevilly, Jules.
1889 *Les Poètes*. Paris: Alphonse Lemerre.

Chasles, Philarète.
1835 "Milton, ses œuvres, sa vie et ses opinions," *Revue Britannique* 16:36–63.
1836 "*Essai sur la littérature anglaise*," *Journal des Débats*, 14 July.
1836 "Le *Paradis perdu* de Milton," *Journal des Débats*, 14 September.
1836 "Le *Paradis perdu*," *Journal des Débats*, 28 September.
1836 "*Essai sur la littérature anglaise*," *Journal des Débats*, 21 October.
1837 "Milton (Jean)," *Dictionnaire de la conversation et de la lecture* 38: 173–80.
Repr. with changes in a new edition of the *Dictionnaire* 13 (1866).
1839 "*Œuvres choisies* de Milton," *Journal des Débats*, 28 August.

Chateaubriand, François René de.
1859–61 *Œuvres complètes*. Paris: Garnier Frères, vols. 7, 10, 11.
1950 *Mémoires d'outre-tombe*. Paris: Flammarion, 4 vols.

Corns, Thomas N.
1982 *The Development of Milton's Prose Style*. Oxford: Clarendon Press.

1990   Milton's Language. Cambridge: Basil Blackwell.

Couffignal, Robert.
1967   "Le Paradis perdu de Victor Hugo à Pierre Jean Jouve," Jacques Blondel, ed., Le Paradis perdu 1667–1967. Paris: Minard, 404–14.

Danielson, Dennis R.
1982   Milton's Good God. New York: Cambridge University Press.

Empson, William.
1965   Milton's God. London: Chatto and Windus.

Filon, Augustin.
1922   Histoire de la littérature anglaise. Paris: Hachette.

Fletcher, Harris F.
1931   Contributions to a Milton Bibliography 1800–1930. Urbana: University of Illinois Press.

French, J. Milton.
1949–58   The Life Records of John Milton. New Brunswick: Rutgers University Press, 5 vols.

Gallagher, Philip J.
1990   Milton, the Bible, and Misogyny. Columbia: University of Missouri Press.

Geffroy, Auguste.
1848   Etude sur les pamphlets politiques et religieux de Milton. Paris: Dezobry, Magdeleine, et Cie.

Geisst, Charles R.
1984   The Political Thought of John Milton. London: MacMillan.

Gillet, Jean.
1975   Le Paradis perdu dans la littérature française de Voltaire à Chateaubriand. Paris: Klincksieck.

Grossman, Marshall.
1987   "Authors to Themselves." Milton and the Revelation of History. Cambridge: Cambridge University Press.

De Guerle, Edmond Héguin.
1868   Milton, sa vie et ses œuvres. Paris: Michel Lévy.

Hughes, Merritt Y.
1965   Ten Perspectives on Milton. New Haven: Yale University Press.

Hughes, Merritt Y., et al., eds.

1970–75   *A Variorum Commentary on the Poems of John Milton.* New York: Columbia University Press, 4 vols. to date.

Kirkconnell, Watson.
1952   *The Celestial Cycle.* Toronto: University of Toronto Press.

Labriola, Albert C.
1981   "'Thy Humiliation Shall Exalt'. The Christology of *Paradise Lost*," *Milton Studies* 15:29–42.

Lamartine, Alphonse de.
1860–63   *Œuvres complètes.* Paris: Chez l'Auteur, vols. 35 and 36.

Lutaud, Olivier
1974   "Le 'Savant Instituteur'" et les 'Labour'd Studies of the French'" *Etudes Anglaises* 27:404–14.

Masson, David.
1946   *The Life of John Milton.* London: Macmillan and Company, 1881–94. Repr. New York: Peter Smith, 7 vols.

McColley, Diane Kelsey.
1983   *Milton's Eve.* Urbana: University of Illinois Press.

Mézières, Alfred.
1861   "La Jeunesse de Milton," *Revue Nationale et Etrangère* 2:346–73, 509–37.

Miller, Dorothy D.
1962   "Eve," *Journal of English and German Philology* 61:542–47.

Miller, Milton.
1951   "*Paradise Lost:* the Double Standard," *University of Toronto Quarterly* 20:183–99.

Milton, John.
1957   *Complete Poems and Minor Prose.* Ed. Merritt Y. Hughes. New York: Odyssey Press.

1953–82   *Complete Prose Works.* Ed. Merritt Y. Hughes. New Haven: Yale University Press, 8 vols.

Parker, William Riley.
1968   *Milton. A Biography.* Oxford: Clarendon Press.

Partridge, Eric.
1924   *The French Romantics' Knowledge of English Literature.* Paris: Champion.

Patrides, C. A.
1987   An Annotated Critical Bibliography of John Milton. Brighton: Harvester Press Ltd.

Planche, Gustave.
1855   Etudes littéraires. Paris: Lévy.

Pongerville, J. B. Sanson de.
1843   "Sur Milton, son époque et ses ouvrages," *Paradis perdu*. Paris: Charpentier.
1861   "Milton (John)," *Nouvelle Biographie générale* 35:570–78. Paris: Firmin Didot Frères.

Prince, F.T.
1954   *The Italian Element in Milton's Verse*. Oxford: Clarendon Press.

Revard, Stella P.
1980   *The War in Heaven.* Paradise Lost *and the Tradition of Satan's Rebellion*. Ithaca: Cornell University Press.

Samuel, Irene.
1965   *Plato and Milton*. Ithaca: Cornell University Press.

Scherer, Edmond.
1876   *Etudes critiques de littérature*. Paris: Calmann Lévy.

Shawcross, John T.
1972   *Milton 1732–1801. The Critical Heritage*. London: Routledge and Kegan Paul.

Sims, James H., and Leland Ryken, eds.
1984   *Milton and Scriptural Tradition*. Columbia: University of Missouri Press.

Steadman, John M.
1984   *Milton's Biblical and Classical Imagery*. Pittsburgh: Duquesne University Press.

Stevens, David H.
1930   *A Reference Guide to Milton from 1800 to the Present Day*. Chicago: University of Chicago Press.

Taine, Hippolyte.
1863–64   *Histoire de la littérature anglaise*. Paris: Hachette, vol. 2.
1857   "Milton, son génie et ses œuvres," *Revue des Deux Mondes* 9:818–54.

Véricour, Louis Raymond de.
1838   *Milton et la poésie épique*. Paris: Delaunay.

Villemain, Abel François.
1823   *Discours et mélanges littéraires.* Paris: Ladvocat.
1819   *Histoire de Cromwell.* Paris: Maradan, 2 vols.
Walker, Julia M., ed.
1988   *Milton and the Idea of Woman.* Urbana: University of Illinois Press.
Wellek, René.
1955–86   *A History of Modern Criticism.* New Haven: Yale University Press, vols. 2, 3 and 4.

Index

Accedence Commenc't Grammar, 128
"Ad Patrem," 9, 51
Adam, 341, 344–45, 370: Chasles on, 82, 87–88; Chateaubriand on, 53, 66, 68, 70–71, 73; de Guerle, 265, 282–83, 296–97, 302; Filon on, 325–26; Lamartine on, 160–63; Taine on, 247–49, 255–56; Véricour on, 105, 106, 107, 108, 114, 115, 118–19; Villemain on, 41–42; Vinet on, 204, 209, 210
Adamo, 10, 24, 29–30, 105, 172, 277
Addison, Joseph, 7, 37, 40, 45, 95, 107, 110, 277, 315, 349
Aeneas, 106, 115, 296–97, 170
Aeneid, 24, 106–11, 301, 341
Ampère, J. J., 351–52
Anchises, 296–97
Andreini, 10, 24, 29–30, 38, 105, 172, 277
Angels, 172–75
Anglican Church, 131–33, 307
Animadversions upon the Remonstrant's Defense: de Guerle on, 261, 288; Stroehlin on, 309; Taine on, 239, 241
Aphrodite, 71
Apology against a Modest Confutation, 309
Apology for Smectymnuus: de Guerle on, 261–63; Geffroy on 126, 146; Mézières on, 230; Scherer on, 291, 295
Arcades, 336: Chateaubriand on, 51; Filon on, 322; Lamartine on, 155; Stroehlin on, 307; Véricour on, 99, 120; Villemain on, 28, 47; Vinet on, 227
Areopagitica, 4, 12, 360: Chasles on, 83, 85; Chateaubriand on, 54; Filon on, 332; Geffroy on, 128–29, 147; Lamartine on, 168; Mézières on, 230, 240–42; Pongerville on, 179; Scherer on, 295; Stroehlin on, 308, 312, 315; Véricour on, 101; Villemain on, 31
Ariel, 229

Ariosto, 105, 108
Aristotle, 349
Arminianism, 274, 311
Arnold, Matthew, 26, 304
Arthur, King, 10, 30
Artis Logicae Plenior Institutio, 36, 65, 142, 349
Art poétique, 5–6, 333
"At a Solemn Music," 244, 335
Athalie, 62, 135
Attendant Spirit, 100, 229, 231, 245

Bacon, Francis, 104, 262, 349
Bailly, M. H., 22
Bandinelli, Bartolommeo, 341
Barberini, Cardinal Antonio, 9, 352
Barberini, Cardinal Francesco, 52, 352
Barbey d'Aurevilly, Jules, 7–8, 333–45: compared to Chasles, 78–79; compared to Mézières, 218; compared to Vinet, 216; critique of Milton, 189–99; notes on, 366–67
Baroni, Leonora, 9–13, 29, 52–53, 150, 352, 318
Baudelaire, Charles, 344
Bayle, Pierre, 3, 269
Belloc, Hilaire, 197
Bentley, Richard, 306
Bible, 105, 108, 124, 217, 281, 286, 301, 331, 340
Biographie universelle, 28
Birch, Marianne, 149
Boadicea, Queen, 102, 162
Bodleian Library, 128
Boileau, 5, 214, 333
Bossuet, Jacques de, 77, 133, 262, 269
Bradshaw, John, 59, 104, 358
A Brief History of Muscovia, 93, 159, 269
Brief Notes upon a Late Sermon, 140
Britannicarum Ecclesiarum, 52
Broadbent, J. B., 70
Bunyan, John, 204, 262, 306

383

384 Index

Calvin, John, 233–34, 268–69, 274, 305
Calvinism, 82, 93, 311–12
Cambridge University, 8, 64, 81, 142, 192, 218, 220, 307
Camoës, 49, 108–12, 115, 165
Carrière, Moriz, 306
Catholicism, 131, 278–79, 310, 315
Cavalier, 103, 130, 313
Censorship, 1–4, 54, 127
Channing, William Ellery, 269, 274–75, 305–06
Chanson de Roland, 109
Characterization, 205–06, 210–12, 248
Character of the Long Parliament, 65
Charles I, 2, 12, 19, 338, 354–55, 362: Chasles on, 85, 93; Chateaubriand on, 49, 54–57, 63; Filon on, 319; Geffroy on, 131–35, 140–42, 146–47; Lamartine on, 152, 156, 158, 162, 166–67, 168; Stroehlin on, 305, 313; Véricour on, 101, 121; Villemain on, 31, 35–36
Charles II, 19, 35–36, 63, 85, 141–42, 158, 167, 331, 354–55
Charles VI, 55
Chasles, Philarète, 7, 333–45: compared to Taine, 237, 333–45; compared to Véricour, 98, 103; compared to Villemain, 47; compared to Vinet, 216; critique of Milton by, 78–96; notes on, 357–59
Chateaubriand, François René de, 4–5, 8, 13, 333–45: compared to Filon, 330; compared to Geffroy, 135; compared to Lamartine, 158, 161; compared to Mézières, 221–22; compared to Scherer, 299; compared to Stroehlin, 316; compared to Taine, 239; compared to Véricour, 98, 101, 110, 117; compared to Villemain, 41; compared to Vinet, 200–01; critique of Milton by, 48–77; notes on, 350–57, 363
Chauvet, Paul, 69, 275
Chénier, André, 259
Christ, 69, 175, 213–14, 246, 276, 287, 330; *see also* Son of God
Cinq-Mars, 15–16
Civil Wars, 81, 94, 168, 180, 187, 198, 253, 302, 314, 334, 338
Colasterion, 264, 311
Coleridge, 277, 283
Comminges, Gaston de, 2
Comus, 3, 23: Barbey d'Aurevilly on, 194; Chasles on, 80, 83;

Chateaubriand on, 51; de Guerle on, 277; Filon on, 321–24; Mézières on, 220, 227–29, 231; Pichot on, 12; Taine on, 239, 243, 245–46, 255; Véricour on, 99–100, 119–20; Villemain on, 28, 47
Considerations Touching the Likeliest Means to Remove Hirelings out of the Church, 64, 138–39, 310, 320
Cooper, James Fenimore, 23
Corinne, 192
Corneille, Pierre, 15–16, 331
Costar, Pierre, 2
Couffignal, Robert, 16
Creation, 10
Cromwell, Oliver: 16–17, 22, 334, 338, 361, 376: Barbey d'Aurevilly on, 193–94; Chasles on, 82; Chateaubriand on, 49, 54, 56, 59–61, 75–77; de Guerle on, 267; Filon on, 320, 330; Lamartine on, 150–51, 145–55, 157, 167–68; Pongerville on, 179–80; Scherer on, 295–96; Stroehlin on, 310; Taine on, 247; Véricour on, 103, 137–38, 147; Villemain on, 32–34
Cromwell, Richard, 60–61, 296

d'Avril, Baron Adolphe, 10
D'Urfé, Anne, 172–77, 188, 365
D'Urfé, Honoré, 172
D'Urfey, Thomas, 178
Dante, 23, 25, 341, 360, 366: Barbey d'Aurevilly on, 195; Chasles on, 90–92, 95; Chateaubriand on, 49, 71–72; de Guerle on, 280–81; Filon on, 328, 341, 360, 366; Lamartine on, 165; Mézières on, 219; Scherer on, 299–300; Véricour on, 97, 112–18; Villemain on, 27
Davenant, Sir William, 17, 36, 50, 85, 141, 181, 222–23
Death (in *Paradise Lost*), 105, 121, 206, 301, 316, 325, 342
De Bonaparte et des Bourbons, 50
Declaration of Indulgence, 142–43
A Declaration of the Lord Protector, 137–38
De Doctrina Christiana: Barbey d'Aurevilly on, 195; Chasles on, 93; Chateaubriand on, 65, 68, 76; de Guerle on, 264, 269–74; Filon on, 311, 316; Geffroy on, 143–44, 148; Lamartine on, 168; Scherer on, 294, 297, 304
Defensio Regia pro Carolo I, 32, 57–58, 135–36, 266, 363

Defensio Secunda, 8, 11–13, 361: Chateaubriand on, 58–59; de Guerle on, 267; Geffroy on, 125, 136–37; Lamartine on, 155; Pongerville on, 179; Scherer on, 291, 295, 361; Véricour on, 102; Villemain on, 32
de Guerle, Edmond Gabriel Héguin, 190, 257–88, 306, 371–72
De Idea Platonica, 9
Delalot, Charles, 4, 25, 201
De la démocratie en Amérique, 39
de Maistre, Joseph, 1
De Monarchia, 195
De Rege et regis institutione, 55
De Rerum Natura, 170, 184
de Sales, François, 193
Descartes, 15–16
Desclozeaux, Ernest, 4, 346
Desmaret, Pierre, 2
Desmarets de St-Sorlin, Jean, 5
de Staël, Germaine, 21, 192, 353
Dickens, Charles, 290, 306
Dictionnaire historique et critique, 3
Dido, 106, 296–97
Discours et mélanges littéraires, 28
Discours sur la servitude volontaire, 268
The Divine Comedy, 26: Chasles on, 92, 96; de Guerle on, 280; Stroehlin on, 302, 315; Véricour on, 108, 116
The Doctrine and Discipline of Divorce, 337, 371: Chateaubriand on, 53–54; de Guerle on, 263–64, 273; Geffroy on, 130–31; Stroehlin on, 311–12; Taine on, 238-39, 241
Dryden, John, 277, 283
Du Bartas, 71, 172
Du Moulin, Pierre, 11, 32, 57, 136, 141, 267

Eden, 71
Eikon Basilike, 32, 56–57, 134, 155, 266, 313
Eikonoklastes, 1, 17, 339, 362: Chasles on, 94; Chateaubriand on, 56; de Guerle on, 266, 277; Filon on, 319; Geffroy on, 134–35, 141; Lamartine on, 155–56, 167; Pongerville on, 180; Stroehlin on, 313; Taine on, 240; Véricour on, 101, 103; Villemain on, 32
"Elegia Septima," 52–53
Eliot, George, 290, 306
Ellwood, Thomas, 11, 286
Encyclopédie des sciences religieuses, 3, 306
England's New Chains Discovered?, 134

Epics, 5–6, 26–27, 107, 111–13, 183–84, 277–79, 295, 341
Epistolarum Familiarum, 269
"An Epitaph on the Marchioness of Winchester," 222, 244
"Epitaphium Damonis," 259–60
Essai sur la littérature anglaise, 50–51, 67, 73, 81, 98, 101, 158, 201
Essai sur le montanisme, 305
Essai sur les révolutions, 50
Essay on Epic Poetry, 3
Essay sur Tite-Live, 241
Esther, 5, 331
Etude sure les pamphlets politiques et religieux de Milton, 146
Euripides, 38, 331
Eve, 341, 344–45, 370: Barbey d'Aurevilly on, 197; Chasles on, 82, 88; Chateaubriand on, 53, 66, 68, 70–72, 73; de Guerle on, 265, 282–83; Filon on, 325–26; Lamartine on, 160–63; Scherer on, 302, 315; Taine on, 247, 248–49, 255–56; Véricour on, 103, 105, 106, 108, 114, 115, 118–19; Villemain on, 41–42; Vinet on, 204, 210
Evidences of Christianity, 274

Faerie Queene, 23, 80
Fairfax, General, 54, 59
Fénelon, 106, 109, 135, 193, 269
Fides Publica, 137, 267
Filon, Augustin, 8, 333–45: critique of Milton by, 317–332; notes on, 375–76
Fletcher, John, 220, 224, 228
Forster, Elizabeth, 269
Free press, 128–29
French Revolution, 4, 27, 56, 81, 90, 152–53, 292, 316, 338, 363

Galileo, 308
Gauden, John, 57, 13, 313
Geffroy, Matthieu Auguste, 316: critique of Milton by, 123–48, notes on, 358, 360–62
Génie du christianisme, 4–5, 48, 50, 66, 117
George III, 312
Gerusalemme liberata, 108, 110–12, 115, 172, 212, 299
Gillet, Jean, 4, 69
Girondin Party, 55
God (as dramatic character), 69, 70, 113, 138, 163, 175–77, 182–83, 202, 207–08, 213–14, 246–47, 278, 281–83, 286, 328, 343

386 Index

Goethe, 23, 190, 219
Gourmont, Rémy de, 48
Grand Remonstrance, 125–26
Griffith, Matthew, 140
Grotius, Hugo, 38, 308
Guarini, Battista, 9, 14, 318

Hall, Joseph, 131, 309
Hallam, Arthur, 222
Handsomeness, 95–96
Hapsburg despotism, 312
Harmonies poétiques et religieuses, 152, 161
Hartlib, Samuel, 312
Hayley, William, 13–14
Heimback, Peter, 65, 314
Henriade, 24, 109, 113, 115, 299
Henrietta Maria, 77, 133, 178, 317, 354
Hesiod, 105
Histoire de Cromwell, 10, 16, 32, 27–28, 34–35, 122
Histoire des Girondins, 153, 195
Histoire de la littèrature, 232, 277, 315, 317, 319–20
Histoire de la Révolution d'Angleterre, 7
History of Britain, 3: Chasles on, 82, 93; Chateaubriand on, 52, 64–65; de Guerle on, 269; Filon on, 332; Geffroy on, 133; Lamartine on, 158, 162; Pongerville on, 172; Stroehlin on, 312; Véricour on, 102, 120; Villemain on, 31, 35–36
Hobson, Thomas, 221, 320
Homer, 25, 325, 341, 342: Chateaubriand on, 49, 58, 71–72, 73, 74; Filon on, 325; Lamartine on, 161, 165; Pongerville on, 183, 188; Scherer on, 302; Véricour on, 105, 108, 111, 113, 116–17; Villemain on, 38; Vinet on, 202, 216
Hors de France, 230
Horton period, 28–29, 99, 307
"How Soon Hath Time," 244
Hugo, Victor, 10, 14, 17–18, 348
Humor, 221, 239
Hymne des anges, 172, 175, 177–78, 188
"Hymn on the Morning of Christ's Nativity," 79–80, 244

Iliad, 24, 341, 360: Chateaubriand on, 74; Filon on, 327; Pongerville on, 182; Scherer on, 301; Véricour on, 105, 107–14
"Il Penseroso," 3, 335: Barbey d'Aurevilly on, 194; Chasles on, 80; Chateaubriand on, 51; de Guerle on, 259, 266; Filon on, 321–22, 324; Mézières on, 223, 225–26; Scherer on, 293; Stroehlin on, 307–08; Taine on, 235, 244–45; Véricour on, 99; Villemain on, 28
Institution chrétienne, 268

James, Henry, 289, 291
Jehovah, 182, 281, 292, 302
Jesus Christ (*see* Christ)
Johnson, Samuel, 29, 277, 306, 331
Jonson, Ben, 222, 228, 307
Journal des Débats, 79
Journal des Savants, 3
The Judgment of Martin Bucer, 264, 311
Jupiter, 113, 117

Kant, Emmanuel, 114
Karcher, Théodore, 274
Keightley, Thomas, 219, 306
Kelley, Maurice, 270
King, Edward, 322
Klopstock, Friedrich, 26, 360: Chateaubriand and, 49; Lamartine and, 165; Scherer and, 299; Stroehlin and, 306; Véricour and, 108, 114, 117–18
Knox, John, 142–43, 309

La Boétie, 268
Lady Alice, 228, 230
"L'Allegro," 3, 335: Chasles on, 80, 99; Chateaubriand on, 51; de Guerle on, 259, 277; Filon on, 321–22, 324; Mézières on, 223; Scherer on, 293; Stroehlin, 307–08; Taine on, 235, 244; Villemain on, 28
Lamartine, Alphonse de, 6, 8, 333–45: compared to Barbey d'Aurevilly, 195, 199; compared to de Guerle, 266; compared to Filon, 321; compared to Mézières, 223; compared to Scherer, 297; compared to Véricour, 121; compared to Vinet, 201–02; critique of Milton by, 149–69; notes on, 362–64, 366, 367
La Mode, 194
La Ramée, Pierre de, 142
La Religion de Milton, 275
La Semaine, 172–73
Latin dictionary, 35, 138
Latin Secretary, 60–61, 84, 136, 141, 155, 269

Index 387

Lauder, William, 38, 104
Le Civilisateur, 150
Le Globe, 4
Le Perroquet de Walter Scott, 8
Les Diaboliques, 189
Les Martyrs, 299
Les Oeuvres et les hommes, 190
Les Poètes, 190
Les Poètes amoureux, 8
Les Quatre Stuarts, 61–63
Letters of State, 312
Lettre à Louis XIV, 135
Liebert, Gustav, 219, 306
Life of John Milton, 219, 334
Life of Milton, 258
Life, Opionion, and Writings of John Milton, 219
Life and Times of Dante, 105, 113
Lilburne, John, 134
Lord Protector, 59–61, 137–38, 156, 267, 310, 312, 320
Lorme, Marion de, 15–16
Lorrain, Claude, 91, 341
Louis XIV, 60, 62, 135, 363
Louis XVI, 55, 81, 153, 155–56, 338, 360–61
Lucan, 24, 108, 112, 115
Lucretius, 170, 184–85, 341
Lusiadas, 108–10, 115
"Lycidas," 3, 335: Chasles on, 79–80; Chateaubriand on, 51; de Guerle on, 259; Filon on, 321; Mézières on, 220, 226, 231; Scherer on, 293; Stroehlin on, 307–08; Taine on, 244–45, 251; Véricour on, 98–99
Lytton, Edward Bulwer, 13

Macaulay, Thomas, 7, 293, 306, 323, 325, 376
"Madrigale XI," 9
Manso, Giovanni Battista, 29, 51, 71, 308
Mariana, Juan, 55
Masenio, Jacopo, 24, 38
Masson, David, 219, 258, 334
Mauvillon, Jacob von, 360
Mazarin, Jules, 2, 60, 352
Medici, Marie de, 173, 178
Méditations poétiques, 149, 159, 223
Mémoire sur gens de lettres des pays êtrangers, 2
Mémoires de littérature, 2
Mercure de France, 4
Mercurius Politicus, 129
Messais, 108–09, 112, 117, 165, 299, 306
Metamorphoses, 170

Mézières, Alfred, 333–45: critique of Milton by, 218–31; notes on, 367–68
Michael, Archangel, 107, 175, 327
Michelangelo, 10, 70, 87, 241, 341
Michiels, Alfred, 47
Milton, Deborah, 19–20, 75, 147, 160
Milton, Elizabeth, 160
Milton, Emma, 19
Milton, 190
Milton Composes his Paradise Lost, 160
Milton Dictating Paradise Lost to his Daughters, 314
Milton et la poésie épique, 97
Milton, sa vie et ses œuvres, 260, 279, 288
Milton and his Two Daughters, 321
Milton's Biblical and Classical Imagery, 177
Minshull, Elizabeth, 13, 75, 160–61, 265–66, 314, 345
Mirabeau, 4, 50, 312, 360
A Modest Confutation, 261
Monck, General George, 139, 140
Monod, Edgar, 21–22
Monthly Review, 118
More, Alexandre, 2, 11, 32, 58–59, 136, 137, 146, 267, 294
Munkacsy, Michael von, 314

Napoléon, 49–50, 59, 64, 354
Napoleon III, 149, 296
The Nice Valour, 224
Nodier, Charles, 24–25
Notes sur l'Angleterre, 254
Nouvelle Biographie générale, 170–71, 179–80
Nouvelles de la république des lettres, 3

Observations upon the Articles of Peace, 154–55
"Ode on the Morning of Christ's Nativity," 222, 307
Odyssey, 74, 109–11, 183, 327
Oedipus at Colonus, 327
Of Education, 52, 128, 146, 260, 312, 369
Of Prelatical Episcopacy, 30, 125, 260, 309
Of Reformation, 30, 125–26, 241–43, 260, 288, 309–10, 375
Of True Religion, 65, 142–43, 158–59, 276–77
Old Wives' Tale, The, 229
Olivier Cromwell, 81
"On the Death of a Fair Infant," 222, 244, 321
"On the Late Massacre in Piedmont," 80, 98, 100, 120, 357

"On May Morning," 221, 259
"On Time," 244, 335
Orlando furioso, 108
Ossian, 108, 161
Ovid, 170
Oxford Movement, 311, 316
Oxford University, 142, 248

Pamela's Prayer, 56, 134, 155
Pamphlets (Milton's): Chateaubriand on, 62; de Guerle on, 262, 264; Filon on, 319; Geffroy on, 125–26, 129, 136, 138, 142, 144–47; Lamartine on, 152; Pongerville on, 178–79; Scherer on, 293–94; Taine on, 238, 242–43; Villemain on, 31–35
Pantheism, 68, 271–72
Paradise Lost, 3, 334–35, 339, 342–43: Addison on, 7; Barbey d'Aurevilly on, 190–99; Boileau on, 6; Chasles on, 83–89, 92, 96; Chateaubriand on, 5, 53, 64–77; de Guerle on, 259, 265, 269, 273, 278–88; Delalot's view of, 4; as drama, 10; Filon on, 321, 323–30; Geffroy on, 124–26; Hugo on, 17–18; Lamartine on, 6, 159–69; Pichot on, 8–13; Pongerville on, 171–78, 181–88; Scherer on, 290, 295–304; Stroehlin on, 311, 315–16; Taine on, 237, 246–52, 255–56; Véricour on, 103–19; Villemain on, 28, 36–47; Vinet on, 200–17
Paradise Regained, 3, 336: Barbey d'Aurevilly on, 190, 198; Chasles on, 93; Chateaubriand on, 65; de Guerle on, 270, 277, 286, 288; Filon on, 315, 330, 332, 336; Lamartine on, 165, 168–69; Mézières on, 231; Scherer on, 293; Taine on, 246; Véricour on, 100, 119; Villemain on, 36
Parker, William Riley, 13, 126, 351
Pascal, Blaise, 269, 356–57, 371
Pastoral Symphony, 259
Paul, St., 5, 294, 310
Petitot, Jean, 55, 305
Petrarch, 219, 292–93
Pharsalia, 24, 108–09
Philaras, Leonard, 58, 65, 136
Phillips, Edward, 306, 353
Pichot, Amédée, 4, 8–14, 132, 192, 218, 318
Pilgrim's Progress, 204, 268, 370
Planche, Gustave, 21, 27, 75

Plato, 38, 100–01, 341
Poetry, 159, 202–03, 285
Pongerville, J. B. Sanson de, 333–45: critique of Milton by, 170–88; notes on, 364–66
Powell, Mary, 335: Chasles on, 82; Chateaubriand on, 53; de Guerle on, 263, 265; Filon on, 318–19; Geffroy on, 129–31, 146; Lamartine on, 151, 161; Mézières on, 221; Scherer on, 296; Stroehlin on, 311; Villemain on, 31
Powell, Richard, 31, 353
Presbyterians, 55, 94, 103, 126–27, 132, 264–65, 309–10
The Present Means and Brief Delineation of a Free Commonwealth, 139
Pro Defensio Regia, 180
Pro Populo Anglicano Defensio, 4, 12, 360: banning of, 1–2; Chasles on, 84–85; Chateaubriand on, 57–58, 63; de Guerle on, 266–67, 277; Filon on, 313–14, 319, 360; Geffroy on, 136, 141; Lamartine on, 155, 179, 180; Scherer on, 295; Stroehlin on, 308; Véricour on, 102; Villemain on, 32
Pro Se Defensio, 137, 146, 267, 320
Prolusiones Quaedam Oratoriae, 269
Prometheus Bound, 331
Protectorate, 10–11, 35, 39, 253, 266
Protestantism, 195–96, 245, 279: Reformation, 315
Puritan(ism), 338: Barbey d'Aurevilly on, 192; Chasles on, 94; Chateaubriand on, 49, 69; de Guerle on, 268; Lamartine on, 168; Mézières on, 225–26; Revolution, 10–11, 81, 148, 156, 302; Scherer on, 291–92, 297; Stroehlin on, 307, 338; Taine on, 245; Véricour on, 103

Racine, 62, 135, 331
Raphael, 341: Chateaubriand on, 70; Filon on, 325–27; de Guerle on, 282; Pongerville on, 174–75; Scherer on, 296–97; Véricour on, 106
The Ready and Easy Way to Establish a Free Commonwealth, 12: Barbey d'Aurevilly on, 194; Chateaubriand on, 59, 61–62, 64, 67, 85; de Guerle on, 267; Filon on, 319–20; Geffroy on, 139, 143, 146; Lamartine on, 156–57

The Reason of Church Government:
Chateaubriand on, 51–52; de Guerle
on, 260–61; Filon on, 320; Ponger-
ville on, 171; Scherer on, 291;
Véricour on, 125–26, 146; Villemain
on, 30
Regii Sanguinis Clamor ad Coelum, 58,
136, 267
Religion de Milton, 69
*Remarks on the Character and Writings of
John Milton*, 274
Renaissance, 233–34, 245, 291, 297
Renan, Ernest, 21, 270
Republicanism, 60–61, 145–46, 266
Restoration, 2, 11, 339–41, 363: Barbey
d'Aurevilly on, 178; Chateaubriand
on, 64; Filon on, 314, 320; Geffroy
on, 141; Lamartine on, 156, 158, 166;
Scherer on, 296; Taine on, 245–46,
253
Revue Britannique, 8, 79, 88
Revue des Deux Mondes, 245, 320, 330
Revue Germanique, 232–33
Rousseau, Jean Jacques, 41, 133

Sabrina, 100, 228
St. Avitus, 71, 105
Sainte-Beuve, Charles Augustin, 23–24,
80, 291, 348
St. Giles, Cripplegate, 269, 314, 363
Salaville, J. B., 4
Samson Agonistes, 3, 5, 7, 11, 14, 335–36:
Barbey d'Aurevilly, 190, 198; Chateau-
briand on, 65; de Guerle on, 263–64,
277, 286–88; Filon on, 330–32;
Geffroy on, 125; Lamartine on, 162,
168–69, 186; Mézières on, 231;
Scherer on, 293; Stroehlin on, 315–
16; Taine on, 237, 246; Véricour on,
82, 92, 119–20; Villemain on, 36, 47
Sand, George, 14
Sarcotis, 24, 38
Satan, 118, 246–47, 296–97, 301–02, 344:
Barbey d'Aurevilly on, 197; beauty of,
72; characterization of, 210; Chasles
on, 87; Chateaubriand on, 66, 67, 72
73; de Guerle on, 279, 282–83; hero,
22, 298; in *Hymne de Anges*, 176–77;
in *Paradise Regained*, 287; parliament
of, 67–68; Filon on, 326; Scherer on,
298; Stroehlin on, 301–02, 315; sun
discourse of, 29–30; Taine on, 246–
47, 250–51, 254; Véricour on, 105,
113–14, 118, 119; Villemain on, 42,
43–44; Vinet on, 210; at war, 176–77

Saumaise, Claude de, 2, 11, 361, 363:
Barbey d'Aurevilly on, 190, 194;
Chasles and, 82, 94; Chateau-
briand and, 57–58; Geffroy and,
135–36, 141; Lamartine and, 156;
180; Scherer and, 293; Véricour
and, 101–03; Villemain and, 32
Scherer, Edmond, 26, 289–304, 305,
372–74
Schmidt, Heinrich, 306
Scott, Sir Walter, 8, 23, 149
Seward, Anna, 13–14
Shakespeare, 10: Chateaubriand on,
71, 73; Mézières on, 228–29;
Scherer on, 292–93; Taine on, 234–
35; Villemain on, 37, 39; Vinet on,
210
Sidney, Sir Philip, 155, 234–35
Sin (in *Paradise Lost*), 105, 121, 206,
301, 316, 325, 342
Skinner, Cyriack, 144, 271, 313
Skinner, Jr., Daniel, 143–44, 271
*Some Account of the Life and Writings of
Milton*, 144
Son of God, 68, 70, 113, 119, 163, 178,
208–09, 214, 272, 274, 283–84, 330
The Spectator, 37, 95
Spenser, Edmund,105, 220, 233–35
Spinozism, 68–69
State Papers, 37
Sterne, Laurence, 290
Stroehlin, Gaspard Ernest, 305–16,
333–45, 374–75
Stuart monarchy, 19, 56, 77, 85, 157, 329

Taine, Hippolyte, 333–45: compared
to de Guerle, 257, 277, 283;
compared to Scherer, 291; compared to Stroehlin, 306; compared
to Véricour, 122; compared to
Vinet, 205; critique of Milton by
232–56; notes on, 368–71, 373
Tasso, 360: Chateaubriand and, 49,
71–72; Lamartine and, 161, 165;
Pongerville and, 172; Scherer and,
299; Stroehlin and, 308; Véricour
and, 105, 108–09, 114; Vinet and,
212, 216
The Tenure of Kings and Magistrates, 12,
339: Chasles on, 84, 94; Chateaubriand on, 55–56; de Guerle on,
266; Filon on, 319; Geffroy on, 133–
36; Lamartine on, 152, 154–56, 167,
180; Stroehlin on, 313; Véricour on,
101, 103; Villemain on, 31

390 Index

Tetrachordon, 264, 270, 311
Théocrite, 259
Theoretical republic, 33, 60–61
Thesaurus Linguae Latinae, 64
Thucydides, 262
Todd, Henry John, 14, 144
Trapham, Dr. Thomas, 362
A Treatise of Civil Power in Ecclesiastical Causes, 64, 138, 320
Treitschke, Heinrich von, 306
Trinity Manuscript, 66
Troy, 106, 111
Turner, Amy Lee, 70
Turnus, 296–97

Una, 80
Unitarian, 269–70, 274–75
Unitarian Christianity, 274
Ussher, Archbishop James, 52, 126

Vatican, 10, 52
Véricour, Louis Raymond de, 24, 333 45: compared to Pongerville, 183, 187; critique of Milton by, 97–122; notes on, 358–60
Vie de Jésus, 270
Vigney, Alfred de, 14–15, 16
Villemain, Abel François, 333–45: critique of Milton by, 27–47; compared to de Guerle, 251; compared to Mézières, 221; compared to Véricour, 122; notes on, 349–50, 360

Villiers, Auguste de, 18–20
Vinet, Alexandre Rodolphe, 200–17, 305, 333–45, 367
Virgil, 9, 341: Chateaubriand on, 49, 71; de Guerle on, 259, 263; Lamartine on, 165; Mézières on, 221; Pongerville on, 170, 183, 188; Scherer on, 297; Taine on, 245; Véricour on, 105–09, 114
Voltaire, 3, 24, 346, 373: Lamartine on, 156; Scherer on, 299; Taine on, 242; Véricour on, 109–10; Villemain on, 29
Voyage historique et littériare, 8–9, 11–12

Wall, Moses, 138
Warton, Thomas, 228, 306
Westhall, Richard, 160
Westminster Assembly, 130–31
Whitelocke, Bulstrode, 319
Whitman, Walt, 255
William III, 77
Williamson, Sir Joseph, 144
Woodcock, Katherine, 35, 319, 363

Yart, Abbé, 3

Zeal, 263, 295

About the Author

Born in Virginia, Harry Redman, Jr., received his higher education at Emory University and the Universities of Wisconsin and Bordeaux. The recipient of a Fulbright Fellowship and other awards, he has taught French at the University of Alabama and Tulane University, from which he recently retired. Interested in French, English and comparative literature, he has worked a great deal with thematic topics. He has authored *German Lyric Poetry's Treatment of the Roland Legend, The Roland Legend in Nineteenth-Century French Literature, Le Côté homosexuel de Flaubert* and about 60 articles on various aspects of French and English literature.

OHIO UNIVERSITY LIBRARY

Please return this book as soon as you have finished with it. In order to avoid a fine it must be returned by the latest date stamped below. All books are subject to recall after two weeks or immediately if needed for reserve.

RETURNED BY:

MAY 1 4 1996

APR 3 0 1996

CF